The French Revolution

It is tempting to respond ... ooh like this c̄ an impatient, "Will somebody just tell me what really happened in the FR? and the answer is, "What really happened in the FR is in this exchange of ideas."

B

Blackwell Essential Readings in History

This series comprises concise collections of key articles on important historical topics. Designed as a complement to standard survey histories, the volumes are intended to help introduce students to the range of scholarly debate in a subject area. Each collection includes a general introduction and brief contextual headnotes to each article, offering a coherent, critical framework for study.

Published

The German Reformation: The Essential Readings
C. Scott Dixon

The English Civil War: The Essential Readings
Peter Gaunt

The Third Reich: The Essential Readings
Christian Leitz

The Counter-Reformation: The Essential Readings
David M. Luebke

The Russian Revolution: The Essential Readings
Martin Miller

The French Revolution: The Essential Readings
Ronald Schechter

In Preparation

The Enlightenment: The Essential Readings
Martin Fitzpatrick

The Cold War: The Essential Readings
Klaus Larres and Ann Lane

The French Revolution

The Essential Readings

Edited by Ronald Schechter

First published 2001

2 4 6 8 10 9 7 5 3 1

Blackwell Publishers Inc.
350 Main Street
Malden, Massachusetts 02148
USA

Blackwell Publishers Ltd
108 Cowley Road
Oxford OX4 1JF
UK

Library of Congress Cataloging-in-Publication Data

The French Revolution : the essential readings / edited by Ronald Schechter.
     p. cm. – (Blackwell essential readings in history)
    Includes bibliographical references and index.
    ISBN 0–631-21270-1 (alk. paper) – ISBN 0–631-21271-X (alk. paper)
    1. France – History – Revolution, 1789–1799 – Historiography.   I. Schechter, Ronald.
  II. Series.

DC147.8 .F73   2001
944.04 – dc21

                                          00-034317

British Library Cataloguing in Publication Data

A CIP catalogue record for this book is available from the British Library.

Typeset in 10$^1/_2$ on 12 pt Photina
by Best-set Typesetter Ltd., Hong Kong
Printed and bound in Great Britain by Biddles Ltd, *www.biddles.co.uk*

This book is printed on acid-free paper

Contents

Acknowledgments

The editor and publishers gratefully acknowledge the following for permission to reproduce copyright material:

American Historical Association for Colin Jones, "The Great Chain of Buying: Medical Advertisement, the Bourgeois Public Sphere, and the Origins of the French Revolution," *American Historical Review* 101:1 (1996) pp. 13–40;

Cambridge University Press for material from François Furet, *Interpreting the French Revolution*, trans. Elborg Forster (1978) pp. 14–17, 36–40, 44–55; and Keith Michael Baker, *Inventing the French Revolution* (1990) pp. 12–27;

Duke University Press for material from Roger Chartier, *The Cultural Origins of the French Revolution*, trans. Lydia G. Cochrane (1991) pp. 3–7, 15–37. Copyright © 1991 Duke University Press;

Harvard University Press for material from Mona Ozouf, *Festivals and the French Revolution*, trans. Alan Sheridan (1988) pp. 267–82. Copyright © 1988 by the President and Fellows of Harvard College;

W. W. Norton & Company for material from Robert Darnton, *The Forbidden Best-Sellers of Pre-Revolutionary France* (1995) pp. 217–46. Copyright © 1995 by Robert Darnton;

The University of California Press for material from Lynn Hunt, *The Family Romance of the French Revolution* (1992) pp. 53–71, 73–88. Copyright © 1992 by the Regents of The University of California;

The University of Chicago Press for Sarah Maza, "Luxury, Morality, and Social Change: Why There Was No Middle-Class Consciousness in Pre-Revolutionary France," *The Journal of Modern History* 69 (1997) pp. 199–229; and Dale Van Kley, "Church, State, and the Ideological Origins of the French Revolution: The Debate over the General Assembly of the Gallican Clergy in 1765," *The Journal of Modern History* 51 (1979) pp. 629–66;

History Workshop Journal for Joan Wallach Scott, "French Feminists and the Rights of 'Man': Oltmpe de Souges's Declanations," History Workshop Journal, 28 (1989), pp 1–21.

The publishers apologize for any errors or omissions in the above list and would be grateful to be notified of any corrections that should be incorporated in the next edition or reprint of this book.

Editor's Introduction

Conceptualizing the French Revolution: Problems and Methods

The Shadow of Furet

In France, for roughly half a century, Marxist historians enjoyed a virtual monopoly over the academic historiography of the French Revolution. Beginning in 1928 the Sorbonne's prestigious chair in the History of the French Revolution was reserved for historians with a demonstrable commitment to socialism. The combination of a rigid hierarchy in French academia and a leftist orientation among French intellectuals more generally – particularly during the quarter century after World War II, when the fabled anti-fascist record of communism provided it with moral authority – made it nearly impossible to challenge the reigning orthodoxy. It was only with the decline of communist hegemony in intellectual circles after 1968, and from a rival institution, the Sixth Section of the École Pratique des Hautes Études (later renamed the École des Hautes Études en Sciences Sociales), that a "revisionist" assault on the prevailing orthodoxy could successfully be launched, opening the way to a rich and diverse historiography of the Revolution.

The first in the Sorbonne's academic dynasty was Albert Mathiez (1874–1932), a disciple of the martyred socialist leader Jean Jaurès (1859–1914) and early supporter of the Bolshevik Revolution, whose roots he traced to the French Revolution. Succeeding Mathiez was Georges Lefebvre (1874–1959), who continued the tradition of Marxist scholarship and spread the word to the Anglo-American world with popular and widely-read English translations of his principal works.[1]

1 See esp. Georges Lefebvre, *The Coming of the French Revolution: 1789*, trans. R. R. Palmer (Princeton University Press, 1947) and *The French Revolution*, trans. Elizabeth Moss Evanson (New York: Columbia University Press, 1962–4), 2 vols.

Finally, Lefebvre's successor, Albert Soboul (1914–82), presided over the dissolution of the Marxist empire in the 1970s when his compatriot François Furet (1927–97) launched the first in a series of challenges to the Sorbonne's supremacy. Although Mathiez, Lefebvre and Soboul were not of one mind on all aspects of the Revolution, they shared Karl Marx's conviction that this world-historical event had occurred because an increasingly wealthy and self-confident class of capitalists known as the bourgeoisie, frustrated with a monarchy that had privileged a landed or "feudal" aristocracy, overthrew it in favor of a "liberal" political and legal order supportive of their own economic interests.

Long before members of the French academic community challenged this interpretation, historians in the United States and the United Kingdom began offering alternative explanations. Indeed, as early as 1929 the Harvard Professor Crane Brinton (1898–1968) argued, on the basis of tax records recording the relative wealth of members of the revolutionary Jacobin clubs, that they "contain[ed] rich and poor, laborer and intellectual, speculator and *rentier*." He concluded that these revolutionaries were "economically so disparate that no simple economic interest [could] hold them together," and suggested rather that "a philosophy, an ideal, a faith, a loyalty," had brought them together.[2] In 1964 Alfred Cobban, a British historian of France, claimed that the bourgeoisie, understood in the Marxist sense of a class of capitalists, played a relatively small role in the Revolution.[3] The following year an American, Elisabeth Eisenstein, argued that " 'France's bourgeoisie' did *not* initiate the protest movement of 1788 and did *not* play a prominent role in the events and reforms of 1789."[4] In 1967 her compatriot George V. Taylor stated that it was "impossible to equate the identifiable leadership of the upper Third Estate – the 'revolutionary bourgeoisie' – with a social class that played a common role in the relations of production, or, more precisely, owned the instruments of production in an emergent capitalist economy."[5]

These Anglo-American objections made little impact in France, and even in the United States the notion that the Revolution stemmed from

2   Crane Brinton, "The Membership of the Jacobin Clubs," *American Historical Review* 34 (July 1929): 751.
3   Alfred Cobban, *The Social Interpretation of the French Revolution* (Cambridge: Cambridge University Press, 1964).
4   Elisabeth L. Eisenstein, "Who Intervened in 1788? A Commentary on *The Coming of the French Revolution*," *American Historical Review* 71 (October 1965): 101.
5   George V. Taylor, "Noncapitalist Wealth and the Origins of the French Revolution," *American Historical Review* 72 (January 1967): 495.

a rising bourgeoisie was a commonplace of many textbooks.[6] Historians around the world paid attention, however, when a former member of the French Communist Party attacked his erstwhile comrades. In 1971, in a widely-read historical journal, François Furet wrote an article denouncing what he called the "revolutionary catechism" by which Marxist historians explained the Revolution.[7] In 1978 he expanded his analysis into a book, *Penser la Révolution française*, which offered a radically new interpretation of the Revolution's origins and character.[8] In that book, a selection of which comprises the first excerpt in this volume, Furet argued that the Revolution was not the result of a triumphant bourgeois class and that its various events and phases could not be explained in terms of class struggle.

Yet Furet did not merely dispute the prevalent orthodoxy. He supplied a sophisticated theory of the Revolution's origins and character. Drawing on the analysis of the nineteenth-century historian and political theorist Alexis de Tocqueville (1805–59), he claimed that the absolute monarchy of Louis XIV and his successors had paradoxically contributed to the development of a democratic or egalitarian ideology among the French.[9] By depriving the old corporate structures of society of their power, according to this theory, the crown induced its subjects to grant moral authority to "men of letters," who necessarily lacked political experience and instead propagated abstract ideas about equality and the sovereignty of the people. Borrowing from historian Augustin Cochin (1876–1916), Furet completed his analysis of the Revolution's origins by describing the "channels" or mechanisms by which the new revolutionary ideology came to permeate French society. It was through the "cafés, salons, Masonic lodges and the so-called *sociétés de pensée*, or 'philosophical societies,'" Furet argued, that the democratic ideology was disseminated.[10] Yet because the state never recognized these "centres of democratic sociability" as legitimate forums

6 R. R. Palmer, whose translation of Lefebvre's *Quatre-vingt-neuf* was a staple of many history courses, summarized the causes of the French Revolution in his own popular textbook: "The Revolution was the collision of two moving objects, a rising aristocracy and a rising bourgeoisie." *A History of the Modern World* (New York: Knopf, 1950), 344.

7 François Furet, "Le Catéchisme révolutionnaire," *Annales E.S.C.* 26 (March–April 1971): 255–89.

8 François Furet, *Penser la Révolution française* (Paris: Gallimard, 1978). The English version is *Interpreting the French Revolution*, trans. Elborg Forster (Cambridge and Paris: Cambridge University Press and Maison des Sciences de l'Homme, 1978).

9 Cf. Alexis de Tocqueville, *The Old Regime and the French Revolution*, trans. Stuart Gilbert (New York: Anchor Books, 1955).

10 Cf. Augustin Cochin, *Les Sociétés de pensée et la démocratie; études d'histoire révolutionnaire* (Paris: Plon-Nourrit et cie, 1921).

The crown made its subjects powerful by rejecting their power. Get rid of power of power them away being seen as the need power. Give power to the people.

through which grievances might be aired, the new, unofficial institutions of an oppressed society acquired a peculiar conception of power. Unlike the English, who supposedly learned through their representative institutions how to negotiate disagreements with the state, the French evidently developed an image of power as absolute, undivided (and indivisible), and of politics as a mortal struggle in which no compromise was possible. When the Revolution broke out, according to Furet, no individuals or groups could admit to holding power, which had been sullied by the reputation it had acquired under absolutism. Only "the people" could rightly exercise power, and politics consequently became a matter of persuasively expressing or interpreting the people's will. The Revolution, according to Furet, therefore "ushered in a world where mental representations of power governed all actions, and where a network of signs completely dominated political life." Finally, because of the absolute conception of power inherited from the Old Regime, all political actors were doomed to view their opponents as wicked conspirators who must be crushed. The result of this "logical evolution," Furet argued, was the Reign of Terror.

It would be difficult to exaggerate the impact of Furet's analysis on the historiography of the French Revolution over the past three decades. Not only did Furet break the monopoly of the orthodox interpretation in France. To a great degree he set the agenda for new and innovative scholarship on the Revolution. Historians committed to some form of class analysis were forced to rethink their assumptions about precisely what the bourgeoisie was and in just what ways the Revolution represented its ascendancy. Historians not holding such a commitment explored aspects of the Revolution's origins and course to which Furet had pointed but that he had not exhaustively analyzed, and addressed questions that he had raised or implied without explicitly or conclusively answering them.

The subsequent historiography has frequently been understood in terms of authors' approval or disapproval of the Revolution and their place on the right, left or middle of the political spectrum. For example, Jack Censer has examined Furet's "negative evaluation of the revolution," determined that Keith Michael Baker and Lynn Hunt (both included in this volume) along with other historians were "critical of the revolution," and wondered how to explain this "common pessimism about the revolution." He believes that "political bias, an expression of the political conservatism of the 1980s," is "too crude an explanation." He nevertheless has recourse to a political explanation, arguing that in recent years "many on the left have been more concerned with individual liberties than with social justice for all" and that "[s]uch an emphasis decreases the likelihood that scholars with leftist views will end up defending a revolution long on equality and short on liberty."[11] Alternatively, Gary Kates has divided recent historians of the French Revolution into Marxists on the left, "Neo-Conservatives" on the right, and "Neo-Liberals" in the center. Moreover, he sees these labels as corresponding to historians' relative sympathy or hostility to the Revolution in its various phases: with Marxists endorsing the entire Revolution, including the Reign of Terror; Neo-Liberals supporting the early, less violent stages of the Revolution, and Neo-Conservatives (including Furet) deploring it altogether.[12] More cautiously, Gwynne Lewis has written, "Some would argue that to identify . . . 'revisionist' historians with liberalism or liberal/conservatism would be going too far. I would, however, be prepared to take a few strides in that direction."[13]

Yet the terms of left and right, liberal and conservative are often so relative and ambiguous that they risk obscuring more than they explain about the historiography of the Revolution. Adding the prefix "neo" does little to clarify matters, as does placing a slash between the terms; and relating these apparent political positions to positive or negative assessments of the Revolution only adds to the confusion. In particular, the notion that the Revolution was "long on equality and short on liberty," which Censer seems to accept and attributes to historians on "the left," is precisely the view of Tocqueville, whose views on democracy were very different from those held by people on "the left" today. More seriously still, the traditional political spectrum is ill-suited to describe much of the feminist scholarship whose impact on the historiography of the Revolution has been decisive.

Specifically, Joan Scott, whose work on the Revolution is excerpted in this volume (chapter 7), argues that the terms by which the Revolution defined citizenship effectively and inevitably excluded women from the national sovereignty that was otherwise loudly proclaimed to be universal. The concept of citizenship was *gendered*,[14] and its gender was masculine. Scott suggests that feminists, beginning with Olympe de Gouges during the Revolution, have been handicapped by a political language that necessarily defined liberation in terms of the rights of "man".

11   Jack R. Censer, "Commencing the Third Century of Debate," *American Historical Review* 94 (December 1989): 1318, 1323, 1324.
12   Gary Kates, ed., *The French Revolution: Recent Debates and New Controversies* (London and New York: Routledge, 1998), 1–20.
13   Gwynne Lewis, *The French Revolution: Rethinking the Debate* (London and New York: Routledge, 1993), unpaginated preface.
14   For an explanation of how the concept of "gender" can be used by historians see Joan W. Scott, "Gender as a Useful Category of Historical Analysis," *American Historical Review* 91 (December 1986): 1053–75, reprinted in her *Feminism and History* (Oxford and New York: Oxford University Press, 1996), 152–80.

Thus she is, on feminist grounds, critical of the Revolution from its very inception, and critical as well of its legacy in political philosophy.[15] Where does this situate her on the familiar left to right political spectrum? Like Furet, she has engaged in a thorough critique of revolutionary ideology. Yet to call her a conservative (or Neo-Conservative) would be absurd. To designate her a liberal would be equally wrong. After all, she concludes, "[T]he recurrence since the Revolution of feminist critiques reminds us not only that the democratic promise of liberal (and socialist and republican) political theory is as yet unfulfilled, but also that it may be impossible of fulfilment in the terms in which it has so far been conceived." Indeed, it is precisely Scott's feminist critique of the gendered terms of the political spectrum that makes the latter inadequate to account for that critique's political meaning.

Kates acknowledges that feminists as well as the "Neo-Conservatives" have criticized the Revolution, yet his attempt to resolve this apparent paradox is highly questionable. He writes, "[I]t is one of the great ironies of historical scholarship that . . . left-wing feminist scholarship has so far been more fruitfully deployed by Neo-Conservative Revisionist scholars than by anyone else."[16] How the "left-wing" character of feminist historiography fits into the definition of political positions according to sympathy or criticism of the Revolution is not explained, and Scott's suggestion that feminism does not have a place on the gendered political spectrum makes this term even less plausible.[17] Moreover, the emphasis on the apparent success of "Neo-Conservative Revisionist scholars" in "deploying" feminism obscures the more obvious success that feminist scholars have had in "deploying" their own claims.[18] As evidence for this apparent appropriation of "left-wing" feminism by the right, Kates refers to Simon Schama's *Citizens*, a narrative history that synthesized and popularized numerous scholarly critiques of the Re-

15   Scott has expanded her analysis in *Only Paradoxes to Offer: French Feminists and the Rights of Man* (Cambridge, MA and London: Harvard University Press, 1996).
16   Kates, *French Revolution*, 15.
17   To be precise, Kates's example of feminist historiography is not Joan Scott but Joan Landes. Yet Landes similarly engages in a thoroughgoing critique of revolutionary ideology on the basis of its masculinist discourse. Joan B. Landes, *Women and the Public Sphere in the Age of the French Revolution* (Ithaca: Cornell University Press, 1988).
18   Feminist historiography of the French Revolution has grown dramatically in little over a decade. In addition to the work of Scott and Landes, see esp. Dorinda Outram, *The Body and the French Revolution: Sex, Class and Political Culture* (New Haven: Yale University Press, 1989); Olwen H. Hufton, *Women and the Limits of Citizenship in the French Revolution* (Toronto: University of Toronto Press, 1992); and Madelyn Gutwirth, *The Twilight of the Goddesses: Women and Representation in the French Revolutionary Era* (New Brunswick: Rutgers University Press, 1992).

volution, feminist and otherwise. Here Kates selectively applies his schema that equates critique of the revolutionaries with conservatism by comparing Schama to Margaret Thatcher. Not only does this implicitly place feminists such as Scott in the same category as Thatcher, an absurdity that Kates does not contemplate but to which his logic inevitably leads. It mutilates Schama's politics as expressed in *Citizens*. Indeed, in one of his own rare allusions to contemporary politics, Schama criticizes the *laissez-faire* economic policy of Louis XVI's minister Turgot as comparable to that of Thatcher's ally in capitalism, Ronald Reagan.[19] Meanwhile, Kates is compelled to dismiss Schama's feminist critique of revolutionary political culture as disingenuous, a mere "appropriation of feminist history for Neo-Conservative purposes," rather than entertaining the more plausible claim that Schama actually believes the feminist views he puts forth.[20] When assumptions about the sincerity of historians are necessary to make one's preferred explanatory categories operate consistently, then it is time to think about just how explanatory those categories are.

To be sure, as Gwynne Lewis rightly observes, it would be naïve "to pretend that history can be written in an ideological vacuum."[21] Whatever the historians' intentions, their work will often be interpreted in light of contemporary politics. This is all the more true when the subject in question is as politically charged as revolution. Yet to see the recent historiography of the Revolution solely in terms of a political contest is to deprive it of much of its conceptual depth and scholarly relevance. Of course, the old debate continues over the bourgeois origins of the Revolution. Colin Jones, in his "Great Chain of Buying: Medical Advertisement, the Bourgeois Public Sphere, and the Origins of the French Revolution" (chapter 5), detects a vibrant and increasingly radical bourgeoisie in the readers of the late eighteenth-century provincial press. Sarah Maza, in her "Luxury, Morality, and Social Change: Why There Was No Middle-Class Consciousness in Pre-Revolutionary France" (chapter 6), argues that the French of the eighteenth century (unlike their British counterparts) did not think of their society as being led by a middle class in the modern sense (as defined in terms of wealth) and that it is anachronistic to attribute a causal role to a "bourgeoisie" that contemporaries would not have recognized. Yet these pieces are more interesting for their methodological implications than for their affinity

---

19   Schama writes of Turgot's policies, "All this was, of course, the direct ancestor of supply-side public finance, and had just about as much chance of success as its version two hundred years later in a different but similarly fiscally overstretched empire." *Citizens: A Chronicle of the French Revolution* (New York: Knopf, 1989), 82.
20   Kates, *French Revolution*, 15.
21   Lewis, *French Revolution*, unpaginated preface.

or antipathy to Marxism, to say nothing of their approval or disapproval of the Revolution. Thus Jones's analysis is interesting largely because it ingeniously combines elements of economic history with the history of communication and "postmodern" understandings of political language. Maza's analysis is interesting primarily because it makes innovative use of contemporary literature and drama to decode prevalent beliefs regarding luxury, morality and the nature of society in pre-revolutionary France.

The excerpts gathered in this volume are therefore not organized according to their authors' political inclinations or feelings about the Revolution. Nor are they categorized, strictly speaking, according to their presumed sub-fields, i.e. intellectual, social, cultural, gender, religious history, since the most creative historians have been remarkably eclectic in combining the methods of the various sub-disciplines. I have tried to place some readings close together on the basis of the shared problems they address. Thus chapters 2, 3 and 4 all problematize the role of ideas in the origins of the French Revolution. Chapters 5 and 6, as mentioned above, ask whether the concept of class, in particular the middle class, can be useful in understanding pre-revolutionary France. Chapters 7 and 8 share a common concern with gender and bodies in revolutionary political culture, and chapters 9 and 10 treat the relationship between religion and the Revolution. Yet my placement of the various readings is not meant to be absolute or exclusive. Chapter 9 is as relevant to the issues raised in chapters 2, 3 and 4 as it is to religious history. Chapters 5 and 6 have important gender aspects that make them worth reading together with chapters 7 and 8. And chapter 8 is as much a reflection on the history of religion as are chapters 9 and 10. I have tried to elaborate on some of these and other connections in the explanatory headnotes to each chapter, but encourage readers to make their own connections, and to look for affinities and tensions between the various excerpts.

What all of the readings from chapter 2 through 10 have in common, at any rate, is that they implicitly or explicitly address questions that Furet raised in his iconoclastic *Penser la Révolution française*. Once Furet is seen as having done more than a demolition job on Marxist orthodoxy, the full relevance of his work for the subsequent historiography of the Revolution can be appreciated. This is not to say that Furet was the sole influence on historians of the Revolution, many of whom would likely have asked similar questions and treated similar problems for other reasons. But the concepts and methods through which Furet sought to understand the Revolution played a crucial role in delineating the contours of future scholarship. The significance of the most important scholarship to come after *Penser la Révolution française*, accordingly, can be best understood not merely as the expression of political positions, but as attempts to address many of those same concepts and methods.

Intellectual History, Discourse and the "Linguistic Turn"

Not the least important of Furet's concepts was that of conceptualization itself. Furet argued that most previous historians, whatever their political sympathies, had insufficiently conceptualized the Revolution that they purportedly sought to understand. What this meant in practice was that they identified with one side or another in the revolutionary struggle and simply narrated its principal events from the perspective of their favorite characters. They did not distance themselves from the events they recounted and therefore fell victim to the illusions from which the historical actors themselves had suffered. The foremost of these illusions, according to Furet, was that of a radical break with the past. The revolutionaries themselves had proclaimed such a break, which their enemies deplored but did not question. Furet enjoined historians to be skeptical of contemporary perceptions and, while he recognized one true break – the rise of mass politics – in the historical fabric characterizing the Revolution, he emphasized the continuities in democratic thinking and conceptions of power that in his view spanned the Old Regime and the revolutionary period.

By underscoring these continuities, Furet highlighted the problem of the Revolution's origins. The question of origins is not an intellectual or scholarly problem if the event in question is seen as a mythical beginning, which is precisely how the revolutionaries understood their moment in history. (Theologians do not inquire into the origins of creation. They simply accept it as a given.) Yet questioning the extent of such a break from the past entails looking for connections between the more and less remote past, conditions that made possible the historical phenomenon one seeks to explain. To be fair to Furet's rivals, they conceptualized the Revolution's origins and did not deny its roots in the previous period, despite his insistence that their explanations involved nothing but the rote repetition of the "catechism" formula: the rise of the bourgeoisie. By presenting the question of origins as explicitly as he did, however, Furet stimulated discussion of this extremely difficult problem. The fact that so many of the excerpts in this volume address the question of the Revolution's origins is merely a reflection of the historiographical tendency of the past quarter-century. Keith Michael Baker, Roger Chartier, Robert Darnton, Colin Jones, Sarah Maza, and Dale Van Kley are among the most distinguished, but by no means the only, historians to ask where the Revolution came from. And if the problem of origins is not new, one of Furet's most important accomplishments was to define, to a great extent, the terms of the investigation.

In particular, Furet emphasized the importance of *ideas* for an understanding of the Revolution. Even the most cursory examination of his writings reveals the prominence of ideas for his historical analysis. The excerpt in this volume begins with a critique of "the *idea* of revolution as experienced and perceived by its actors" (my emphasis). Elsewhere Furet wrote of "political ideas," the "idea of equality," the "idea of plot," and the "idea that power is the people." Variations on the theme of ideas are the repeated reference to "notions," "concepts," "principles," "values," and "ideology." Moreover, Furet highlighted the importance of "men of letters" for the creation and propagation of ideas, and attributed particular importance to Rousseau. He called the Revolution "this strange offspring of '*philosophie*,'"[22] suggesting that the Enlightenment thinkers or *philosophes* had engendered it.

But what was the precise relationship between ideas and the events known as the French Revolution? It is this question that Keith Michael Baker addresses in his essay, "On the Problem of the Ideological Origins of the French Revolution" (chapter 2). The results of his inquiry are relevant not only to the historiography of the Revolution, but also to an understanding of that branch of the historical discipline known alternately as intellectual history or the history of ideas. For Baker the relationship between ideas and events is not as straightforward as often suggested. Baker criticizes historians for treating ideas as though they were objects capable of influencing action, as though, for example, "the Enlightenment" or its constituent "doctrines" could be shown to have caused the events later grouped under the heading of the French Revolution. He argues: that the perceived influence of ideas on events is an illusion of hindsight; that the "ideas" themselves are in fact collections of statements that can be (and have been) used in a variety of ways; and that the proper object of intellectual history is therefore the ways in which people have used particular kinds of statements to make particular claims. These ways, or instruments, of making claims Baker calls *discourses*.

What is a discourse? This word appears not only throughout Baker's work but in so much of the recent scholarship on the French Revolution that an understanding of its meaning is crucial. The term was popularized by French philosopher Michel Foucault (1926–84).[23] For

22   Furet, *Interpreting the French Revolution*, 27–8.
23   See esp. Michel Foucault, *The Archaeology of Knowledge and the Discourse on Language*, trans. A. M. Sheridan Smith (New York: Pantheon, 1972).

Foucault a discourse was a special kind of language that governed power relations in any given society. Its power consisted in its ability to define key words such as "normal" and "abnormal," "natural" and "unnatural," "rational" and "irrational," "healthy" and "sick." By conferring positive attributes to some people and activities and negative traits to others, discourses assured the power and legitimacy of certain groups and the exclusion or oppression of others.

For Baker it was the interaction between competing discourses that defined the political culture out of which the Revolution emerged. In particular, Baker argues that in the second half of the eighteenth century three discourses vied for dominance. One discourse praised *justice*, ostensibly the activity of the law courts known as the *parlements*, and was therefore popular among many of the magistrates who wished to limit the power of the monarchy. A second discourse valorized *will*, reputedly the principal feature of the sovereign "people" or "nation," and defined the thinking of more radical politicians who argued for popular sovereignty (as opposed merely to limited monarchy). The third discourse lauded *reason* and legitimized the power of "enlightened" bureaucrats who wished to reform the country from above without interference from below. Ultimately, according to Baker, the discourse of the will defeated the other two and therefore opened the way for the radicalism of the Revolution.

Joan Scott's article, "French Feminists and the Rights of 'Man': Olympe de Gouges's Declarations" (chapter 7), similarly relies upon discourse analysis. According to Scott, revolutionary discourse defined citizenship in universal terms. It suggested that all individuals, as a sole consequence of being human beings, were endowed with the right to share in the creation of the laws to which they would be subject. The revolutionary principle of equality precluded the special treatment or disproportionate empowerment of any particular individual or group. At the same time, Scott observes, revolutionary discourse contradicted itself by defining this ostensibly "universal" being, the citizen, in terms that only applied to certain kinds of people: i.e. white men. Not only did the deputies in the various revolutionary assemblies refuse to recognize the political rights of women, and only "emancipate" enslaved blacks after the successful slave uprising in Saint-Domingue. The very terms in which revolutionaries understood the qualities of citizens were thought to apply exclusively to white men, not to women or blacks. In her analysis of the contrasting revolutionary representations of men and women, Scott observes that citizens were seen as active, free, rational and concerned with the public good, attributes typically associated with men (i.e. gendered male), while women were typically defined as passive, dependent, emotional and preoccupied with private or domestic concerns. Scott shows that in this linguistic or discursive climate, all attempts to argue for women's rights were doomed. The attempts of Olympe de Gouges are a case in point. When this revolutionary feminist challenged the exclusion of women from the rights of "man," she argued on the basis of features that women alone possessed or were thought to possess: parental and familial love, courage during childbirth, and superior physical beauty. These assumptions about the special or particular character of women undermined the attempt to take part in "universal" citizenship and gave de Gouges's writings the appearance of a lobbying effort on behalf of special interests. Yet they underscore, in Scott's view, the inescapable strength of the discourse that guaranteed the dominance of men over women. Even today, Scott argues, "liberal" as well as republican and socialist political ideas defined in gendered terms threaten to make feminist critiques ineffective, and true equality may only be achieved once the old discourses are discarded.

On the surface there would appear to be little in common between Scott and Furet. Furet had little if anything to say about the exclusion of women from political life. His was an exclusively male story. Yet like Scott he was interested in exposing the internal contradictions in revolutionary ideology. More specifically, he shared Scott's sense that the universalistic language of the revolutionaries masked the fact that only a fraction of the population held power at any given time. Apart from the specifics of their arguments, Scott and Furet share the method of discourse analysis. And they are not alone in this respect. Other historians included in this volume have similarly emphasized the importance of discourse for an understanding of the Revolution. Sarah Maza (chapter 6) argues that the absence of a discourse valorizing the middle classes and the presence of one that defined society in terms of a moral community or family explains why the economic middle of French society did not acquire the authority in politics that its English counterpart enjoyed. Dale Van Kley (chapter 9), though he does not use the term "discourse," shows how conservative champions of absolutism and ecclesiastical authority shared with liberal advocates of secular, representative government the same legitimizing vocabulary that historians have since identified with "the Enlightenment." Even Colin Jones, an erstwhile opponent of discourse analysis, has made use of this method in his "Great Chain of Buying" article (chapter 5), as will be shown below.

Although historians have had many reasons for their methodological preferences, Furet himself arguably did much to prompt a discussion of revolutionary discourse, not only because his emphasis on the role of ideas called for a more sophisticated methodology than that of traditional intellectual history, but also because he used the term himself. He complained, for example, that "the historians of the French Revolution have taken the revolutionary *discourse* at face value because they them-selves have remained locked into that *discourse*." Elsewhere he argued that the Revolution "replaced the conflict of interests for power with a competition of *discourses* for the appropriation of legitimacy" (my emphasis). Although he never referred explicitly to Foucault and may well have developed his ideas on political language independently of him,[24] Furet shared Foucault's insight into the relationship between lan-guage and power. He saw that, at least under certain circumstances, power was not simply a matter of making and executing laws, but of defining terms. Unlike Baker, who has generalized the claim that "politi-cal authority is . . . essentially a matter of linguistic authority,"[25] and others who have implicitly accepted this maxim, Furet limited his lin-guistic analysis to the revolutionary period and suggested that under "normal" circumstances language has less influence in determining power relations. Nevertheless, his observations about the role of lan-guage in conferring power during the French Revolution gave special significance to the work of historians who would apply Foucault's theories to their analyses of the Revolution.

The emphasis on language, which Furet and other historians have used to revitalize both the historiography of the French Revolution and the sub-field of intellectual history more generally, is typically called "the linguistic turn." It has been criticized not only for its tendency toward difficult jargon – itself ironically providing evidence of the claim that discourses serve to empower certain groups and exclude others – but for its apparent lack of concern for action in history. When reading Furet's observation that the Revolution "ushered in a world where mental representations of power governed all actions, and where a network of signs completely dominated political life," one is tempted to ask impatiently, What about the storming of the Bastille? What about the insurrections, coups d'état and political executions? What about the war with France's neighbors and the civil war within its borders? Was the Revolution nothing but a linguistic event? Keith Baker defines the term revolution as "a transformation of the discursive practice of the community, a moment in which social relations are reconstituted and the discourse defining the political relations between individuals and groups is radically recast." But not everyone will be satisfied with such

24   For a more complete analysis of Furet's relationship to Foucault and other the-orists of language and power see Lynn Hunt's review essay on *Penser la Révolution française, History and Theory* 20 (1981): 313–23.
25   Keith Michael Baker, *Inventing the French Revolution: Essays on French Political Culture in the Eighteenth Century* (Cambridge: Cambridge University Press, 1990), 5.

a definition. David Bell objects that Baker "comes perilously close to suggesting that the French Revolution had its origins in a kind of rhetorical exercise, in which the rumbling sea of discursivity cast forth a new set of meanings that, through their own perverse logic, unconnected to France's social and economic turmoil, then unleashed political chaos, civil war, the Terror, and ultimately a European conflagration with a death toll surpassed only by the holocausts of the two World Wars."[26] The same criticism might also be applied to the other historians who focus on ideas and language at the expense of other aspects of human experience.

The Continuing Relevance of Social Analysis

Has the historiography of the French Revolution become too focused on ideas and language and too inattentive to other forms of activity? Readers will have to answer this question for themselves. Yet it is important to emphasize that Furet's analysis focused on many aspects of human experience, not only language, and that these concerns have also played an important role in the work of other historians of the Revolution. In many ways, Furet was a traditional social historian. That is to say, he relied on the methods of sociology when undertaking historical analysis. He is normally not categorized as a social historian and is typically seen as an intellectual or political historian. Part of the reason for this confusion comes from Furet's own writing. After all, Furet praised Tocqueville for attempting a "history in the inverse mode of a sociological interpretation." Yet what he meant by "sociological interpretation" was a particularly narrow kind of social analysis that explained all ideology in terms of class interest. Otherwise, the basic categories of the social sciences were vital to his analysis. The most basic of these categories was "society" itself.

Daniel Gordon has argued against speaking of "society," "the social," and "sociability" before asking what these terms meant to the women and men of the eighteenth century who first employed them.[27] Maza similarly opposes the tendency of historians "to take [the] 'social' for granted" and prefers to ask how the people she studies imagined the human groupings in which they found themselves. Yet Furet, for better or worse, had no such qualms about speaking of society. Using categories invented by the German philosopher Hegel in the aftermath of

26   David A. Bell, "Is the Revolution a Text?" *Partisan Review* 59 (Spring 1992): 324.
27   Daniel Gordon, *Citizens without Sovereignty: Equality and Sociability in French Thought, 1670–1789* (Princeton: Princeton University Press, 1994), 139.

the French Revolution (and in part in order to explain it), he distinguished between "the state" and "civil society." He saw these categories as real things and analyzed their relationship to each other before, during, and after the Revolution. He made his debt to social science even more explicit when he wrote that Tocqueville's explanation of the role of intellectuals in the radicalization of the French "is not sufficient to account for *the sociological conditions* that shaped . . . what was to become the revolutionary consciousness" (my emphasis). Indeed, his recourse to Cochin resulted from his conviction that Tocqueville was insufficiently attuned to sociological structures. Cochin did not merely study what "men of letters" wrote and thought. He asked where and how they and their readers met. In this respect he was a social historian and Furet, by adopting his findings, was a social historian as well.

Other historians, despite their affinity for the "linguistic turn," have managed to combine this methodological tendency with a commitment to social analysis. They are interested in what people did as well as what they said (or wrote). Indeed, for Baker, the distinction between doing and saying is specious. His thinking is informed by the "Cambridge school" of linguistics, which asserts that language not only describes; it *acts* as well.[28] (For example, when the police officer says, "You are under arrest," this is not merely a description. It is also an act.) Moreover, Baker observes that actions without words, such as that of the rioter who picks up a stone, nonetheless have an "intellective" element to them. They *mean* something, just as words mean something, and those meanings are determined by the social context.

Roger Chartier (chapter 3) is even more indebted to the categories of social science, for if Baker considers his intellectual history a form of social history, Chartier calls for an "enlargement of perspective" that includes the analysis of other practices. It is not sufficient, he maintains, to study ideas or ideologies and instead he calls for "an approach in terms of cultural sociology." Like Furet, he insists on the importance of the forms of "intellectual sociability" out of which the ideas of the Enlightenment emerged. This involves examining what Cochin (and Furet) believed crucial to the formation of revolutionary ideas: the philosophical societies, Masonic lodges, literary clubs and other "associations of the eighteenth century." Chartier expands the field of investigation still further by adapting insights from the German social philosopher Jürgen Habermas. According to Habermas, the eighteenth century saw the rise of a "political public sphere," a metaphorical space between the state and "civil society" in which private individuals came together to

---

28   On the performative function of language see J. L. Austin, *How To Do Things With Words* (Cambridge, MA: Harvard University Press, 1962).

discuss matters of public importance and, eventually, to criticize the policies of the state and promote revolutionary ideology.[29] Its institutions included salons, cafés, academies, and journals and it depended upon the circulation of printed material. Chartier does not believe that the forms of intellectual sociability or the institutions of the public sphere themselves necessarily produced democratic or radical ideas. He emphasizes the "discordances" between the "discourses that in representing the social world proposed its reorganization" and the "practices" such as the exclusion of the uneducated from the "public sphere," which "created new differentiations and new divisions." Indeed he argues that these discordances produced the cultural climate that made the Revolution possible. Yet he regards the public sphere as a real object of investigation, even if his interpretation of its role in the origins of the Revolution is not identical with that of Habermas. Thus an understanding of discourses is necessary, but not sufficient, for Chartier, who like Furet is both an intellectual and a social historian.

Robert Darnton (chapter 4) similarly attempts to combine intellectual and social history by placing the history of political ideas in the context of specific social practices. In particular, he is interested in the history of communication, a sub-field of historical scholarship that Habermas has done much to promote. The history of communication involves the study of how ideas were circulated and has included important studies of such topics as the book trade and the publication of newspapers and periodicals.[30] Darnton himself has written extensively on the history of

29   Jürgen Habermas, *The Structural Transformation of the Public Sphere: An Inquiry into a Category of Bourgeois Society*, trans. Thomas Burger and Frederick Lawrence (Cambridge, MA: MIT Press, 1991).

30   The history of communication, and of book publishing and the press in particular, has attracted enormous interest in the past few decades. Among the most important of these works for the history of the French Enlightenment and Revolution are: Robert Darnton, *The Business of Enlightenment: A Publishing History of the Encyclopédie, 1775–1800* (Cambridge: Harvard University Press, 1979); *The Forbidden Best-sellers of Pre-Revolutionary France* (New York: Norton, 1995); Jack R. Censer and Jeremy D. Popkin, eds., *Press and Politics in Pre-Revolutionary France* (Berkeley: University of California Press, 1987); Popkin, *Revolutionary News: The Press in France, 1789–1799* (Durham: Duke University Press, 1990); Censer, *The French Press in the Age of Enlightenment* (New York and London: Routledge, 1994); Sarah Maza, *Private Lives and Public Affairs: The Causes Célèbres of Prerevolutionary France* (Berkeley: University of California Press, 1993); and Carla Hesse, *Publishing and Cultural Politics in Revolutionary Paris, 1789–1810* (Berkeley: University of California Press, 1991). On the role of the *salons* in the communication of Enlightenment ideas see Dena Goodman, *The Republic of Letters: A Cultural History of the French Enlightenment* (Ithaca: Cornell University Press, 1994).

book publishing and has more recently begun examining the character of "the news" in eighteenth-century France. In the selection excerpted for this volume, he addresses the question of "the influence of forbidden books" on the Revolution.

Previous historians, most notably Daniel Mornet, have attempted to determine the extent to which books influenced the opinions of eighteenth-century readers. For Mornet the result of Enlightenment literature was a product that he vaguely called "intelligence," and this quality he saw as one of the principal causes of the Revolution.[31] Baker has criticized Mornet for the lack of clarity in his concept of "intelligence" and for drawing a false dichotomy between "intellectual causes" (deriving from books) and "political causes" (deriving from "situations or events"). Chartier has criticized him on similar grounds, adding that "the diffusion of ideas" is not "a simple imposition." In other words, he argues, eighteenth-century readers did not simply absorb ideas from the books they read in an uncritical or unquestioning manner, but rather interpreted and thus transformed the content of what they read in light of their own beliefs and experiences.

Darnton's analysis of the impact of books departs from Mornet's in three ways. First, whereas Mornet was primarily interested in the influence of the High Enlightenment, i.e. books written by *philosophes*, Darnton takes as his subject matter the anonymous libels, often pornographic in nature, which attacked the royal family, the French court and the clergy. Second, like Chartier, Darnton rejects the notion that readers simply accept what they read, that their minds are like "soft wax," and emphasizes the need to understand *how* readers appropriate and transform the messages conveyed by authors. Third, he places his study of books in the context of other media, noting that ideas spread via "gossip, songs, letters, prints, posters, books, pamphlets, manuscript gazettes, and newspapers of sorts – foreign periodicals and the official, heavily censored French press." In studying larger networks of communication, he argues, one sees the prominence and persistence of certain ideas, which have a longer life and greater impact than if they had been conveyed from books alone. For Darnton the most important of these ideas is that of a monarchy having degenerated into despotism. He does not argue that this idea "caused" the Revolution, but that its acceptance by a large number of French subjects made them more sympathetic to an anti-monarchical position when the revolutionary situation came about.

31   Daniel Mornet, *Les Origines intellectuelles de la Révolution fraçaise* (Paris: A. Colin, 1933).

Colin Jones also combines the methods of intellectual and social history. Like Furet, Chartier and Darnton, he is interested in ideas as well as practices, language as well as institutions, discourse as well as the interests of classes and professional groups. Indeed, it is a sign of the strength of the "linguistic turn" that Jones, who in 1991 lamented that for Baker and likeminded historians "discourse reigns supreme and social factors bulk exceeding small,"[32] by 1996 was employing discourse analysis himself. In his "Great Chain of Buying" (chapter 5), Jones argues that the bourgeoisie used a medical discourse, employing terms such as "constitution," "regime," and "circulation" to expose the reputed deficiencies in the French state and thereby to legitimize their attempts at political reform. His analysis, however, is not limited to language. Like Furet, Chartier and Darnton, Jones is interested in the sociological conditions that made specific discourses possible. As with Chartier and Darnton, he approaches his topic from the perspective of a historian of communication; his particular topic here involves the history of the provincial press. Like other historians with similar interests, he invokes Habermas's concept of the public sphere, yet he follows the Marxist social philosopher more scrupulously by insisting on the *bourgeois* character of the public sphere and, like Habermas, connecting it "to the growth of capitalist relations of production." Paradoxically, then, Jones has used the very methods that Furet advocated in his critique of Marxist interpretations to rehabilitate their claim that a rising bourgeoisie led to the Revolution. Like Furet, and Cochin before him, Jones examines the "sociological conditions" of revolutionary consciousness, yet these conditions turn out to be determined by economic factors. Still, if Jones is more of a Marxist than others who have shown an interest in the social structures behind the production of ideas, he is no more of a "social" historian than many of his non-Marxist, linguistically-inclined colleagues.

Religion and Revolution

If Furet informed discussions of the relationship between ideas, social configurations and history, it is perhaps not surprising that he displayed an interest in the role of religion in the French Revolution. After all, as the sociologist Emile Durkheim (1858–1917) observed, religion is inseparable from the workings of any society and indeed functions as a

---

32   Colin Jones, "Bourgeois Revolution Revivified: 1789 and Social Change," in Colin Lucas, ed., *Rewriting the French Revolution* (Oxford: Oxford University Press, 1991), 75.

means of holding societies together.[33] Furet saw political convictions in particular as greatly resembling religious faith. He described his academic opponents in religious or clerical terms, referring to them as "true believers" in the "revolutionary catechism" or "Lenino-populist vulgate." He called them "disciples" who denounced any differing interpretation of the Revolution as "heresy."[34] This language had rhetorical value insofar as it ironically suggested that Furet's adversaries were more like priests than the revolutionaries they claimed to be. Yet it was not merely a rhetorical flourish. The use of religious terminology was rooted in Furet's conception of the religious character of revolutionary ideology more generally.

Like Tocqueville, who noticed that "though its objectives were political, the French Revolution followed the lines of a religious revolution,"[35] Furet compared the object of his investigation to "the religious wars of the sixteenth century." He found that in both cases human action was heavily invested with moral meaning, but that in the French Revolution "man . . . knew that he was saved or condemned" depending upon the history that "he" was evidently in the process of making. Furet called this belief a "lay eschatology," referring to the prophetic End of Days at which time, according to Christian theology, God will judge all human actions. Combined with the conviction that "the Revolution had no objective limits, only enemies," this belief constituted "a credo whose acceptance or rejection separated the good from the wicked." Furet's analysis of revolutionary ideology in religious terms, like that of Tocqueville, is suggestive, yet neither the one nor the other explains where the fervor that supposedly characterized the revolutionaries came from. This failure in turn highlights the larger problem, which Furet raised and other historians have examined, of the relationship between the Revolution and its "origins." In particular, how could a "religious revolution" have come out of a period known for its secular character? How could it have been the product of the famously irreligious Enlightenment or, in Furet's own terms, the "offspring of *philosophie*"?

Dale Van Kley addresses this question in his "Church, State, and the Ideological Origins of the French Revolution: The Debate over the General Assembly of the Gallican Clergy in 1765" (chapter 9). In this article Van Kley argues that many of the political ideas that would characterize the revolutionary and post-revolutionary periods developed in pre-revolutionary disputes between believing Catholics over the proper

---

33   For Durkheim's theories on religion and society see his *Elementary Forms of the Religious Life*, trans. Joseph Ward Swain (New York: Free Press, 1965).
34   Furet, *Interpreting the French Revolution*, 81, 82, 89.
35   Tocqueville, *The Old Regime and the French Revolution*, 10–13.

organization of the French church. Liberal ideas of representative government and radical notions of the sovereignty of the "nation," Van Kley maintains, were largely developed by "conciliarists" who preferred to see the church governed by lay councils and parish priests rather than bishops. Meanwhile, bishops jealous of their power within the church allied themselves with the crown, thus promoting the conservative ideology of "throne and altar." On the right as well as the left – and Van Kley suggests that these terms are not anachronistic when applied to the pre-revolutionary period – disputants made use of the language of the Enlightenment. By extension, Van Kley argues that the Enlightenment itself, which was more a "set of appeals" (to reason, nature, rights, happiness, etc.) than a coherent doctrine, was not inevitably anti-religious.

Like Tocqueville's and Furet's analysis of the Revolution's origins, Van Kley's interpretation of the religious roots of revolutionary and post-revolutionary political thought emphasizes continuities. Yet other historians interested in the Revolution's religious aspects have focused on the discontinuities or breaks that they have seen as distinguishing the Old Regime from the revolutionary and post-revolutionary periods. In her landmark book *La Fête révolutionnaire*, Mona Ozouf explains the phenomenon of revolutionary festivals, which previous historians had dismissed as curiosities or exercises in partisan propaganda, as a manifestation of the collective human need for the sacred. The conclusion to the English translation of Ozouf's study, excerpted in this volume (chapter 10), summarizes the book's findings. Ozouf argues that the revolutionaries, after attacking traditional Catholic worship as "fanatical," "superstitious" and supportive of "tyranny," nevertheless understood the urgent need to substitute the old forms of religious life with new doctrines, symbols and, above all, rituals. Ozouf judges the revolutionary festivals as successful in providing the sense of the sacred that Catholicism had previously furnished. Here she appears indebted to Durkheim's insight, which Furet seems to have shared, that all societies, whether "modern" or "pre-modern," need rituals in which they recognize and sacralize themselves. Ozouf emphasizes a particular aspect of the sacred experience that the revolutionary festivals apparently manifested: namely the sense of inauguration or beginning anew. She finds in the symbolism, language, and rituals of the revolutionary festivals a conviction that humanity was transcending its unhappy past and embarking on an entirely new period in history. This new age, according to the revolutionary faith, would be characterized by the perfect integration of individuals with the social order and the achievement of the creative potential inherent in human beings. Yet whereas Furet warned against taking the revolutionaries at their word when they proclaimed (through their principal documents) that they were breaking from their past, Ozouf suggests that they were doing precisely what they said they were doing. By the time Napoleon took power in 1799, she argues, the "transfer of sacrality" was complete. The new "social and political values" that the Revolution had promoted, "[r]ights, liberty, and the fatherland," were now widely treated as sacred. Thus the "Revolutionary festival" was "exactly what it wanted to be: the beginning of a new era."

Like Ozouf, Lynn Hunt understands the Revolution as truly marking a break from the preceding period. She also shares Ozouf's Durkheimian sense that the Revolution involved an attempt to sacralize new values. In her *Family Romance of the French Revolution* she describes the process by which revolutionaries broke with the traditional way of imagining the state, i.e. as a family with the king as father, queen as mother and subjects as children, and replaced this configuration with "one in which the parents were effaced and the children, especially the brothers, acted autonomously."[36] In her chapter "The Band of Brothers" (chapter 8), she examines the attempts of revolutionaries to sacralize the fraternal community that they believed themselves to be instituting. Focusing on the period between the arrest of the king and queen and the end of the Reign of Terror, Hunt studies the revolutionaries much as an anthropologist might study the religious beliefs and practices of a particular group. In this guise she tests the claims of a prominent theorist of religion, René Girard. According to Girard, violence is endemic to all societies, yet those that channel it into a symbolic sacrificial object or scapegoat are able to achieve domestic peace.[37] Hunt observes that the revolutionaries were engaged in precisely such a scapegoat killing when they executed the king in January 1793, that contemporaries referred to the event as though it had sacred meaning, but that this act of violence did not function as Girard's theory would suggest, as "[t]housands more victims of every social class, both men and women, proceeded to the guillotine after him."

Psychology: "the historian's unacknowledged principal aide"

Speculation on the religious needs of societies, the relationship between guilt, punishment and the sacred, borders inevitably on the field of psychology. Hunt makes her debt to psychoanalytical theory explicit. Indeed, the very title of her book alludes to Sigmund Freud's concept of

---

36 Lynn Hunt, *The Family Romance of the French Revolution* (Berkeley: University of California Press, 1991), xiv.
37 René Girard, *Violence and the Sacred*, trans. Patrick Gregory (Baltimore: Johns Hopkins University Press, 1977).

the "family romance." According to Freud, certain children (primarily boys) responded to anger at their parents by imagining that they were not, in fact, their true parents. Their real parents, according to the form the fantasy typically took, were of a higher social rank.[38] Hunt does not apply Freud's theory literally to the case of the French Revolution. After all, the revolutionaries, having abolished inherited rank and proclaimed the principle of human equality, could not easily have imagined any family to which they belonged, literally or metaphorically, in terms of elevated rank. Yet Hunt notes that family metaphors were a primary way of imagining the French state and society, both before and during the Revolution. And if the king and queen had functioned as father and mother to their French "children," then the replacement of this family arrangement with a "band of brothers" must have had psychological implications. In particular, Hunt suggests, the "parricides" felt guilty about the murder of their figurative parents. Here she draws on another work of Freud's, *Totem and Taboo*, in which the founder of psychoanalysis speculated that law and society originated from the psychological consequences of an act of parricide.[39] Hunt's subjects apparently betrayed their sense of guilt through their silence regarding the killing of their monarchs, or, alternatively, through their passionate demands for silence on the matter. Yet this urge to silence and forgetting competed with the need to commemorate and legitimize the founding of the new family: the "nation." Silence and speaking, suppressing and remembering thus alternated in a neurotic cycle.

Ozouf's investigation of the religious or sacred aspects of the revolutionary experience similarly crosses the border into the field of psychology. Ozouf also considers Freud in her analysis of the revolutionary festivals. She notes (in a section of her book not excerpted in this volume) that if Durkheim saw festivals as opportunities for any given society's integration and redoubled commitment to its rules, Freud understood festivals as moments of transgression, points at which the normal rules governing social behavior were violated. On the basis of her examination of thousands of revolutionary festivals, Ozouf concludes that Durkheim was closer to the truth than Freud.[40] Despite her criticism of Freud, however, she does not reject the attempt to understand the psychology of the historical actors she has chosen to investigate. Indeed, she repeatedly describes the psychological condition of

---

38   Sigmund Freud, *The Standard Edition of the Complete Psychological Works of Sigmund Freud*, trans. James Strachey (London: Hogarth Press, 1959), vol. 9, 235–41. Cf. Hunt, *Family Romance*, xiii.

39   Freud, *Standard Edition*, vol. 13, 1–162.

40   Mona Ozouf, *Festivals and the French Revolution*, trans. Alan Sheridan (Cambridge, MA: Harvard University Press, 1988), 102–3.

people who lived at the time of the Revolution. She refers to the "visceral . . . fear" that prevented revolutionary officials from intervening in unauthorized nocturnal burials. She tries to "imagine the feelings of the civil servants" when they saw the persistence of Christmas pageants despite the attempt of revolutionaries to suppress them. She credits "the emotion aroused among the sans-culottes" for the ceremonial acclamation of Marat. Finally, she describes the "obsession with ceremonies" among the revolutionaries, their "obsessive . . . recourse to antiquity" and "frantic desire to purge."

The combination of psychological and historical analysis is typically called "psychohistory." After enjoying a brief vogue from the late 1950s into the 1970s, it has lost much of its prestige, though vociferous critics were present from the beginning. Today the very word "psychohistory" is practically a term of abuse among professional historians.[41] This bias is particularly ironic when one considers that psychological conditions are among the most fundamental of historical data. How people in the past felt, what attracted them and what repelled them, what they feared and what hopes they maintained, are not only questions that stimulate the curiosity of so many historians. They are crucial in the formulation of historical explanations. In other words, psychological conditions *matter*. They are not the only things that matter. Nor are they easily discovered. Indeed, they are among the most elusive of historical facts. Yet they matter nonetheless. Moreover, historians often acknowledge the importance of understanding psychological conditions, even if they fail to make this explicit or to avail themselves of psychological theories. Peter Gay writes:

> The professional historian has always been a psychologist – an amateur psychologist. Whether he knows it or not, he operates with a theory of human nature; he attributes motives, studies passions, analyzes irrationality, and constructs his work on the tacit conviction that human beings display certain stable and discernible traits, certain predictable, or at least discoverable, modes of coping with their experience . . . Among all his auxiliary sciences, psychology is the historian's unacknowledged principal aide.[42]

Any review of the historiography of the French Revolution would seem to support Gay's contention. Indeed, Furet himself, who stimulated the

41   Perhaps the best-known denunciation of psychohistory is still David E. Stannard's *Shrinking History: On Freud and the Failure of Psychohistory* (New York and Oxford: Oxford University Press, 1980).
42   Peter Gay, *Freud for Historians* (New York and Oxford: Oxford University Press, 1985), 6.

discussion of so many matters relating to the French Revolution, also raised crucial psychological questions. In some places he seems to have disparaged psychological speculation. He criticized Michelet for having written "a history . . . made up of discoveries of the heart and marked by an intuitive grasp of men's souls and actors' motives." Yet he praised Tocqueville for having seen "the discrepancy . . . between the intentions of the actors and the historical rôle they played," thus implying that Tocqueville similarly understood their intentions. Furthermore, Furet repeatedly used psychological language in his analysis. He claimed that the monarchy's concessions in 1788 "opened up a vast field for the deployment of ideas and social passions." He stated that by the summer of 1789 "thought and speech were liberated, not only from censorship and the police – as, in fact, they had been for some years – but from the internal inhibition created when voluntary consent is given to age-old institutions." Curiously, he also claimed that "revolutionary society exorcised the curse that weighed upon it by reconsecrating [power] in a manner that was the very opposite of that of the Ancien Régime," thus suggesting that the psychological legacy of the Old Regime was not yet overcome and had to be "exorcised." Yet both statements reveal a common interest in the feelings and inhibitions of the revolutionaries. Furet described "the frenzied collective preoccupation with power that . . . shaped the political battles of the Revolution" and wrote that "the plot was the figment of a frenzied preoccupation with power." Elsewhere he depicted this "collectively shared image of power" as a "phantasm," and suggested a kind of collective paranoia when he wrote that "the Revolution invented formidable enemies for itself." Even when he was not using terms such as "frenzied," "figment," and "phantasm" to describe the revolutionaries, Furet implicitly analyzed their psychological state and moreover judged it to be abnormal. He faulted historians for presuming that the Revolution was the "normal" response to supposedly intolerable conditions. The implication is that revolutionary behavior was abnormal. Consequently, Furet underscores the question of precisely what sort of mental state characterized the revolutionaries.

It is not surprising, therefore, that other historians have raised psychological questions about the origins or character of the French Revolution. Roger Chartier stresses the importance of "automatic and obligatory loyalties" or, more exactly, the erosion of these loyalties, in the fall of the French monarchy. He also authorizes speculation on the "temperament" of the historical actors in question, contrasting, with the nineteenth-century historian Edgar Quinet (1803–75), "the inflexible nature of the religious reformers of the sixteenth century and the more malleable temper of the revolutionaries of the eighteenth century." He suggests the possibility of understanding "variations in the structure of personality" in order to learn what was distinctive about the "psychic economy" – a term he borrows from the German sociologist Norbert Elias (1897–1990) – of the eighteenth-century French. Robert Darnton, although he disagrees with Chartier on when and how the French lost their affection for the king and queen, nevertheless presumes that by 1785 "[y]ears of slander had damaged something fundamental in the people's attachment to the monarchy." He attributes much of this disaffection to books, which "aroused emotions and stirred thoughts with a power we can barely imagine today," whereas for Chartier anti-monarchical literature only reflected a "previous . . . affective disinvestment."[43] Yet both historians seem to believe that the emotions of the eighteenth-century French are not only discernible, but crucial for understanding the origins of the French Revolution. Similarly, Jones reports on the mental condition of provincial editors of advertising supplements, calling them "happy . . . to a man" and noting that for them "the market held few terrors." Maza presents a very different picture of literate French people in the second half of the eighteenth century. She finds a "fear of 'luxury'," "panic over its effects," and "an acute sense of moral void and social dissolution" resulting from the burgeoning of the consumer market. Yet both historians are confident in their ability to detect such emotions as fear, dread, and happiness. Indeed, Maza goes so far as to generalize her claims about the psychological condition of the French, as she writes of "the devastating effects of the Seven Years' War on the national psyche." Combining the related phenomena of psychology and religion, moreover, she explains the late eighteenth-century enthusiasm for sentimental art forms and "social morality" as "an attempt to promote new forms of spiritual fulfillment in one's sense of connectedness to a community of fellow human beings."

If one expands the realm of the psychological from that of emotions to the workings of the mind more generally, to thinking as well as feeling, then the presence of psychology in the historiography of the French Revolution is more pervasive still. The prevalence of the word "consciousness" is merely one indication of this phenomenon. Furet referred repeatedly to the term, though without ever precisely defining it. Jones writes of "class consciousness" among members of the bourgeoisie. Maza highlights the question of "middle-class consciousness" in the very title of her article, and though she finds it to be non-existent, she discovers another kind of consciousness, which imagined society as a single family held together by altruistic feelings and behavior. Baker

43   Roger Chartier, *The Cultural Origins of the French Revolution*, trans. Lydia Cochrane (Durham: Duke University Press, 1991), 86.

focuses on "intellection," Chartier writes of "systems of perception," and Darnton attempts to reconstruct the "mental world" of eighteenth-century French readers, yet all of these terms are simply different ways of expressing a single goal: an understanding of how human minds made sense of or constructed reality. If one adds the unconscious to the elements of the mind one wishes to study, then the full range of mental activity, the full scope of psychological investigation, can be understood as falling under the purview of the historian. Yet even if one excludes this arena as inaccessible, the points of connection between history and psychology are quite numerous indeed.

Thus history cannot be separated from psychology, and historians will return to psychological questions whether they explicitly address psychological theories (as Hunt does) or engage in a lay analysis of cognitive processes, "mental representations," anxieties, "frenzies" and "phantasms." In this respect, what is striking about the historiography of the French Revolution, a subject in which emotions and ideas play as great a role as in any historical period, is not the prevalence of psychological theory, but its relative absence. Hopefully, future work on the Revolution will profit from the vast discipline of psychology. After all, if attempts to combine history with various other fields have invigorated historiography, why should the combination of history and psychology prove any less fruitful?

History among the Disciplines

But here I am begging the question of just how valuable such combinations have been. The key word in this discussion is *interdisciplinarity*, or the crossing of boundaries between academic disciplines. Should scholars strive for interdisciplinarity? Should they borrow concepts, models and methods from other fields, or ought they to remain within the boundaries assigned by the conventions of their own disciplines? This is a very large pair of questions, which has been repeatedly debated and will no doubt continue to attract attention in academic publications as well as departmental and faculty meetings at colleges and universities throughout the world. It cannot be treated exhaustively here, yet the readings collected in this volume afford an opportunity to examine the implications of interdisciplinarity for the historiography of the French Revolution in particular and the field of history more generally.

As these readings show, the historiography of the Revolution over the last three decades has been highly interdisciplinary indeed. In order to describe and explain the Revolution historians have borrowed concepts, models and methods from sociology, political science, economics, anthropology, literary criticism, linguistics, philosophy, psychology, religion, art history, and the already highly interdisciplinary fields of gender studies and cultural studies. A common complaint about this sort of eclecticism is its perceived tendency to pollute historical writing with jargon. Yet the historian Peter Burke has pithily defined jargon as "little more than the other person's concepts."[44] Terms like "discourse," "public sphere," and "sacrality" might offend one's sensibilities when read or heard for the first time. This reaction, however, is more a result of unfamiliarity than anything inherent in the words themselves. Once understood, they can be rejected as lacking sufficient relevance or explanatory power, yet in some cases at least they will clarify more than they obscure. Advanced students and professional scholars often assume that they are finished learning "vocabulary" and therefore impatiently reject unfamiliar terms as useless, especially if these come from disciplines in which they have had little instruction. A commitment to learn "other people's concepts" and at least to consider their applicability to one's own subject matter is well worth the required time and effort.

Learning from other disciplines is all the more advisable insofar as the scope of history inevitably includes their subject matter. The *Oxford English Dictionary* defines "history" as "[t]hat branch of knowledge which deals with past events, as recorded in writings or otherwise ascertained; the formal record of the past, esp. of human affairs or actions." Of course, in practice historians necessarily reduce this unimaginably vast purview by specializing according to period, place, and a comparatively manageable set of themes. But what are these themes? It would be impossible to write an exhaustive list, but some of the most obvious candidates are: the pursuit of power, wealth and status; the production and consumption of objects and use of technologies; the organization of communities; the perception and treatment of insiders and outsiders; attempts at creating and communicating meaning through symbols and rituals; mental divisions between good and evil, sacred and profane; feelings of attraction and aversion, impulses toward creation and destruction, peace and war; and the complicated relationship between human beings and the natural world. In short, history concerns itself, at least potentially, with nothing less than the totality of the human condition. It is therefore the natural partner of other disciplines that take as their subject any aspect of that condition.

This defense of interdisciplinarity is not new. It echoes the call for "total history," articulated in 1966 by Emmanuel Le Roy Ladurie but

44   Peter Burke, *History and Social Theory* (Ithaca: Cornell University Press, 1992), 44.

implicitly advocated as early as the 1920s by his predecessors in the so-called *Annales* school, who combined such diverse interests as geography, demography, meteorology, sociology, psychology, and anthropology.[45] One finds sympathy for interdisciplinarity earlier still in the "New History" of James Harvey Robinson, an American historian of the French Revolution who in 1912 declared that since "History includes every trace and vestige of everything that man has done or thought since he first appeared on the earth," it would be necessary for historians to study, among other things, anthropology, sociology, "Prehistoric archaeology," "Social and Animal psychology," "the Comparative study of religions," and "Political economy."[46] This optimism about the ability of historians to synthesize the knowledge of so many fields might appear naïve, perhaps even arrogant. The project appears more defensible, however, if the knowledge of the human past as informed by the relevant disciplines is seen as a goal that can never truly be reached but toward which it is worth striving, an ideal standard against which scholarship can be measured.

In some respects, moreover, history can be understood as an inherently interdisciplinary subject, which in fact conformed to the principles of *Annales* and the New History long before they were articulated. One could argue that Herodotus, the ancient Greek historian and reputed "father of history," was an anthropologist, a geographer, a political scientist and moral philosopher in addition to being a historian. Closer to the period with which we are concerned here, David Hume, who was at once a philosopher, psychologist, sociologist and historian, believed history capable of revealing "the constant and universal principles of human nature" and "the regular springs of human action and behaviour."[47] His polymath contemporary, Voltaire, wrote histories that paid attention to laws and customs, religious beliefs, economic practices, scientific endeavors, as well as politics, diplomacy and war. Both Hume and Voltaire exemplified the Enlightenment belief, best expressed in the project of the *Encyclopédie*, in the underlying unity of disparate branches of knowledge. The nineteenth-century historians of the French Revolu-

45   Emmanuel Le Roy Ladurie, *The Peasants of Languedoc*, trans. John Day (Urbana: University of Illinois Press, 1974). On the "*Annales* school" see Peter Burke, *The French Historical Revolution: The Annales School 1929–89* (Stanford: Stanford University Press, 1990).
46   James Harvey Robinson, *The New History: Essays Illustrating the Modern Historical Outlook* (New York: Macmillan, 1912), cited in Burke, *French Historical Revolution*, 9. On Robinson's continuing relevance for an understanding of the French Revolution see Lynn Hunt, "Forgetting and Remembering: The French Revolution Then and Now," *American Historical Review* 100 (October 1995): 1119–35.
47   David Hume, *An Enquiry Concerning Human Understanding*, ed. P. H. Nidditch (Oxford: Clarendon Press, 1975), 83.

tion inherited the conviction that history must inform and be informed by other branches of knowledge. Tocqueville, for example, was not simply interested in recounting the history of the Old Regime and seeking the origins of the French Revolution. He wished to know when and why revolutions occur, under what conditions status matters more than wealth or power, how religious inclinations affect political ideas and actions, how and when the organization of a polity influences the beliefs of its members, and under what conditions democracy is possible. He therefore shared the concerns of the political scientist and sociologist with those of the historian. Similarly, Karl Marx maintained theories of human nature, psychological notions of consciousness and alienation, economic theories of value and a dialectical model of history (inherited from Hegel) in which primitive forms of social and economic organization would collapse under the weight of their contradictions and give way to higher stages of historical development. Insofar as his disciples, including the Marxist historians of the French Revolution, have shared his assumptions, they too have crossed disciplinary boundaries.

Thus the interdisciplinarity of the work collected here is not in and of itself new. What is new is the precise combinations between history and the other branches of knowledge. The decline – relative though not definitive – of Marxist assumptions has opened up the historiography of the French Revolution to possible combinations unthinkable during the heyday of the old orthodoxy. The study of political ideas, once widely viewed as mere "ideology" masking more fundamental class interests, has flourished in the new historiography. Language and symbols are no longer seen merely as tools of class domination, but as defining features of social identity as well as political contestation. The relative status of women and men, once overshadowed by the presumably more fundamental relationship between those who owned the means of production and those who did not, can now be viewed as integral to an understanding of the character and legacy of the Revolution. The study of religion, once dismissed as the "opium of the masses," can take its rightful place in the endeavor to explain how the Revolution came about and why it took the form it took.

As these readings show, history can benefit greatly from the freedom and willingness to explore other fields. Yet it does not merely take. It offers something in return. It provides a temporal aspect, an account of human experience at a time that no longer exists. Only the collection and interpretation of the traces of the past, whether in documents or artifacts, can enable us to know which aspects of the human condition are new and which are old, how and to what extent the past is like the present. Whether the historian will find "regular springs of human action and behavior," as Hume would contend, or irregular springs, or different mechanisms altogether, are hypotheses that only the study of history can test. And if one determines that people have changed in some fundamental way from the past to the present, this does not tell us whether that difference was continuous. There is no better way to examine such questions of continuity and change than to study a revolution, which by definition is a break but which, upon closer investigation, might yield surprising continuities, perhaps even toward our own day.

1

Interpreting the French Revolution

François Furet

Originally appeared as François Furet, *Interpreting the French Revolution*, trans. Elborg Forster (1978), pp. 14–17, 36–40, 44–55 (Cambridge: Cambridge University Press).

Editor's Introduction

The selection excerpted below begins with a plea for historians to distance themselves mentally from the events they seek to understand. Furet praises his nineteenth-century predecessor, the historian and political philosopher Alexis de Tocqueville, for having taken a dispassionate, critical, *conceptual* approach to the subject of the French Revolution. By questioning the revolutionaries' claim of having broken radically from the past, Furet argues, Tocqueville had been able to make his paradoxical argument that the Revolution only completed the work of the absolute monarchy. Its administrative centralization and consequent democratization of society, in Tocqueville's view, had already begun in the seventeenth century; thus the Revolution represented a continuity, not a break. Furet contrasts this conceptual stance with that of one of Tocqueville's contemporaries, Jules Michelet, whom he criticizes for his *commemorative* approach to the Revolution. Because Michelet identified with the aspirations of the revolutionaries themselves, Furet argues, he was unable to see the extent to which they misunderstood the historical significance of the events of their day. He was bound to narrate the history of the Revolution without truly understanding it. Nor do counter-revolutionary writers escape the trap of commemorative historiography, Furet maintains, since they similarly take the revolutionaries' claims at face value.

Nevertheless, Furet does not see Tocqueville's analysis as sufficient to explain the Revolution's origins. He endorses his predecessor's observation that "men of letters" came to wield moral authority (though not actual power) in the eighteenth century and that their "abstract" political and social theories took hold of subjects who had no practical experience in government. At the same time, he argues that Tocqueville lacked an understanding of the "sociological conditions" by which French society acquired its "revolutionary consciousness." Still, he stays close to the spirit of Tocqueville's reputedly "conceptual" approach by introducing a key concept intended to complete the explanation: *political sociability*, or the "mode of organising the relations between citizens (or subjects) and power, as well as among citizens (or subjects) themselves in relation to power." Traditionally, Furet argues, political sociability in France bound subjects to each other and to the government through corporate institutions, e.g. estates, *parlements*, municipalities, guilds and religious communities, each of which had a known and accepted place in the hierarchy of power extending from the king downward to the "people." Yet beginning in the seventeenth century the absolute monarchs attempted to concentrate power in their own hands, thus depriving the traditional *corps* of their power, authority, and social significance. In the eighteenth century, however, a new form of political sociability emerged, which Furet, drawing on the historian Augustin Cochin, calls *democratic sociability*. Its institutions were the Masonic lodges, philosophical societies and cafés, where individuals met in democratic fashion, that is without regard to social rank. Because these institutions enjoyed no official status, and indeed were suspect to the monarchy, they had no way of communicating with the state. Lack of communication bred mutual mistrust, and both the state and society attributed conspiratorial designs to the other. Under these circumstances no negotiated settlement to disagreements was possible. The only solution to the burden of absolutism, according to Cochin and Furet, was "pure democracy," that is, revolution.

Revolution came in 1787, Furet argues, insofar as that year marked the first "capitulation" of the state to the demands of society: the sharing of power between the administrative officials known as *intendants* and elected representatives of the Third Estate (i.e. non-nobles). The following year saw additional acts of surrender, most spectacularly the calling of the Estates General, yet only in spring and summer 1789 did the truly revolutionary transformation take place. The king's acceptance of the National Assembly and the taking of the Bastille made it clear for the first time that the old monarchy had, for all practical purposes, abdicated. Now it was possible for a "new historical consciousness" to dispense with the age-old respect for the monarchy and the church, and it became possible to imagine a new social and political order based on democratic principles. Simultaneously, "the masses had broken in on the stage of history," and revolutionary leaders had to appeal to "the people."

Despite this undeniable break in the course of history – a break about which Tocqueville had little to say – the legacy of the Old Regime cast a shadow on the Revolution that succeeded it. Specifically, Furet argues, the very idea of power had been so closely associated with abuses and despotism that revolutionary leaders were forced to dissociate themselves from it. Revolutionary ideology therefore required that power be held by society, "the people" as a collectivity, not this or that party or ministry, though the everyday activity of politics necessitated the concentration of power in the hands of certain groups or individuals. Revolutionaries attempted to resolve this paradox, according to Furet, by resorting to the concept of *opinion*. Unlike our idea of opinion as relative or debatable, the revolutionaries inherited from the democratic sociability of the eighteenth century the notion that opinion was a single, indisputable object held in common by "the people" and true because the people were, by definition, the best judge of what was right. At the same time, not everyone was thought to belong to "the people." Selfish individuals and groups, labeled "aristocrats" whether they possessed titles of nobility or not, were presumed to be enemies of revolutionary equality. Thus some groups were simply factions, or cabals, whereas others spoke for "the people" and generated infallible *opinion*. Distinguishing the one from the other was precisely what revolutionary politics amounted to, according to Furet. The "job" of revolutionaries was "not to act," but "to interpret action," to announce when the people had made its will apparent and to identify their own will with that of the people. By the same token, revolutionaries were compelled to denounce rivals as conspirators bent on returning the nation to despotism.

And rivals were inevitable, Furet suggests, precisely because the notions of "the people" and "opinion" were fictions. Real politics entailed conflicting interests and beliefs, but whereas a system of representative government would have permitted these conflicts to occur without violence, the revolutionary ideology of direct democracy only guaranteed violence. Leaders of factions, denying their factional character, would repeatedly attempt to stop the revolution when the groups with which they identified attained power. Yet rival groups, denounced as traitors, would necessarily fight those in power – as they would be fighting for their lives. Should they gain control momentarily, the cycle would nevertheless continue.

The tendency to demonize one's opponents was only exacerbated, Furet argues, by the recent development in "historical consciousness" according to which human beings are responsible for everything that happens to them and "every historical fact can be reduced to a specific intention and to a subjective will." Rather than attributing at least some occurrences to God, nature, magic, fate, or accident, the revolutionaries presumed that anything that went wrong was the result of a plot, and that all positive developments had well-intentioned human authors. This way of thinking encouraged the tendency to divide the world into good and evil, patriotic advocates of equality and "aristocratic" conspirators against the nation. And just as it placed no boundaries on the human potential for good, it authorized the relentless search and pitiless punishment of "conspirators," whose existence was confirmed (in a circular form of reasoning) by the simple fact of human unhappiness.

Such was the "dynamic" that Furet attributes to the Revolution from the spring of 1789 to the summer of 1794. His interpretation of the French Revolution is therefore both a set of claims about its origins and an analysis of the course it (in his view, inevitably) took. Historians have challenged his interpretation, yet they have been forced to contest him on his own terms, that is, by conceptualizing. How they have done so can be seen in this volume's other excerpts.

Interpreting the French Revolution

François Furet

Any conceptualisation of the history of the Revolution must begin with a critique of the idea of revolution as experienced and perceived by its actors, and transmitted by their heirs, namely, the idea that it was a radical change and the origin of a new era. So long as that critique is absent from a history of the Revolution, superimposing a more social or more economic interpretation upon a purely political interpretation will not change what all those histories share, a fidelity to the revolutionary consciousness and experience of the nineteenth and twentieth centuries. Nonetheless, the social and economic deposits added by Marxism may have one advantage, for the absurdities to which they lead bring into sharp focus the dilemmas of any history of the Revolution that remains founded on the personal consciousness of those who made that history.

It is here that I encounter Tocqueville, and that I take the measure of his genius. At the very time when Michelet was working out the most penetrating of the histories of the Revolution written in the mode of personal identification – a history without concepts, made up of discoveries of the heart and marked by an intuitive grasp of men's souls and actors' motives – Tocqueville, and Tocqueville alone, envisaged the same history in the inverse mode of a sociological interpretation. It does not matter, therefore, that the Norman aristocrat did not hold the same *opinions* as the son of the Jacobin printer. Tocqueville, after all, did not write a more 'right-wing' history of the Revolution than Michelet. He wrote a *different* history of the Revolution, basing it upon a critique of revolutionary ideology and of what he saw as the French Revolution's illusion about itself.

. . .

'So you think that the French Revolution is a sudden break in our national history?', [Tocqueville] asked his contemporaries. In reality it is the fruition of our past. It has completed the work of the monarchy. Far from being a break, it can be understood only within and by historical continuity. It is the objective achievement of that continuity, even though it was experienced subjectively as a radical break.

Thus, Tocqueville developed a radical critique of any history of the French Revolution based only on the consciousness of the revolutionaries themselves. His critique is all the more penetrating as it remains within the political sphere – the relation between the French people and the governing power – which is precisely the sphere that *seems* to have been most profoundly transformed by the Revolution. Tocqueville is mainly concerned with the domination of local communities and civil society by the administrative power following the growth and extension of the centralised State. The takeover of society by the administrative State was more than the permanent feature linking the 'new' régime with the 'old', Bonaparte with Louis XIV. It also explained the developments by which 'democratic' (i.e. egalitarian) ideology penetrated throughout traditional French society. In other words, Tocqueville saw in the constitutive aspects of the 'Revolution', that is, an administrative State ruling a society informed by an egalitarian ideology, a work largely accomplished by the monarchy before it was completed by the Jacobins and the Empire. And what is called 'the French Revolution', an event later inventoried, dated, and magnified as a new dawn, was but the acceleration of a prior political and social trend. By destroying, not the aristocracy, but the aristocratic principle in society, the Revolution put an end to the legitimacy of social resistance against the central State. But it was Richelieu who set the example, and so did Louis XIV.

If Tocqueville never wrote a real history of the French Revolution it was, I believe, because he conceptualised only one aspect of that history, namely its continuity. He presented the Revolution in terms of its outcome, not as an event; as a process, not as a break. At the time of his death, he was working on his second volume and was confronting the problem of how to account for that break. But what remains fundamental in the work of this deductive and abstract mind, providentially wandering in a field suffused with the narrative method, is that it escaped the tyranny of the historical actors' own conception of their experience and the myth of origins. Tocqueville was not personally immersed in the choices that Necker, Louis XVI, Mirabeau or Robespierre had to make. He was a bystander. He was speaking of other things.

That is why his book is even more important for the method it suggests than for the thesis it advances. It seems to me that historians of the Revolution have, and always will have, to make a choice between Michelet and Tocqueville. By that I do not mean the choice between a republican and a conservative interpretation of the French Revolution, for those two kinds of history would still be linked together in a common definition of the problem, which is precisely what Tocqueville rejected. What separates Michelet and Tocqueville is something else: it is that Michelet brings the Revolution back to life from the inside, that he communes and commemorates, while Tocqueville constantly examines the discrepancy he discerns between the intentions of the actors and the historical rôle they played.

That is why, in my opinion, *L'Ancien Régime et la Révolution* remains the most important book of the entire historiography of the French Revolution. It is also why it has always been, for more than a century now, the stepchild of that historiography, more often cited than read, and more read than understood.[1] Whether of the Right or of the Left, royalist or republican, conservative or Jacobin, the historians of the French Revolution have taken the revolutionary discourse at face value because they themselves have remained locked into that discourse. They keep putting on the Revolution the different faces assumed by the event itself in an unending commentary on a conflict whose meaning, so they think, the Revolution itself has explained to us once and for all through the pronouncements of its heroes. They must therefore believe, since the Revolution says so, that it destroyed the nobility when it negated its principle; that the Revolution founded a new society when it asserted that it did; that the Revolution was a new beginning of history when it spoke of regenerating the human race. Into this game of mirrors, where the historian and the Revolution believe each other's words literally, and where the Revolution has become history's protagonist, the absolutely trustworthy Antigone of the new era, Tocqueville introduces a doubt that strikes at the very heart of the matter: what if that discourse about a radical break reflects no more than the illusion of change?

The answer to that question is not simple, nor would answering it take care of the whole history of the Revolution. Yet it is probably indispensable to a conceptualisation of that history. Its importance can be measured negatively: unless the historian comes to grips with it, he is bound to execrate or to celebrate, both of which are ways of commemorating.

. . .

French society in the eighteenth century was desperately searching for responsible spokesmen. It was too highly 'developed', as we would say today, to be kept, as in the preceding century, in silent and obedient submission to the State. But in its search for political representation

---

1   Georges Lefebvre's rather condescending introduction to *L'Ancien Régime et la Révolution* (Paris: Gallimard, 1952) is characteristic of that situation. Even so, Lefebvre was the only historian of the French Revolution to have read Tocqueville with some care. All my references to *L'Ancien Régime* are to the above-mentioned critical edition in two volumes, respectively vol. II:1 and II:2 of Tocqueville's *Oeuvres complètes* (J. P. Mayer, general editor): vol. I (1952; 2nd edn, 1964), contains the published text, with introductions by Lefebvre and J. P. Mayer; vol. 2 (1953), edited by André Jardin, contains Tocqueville's working notes and unfinished chapters.

it was hampered by the legacy of Louis XIV, who had systematically closed off the channels of communication between society and the State (such as the Estates General, the remonstrances of the *parlements*, the municipalities and the town councils) yet also maintained and even consolidated the structure of the society of orders. It was only natural that after the death of Louis XIV, society should attempt to revive the traditional circuits of representation, especially the rôle of the *parlements*. But since these same *parlements*, throughout the century, gave repeated proof of their conservatism, since they condemned the *Encyclopédie*, and *Émile*, and the unfortunate Calas, they hardly constituted the best spokesmen for an 'enlightened' society. They could perpetuate the illusion of their representative character only so long as the monarchical State – before or after it yielded to them – fought them; but the illusion was short-lived.

That is why eighteenth-century society increasingly turned to other spokesmen, namely to the *philosophes* and men of letters. No one has understood and expressed that better than Tocqueville in the first chapter of Book 3 of *L'Ancien Régime*. He felt that, by abolishing the ancient 'liberties' and destroying the political function of the nobility without also permitting the formation of a new ruling class on a different basis, the monarchy unwittingly set up the writers as imaginary substitutes for that ruling class. Hence literature took on a political function:

> Considering that this same French nation – so unfamiliar with the conduct of its own affairs, so deprived of experience, so hampered by its political institutions, and so powerless to improve them – was also at that time the most literate nation on earth and the one that cared most deeply about the things of the mind, one can easily understand how its writers came to be a political power and eventually became the foremost of these powers.

That confusion of rôles, in which men of letters assumed a function they could fulfil only in its imaginary aspects, that is, as opinion-makers who wielded no practical power whatsoever, was to shape political culture itself. The men of letters tended to substitute abstract right for the consideration of facts, principles for the weighing of means, values and goals for power and action. Thus the French, deprived as they were of true liberties, strove for abstract liberty; incapable of collective experience, lacking the means of testing the limits of action, they unwittingly moved toward the *illusion of politics*. Since there was no debate on how best to govern people and things, France came to discuss goals and values as the only content and the only foundation of public life.

Since there was no outlet for political change, the F. chose an abstract one.

Yet Tocqueville's brilliant analysis, which explains so much about the intellectuals' rôle in French political debate since the eighteenth century, is not sufficient to account for the sociological conditions that shaped the elements of what was to become the revolutionary consciousness. What is missing in his general intuition is an examination of the channels by which the new power of public opinion, existing side by side with power *tout court*, came to act upon society. For society produced, and maintained, alongside the traditional one, a new *political sociability*, waiting in the wings to take over the entire stage: that was Augustin Cochin's discovery.

By political sociability, I mean a specific mode of organising the relations between citizens (or subjects) and power, as well as among citizens (or subjects) themselves in relation to power. An 'absolute' monarchy implies and presents a type of political sociability in which all of society is arranged concentrically and hierarchically around the monarchy, which is the central organising force of social life. It occupies the summit of a hierarchical arrangement of *corps* and communities whose rights it guarantees and through which authority flows downward, while obedience (tempered by grievances, remonstrances, and negotiations) flows upward. Under the Ancien Régime, however, the circuits of the old political sociability were increasingly stripped of their traditional meaning and their symbolic content; the administrative monarchy dealt a severe blow to ranks and *corps* when it taxed them. To the very end it clung to the image of a society it had done its best to destroy; but nothing in that theoretical society allowed it to communicate any longer with real society. Everything, beginning with the court, had become a screen.

Yet real society did reconstruct, in other ways and other places, beyond the monarchy, a world of political sociability. This new world was based on individuals, and no longer on the institutional groups to which they belonged; it was founded on the confused notion called 'opinion' that came into being in cafés, salons, Masonic lodges and the so-called *sociétés de pensée*, or 'philosophical societies'. One can call it democratic sociability – even though its network did not extend to all of the people – simply to express the idea that its lines of communication were formed 'below' and ran horizontally in a disjointed society, where all individuals were equal. 'Opinion' was precisely the obscure way of expressing the idea that something new had emerged from the silence that had engulfed the pyramid of the king's traditional interlocutors. That 'something' was based on new principles, but nobody clearly understood what they were.

The reason is that while democratic sociability did indeed begin to reunify a disintegrating society – for it played, on a practical level, the same integrating rôle as ideologies of the 'nation' on the intellectual level – it remained in many respects, like its older counterpart, impenetrable. The new centres around which it took shape, such as the philosophical societies or the Masonic lodges, lay by definition outside the traditional institutions of the monarchy. They could not become 'corporate bodies' in the traditional pyramid since they were not only of a different, but indeed of an incompatible order. The elements they were made of did not exist prior to society, as so many indivisible nuclei that together might constitute a hierarchical organisation. They were, on the contrary, *products* of a society, albeit of a society emancipated from power and engaged in creating a new social and political fabric based on the individual. Such a principle could not be openly proclaimed and had, in fact, long been fought against by the kings of France, so that for a very long time those new centres of democratic sociability seemed suspect and were often secret or semi-secret.

The new circuit of sociability thus had no communication with the traditional one; it was totally unrelated to the network of relationships woven by the authorities. It produced opinion, not action – or, better, it produced opinion that had no effect on action. Its image of power was thus substitutive, yet patterned on the 'absolute' power of the monarch, simply inverted in favour of the people. The very fact that a philosophical society or club claimed to be speaking for the nation, or for the people, was sufficient to transform individual opinions into plain 'opinion' and opinion into imaginary absolute power, for in that kind of alchemy there was no room for either legitimate disagreement or legitimate representation. The two symmetrical and opposite images of undivided power furnished the ingredients for notions and reciprocal imputations of conspiracy: enlightened 'opinion' believed in a conspiracy of ministers or a plot to institute a ministerial despotism; the royal administration believed in a conspiracy among the grain merchants or the men of letters.

It is precisely in that sense that the eighteenth-century French monarchy was *absolute*, and not – as has been said again and again by republican historiography on the basis of what the Revolution asserted – because of the way it exercised its authority. Its power was weak, but it conceived of itself as undivided. That notion, which remained intact even after its actual content had eroded, was precisely the sufficient and necessary reason for the concealment of the political circuit. As society wrested – or reconquered – more and more power from the monarchy, the notion of absolutism proved so persuasive that it became necessary to refashion that power in an outwardly radically different manner and yet on the model of absolutism. The two circuits were incompatible precisely because they had so much in common. If they excluded any means of communicating with each other, it was because they shared the same idea of power. The French Revolution is inconceivable without that idea, or that phantasm, which was a legacy of the monarchy; but the Revolution anchored power in society instead of seeing it as a manifestation of God's will. The revolutionary consciousness took form as an attempt to recreate undivided power in a society free of contradictions. The new collectively shared image of politics was the exact reverse of that of the Ancien Régime.

It is clear that ever since the death of Louis XIV the idea of absolute monarchy had blocked all efforts at revamping the political system, in particular the attempt at establishing a representative régime. The *parlements*, being an integral part of the traditional structure, usurped rather than exercised a representative rôle. Yet when they too finally claimed to embody 'the nation', as in the famous episode of 1769–71,[2] they unwittingly based their stand on the system of fictive equivalences that was just beginning to form the democratic texture of the philosophical societies. Nothing shows more clearly the identical though opposite character of the two sets of political assumptions, and the mutual exclusiveness this implied, than that oligarchy of privileged men who started speaking of the 'nation' and the 'people', and who could break out of the absolute monarchy only by espousing pure democracy.

. . .

I have long thought that it might be intellectually useful to date the beginning of the French Revolution to the Assembly of Notables in early 1787, for that chronological transfer has the double advantage of dating the crisis of traditional authority more precisely and of integrating what has come to be called the 'aristocratic revolution' into the Revolution itself. For the absolute monarchy died, in theory and in practice, in the year when its *intendants* were made to share their responsibilities with elected assemblies in which the Third Estate was given twice as many representatives as in the past.[3] What foundered in the void

---

2   I am referring to the series of remonstrances of the *Cour des aides* [tax court], many of which were written by Malesherbes himself, who was First President during these years of bitter conflict with Louis XV. The most explicit text is that of 18 February 1771. Written after the most active members of the *parlement* had been exiled and their offices confiscated, it protests against the 'destructive system that threatens the entire nation', and against the arbitrary royal power that 'deprives the nation of the most essential rights of a free people'.

3   The basic book on this question is still P. Renouvin, *Les Assemblées provinciales de 1787* (Paris: Picard, 1921).

created by the rapid collapse of the monarchy's authority was not only the 'aristocracy' or the *parlements*, but indeed political society as a whole. And the break that occurred in late 1788 between the *parlements*, which favoured a traditional summoning of the Estates, and the rest of that political society – which already called itself 'the nation' – was, as Cochin already realised, the first of the many schisms that were to divide the revolutionary camp.

In fact, Tocqueville dates what he calls the 'true spirit of the Revolution' from September 1788. He wrote long passages about it, but never put them into a definitive form, and they were published together with his working notes (*L'Ancien Régime*, vol. 2, Book 1, ch. 5). He defines that 'spirit' less exclusively than I do, tracing its various manifestations, such as the abstract search for the perfect constitution to be established once the slate of the past has been wiped clean, or the will to transform 'the very foundation of society' (p. 106). Yet he comes close to the definition I am trying to develop when he characterises the evolution of ideas in late 1788 as follows:

> At first people spoke only of working for a better adjustment in the relations between classes; soon they advanced, ran, rushed toward the idea of pure democracy. In the beginning they quoted and commented Montesquieu; in the end they talked of no one but Rousseau. He became and was to remain the only tutor of the Revolution in its youth. (pp. 106–7)

I am not sure that the evolution of ideas was that simple. In order to find out, one would have to be able not only to read but to date all the pamphlets of the period, which are for the most part anonymous and undated. Tocqueville made extensive use of Sieyès's pamphlet, which he considered typical, while I feel that at that date it was prophetic and therefore exceptional. It was no doubt because he wanted to keep to his timetable of radicalisation that Tocqueville saw the *Cahiers* as a corpus of revolutionary texts. But I believe that in fact the current of traditional political ideas (or what I have called the old political sociability) lived on in the *Cahiers* and also in many political pamphlets, even those written after September 1788.

Yet the chronological break of September is important, and Tocqueville's intuition was fundamentally correct. The summoning of the Estates General, the appointment of Necker, the recall of the *parlements*, all in the summer of 1788, were so many acts of capitulation by Louis XVI that created a general power vacuum. They touched off a war among the classes who wanted that power, a war that was fought over the modes of representation in the Estates and thus opened up a vast field for the deployment of ideas and social passions. Here was the opening through which the ideology of pure democracy surged in, even though it did not gain full control until the spring of 1789.

If one defines the Revolution as the collective crystallisation of a certain number of cultural traits amounting to a new historical consciousness, the spring of 1789 is indeed the key period. For while power had been available for at least two years, the fact became fully apparent only at this point, with the victorious revolt of the 'Commons' against the king's orders. Until May, the old mode of political sociability, centred on the king of France at the summit of the social order, more or less held up – as the *Cahiers* indicate – for the area of power he had in fact relinquished had not yet been discovered. But all that changed with the events of May, June and July. The victory of the Third Estate over the king, the capitulation of the First and Second Estates, the taking of the Bastille, and the vast popular excitement that preceded and followed it clearly went beyond the framework of the old legitimacy. Thought and speech were liberated, not only from censorship and the police – as, in fact, they had been for some years – but from the internal inhibition created when voluntary consent is given to age-old institutions: the king was no longer the king, the nobility was no longer the nobility, the Church was no longer the Church. Moreover, once the masses had broken in on the stage of history, political education gained a vast new public, whose expectations called for completely new modes of social communication. Speeches, motions and newspapers ceased to be aimed at educated people, and were henceforth submitted to the judgment of the 'people'. The Revolution marks the beginning of a theatre in which language freed from all constraints seeks and finds a public characterised by its volatility. This two-fold shift in the functioning of the symbolic circuit that surrounds and protects power was the outstanding development in the spring of 1789.

That is why, in a sense, everything indeed 'began' here: 1789 opened a period when history was set *adrift*, once it was discovered that the actors in the theatre of the Ancien Régime were mere shadows. The Revolution is the gap that opened up between the language of the *Cahiers* and that of the *Ami du peuple* in the space of only a few months.[4] It must be seen as not so much a set of causes and consequences as the opening of a society to all its possibilities. It invented a type of political discourse and practice by which we have been living ever since.

By the spring of 1789, then, it had become clear that power no longer resided in the royal Councils and *bureaux*, from which a steady stream

4   The first issue of Marat's paper is dated 12 September 1789. Its definitive title appeared on the 16th.

of decisions, regulations and laws had been sent out for so many centuries. All of a sudden power had lost its moorings; it no longer resided in any institution, for those that the Assembly tried its best to reconstruct were bound to be swept away, rebuilt, and destroyed again, like so many sandcastles assaulted by the tide. How could the Ancien-Régime king accept them when everything about them expressed distrust of him and the will to dispossess him? And how, in any event, could so recent a creation, so new a State, rebuilt or rather reconceived on such precarious ground, quickly produce a minimum of consensus? No one believed it, though everyone professed to do so, since everyone was speaking in the name of the people. Nor did anyone have the power to create that consensus, even among those who might be called the 'men of 1789', and who were in agreement about the society and the kind of political régime they wanted. There was an essential instability inherent in revolutionary politics, as a consequence of which the periodic professions of faith concerning the 'stabilisation' of the Revolution unfailingly led to renewed bursts of revolutionary activity.

Leaders and factions spent their time wanting to 'stop' the Revolution, always for their own benefit, at a time that suited them, and in opposition to others. Mounier and the *monarchiens*, spokesmen for a kind of French Whiggism, did so as early as August 1789. Mirabeau and Lafayette pursued the same aim throughout 1790, simultaneously, but each for his own ends. Finally, the Barnave–Duport–Lameth triumvirate was the last to rally, after Varennes, to the moderate politics of a constitutional monarchy. But each of these successive rallyings took place only after its leaders had taken the Revolution a step further in order to keep control of the mass movement and to discredit rival factions. Unable to attain the first objective, the moderates succeeded so well in the second that the weapon soon turned against them and against 'moderatism' of any kind. Thus, even during the apparently 'institutional' phase of the Revolution, when France had a rather widely accepted Constitution, every leader – from La Fayette to Robespierre – and every group took the risk of extending the Revolution in order to eliminate all competitors instead of uniting with them to build new national institutions. That seemingly suicidal behaviour was due to exceptional circumstances, which explain the blind determination of the protagonists. The *Constituants* of 1789, unlike those of 1848, were not primarily interested in bringing the Revolution to a 'close'. But then 1848 had its eyes riveted on 1789. There was no precedent for 1789. The politicians of that time had, as Mirabeau put it, 'far-reaching ideas'; but when it came to political action they had to improvise.

The reason is that they were caught up in a new system of action that severely constrained them. The characteristic feature of the Revolution was a situation in which power was perceived by everyone as vacant, as having become intellectually and practically available. In the old society exactly the opposite had been the case: power was occupied for all eternity by the king; it could not become available except at the price of an act that would be both heretical and criminal. Moreover, power had owned society, and decided what its goals should be. Yet now it had not only become available, it had become the property of society, which was called upon to take it over and subject it to its own laws. Since power was held responsible for all the ills of the Ancien Régime and considered the locus of arbitrariness and despotism, revolutionary society exorcised the curse that weighed upon it by reconsecrating it in a manner that was the very opposite of that of the Ancien Régime: henceforth it was the people that was power. But by the same token society forced itself to keep that equation alive through opinion alone. Language was substituted for power, for it was the sole guarantee that power would belong only to the people, that is, to nobody. Moreover, language – unlike power, which is afflicted with the disease of secrecy – is public, and hence directly subject to scrutiny by the people.

Democratic sociability, which had characterised one of the two systems of political relations coexisting in the eighteenth century, because, like two parallel lines, they could never meet, now took over the sphere of power. But it did so only with what it was able to produce, that is, the ordinarily soft and pliable thing we call opinion. In those special circumstances, however, that material suddenly became the object of the most meticulous attention, the core, indeed the stake, of the entire political struggle. Once it had become power, opinion had to be at one with the people; language must no longer serve to hide intrigues but reflect values as in a mirror. In the frenzied collective preoccupation with power that henceforth shaped the political battles of the Revolution, representation was ruled out or perpetually put under surveillance; as Rousseau had stated, the people cannot, by definition, alienate its rights to particular interests, for that would mean the instant loss of its freedom. Legitimacy (and victory) therefore belonged to those who symbolically embodied the people's will and were able to monopolise the appeal to it. It is the inevitable paradox of direct democracy that it replaces electoral representation with a system of abstract equivalences in which the people's will always coincides with power and in which political action is exactly identical with its legitimacy.

If the Revolution thus experienced, in its political practices, the theoretical contradictions of democracy, it was because it ushered in a world where mental representations of power governed all actions, and where a network of signs completely dominated political life. Politics was a matter of establishing just *who* represented the people, or equality, or the nation: victory was in the hands of those who were capable of occupying and keeping that symbolic position. The history of the Revolution between 1789 and 1794, in its period of development, can therefore be seen as the rapid drift from a compromise with the principle of representation toward the unconditional triumph of rule by opinion. It was a logical evolution, considering that the Revolution had from the outset made power out of opinion.

Most histories of the Revolution fail to assess the implications of that transformation; yet none of the leaders who successively dominated the revolutionary scene wielded power in the normal sense, by giving orders to an army of underlings and commanding a machinery set up to implement laws and regulations. Indeed, the régime set up between 1789 and 1791 made every effort to keep the members of the Assembly away from executive power, and even to protect them from any such contamination. The suspicion of ministerial ambitions under which Mirabeau had to labour until the very end and the parliamentary debate about the incompatibility between the functions of representative and minister are telling illustrations of that attitude.[5] It was related to more than political circumstance and the Assembly's distrust of Louis XVI. It was inherent in a specific idea of power, for the Revolution held that executive power was by its very nature corrupt and corrupting, being separate from the people, out of touch with it and hence without legitimacy.

In actual fact, however, that ideological disqualification simply led to a *displacement of power*. Since the people alone had the right to govern – or at least, when it could not do so, to reassert public authority continually – power was in the hands of those who spoke for the people. Therefore, not only did that power reside in the word, for the word, being public, was the means of unmasking forces that hoped to remain hidden and were thus nefarious; but also power was always at stake in the conflict between words, for power could only be appropriated through them, and so they had to compete for the conquest of that evanescent yet primordial entity, the people's will. The Revolution replaced the conflict of interests for power with a competition of discourses for the appropriation of legitimacy. Its leaders' 'job' was not to act; they were there to interpret action. The French Revolution was the set of new practices that added a new layer of symbolic meanings to politics.

Revolutionary activity *par excellence* was the production of a maximalist language through the intermediary of unanimous assemblies mythically endowed with the general will. In that respect, the history of the Revolution is marked throughout by a fundamental dichotomy. The deputies made laws in the name of the people, whom they were pre-

5   Debate of November 1789.

sumed to *represent*; but the members of the *sections* and of the clubs acted as the *embodiment* of the people, as vigilant sentinels, duty-bound to track down and denounce any discrepancy between action and values and to reinstate the body politic at every moment. As regards domestic politics, the salient feature of the period between May–June 1789 and 9 Thermidor 1794 was not the conflict between Revolution and counter-revolution, but the struggle between the representatives of the successive Assemblies and the club militants for the dominant symbolic position, the people's will. For the conflict between Revolution and counter-revolution extended, with nearly unchanged features, far beyond 9 Thermidor, while the fall of Robespierre marked the end of a politico-ideological system characterised by the dichotomy I am trying to analyse here.

One of the most frequent misunderstandings of the historiography of the French Revolution is its attempt to reduce that dichotomy to a social cleavage by granting in advance to one of the rival powers a status that was precisely the undefined and quite literally elusive stake in the conflict, namely the privilege of being the people's will. In substituting the opposition between the bourgeoisie and the people for the one between aristocratic plot and the people's will, that misunderstanding turns the 'public safety' period into the culminating though temporary episode in which the bourgeoisie and the people marched hand in hand in a kind of Popular Front.[6] That rationalisation of the political dynamic of the French Revolution has one major flaw, for in reifying revolutionary symbolism and in reducing political motivation to social concerns, it makes 'normal' and obliterates what calls for explanation: the fact that the Revolution placed that symbolic system at the centre of political action, and that it was that system, rather than class interest, which, for a time at least, was decisive in the struggle for power.

There is little need, therefore, to launch upon a critique of that type of interpretation and to point out its incoherences with respect to the strictly social aspects of the problem. Not only has that critique already been made, notably by the late Alfred Cobban,[7] but, more important, that type of interpretation is *irrelevant to the problem at hand*. Even if it were possible to show – and that is not the case – that, for instance, the conflict between the Girondins and the Montagnards had its roots in the contradictory class interests of the antagonists or, on the contrary, that the period dominated by the Committee of Public Safety was characterised by a compromise between 'bourgeois' and 'popular' interests,

6   The expression was used by Georges Lefebvre.
7   Alfred Cobban's most important articles were collected in *Aspects of the French Revolution* (London: Jonathan Cape, 1968).

such a demonstration would still be altogether beside the point. The 'people' was not a datum or a concept that reflected existing society. Rather, it was the Revolution's claim to legitimacy, its very definition as it were; for henceforth all power, all political endeavour revolved around that founding principle, which it was nonetheless impossible to embody.

That is why the history of the French Revolution, in the narrow sense, is characterised throughout by violent clashes between the different versions of that legitimacy and by the struggle between the men and the groups who found ways to march under its banner. The successive Assemblies embodied the legitimacy of representation, which, however, was from the very outset fought against by direct democracy, as supposedly expressed in the revolutionary *journées*. Moreover, in between *journées*, a vast range of organisations – newspapers, clubs and assemblies of all kinds – were contending for the right to express direct democracy, and so for power. That double system gradually came to be institutionalised in the Jacobin Club, which, as early as 1790, functioned as the symbolic image of the people controlling the Constituent Assembly and preparing its decisions. Its structure may have remained very diffuse – as diffuse, by definition, as direct democracy, since every *section*, every meeting, indeed every citizen was in a position to produce the people's will – but the fact remains that Jacobinism laid down the model and the working of direct democracy by dictating opinion in the first organised group to appropriate the Revolution's discourse on itself.

Augustin Cochin's fundamental contribution to the history of the French Revolution was to examine how that new phenomenon came into being through the production and manipulation of revolutionary ideology. But because his study sets out to show that the phenomenon worked in a nearly mechanical manner – as soon as the discourse of pure democracy, concealing an oligarchic power, had appropriated the consensus – it underestimates the cultural links that were also vitally necessary for that system. Although the exact congruity between revolutionary democracy – as proclaimed and practised by the club militants – and the 'people' was a fundamental and mythical image of the Revolution, it is nonetheless true that this notion gave rise to a special relationship between politics and a section of the popular masses: the tangible 'people' – a minority of the population to be sure, but very numerous compared to 'normal' times – who attended revolutionary meetings, took to the streets on important *journées* and provided visible evidence for the abstraction called 'the people'.

The birth of democratic politics, which is the only real 'advent' of those years, could not have occurred without a common cultural environment in which the world of action and the world of conflicting values overlapped. Such a congruity is not unprecedented: that was how the religious wars of the sixteenth century, for example, had mustered most of their recruits. What is new in the laicised version of revolutionary ideology – the foundation of modern politics – is that action totally encompassed the world of values, and thus became the very meaning of life. Not only was man conscious of the history he was making, but he also knew that he was saved or condemned in and by that history. That lay eschatology, which was destined to so great a future, was the most powerful driving force of the French Revolution. We have already noted its integrating function for a society in search of a new collective identity, as well as the extraordinary fascination it exerted by promoting the simple and powerful idea that the Revolution had no objective limits, only enemies. Those premises gave rise to an entire system of interpretation, which, strengthened by the first victories of the Revolution, became a credo whose acceptance or rejection separated the good from the wicked.

The central tenet of that credo was the idea of equality, experienced as the reverse of the old society and perceived as the condition and purpose of the new social compact. But the notion of equality did not directly produce revolutionary energy, which first had to pass, as it were, through a relay to which the idea of equality was directly connected. That relay was the opposite principle, which created conflict and justified the use of violence: the aristocratic plot.

To review the uses and acceptations of the idea of plot in revolutionary ideology would be an unending task, for it was truly a central and polymorphous notion that served as a reference point for organising and interpreting action. It was the notion that mobilised men's convictions and beliefs, and made it possible at every point to elaborate an interpretation and justification of what had happened. From the very first events of the French Revolution one can see it function in those two ways and observe how it gained currency at all cultural levels, thereby unifying them: during the 'Great Fear' (*Grande Peur*), the peasants armed themselves to forestall the conspiracy of the brigands; the Parisians stormed the Bastille and then Versailles to forestall the Court plot; the deputies to the Estates General gave legitimacy to the insurrection by invoking the plots it had foiled. The idea appealed not only to a religiously oriented moral sensibility that had always seen evil as the work of hidden forces, but also to the new democratic conviction that the general, or national, will could not be publicly opposed by special interests. Above all, it was marvellously suited to the workings of revolutionary consciousness, for it produced the characteristic perversion of the causal schema by which every historical fact can be reduced to a specific intention and to a subjective act of will; thus the crime was sure to be heinous, since it was unavowable, and crushing the plot became a laudable and purifying act. Moreover, there was no need to name the perpetrators of the crime and to present precise facts about their plans, since it was impossible to determine the agents of the plot, who were hidden, and its aims, which were abstract. In short, the plot came to be seen as the only adversary of sufficient stature to warrant concern, since it was patterned on the Revolution itself. Like the Revolution, it was abstract, omnipresent and pregnant with new developments; but it was secret whereas the Revolution was public, perverse whereas the Revolution was beneficial, nefarious whereas the Revolution brought happiness to society. It was its negative, its reverse, its anti-principle.

The idea of plot was cut from the same cloth as revolutionary consciousness because it was an essential aspect of the basic nature of that consciousness: an imaginary discourse on power. That discourse came into being, as we have seen, when the field of power, having become vacant, was taken over by the ideology of pure democracy, that is, by the idea that the people are power, or that power is the people. But the revolutionary consciousness believed in historical action: if its advent was made possible only by the intervention of the people, it was because it had been blocked and continued to be threatened by a counter-power potentially more powerful than power itself: the plot. Hence the plot revived the idea of absolute power, which had been renounced by democratic power. Once the transfer of legitimacy, the very hallmark of the Revolution, had been accomplished, that absolute power became a hidden though formidable threat, while the new one was supreme though fragile. Like the people's will, the plot was the figment of a frenzied preoccupation with power; they were the two facets of what one might call the collectively held image of democratic power.[8]

That figment turned out to be almost indefinitely expandable. It adapted itself to every situation, rationalised every form of conduct, and penetrated all sections of the public. It started out as a vision of power held by those who had been excluded from power and were free to express their vision once the existing power had become vacant. In the initial revolutionary situation the denunciations of the 'aristocratic plot' coalesced into a call for action. At a time when its opponents were still very weak and poorly organised – in 1789–90 – the Revolution invented

---

8   This analysis owes a great deal to the discussion in Pierre Nora's seminar at the École des Hautes Études en Sciences Sociales in 1977 about the idea of plot and the French Revolution. M. Gauchet and L. Theis in particular helped me refine the terms of my analysis.

formidable enemies for itself, for every Manichaean creed needs to overcome its share of eternal evil. The adjective 'aristocratic' brought to the idea of plot a definition of its content, referring no longer to the methods but to the nature of the adversary. In fact, it was a rather vague definition, since it very soon came to encompass not only the aristocracy but also royal authority, all the old society, the inertia of a world confronted with change, and impersonal as well as human resistance. But if the word was – as it had to be – obscure, since it was the abstract and expandable designation of a hidden enemy, it was perfectly clear about the values it celebrated *a contrario*: just as aristocracy was seen as the reverse of equality, so the plot was seen as a power directly opposed to that of the people. It stood for inequality, privilege, a society splintered into separate and rival 'bodies', and the entire universe of rank and difference. The nobility – less as an actual group than as a social principle – was seen as the symbol of that 'difference' in the old world and made to pay the full price of the reversal in values. Only its formal exclusion from society could lend legitimacy to the new national pact.

The 'aristocratic plot' thus became the lever of an egalitarian ideology that was both exclusionary and highly integrative. Here again, two complementary systems of symbols came into play: the nation was constituted by the patriots only in reaction to its adversaries, who were secretly manipulated by the aristocrats. The potential applications of that basic proposition were practically unlimited, since equality, being a value more than a state of society, could never be taken for granted, and since its enemies were not real, identifiable and circumscribed forces, but constantly renewed incarnations of its anti-values. The symbolic content of the revolutionary struggle was the most immediate reality to act on attitudes and behaviours. In that sense it is quite true that there was no break between the two revolutions that can be dated to 1789 and 1792. From the meeting of the Estates General to the dictatorship of the Committee of Public Safety, the same dynamic was at work; it was fully developed, though not yet supreme, as early as 1789. Considered from that angle, the history of the Revolution spans the years during which that dynamic came to fill the entire sphere of power, up to the fall of Robespierre.

2

On the Problem of the Ideological Origins of the French Revolution

Keith Michael Baker

Originally appeared as Keith Michael Baker, *Inventing the French Revolution* (1990) pp. 12–27 (Cambridge: Cambridge University Press).

Editor's Introduction

In this essay, the first chapter of his book *Inventing the French Revolution*, Keith Michael Baker seeks to clarify "the problem of the ideological origins of the French Revolution" and simultaneously to redefine the field of intellectual history. For Baker intellectual history is not merely the history of "intellectuals," or of those individuals who have devoted their lives to the formulation of ideas. It is the history of "intellection," the process by which human beings understand or attribute meaning to what they experience.

In order to describe the material that intellectual historians use, Baker draws on metaphors from anthropologist Claude Lévi-Strauss (1908–) and philosopher Michel Foucault (1926–84) respectively. Lévi-Strauss furnishes the image of random objects filling the workshop of a *bricoleur* or "jack-of-all-trades." Foucault provides a more precise description of these objects. They are *discourses*, those languages that govern power relations in any given human group by granting positive qualities to some people and negative ones to others. (See the Introduction for a more extended discussion of the term.) Thus the intellectual historian's materials are the discourses that history has left behind in a disorderly fashion; her job is to fit them together in a way that offers a coherent explanation of both thought categories and power relations from her chosen place and time in history.

The models provided by Lévi-Strauss and Foucault are problematic, however, since Lévi-Strauss has insisted on studying cultures without reference to history and Foucault criticized historians for allegedly ignoring ruptures and presenting a false picture of continuity. Both thinkers have taken a *synchronic* approach to their subject, i.e. one that focuses on a particular moment in time, whereas history would seem to demand a *diachronic* perspective that treats events successively "over" or "across" time. Hence the "Faustian bargain" in which "structuralists" such as Lévi-Strauss and Foucault offer an explanation of human activity as essentially involving the production of *meaning* and historians accept this wisdom "at the cost of [their] historical souls."

Baker proceeds to offer a solution to the dilemma. He argues that discourses are and always have been multiple and related to each other in unpredictable ways. Sometimes they reinforce one another; sometimes they compete with each other. Which discourses will rise to prominence and which will become obscure is not self-evident or inevitable. Only the historian, through a careful study of the historical evidence, can tell us what the outcome of this configuration was and why it was so. As a case study Baker draws on his area of expertise, eighteenth-century France, and takes on the classic question of the "ideological origins of the French Revolution." He chooses the term "ideological" over "intellectual" because the former is more suggestive of the contestation or disagreement that in his view characterized the political culture of France in the second half of the eighteenth century.

Baker argues that prior attempts to explain the Revolution in intellectual–historical terms have failed. The "Marxist paradigm" discouraged such investigation because it treated ideas as little more than weapons in the class struggle that led inevitably to the Revolution, and preferred to focus on what it regarded as the real cause: the class struggle itself. Moreover, Baker argues, drawing on François Furet, the reputedly Marxist tendency to view the Revolution as an "advent," i.e. as the beginning of something (in this case modernity), discouraged serious attempts at explaining its origins; its emphasis was rather on *future* developments that the inaugural or original event seemed to prefigure.

Insofar as non-Marxists have attempted to explain the ideological origins of the French Revolution, Baker sees their work as deficient. In particular, he opposes what he regards as a tendency to frame the question in terms of "The Influence of the Enlightenment on the French Revolution." This approach, in his opinion, *reifies* or treats as fixed, concrete objects what in fact are multifaceted and rapidly-changing phenomena; it thus gives a misleading impression of "influence." Equally fallacious in his view is the "linear history of doctrines" in which the supposed "logic" of a particular thinker's philosophy leads inevitably to its culmination in the

Revolution. Moreover, Baker assesses as inadequate the "quantitative studies of the book trade" and similar attempts to specify the impact of ideas on readers since they are (in his view) insufficiently attuned to *how* these ideas were interpreted, and naïvely treat "ideas as if they were causal, individual agents of motivation."[1] Finally, before offering his own explanation of the French Revolution, Baker takes on the work of two venerable historians: Alexis de Tocqueville (1805–59) and Daniel Mornet (1878–1954). He faults Tocqueville for having underestimated the degree of opposition to the alleged "despotism" of the monarchy in the eighteenth century; and he criticizes Mornet for having distinguished between "purely political" factors on the one hand and an ill-defined but somehow decisive "intelligence" on the other.

Baker's own theory of the ideological origins of the French Revolution depends upon his definition of revolution: "a transformation of the discursive practice of the community, a moment in which social relations are reconstituted and the discourse defining the political relations between individuals and groups is radically recast." In his search for the origins of this transformation toward the end of the eighteenth century in France, Baker has located three principal discourses that each served toward a rethinking of the relationship between the "public authority" (i.e. the state) and the people subject to it: (1) a *judicial* discourse, (2) a *political* discourse, and (3) an *administrative* discourse. The judicial discourse, most popular with the *parlements* and opponents of monarchical "despotism," emphasized what it called *justice*; it defined proper relations between individuals and groups in terms of historical precedent, a (largely imaginary) "constitution," and a hierarchical sense of rights as dependent upon one's rank. The political discourse, first articulated by theorists such as Rousseau and adopted by some of the more radical spokesmen for the *parlements*, emphasized *will*; it denigrated the will of individuals (including the king) as despotic, and valorized the "general will," the will of the "people" or "nation," as guaranteeing true liberty. The administrative discourse was favored by the *physiocrats*, those early economists who aimed at dismantling all obstacles to free trade within the kingdom; it was a discourse of *reason* that praised "nature" as the principle upon which human relations should be organized. According to Baker, these three discourses did not "cause" the Revolution, but they endowed the "events that destroyed the Old Regime" (e.g. the proclamation of the National Assembly, the storming of the Bastille) with "explosive meaning." At the same time, they competed with and contradicted one another. Ultimately it was the political discourse, the discourse of the *will*, that took precedence over the others,

1   Among Baker's targets here is Robert Darnton, who addresses his criticisms, as well as those of other historians, in chapter 4 of this volume.

and this victory played a crucial role "in patterning the history of the Revolution after 1789." Just how it did so is elaborated elsewhere in *Inventing the French Revolution*, but insofar as Baker explains the *origins* of the Revolution, this essay on its own serves as a powerful alternative to previous attempts.

Rousseau's "general will - denigrates the will of individuals

On the Problem of the Ideological Origins of the French Revolution

Keith Michael Baker

In recent years, intellectual historians have found themselves in an ironic position. Once under sentence of confinement to the scholastic irrelevance of the superstructure, they have seen the base–superstructure distinction almost entirely abandoned in modern social thought. Once threatened by the imperialism of behavioral social science among historians, they have witnessed a reorientation of the social sciences generally toward problems of meaning. They have watched those who dismissed ideas as the most ephemeral of appearances – and the history of ideas as a narrative cobweb to be swept away by the *Annalistes'* broom – rediscover the domain of the event as the play of meanings in human action. Structuralists have offered them the world as a text without history; poststructuralists have threatened them with the specter of history without a text. It is scarcely surprising, then, that intellectual historians have shown some of the disorientation of ghetto dwellers after the walls have been broken down, uncertain whether they have been invaded or liberated.

I can best state my own view by saying that I regard intellectual history as a mode of historical discourse, rather than as a distinct field of inquiry with a clearly demarcated subject matter. It is a way of addressing the past, a certain orientation toward history generally, rather than a separate or autonomous branch of historical scholarship in any strict or categorical sense. The intellectual historian analyzing a text, concept, or movement of ideas has the same problem as the historian faced with any other historical phenomenon, namely to reconstitute the context (or, more usually, the plurality of contexts) in which that phenomenon takes on meaning as human action. History, in other words, is a diagnostic discipline: Given the scratch, the historian seeks to discover the itch; or, to offer a less behavioristic formulation, given the solution, the historian tries to reconstitute the problem. I do not think the intellectual historian differs (or, at least, should differ) in this respect from other historians with other concerns. Let us rebuild no walls.

What, then, is the orientation characteristic of intellectual history? I would say that the intellectual historian seeks particularly to attend to the intellective dimensions of social action as historically constituted. This may seem a rather general definition, perhaps even an empty one.

But I choose it for several reasons. The first is that I want to set aside from the outset the idea that intellectual history is confined to the history of "intellectuals." This is not to say, of course, that their activities have no place in intellectual history: The nature and definition of cognitive functions in particular societies, the institutional position, social role, and conceptual claims of those who engage in more or less specialized intellectual activities, remain among the most interesting problems with which the intellectual historian is presented. They offer a rich field for comparative research of a kind that intellectual historians have barely begun to consider. However, such problems do not exhaust the domain of intellectual history, nor, indeed, could they be answered adequately if they did. Intellectual history is not simply the history of intellectuals, broad as that history may be. It is the history of "intellection," which (according to the *Oxford English Dictionary*) derives from a Latin root that implies "perceiving, discerning, discernment, understanding, meaning, sense, signification." In a word, it is the history of meaning.

But meaning is a dimension of all social action. We can therefore set aside the untenable distinction between ideas and events – and the artificial and sterile problems about the relationship and priority between them – that has so often introduced confusion and absurdity into discussion of intellectual history. The action of a rioter in picking up a stone can no more be understood apart from the symbolic field that gives it meaning than the action of a priest in picking up a sacramental vessel. The philosopher picking up a pen is not performing a less social action than the ploughman picking up a plough, nor does the latter act lack intellectual dimensions. Action implies meaning; meaning implies cultural intersubjectivity; intersubjectivity implies society. All social activity has an intellective dimension that gives it meaning, just as all intellectual activity has a social dimension that gives it point.

I do not mean to assert here that all history is intellectual history. But I think it does follow from this argument that intellectual history can have no precise boundary with other fields. On the one hand, it will seek to elicit the intellective dimensions in those forms of social action which present themselves as stable forms of behavior – those patterns of action constituted by implicit meanings that often seem indistinguishable from a description of the actions themselves. To this extent, it will merge with institutional or social history as the *histoire des mentalités*. On the other hand, it will seek to analyze those more explicit forms of intellectual activity that have been established as specialized kinds of knowledge, recognizing that the more explicit play of ideas that characterizes such activity occurs within a structured field of discourse that defines its purposes and procedures internally and establishes its existence externally as part of a set of social constraints. To this extent, intellectual history will take shape as the history of particular disciplines, genres, theories, or problems: for instance, the history of the sciences, the history of theology and philosophy, legal history, and the history of historiography. Indeed, insofar as the identity of any such discipline depends upon establishing and maintaining an appropriate genealogy, intellectual history merges imperceptibly into the practice of the discipline itself.

I should emphasize here that I am not trying to reinstate the distinction between popular and elite culture, one dominated by habit, custom, passivity, the other by creativity and the "free play" of ideas. Inherited reifications of constituted experience form many dimensions of the consciousness of the elite, no less than those of other social groups; intellectual creativity occurs within the domain of popular culture, just as it does in more specialized cognitive activities. Nor do I regard the distinction between implicit social meanings and explicitly articulated intellectual activities as an exhaustive one. On the contrary, it defines two more or less stabilized limits in the relationship between intellection and social life: two limits between which there exists a complex middle ground, where ideas seem neither to merge with the practice of concrete social life nor to separate out as the object of a set of specialized intellectual activities. This is the middle ground – more or less vast in any particular society at any particular time – in which there is a consciousness of ideas at play in social life, in which mental sets appear to form and disaggregate, in which domains of experience are claimed for competing fields of discourse, in which the relationship between words and things presents itself as problematic.

In the body of this essay, I shall consider a classic problem that falls within this domain: the problem of the ideological origins of the French Revolution. Before doing so, however, I feel obliged to return to one aspect of this brief initial effort to characterize intellectual history. I said that the intellectual historian seeks particularly to attend to the intellective dimensions of social action as historically constituted. But I have not yet touched on the problem of how one might think of these dimensions as historically constituted. I have not, that is, suggested how one might counter the Faustian bargain we seem to be offered by the structuralists: an offer of the entire world as a domain of meaning, but at the cost of our historical souls.

I can perhaps approach this problem by appealing to the metaphor of *bricolage* offered by Claude Lévi-Strauss.[1] *Bricolage* is the activity of the *bricoleur*, the jack-of-all-trades who is good with his hands, putters around in his workshop, and finds fulfillment in creating (or

---

1   Claude Lévi-Strauss, *The Savage Mind* (Chicago, 1966), 16–36.

undertaking) odd jobs. The *bricoleur* does not throw things away. He collects "bits and pieces," "odds and ends," on the assumption that they will eventually come in handy. He uses them for his purposes in an improvisational way, combining objects that had been fashioned for a variety of prior uses. Thus the distinctive features of the *bricoleur's* stock are finiteness and heterogeneity. He defines his projects in terms of what he has; his activities are preconstrained by the nature of the materials he has collected. These materials are heterogeneous, in the sense that they have no necessary or systematic relationship. They are remains, the end results of previous activities, the remnants of previous constructions. Thus their actual relationship one to another is contingent: They exist in the stock as the result of the occasions the *bricoleur* has taken to extend and renew it. And their potential relationship is unpredictable, in the sense that the *bricoleur* chooses among and combines them in ways, and for purposes, that do not derive from any necessary relationships underlying their coexistence within the stock. In this manner, Lévi-Strauss suggests, the *bricoleur* "builds up structures by fitting together events, or rather the remains of events," whereas the scientist or engineer (with whom he is contrasted) creates events by elaborating structures.[2]

If this is to be a useful metaphor for intellectual history, we must begin by avoiding the temptation to regard the *bricoleur* as a transcendent, suprahistorical subject: *Bricolage* is not the Cunning of Reason. But we can perhaps consider the intellectual stock of any society, at any particular time, as in some ways resembling that of the *bricoleur*. An inventory of that stock, which would look very much like Michel Foucault's "archive,"[3] would reveal a multiplicity of separate discourses constituting separate domains of meaning. Each of these discourses would have its own history; each would have its own "logic"; each would constitute a field of social action by categorizing the world of social actors in accordance with its own terms of reference. These discourses would coexist within the society as a whole, some remaining quite separate one from another, many overlapping in the practice of social life, as well as in the consciousness of individuals. They would be heterogeneous in the sense that they would often involve assumptions and implications that, if elaborated far enough, would contradict the assumptions and implications of others. Their relationship would be contingent in the sense that they could not be integrated into a total

2   Ibid., 22.
3   Michel Foucault, *The Archaeology of Knowledge* (1969), tr. A. M. Sheridan Smith (New York, 1972), 126–31. The following discussion draws generally on Foucault's approach to what he calls the "historical a priori" (127).

system or structure, as parts to a whole, according to a strict enchainment of logical relations. They would be arranged hierarchically in the sense that some would be regarded as controlling and some thought of as controlled, that some would be thought of as more powerful than others. But this hierarchy would be conventional rather than apodictic, political rather than logical.

How, then, could we move from a synchronic view of such an intellectual universe to a diachronic one? If we set aside the *bricoleur* as a transcendent historical agent, how can we think of the process of transformation and change that would correspond to his activity? The answer would seem to lie in emphasizing that the multiplicity of discourses we have been considering are not dead remnants, the archaeological remains of some vanished constructions. On the contrary, they are fields of social action symbolically constituted, social practices, "language games" each subject to constant elaboration and development through the activities of the individual agents whose purposes they define. Coexisting in a given society, often overlapping in social practice and in the consciousness of individuals, they are not insulated one from another in any strict way. Drawing upon common linguistic resources, they will have a greater or lesser degree of interpenetration, so that individual acts and utterances will often take on meaning within several fields of discourse simultaneously. Changes in one realm of discourse will redound upon others in unanticipated and unpredictable ways; elements from several discourses will be combined to define new domains of experience and social action. In some cases, these changes will support and reinforce one another. In others, they will create a state of tension and contradiction still negotiable within the conventional hierarchization of discourse. In others, competing claims and implications will be elaborated to such an extent that their resolution will threaten – and eventually force a redefinition of – that hierarchization in more or less radical ways.[4]

Rather than elaborating these considerations further in purely abstract terms, I shall explore the kind of approach they seem to suggest to one of the classic problems of European intellectual history, the problem of the ideological origins of the French Revolution. Why speak of "ideological," rather than "intellectual" origins? At this point, I have two answers to that question. The first is that I think it inconsistent with what I have already said to offer any strong distinction between these terms. In its original sense, "ideology" was concerned with the study of the process by which the world of phenomena is given order and

4   For what I take to be an essentially similar view of this process, see J. G. A. Pocock, "Political Languages and Their Implications," in Pocock, *Politics, Language and Time: Essays on Political Thought and History* (New York, 1971), 3–41.

meaning through the activity of signification. For the Idéologues – the fascinating and much maligned group of philosophers to whom we owe the term – that process was to be understood as an essentially individual one, grounded in a universalistic conception of natural human reason.[5] If we understand it as a social – that is [to] say, intersubjective – process, grounded in a pluralistic theory of discourse, then "ideology" and "intellection," "ideological" and "intellectual," are not strictly distinguishable.

At the same time, it may in another respect be useful to maintain a differentiation between the two sets of terms. The various uses of "ideology" have generally involved some notion of contested meaning, of the process of signification itself as problematic, of a tension between alternative – usually true (objective) and false (subjective) – constructions of the world. For the Idéologues, "ideology" offered a scientific, objective, rational understanding of the logic of the human mind: an understanding of the order of sensations and ideas that would sweep away false reasoning and establish the basis for a rational social order. In appropriating the term, Marxism inverted the relationship between "science" and "ideology," identifying the latter with the false, subjective reasoning to which the Idéologues had opposed it. But Marxism also maintained the sense of "ideology" as a matter of contested meanings – of representations of the world that are either explicitly contested by historical actors in the course of class struggle, or implicitly contested by the philosopher-historian in terms of the dichotomy between ideology and science. I would like to retain "ideology" and "ideological" in a related sense, as terms to characterize those activities and situations in which signification itself seems to be at issue in social life, in which there is a consciousness of contested representations of the world in play, in which social action takes the form of more or less explicit efforts to order or reorder the world through the articulation and deployment of competing systems of meaning.[6]

Perhaps I should add, to avoid possible misunderstanding, that I see nothing in this view that commits me to a notion of ideology as the mere

5 See George Lichtheim, "The Concept of Ideology," *History and Theory* 4 (1964–5): 164–70; Emmet Kennedy, " 'Ideology' from Destutt de Tracy to Marx," *Journal of the History of Ideas* 40 (1979): 353–68. As a result of recent work, the Idéologues are now much better understood. See Sergio Moravia, *Il tramonto dell'illuminismo: Filosofia e politica nella società francese (1770–1810)* (Bari, 1968), and *Il pensiero degli Idéologues: Scienza e filosofia in Francia (1780–1815)* (Florence, 1974); Georges Gusdorf, *Les sciences humaines et la pensée occidentale*: vol. 8, *La conscience révolutionnaire, les Idéologues* (Paris, 1978); Emmet Kennedy, *A Philosophe in the Age of Revolution: Destutt de Tracy and the Origins of "Ideology"* (Philadelphia, 1978); Martin Staum, *Cabanis: Enlightenment and Medical Philosophy in the French Revolution* (Princeton, 1980).
6 See Clifford Geertz, "Ideology as a Cultural System," in Geertz, *The Interpretation of Cultures* (New York, 1973), 193–233.

reflection of some more objective or real interests of social groups or classes. I think it points toward a conception of a "politics of language" (in the way Pocock has used that term) rather than a sociology of ideas. Group interests are not brute, objective phenomena; they rest on cognitive principles of social differentiation. A community exists only to the extent that there is some common discourse by which its members can constitute themselves as different groups within the social order and make claims upon one another that are regarded as intelligible and binding. The interaction involved in the framing of such claims is constrained within that discourse, which it in turn sustains, extends, and on occasion transforms. Political authority is, in this view, a matter of linguistic authority, both in the sense that public functions are defined and allocated within the framework of a given political discourse, and in the sense that their exercise takes the form of maintaining that discourse by upholding authoritative definitions of (and within) it. In these terms, then, a revolution can be defined as a transformation of the discursive practice of the community, a moment in which social relations are reconstituted and the discourse defining the political relations between individuals and groups is radically recast. Some such revolution, it seems safe to say, occurred in France in 1789.

Yet there has been relatively little explicit or systematic attention in recent years to the question of the ideological origins of the French Revolution: that is, to the elaboration of the field of political and social discourse – the pattern of meanings and implications – that constituted the significance of the events of 1789 and gave them explosive force. In large part, this problem has been obscured by prevailing approaches to the field, particularly by the Marxist paradigm that has dominated historical interpretation of the French Revolution until very recently. As François Furet has argued very effectively, the Marxian conception of the French Revolution as an "advent" – the rise of the bourgeoisie to power as the expression of an objective historical necessity – has obscured its nature as an "event" – as the invention of a new form of discourse constituting new modes of political and social action.[7] To the extent that competing modes of political discourse have been treated as functions of a sociological infrastructure, parlementary constitutional-

---

7   François Furet, *Penser la Révolution française* (Paris, 1978). Further references to this work will cite the English version, *Interpreting the French Revolution*, tr. Elborg Forster (Cambridge, 1981). I have considered the argument of this work more fully in a review essay, "Enlightenment and Revolution in France: Old Problems, Renewed Approaches," *Journal of Modern History* 53 (1981): 281–303. For a brief review of the historiographical collapse of the broadly Marxist consensus regarding the origins of the French Revolution, see William Doyle, *The Origins of the French Revolution* (Oxford, 1980), 7–40.

ism as noble reaction, and Enlightenment political theory as bourgeois consciousness, the question of the ideological origins of the Revolution has disappeared as an independent problem. Perhaps not surprisingly, then, one of the most telling symptoms of the weakening of the Marxist paradigm in the study of the French Revolution is the growing interest in the more directly political aspects of the period, in the goals and strategies of the political actors, in the political vocabulary of the French Revolution, not as "mere rhetoric" (two words which the last generation of historians welded together almost as inseparably as "rising" and "bourgeoisie"), but as a means of transforming the symbolic grounding of the national community, the supremely political act of redefining the body politic. The most pressing task for the historiography of the French Revolution, Furet has rightly argued, is precisely this: "to rediscover the analysis of its political dimension. But the price to pay is two-fold: not only must we stop regarding revolutionary consciousness as a more or less 'natural' result of oppression and discontent; we must also develop a conceptual understanding of this strange offspring of '*philosophie*' (its offspring, at least, in a chronological sense)."[8] In short, we must understand the language of the French Revolution as an intellectual creation.

But if, as Furet suggests, the revolutionary consciousness is the offspring of *philosophie*, we should be able to draw on the vast body of work on the Enlightenment in discussing the ideological origins of the French Revolution. Efforts to do so, however, are often obscured by a false problematic (which I am tempted to call the "Heath Pamphlet Problematic") which presents itself as the question of "The Influence of the Enlightenment on the French Revolution." To my mind, no very helpful response is likely to emerge from a question posed in these terms. "Enlightenment" and "Revolution" simply become so reified that they face one another like two blocs – or, perhaps more accurately, like two opposing pieces at the end of a game of checkers, which can be manipulated through an indefinite series of relationships without ever making contact. There have, of course, been attempts to break this issue down analytically, but they have tended to take two forms, neither of which seems to pose the question effectively. The most obvious form has been a linear history of doctrines, cast in terms of a necessary logic of ideas, usually with an emphasis on the influence of a particular doctrine or thinker. This, I suppose, is what one would call the "C'est la faute à Rousseau" style of interpretation. The most obvious example in relatively recent historiography is probably J. L. Talmon's work on the origins of totalitarian democracy, a work that, in my view, reveals some

8   Furet, *Interpreting the French Revolution*, 27–8.

of the worst excesses of the teleological tendencies in intellectual history so ably criticized by Quentin Skinner.[9]

This kind of approach can be distinguished from a second one (with which it can merge in practice), which might be called the "diffusionist" or "trickle-down" approach. Here the issue comes to rest on questions regarding the extent to which certain writings have been circulated or certain ideas diffused, and the extent to which those acting in the Revolution can be regarded as motivated to act by such ideas. I do not wish to diminish the relevance of quantitative studies of the book trade, or of efforts to investigate the circulation of ideas among particular social groups. They are important for our understanding of the nature of intellectual and social life during any period. But books are not mere objects, nor are ideas isolated units. Texts, if read, are understood, and hence reinterpreted, by their readers in con-*texts* that may transform their significance; ideas, if received, take on meaning only in relation to others in the set of ideas into which they are incorporated. Thus it is important to insist upon the distinction between examining the circulation of ideas and understanding their meaning to social actors, and to avoid treating ideas as if they were causal, individual agents of motivation and determination. Understanding the ideological origins of the French Revolution is not a matter of establishing a causal chain linking particular ideas, individual or group motivations, and events in a series of one-to-one derivations. It is not necessary, for example, to establish that everyone in the crowd attacking the Bastille in July 1789 was motivated to overthrow despotism, for that event to take on the meaning of an attack on despotism within the field of political discourse created in the course of the earlier events of that year. Nor is it necessary to deny that the Great Fear retained many elements of traditional behavior in order to recognize its significance as revolutionary action. The Revolution of 1789 depended, in effect, on the creation and deployment of a political language that cast many different kinds of behaviors, from aristocratic resistance to popular fears, into the same symbolic order. In order to understand the Revolution as a political – that is to say, public – event, we need to reconstitute the field of political discourse in which it occurred, a field in which certain kinds of actions took on meanings that often went far beyond what particular actors intended.

Yet there has been relatively little effort in contemporary historiography (though there is a body of older historiography to be recovered

9 J. L. Talmon, *The Origins of Totalitarian Democracy* (London, 1952). See Quentin Skinner, "Meaning and Understanding in the History of Ideas," *History and Theory* 8 (1969): 3–53.

on this theme) to consider the political discourse of the prerevolutionary period as an object of study in its own terms. If the power of the "social interpretation" of the French Revolution has been one reason for this lack, another seems to have been what I will call the "Tocqueville syndrome": the tendency to identify French political reflection with the activity of men of letters engaged in an "abstract and literary politics," by definition divorced from immediate problems of political and social life.

Tocqueville's characterization of the Enlightenment can be challenged in a number of ways. It can be insisted that much of its thinking, far from being abstract, was intimately related to the immediate social and political issues of the day. It can be pointed out that many of its principal spokesmen were by no means innocent of the practice of public affairs: that Montesquieu, for example, served as a magistrate in the parlement of Bordeaux; that Mably acted as a ministerial adviser on international affairs and wrote one of the standard works on international law; that Helvétius engaged in tax-farming; that Voltaire produced political tracts, at request, for several ministers; that Turgot was no less a philosophe for all his experience as intendant. And it can be demonstrated that its principal institutional expression – the provincial academies so ably studied by Daniel Roche – is characterized precisely by "the solidarity of command and power" of a ruling elite, united "in a vocation of common service to city, province or State."[10]

But these arguments do not entirely engage the argument of L'ancien régime et la Révolution. Tocqueville in fact acknowledged, both explicitly and implicitly, that the tendency to abstract radical thinking was not simply a function of a lack of practical public responsibilities. On the one hand, he allowed that eighteenth-century French thinkers, contemplating the confused and antiquated spectacle of their social order, "were *naturally* led to want to rebuild the society of their time according to an entirely new plan, which each of them drew up according to the sole light of his reason";[11] on the other, he acknowledged that even those in power yielded on occasion to the claims of abstract thinking.[12] The participation in public affairs he found lacking in France was a

---

10   Daniel Roche, *Le siècle des lumières en province: Académies et académiciens provinciaux, 1680–1789*, 2 vols. (Paris, 1978), 1:206.

11   Alexis de Tocqueville, *L'ancien régime et la Révolution*, in Tocqueville, *Oeuvres complètes*, ed. J. P. Mayer, 2(i), 6th ed. (Paris, 1952), 195, emphasis added. Although I have not followed the Gilbert translation at all points, I will also cite relevant page numbers in the standard English edition, *The Old Regime and the French Revolution*, tr. Stuart Gilbert (Garden City, N.Y., 1955), in this case 140.

12   Tocqueville, *L'ancien régime*, 200 (*Old Regime*, 147).

special kind of participation, the kind that comes only with free political institutions. Ultimately, he explained the central importance of men of letters in French public life, the radical, abstract quality of their language, and its power over the mass of Frenchmen, all in terms of a single factor: "the complete absence of all political liberty."[13] Denied the acquaintance with the nature of public affairs that comes only with free political institutions, the philosophes became even bolder in their speculations than they otherwise would have been. Innocent of the experience of self-government, and lacking any constitutional means to express their concerns, the mass of Frenchmen readily accepted these speculations as a surrogate for the expression of their political passions. Deprived of their traditional authority, even the nobility engaged in the philosophical parlor game, forgetful, owing to their lack of political freedom, of the obvious knowledge "that general theories, once accepted, are inevitably transformed into political passions and reappear in actions."[14] Thus all sections of French society, Tocqueville would have us believe, were mindless of the fact that ideas have consequences.

> But what will seem more extraordinary to us, as we contemplate the debris left by so many revolutions, is that the very idea of a violent revolution never occurred to our parents' minds. No one talked of it, no one even imagined it. The small disturbances which public liberty constantly inflicts on the most stable societies serve as a daily reminder of the possibility of upheavals and keep the public on the watch. But in this French society of the eighteenth century, which was about to fall into the abyss, there had as yet been no warning of danger.[15]

This picture is surely overdrawn. If France lacked English political liberties, it was by no means devoid of the kind of constitutional contestation many contemporaries associated with that turbulent state across the Channel. Acute observers detected revolutionary English weather in the storms that dominated the French constitutional climate in the mid-eighteenth century. "There is a philosophical wind blowing toward us from England in favor of free, anti-monarchical government," wrote the marquis d'Argenson in 1751; "it is entering minds, and one knows how opinion governs the world. It could be that this government is already accomplished in people's heads, to be implemented at the first chance, and the revolution might occur with less conflict than one thinks. All the orders of society are discontented together . . .

13 Tocqueville, *L'ancien régime*, 195 (*Old Regime*, 140).
14 Tocqueville, *L'ancien régime*, 196 (*Old Regime*, 142).
15 Tocqueville, *L'ancien régime*, 197 (*Old Regime*, 143).

a disturbance could turn into revolt, and revolt into a total revolution."[16] Considered in this context, "liberty" and "despotism," "property" and "representation," were not abstract literary counters: They were ideological claims that Jansenists hurled against oppressive clergy, that parlementary magistrates elaborated in exile and circulated in clandestinely published remonstrances, that provincial Estates mobilized against ministerial enemies. As a result of these conflicts, d'Argenson observed, the nature of *nation* and *état* were debated in mid-eighteenth-century France as never before: "These two terms were never uttered under Louis XIV; even the idea of them was lacking. We have never been so aware as we are today of the rights of the nation and of liberty."[17]

Tocqueville, who cites d'Argenson's *Mémoires* for his own purposes, did not entirely disregard the constitutional struggles which the marquis followed with such interest and apprehension. But it was crucial, for the political argument of his work, to minimize their importance. He therefore relegated them to a relatively unobtrusive chapter of *L'ancien régime et la Révolution* devoted to the "singular sort of liberty" that did still exist amid the institutions of absolutism.[18] Here the constitutional activities of the parlements are praised as "the only part of a free people's education the Old Regime gave us;" and their resistance to Maupeou in 1770 is held out as an action as noble as any in the history of free nations, even though they were "doubtless more preoccupied with their own interests than the public good."[19] Yet several chapters later, in the chapter upon which his entire work hinges, Tocqueville can still insist that Frenchmen had no interest in liberty in the mid-eighteenth century, that they had lost the very idea of it along with the practice.[20] Why the contradiction? The answer becomes clear in Tocqueville's discussion of the physiocrats, whom he in fact cites far more frequently than the philosophes in his consideration of the ideological origins of the French Revolution. The physiocrats, he argues, reveal more clearly than the

---

16   [René Louis de Voyer de Paulmy, marquis d'Argenson], *Journal et mémoires du marquis d'Argenson*, ed. J. B. Rathéry, 9 vols. (Paris, 1859–67), 6:464 (3 September 1751). Impending revolution became a recurrent theme in d'Argenson's journal during the 1750s, as the struggle between crown and parlements unfolded: See, for example, 7:23; 7:51; 7:242; 7:271; 7:295; 8:153; 9:294; 9:370. Lord Chesterfield expressed a similar view in 1752: See Charles Aubertin, *L'esprit public au XVIIIᵉ siècle*, 2d ed. (Paris, 1873), 279, n. 2.

17   *Journal et mémoires du marquis d'Argenson*, 8:315 (26 June 1754). For a concise general discussion of these constitutional conflicts, see Jean Egret, *Louis XV et l'opposition parlementaire, 1715–1774* (Paris, 1970).

18   Tocqueville, *L'ancien régime*, 168–77 (*Old Regime*, 108–20).

19   Tocqueville, *L'ancien régime*, 174–75 (*Old Regime*, 116–17).

20   Tocqueville, *L'ancien régime*, 214 (*Old Regime*, 165).

philosophes the "true nature" of the French Revolution,[21] that combination of the desire for equality with the acceptance of the despotism of centralized public authority which had emerged again in France, in his own day, with the coup d' état of Napoleon III. It was this latter phenomenon (as Richard Herr has ably demonstrated) that Tocqueville set out to explain in *L'ancien régime et la Révolution*. And he did so by maintaining that the French were infected with the egalitarian, centralizing, despotic ideology exemplified by the physiocrats ("false ideas, vicious habits and pernicious tendencies" contracted by long exposure to absolute authority) *before* they reacquired their taste for liberty.[22] Ideas of equality as implemented by centralized authority established themselves first; ideas of liberty as an alternative to centralized authority appeared only as a weaker (and ultimately incompatible) second.[23] To buttress this argument, Tocqueville was therefore obliged to set aside the actual political conflicts of the mid-eighteenth century (in which the conflict between liberty and despotism became clearly defined as the central issue), despite the quite compelling evidence of their importance in the development of French political consciousness. Later historians have tended to follow his lead in minimizing the importance of these constitutional struggles or writing off the political language of the parlements as a mere guise for the defense of particular social interests.

Thus it was the effect of Tocqueville's analysis to emphasize the gap between philosophical thinking and immediate realities of political life, on the one hand, and to divert attention from the ideological significance of the actual political conflicts that occurred in eighteenth-century France on the other. Both of these issues need to be reexamined. The philosophes need to be considered within the spectrum of political language existing in their own day, not artificially insulated from it; the nature of eighteenth-century French political culture needs to be

21   Tocqueville, *L'ancien régime*, 209 (*Old Regime*, 158).
22   Tocqueville, *L'ancien régime*, 213–16, 190 (*Old Regime*, 163–7, 137). See Richard Herr, *Tocqueville and the Old Regime* (Princeton, 1962), esp. 56–63.
23   "It was this desire to introduce political liberty in the midst of ideas and institutions that were incompatible with it but that had become ingrained in our tastes and habits – it was this desire that has, over the last sixty years, produced so many vain attempts to create free government, followed by such disastrous revolutions. Finally, tired by so much effort, disgusted by such a painful and sterile undertaking, many Frenchmen abandoned their second objective [political liberty] in order to return to their first [efficient administration and social equality] and found themselves welcoming the realization that to live in equality under a master still had, after all, a certain attraction. Thus it is that we resemble much more today the economists of 1750 than our fathers of 1789." (*L'ancien régime*, 216 [*Old Regime*, 167–8]. In this case, I have followed the translation by Herr, *Tocqueville and the Old Regime*, 61–2, including his interpolations.)

reconsidered in its own terms, rather than denied by comparison with English political liberties. Neither of these suggestions is new.[24] Yet, oddly enough, there has been no systematic effort to reconstitute the discourse of French public life in the decades preceding the French Revolution, nor has there been a full-scale attempt to recover the competing representations of social and political existence from which the revolutionary language ultimately emerged. Despite the wealth of material available (though perhaps, in part, because of it), there is no equivalent for prerevolutionary France of Bernard Bailyn's *Ideological Origins of the American Revolution*.[25]

Daniel Mornet's classic work is a particularly interesting contrast in this respect. *Les origines intellectuelles de la Révolution française* is presented as "a history of the intellectual origins of the Revolution and not a history of revolutionary ideas."[26] Since these latter (liberty, equality, fraternity, the social contract, and so on) have existed more or less confusedly in all human societies, Mornet argued, a history of revolutionary ideas would require an endless genealogical regression into the history of political doctrines. But what, then, does Mornet mean by the "intellectual origins" of the Revolution? Can one, indeed, write such a history without also writing a history of ideas? The effort to do so seems to me one explanation of why Mornet's erudite and far-ranging work is yet so concrete in some respects and so elusive in others. Something is being diffused in Mornet's prerevolutionary France, but it is difficult to say precisely what it is. It seems to be a critical attitude of mind or habit of thinking, subversive of authority in all aspects. Mornet's favorite term for it is *intelligence*.[27] Yet, in an odd way, he appears to offer us a story of the growth of a habit of thinking, without any sustained analysis of its categories of thought.

This lack is particularly noticeable in relationship to political thinking. In this respect, Mornet suggests another distinction that is quite revealing: a distinction between "intellectual causes" of the Revolution and "purely political" causes. Purely political causes involve "situations

---

24 See, for example, Peter Gay, *Voltaire's Politics* (Princeton, 1959), and *The Enlightenment: An Interpretation*: vol. 2, *The Science of Freedom* (New York, 1969); Furio Diaz, *Filosofia e politica nel Settecento francese* (Turin, 1962).

25 Bernard Bailyn, *The Ideological Origins of the American Revolution* (Cambridge, Mass., 1967).

26 Daniel Mornet, *Les origines intellectuelles de la Révolution française (1715–1787)*, 6th ed. with preface by R. Pomeau (Paris, 1967), 1.

27 "Our study proposes precisely to examine this role of intelligence in the preparation of the French Revolution," Mornet explains by way of introduction (*Les origines intellectuelles*, 2). In his conclusion, he speaks of "this vast, active, passionate awakening of intelligence [which] was not limited to Paris or some large towns" (475). See also the text to note 30 in the present chapter.

or events intolerable enough to inspire the desire to change or resist, without any other reflection than the sentiment of suffering and the search for immediate causes and remedies." This latter search is revealed in "purely political works . . . limited to setting out these situations and events, these causes and these remedies, without ever seeking to generalize, or to base themselves on principles and doctrines." By contrast, purely intellectual causes express themselves in "the study of these principles and doctrines without concern, at least in appearance, for the political realities of the present time."[28] Of course, Mornet insisted that this dichotomy was more theoretical than real, particularly in relation to eighteenth-century France: "The purely political actor [*le politique pur*] will seek to fortify his claims by appealing to philosophical justice and reason; the philosopher will construct his doctrine to resolve the problems that real life and contemporary politics have posed."[29] Yet what is missing in this formulation – or, more properly, precluded by it – is exactly the sense of politics as constituted within a field of discourse, and of political language as elaborated in the course of political action. This is perhaps the reason for the striking absence in Mornet's work of any sustained discussion of the constitutional conflicts that were so central a feature of French public life after the middle of the century, and of the conflicting representations of the social order that were elaborated in response to them. "It is intelligence," Mornet insists in the very last words of his book, "that produced, organized the consequences, and gradually came to demand the Estates General. And from the Estates General, but without intelligence suspecting it, would come forth the Revolution."[30] Unfortunately, Mornet offers us a history of that intelligence without providing us with the language in which it was articulated. It is difficult to imagine how from an intelligence so inarticulate so profound an utterance could spring.

This does not mean that we must resort to the endless genealogy of revolutionary ideas that Mornet regarded as the logical alternative to his own approach. On the contrary, we should aim not to write the history of particular unit ideas, but to identify a field of political discourse, a set of linguistic patterns and relationships that defined possible actions and utterances and gave them meaning.[31] We need, in short, to reconstitute

28   Mornet, *Les origines intellectuelles*, 431.
29   Ibid.
30   Ibid., 477.
31   For a suggestive move in this direction, informed by a sophisticated linguistic analysis, see the work of Régine Robin: "Fief et seigneurie dans le droit et l'idéologie juridique à la fin du XVIIIᵉ siècle," *Annales historiques de la Révolution française* 43 (1971): 554–602; Régine Robin and Denise Maldidier, "Polémique idéologique et affrontement discursif en 1776: Les grands édits de Turgot et les remontrances du

the political culture within which the creation of the revolutionary language of 1789 became possible. It is the burden of the essays gathered in the first two parts of this volume to suggest that this political culture began to emerge in the 1750s and 1760s and that its essential elements were already clear by the beginning of Louis XVI's reign.[32] In the course of these two decades, politics broke out of the absolutist mold. *Opinion* became *opinion publique*: not a social function but a political category, the *tribunal du public*, the court of final appeal for monarchical authority, as for its critics.[33] *Droit public* – the nature of the political order and the conditions under which the nation existed as a collective body – became the ultimate question upon which that tribunal was called to decide. And the *publiciste* as learned authority on the nature of *droit public* began to give way to the publicist as man of letters whose ambition it was to define the language of the court of public opinion by laying down the meaning of terms.[34]

The various efforts to reconstitute the meaning of *droit public* and redefine the nature of the social order in France were remarkable in their number and complexity. But I think they can be understood in terms of three basic strands of discourse. These strands represent a disaggregation of the attributes traditionally bound together in the concept of monarchical authority – reason, justice and will – and their reconceptualization as the basis of competing definitions (or attempted redefinitions) of the body politic. According to the traditional language of absolutism, monarchical authority is characterized as the exercise of justice, that justice by which each receives his due in a hierarchical

Parlement de Paris," in J. Guilhaumou, D. Maldidier, A. Prost, and R. Robin, *Langage et idéologies: Le discours comme objet de l'histoire* (Paris, 1974), 13–80: Régine Robin, *Histoire et linguistique* (Paris, 1974). The *cahiers* of 1789 have also been the subject of an important study by George Taylor, "Revolutionary and Non-Revolutionary Content in the *Cahiers* of 1789: An Interim Report," *French Historical Studies* 7 (1971–2): 479–502.

32   Several paragraphs, sketching arguments now developed more fully in later essays in this volume, have been deleted here from the version of this essay originally published.

33   On the *tribunal du public*, see Edmond Jean François Barbier, *Chronique de la régence et du règne de Louis XV (1718–1763)*, 8 vols. (Paris, 1885), 6:512 (March 1757), citing the denunciation of unauthorized writings concerning the Damiens affair by Joly de Fleury, *avocat général* of the parlement of Paris. On the emergence of the term *opinion publique* more generally, see Jürgen Habermas, *Strukturwandel der Oeffentlichkeit* (Neuwied, 1962), 104–18.

34   On the term *publiciste*, see Ferdinand Brunot, *Histoire de la langue française des origines à 1900*, new ed., 13 vols. (Paris, 1966–1972), 6(i):36; Walther von Wartburg, *Französisches etymologisches Wörterbuch*, 21 vols. (Bonn, 1928–65), 9:508. Malesherbes offered an interesting historical view of this process in the *Remontrances* of the Cour des aides in 1775.

society of orders and estates. Justice is given effect by the royal will, which is preserved from arbitrariness by reason and counsel. In the second part of the eighteenth century, this cluster of attributes seems to separate into three strands of discourse, each characterized by the analytical priority it gives to one or the other of these terms. What I shall call the judicial discourse emphasizes *justice*. What I shall call the political discourse emphasizes *will*. What I shall call the administrative discourse emphasizes *reason*. These three competing vocabularies structure the language of opposition to monarchical authority, just as they define the efforts and claims of its defenders.

The idea that royal power is essentially judicial remains a constant theme of monarchical theorists throughout the eighteenth century. At the same time, it provides the essential topos in the parlementary constitutionalism that becomes so important in focusing the attack on royal despotism in the 1750s and afterward. It finds its clearest expression in the argument for a traditional constitution, a historically constituted order of things which both defines and limits royal power, and which it is the function of royal authority to uphold. The essential notions in this discourse are justice as the recognition of that which is fitting and proper (giving each his due in a hierarchical society of orders and Estates); social order as constituted by prescription, tradition, and continuity; the exercise of public power according to constitutionally prescribed legal forms; and public participation understood in the most traditional sense of making representations, that is, framing particularistic claims. This is the prevailing language of parlementary attacks on ministerial despotism. It is still perceptible in the more liberal constitutionalism of figures such as Malesherbes, and it informs much of the resistance to monarchical reform in the immediate prerevolutionary period.

Alongside this discourse of justice, however, and increasingly in tension with it, there emerges a discourse of will. Again this remains a characteristic of defenses of royal sovereignty in more or less traditional terms. But it also becomes the central feature of a vocabulary of opposition to monarchical authority that is couched in explicitly political, rather than quasi-judicial or quasi-constitutional terms. In this discourse, social order is defined not in terms of justice, law, prescription, adjudication, but in terms of will, liberty, contingency, choice, participation. If, in the judicial discourse, will is opposed to justice as the arbitrary and contingent to the lawful and constituted, in the political discourse will is opposed to will. Royal power is despotic, not because it is the exercise of will per se, but because that will is royal or particular, not national or general. The discourse of will provides the dominant language in Rousseau and Mably, in some of the works of the radical parlementary propagandists, and eventually in Sieyès's famous pamphlet *Qu'est-ce que le Tiers Etat?*

This discourse of will can in turn be distinguished from a third discourse, a discourse of reason. In its terms, the ancient constitution has become a present contradiction, of which the arbitrariness of royal will is but one expression. The contingency of royal will must give way, not to the assertion of the political will of the nation, but to the exercise of reason and enlightenment. The social order must be reconstituted on the basis of nature – which is to say, property and civic equality – in order to transform political contingency into rational order, arbitrary government into rational administration, law into education, and representation into an institutional means for the expression of rational social choice. Thus, in contrast to the discourse of will which frequently appeals to the model of the ancient city states, the discourse of reason is a discourse of modernity that emphasizes the growth of civilization and the progress of civil society. Elements of this language pervade much of the political thought of the Enlightenment, as well as the thinking of some of the enlightened administrators of the period; it is at its clearest in the discourse of Turgot and the physiocrats, whose aim is to transpose the problem of social order into the language of social science. At the end of the Old Regime, it sustains the reform program of the monarchy for greater administrative uniformity, civil rights, and fiscal equality, and for the representation of social interests through the participation of property owners in the rational conduct of local government by provincial assemblies.

The emergence, elaboration, and interpretation of these three discourses, I think it can be argued, defined the political culture that emerged in France in the later part of the eighteenth century and provided the ideological framework that gave explosive meaning to the events that destroyed the Old Regime. The origins of the political language of 1789, the language that came to constitute the grounding of the new order, cannot be found solely in any one of them. Instead, it seems to have been created from the competition among them. The revolutionaries replaced the historical jumble they characterized as "feudalism" with a rational social order grounded in nature; in doing so, they based their reconstitution of society on such principles as property, public utility, and the rights of man. To this extent, they achieved the goals and accepted a language defined within the discourse of reason. At the same time, they established responsible government subject to the rule of law and insisted that public authority be limited constitutionally in a system of representative government. To this extent, they fulfilled the purposes and accepted some of the language of the constitutionalism that I have associated with the discourse of justice. But all of this was construed as an act of will, as an expression of the general will of a nation that declared itself one and indivisible in the assertion of its inalienable sovereignty. All of this was bracketed, in short, within the discourse of will. The result was a transformed political discourse with its own tensions and contradictions, which in turn played their part in patterning the history of the Revolution after 1789.

3

The Cultural Origins of the French Revolution

Roger Chartier

Originally appeared as Roger Chartier, *The Cultural Origins of the French Revolution*, trans. Lydia G. Cochrane (1991) pp. 3–7, 15–37.

Editor's Introduction

Roger Chartier shares several of Keith Baker's inclinations. In particular, he maintains his colleague's belief that Daniel Mornet (1878–1954) was wrong to draw a strict distinction between "intelligence" and "political causes" of the French Revolution, and that Alexis de Tocqueville (1805–59) presented a similarly misleading dichotomy between ideas and politics. Moreover, like Baker, he maintains an ambivalent stance toward the philosophy of Michel Foucault (1926–84). Both embrace Foucault's concept of *discourse*, yet both confront his critique of historiography. If Baker attempts to avoid the "Faustian bargain" that seems to impart insights into human activity at the price of the historian's "soul,"[1] Chartier addresses Foucault's objections to the tendency of historians to search for *origins*. For Foucault this project was *teleological*, i.e. it falsely attributed a *telos* or "goal" to historical events and simultaneously created the illusion of *continuity* over time and space. Chartier suggests that the search for origins is the only means by which historians can impose order upon the chaos of the past, yet he recognizes the danger of falsification that such searches entail. With respect to the origins of the French Revolution in particular, he attempts to reduce this danger by seeking *cultural* as opposed to merely *intellectual* origins.

What is the difference between cultural and intellectual origins? For Chartier, who draws on the field of *cultural sociology*, cultural origins would

1 See chapter 2.

include "well-elaborated thoughts," i.e. the presumed activity of intellectuals, as well as "unmediated . . . representations" (read: impressions
people send and receive without reflection) and "automatic . . . loyalties."
He suggests, moreover, that these latter phenomena are a better guide to
origins because they remain unconscious to future generations actively in
search of a legitimizing "paternity," whereas those same later generations
could easily construct a "genealogy" (which historians would accept
uncritically) with the discourse of well-known philosophical texts. Yet
where does one find these unarticulated "representations" and "loyalties"?
Chartier claims that one must look at *practices*, which for the purposes
of his study involve what and how people read, wrote, and discussed the
"well-elaborated thoughts" of the day. Alternatively, he designates these
practices as *forms of intellectual sociability*. Here he departs from Baker,
who, while acknowledging the social aspects of "intellection," does not
examine them systematically. As to the "well-elaborated thoughts" themselves, however, Chartier echoes Baker's (and Foucault's) call for considering them as *discourse* and thus restoring the *political* dimension to the
culture in question. Thus the proper object of study is not culture *per se*,
but *political culture*.

Crucial to Chartier's argument is the relationship it establishes
between discourse and practice.[2] In particular, Chartier is skeptical of the
notion that "practices can be deduced from the discourses that authorize
or justify them." As an example of this error he points to the approach
that "sees the diffusion of philosophical ideas as leading to acts of rupture
directed at the established authorities, on the assumption that actions are
engendered by thoughts." Although he claims that this mistake is "typical
of all the literature devoted to the Enlightenment," his apparent target is
Robert Darnton, whose work he explicitly challenges elsewhere in his *Cultural Origins*. (For a sample of Darnton's work, including his response to
Chartier's criticism, see chapter 4.) Furthermore, just as Chartier questions the assumption that one can deduce practice from discourse, he
similarly doubts that one can derive discourse from practice, or "that it
is possible to translate into the terms of an explicit ideology the latent
meaning of social mechanism." Among those explicitly charged with this
error is Augustin Cochin (1876–1916), who had assumed the "Jacobin"
character of the Old Regime philosophical societies on the basis of their
"democratic" forms of organization. Implicitly guilty by association is

---

2   Baker would no doubt deny the distinction between doing on the one hand and
writing or saying on the other. As a follower of the "Cambridge school" of linguistics,
he is committed to the notion of the *performative* nature of language, or, as philosopher of language J. L. Austin (1911–60) put it, that one can "do things with words."
How To Do Things With Words (Cambridge, MA: Harvard University Press, 1962). Indeed,
Foucault himself considered discourse inseparable from practice.

François Furet (1927–97) who drew on Cochin's analysis in his own explanation of "Jacobinism."[3]

In contrast to an approach that assumes "harmony" between what people said and what they did, Chartier emphasizes the "discordances" that he believes existed not only between any given practice and the discourse that served to justify it, but from one discourse to the next and from one practice to the next. "If the Revolution did indeed have cultural origins," he claims, "they resided" in these "discordances." The section (a complete chapter in his *Cultural Origins*) entitled, "The Public Sphere and Public Opinion," can be seen as a case study of such discordances. For his definition of the public sphere, or more precisely, the "political public sphere," Chartier relies on the German social philosopher Jürgen Habermas (1929–), who characterizes this eighteenth-century phenomenon as a space in which autonomous, "bourgeois" individuals gathered to discuss matters of government, thus implicitly or explicitly undermining the authority of the state. (Chartier observes that the political public sphere undermined the church as well by engaging in the long-forbidden discussion of the "mysteries of religion.") In *practice*, this sphere was based in *salons* (drawing-room meetings of writers, artists, and scientists typically hosted by wealthy women), cafés, clubs (including "philosophical societies") and, most crucial for Habermas, the scholarly journals through which ideas were distributed. The *discourse* that authorized or legitimized these practices was the notion of "public opinion."

Like Habermas himself, Chartier looks to the moral philosopher Immanuel Kant (1724–1804) for a description of the public opinion ideal. According to Kant, the "public" use of reason was not, as the term would seem to imply, the activity of a public official, but that of a private person whose thoughts were communicated to a *universal* audience, which Kant called "a society of world citizens." Yet Kant's precondition for membership in this universal society was the ability to communicate one's thoughts in the "universal" medium of print. Thus the "society of world citizens" was in fact a "reading public" composed of "scholars" who were capable not only of reading but of writing as well. Paradoxically, then, an activity deemed universal (i.e. the public use of reason) was limited to a tiny minority of private individuals with the financial means and education to publish. The "people," that is the majority of the population, were thus excluded from the "public."

Chartier descibes a similar discrepancy between discourse and practice in France. Following Baker as well as historian Mona Ozouf, he notes that the term "people" held negative connotations in France but that after 1750, in the wake of "constitutional" conflicts between the *parlements* and

3   See chapter 1.

the monarchy, the notion of "public opinion" suddenly emerged.[4] According-ing to its proponents, public opinion was a kind of "tribunal" in which "men of letters" – again access to the machinery of publication is crucial – were authorized to make judgments on everything from aesthetic matters to the question of the best form of government. Its legitimacy derived from its *universality*, which in turn came from the fact that it did not reside in any particular institution. Yet the discourse of public opinion, while claiming universality, masked the real social fact that a "line of demar-cation ran between those who could read and produce written matter and those who could not." Once this contradiction was exposed, Chartier suggests, further "discordances" were inevitable.

4   Here Chartier draws again on the work of Keith Baker, as well as scholarship by Mona Ozouf, whose work on a different subject is excerpted in chapter 10 of this volume.

The Cultural Origins of the French Revolution

Roger Chartier

Enlightenment and Revolution; Revolution and Enlightenment

Any reflection on the cultural origins of the French Revolution leads ineluctably back to a classic, Daniel Mornet's *Les Origines intellectuelles de la Révolution française 1715–1787*.[1] Mornet's work seems to dictate the only possible perspective for further work, a perspective that postulates an evident and obligatory connection between the progress of new ideas throughout the eighteenth century and the emergence of the Revolution as an event. For Mornet, three laws governed the penetration of the new ideas that he identified with the Enlightenment into general public opinion. First, ideas descended the social scale from "the highly cultivated classes toward the bourgeoisie, the petty bourgeoisie, and the people."[2] Second, this penetration spread from the center (Paris) toward the periphery (the provinces). Finally, the process accelerated

---

1 Daniel Mornet, *Les Origines intellectuelles de la Révolution française 1715–1787* (Paris: Armand Colin, 1933, 1967). This work was written roughly at the midpoint of Mornet's career; he was a faithful disciple of Gustave Lanson, professor of letters at the Sorbonne. Before World War I Mornet published *Le Sentiment de la nature en France. De Jean-Jacques Rousseau à Bernardin de Saint-Pierre* (Paris: Hachette, 1907); "Les enseignements des bibliothèques privées (1750–1780)," *Revue d'Histoire Littéraire de la France* (July–September 1910): 449–96; and *Les Sciences de la nature en France au XVIIIe siècle* (Paris: Armand Colin, 1911). Three requirements, strongly expressed in his *Origines intellectuelles*, underlay Mornet's approach and distanced him from aesthetically inclined and ahistorical literary criticism: the demand to grasp the literary production of an epoch in its totality rather than limiting study to the "great" authors and "great" texts of tradition and the literary canon; the need to investigate not only the texts but the literary institutions, the works' circulation, and their audience (which led Mornet in his 1910 article to a pioneering interest in library inventories); the importance of using counts and percentages to measure circulation ("what matters just as much as the number is the proportion of the number," *Origines intellectuelles*, p. 457). In his later works – the *Histoire de la littérature française classique, 1600–1700, ses caractères véritables et ses aspects inconnus* (Paris: Armand Colin, 1940), for example – Mornet shifted away from Lanson's perspective, which earned him a biting critique from Lucien Febvre in "De Lanson à Daniel Mornet. Un renoncement?" *Annales d'Histoire Sociale* 3 (1941), an article reprinted in Febvre's collected essays in *Combats pour l'histoire* (Paris: Armand Colin, 1953).
2 Mornet, *Origines intellectuelles*, p. 2.

during the course of the century, beginning with minorities who anticipated the new ideas before 1750 and continuing in the decisive and mobilizing conflicts of the mid-century to arrive, after 1770, at a universal diffusion of the new principles. This led Mornet to the book's underlying thesis, that "it was, in part, ideas that determined the French Revolution."[3] Even if he did not deny the importance – indeed, the primacy – of political causes, Mornet set up Enlightenment thought, in both its critical and its reforming aspects, as a necessary precondition for the final crisis of the old monarchy as it moved toward revolution: "Political causes would doubtless not have been sufficient to determine the Revolution, at least not as rapidly. It was intelligence that drew out and organized its consequences."[4]

In spite of his prudence and his rectifications (clearly signaled in his writing by expressions such as "in part," "doubtless," and "at least"), Mornet postulated a necessary connection between the Enlightenment and the Revolution. The reasons for the Revolution were, of course, not entirely contained in philosophy, but without transformations in "public thought" wrought by "the intelligence," that event could not have occurred when it did. This led Mornet to a working hypothesis that for the last fifty years has haunted both the intellectual history and the cultural sociology of the eighteenth century.

The Chimera of Origins

Doubts have arisen, however, that insinuate that the question may have been badly put. First of all, under what conditions is it legitimate to set up a collection of scattered and disparate facts or ideas as "causes" or "origins" of an event? The operation is not as self-evident as it may seem. On the one hand, it supposes a sorting-out process that retains, out of the innumerable realities that make up the history of an epoch, only the matrix of the future event. On the other hand, it demands a retrospective reconstruction that gives unity to thoughts and actions supposed to be "origins" but foreign to one another, heterogeneous by their nature and discontinuous in their realization.

Following Nietzsche, Michel Foucault has offered a devastating criticism of the notion of origin understood in this sense.[5] Assuming the

---

3   Ibid., p. 3.
4   Ibid., p. 477.
5   Michel Foucault, "Nietzsche, la Généalogie, l'Histoire," in his *Hommage à Jean Hyppolite* (Paris: Presses Universitaires de France, 1971), pp. 145–72, available in English as "Nietzsche, Genealogy, History," in Foucault, *Language, Counter-Memory, Practice: Selected Essays and Interviews*, trans. Donald F. Bouchard and Sherry Simon (Ithaca: Cornell University Press, 1977), pp. 139–64.

absolute linearity of the course of history, justifying a never-ending search for beginnings and annulling the originality of the event as already present before it happens, recourse to this category obliterates both the radical discontinuity of abrupt historical changes and the irreducible discordance separating the various series of discourses and practices. When history succumbs to "the chimera of origins," it burdens itself, perhaps unconsciously, with several presuppositions: that every historical moment is a homogeneous totality endowed with an ideal and unique meaning present in each of the realities that make up and express that whole; that historical becoming is organized as an ineluctable continuity; that events are linked together, one engendering another in an uninterrupted flow of change that enables us to decide that one is the "cause," another the "effect." For Foucault, however, it was precisely these classical notions of totality, continuity, and causality that "genealogical" or "archaeological" analysis had to escape if it wanted to render an adequate account of rupture and divergence. Like the *wirkliche Historie* of Nietzsche, such an analysis "transposes the relationship ordinarily established between the eruption of an event and necessary continuity. An entire historical tradition (theological or rationalistic) aims at dissolving the singular event into an ideal continuity – as a teleological movement or a natural process. 'Effective' history, however, deals with events in terms of their most unique characteristics, their most acute manifestations."[6] If history is to replace a search for origins with "the systematic deployment of the notion of discontinuity,"[7] the very pertinence of the question with which we began is undermined.

This is all the more true since the notion of origin entails the further risk of proposing a teleological reading of the eighteenth century that seeks to understand it only in relation to the phenomenon deemed to be its necessary outcome – the French Revolution – and to focus only on the phenomenon seen to lead to this outcome – the Enlightenment. However, precisely what should be questioned is the retrospective illusion inherent in "the regressive movement that enables us to read premonitory signs when the event has arrived at completion and when we regard the past from a point of arrival that perhaps was not necessarily its future."[8] In affirming that it was the Enlightenment that produced the Revolution, the classical interpretation perhaps inverses logical order: should we not consider instead that it was the Revolution that invented the Enlightenment by attempting to root its legitimacy in a corpus of texts and founding authors reconciled and united, beyond

6 Foucault, "Nietzsche," p. 161; *Language*, p. 154.
7 Foucault, "Réponse au Cercle d'Epistémologie," *Cahiers pour l'Analyse* 9, Généalogie des Sciences (Eté 1968): 9–40, quotation p. 11.
8 Jean Marie Goulemot, "Pouvoirs et savoirs provinciaux au XVIIIe siècle," *Critique* 397–398 (1980): 603–13.

their extreme differences, by their preparation of a rupture with the old world?[9] When they brought together (not without debate) a pantheon of ancestors including Voltaire, Rousseau, Mably, and Raynal, when they assigned a radically critical function to philosophy (if not to all the Philosophes), the revolutionaries constructed a continuity that was primarily a process of justification and a search for paternity. Finding the "origins" of the event in the ideas of the century – which was Mornet's program – would be a way of repeating, without knowing it, the actions of the persons involved in the event itself and of holding as established historically a filiation that was proclaimed ideologically.

Can the difficulty be circumvented by a reformulation that replaces the category of *intellectual* origins with that of *cultural* origins? Such a substitution would undoubtedly do much to increase the possibilities for comprehension. On the one hand, the notion of cultural origins assumes that cultural institutions are not simple receptacles for (or resistances to) ideas forged elsewhere. This permits us to restore a dynamic of their own to forms of sociability, means of communication, and educational processes that is denied them by an analysis like Mornet's that considers them only from the point of view of the ideology that they contain or transmit. On the other hand, an approach in terms of cultural sociology opens a large range of practices that must be taken into consideration: not only clear and well-elaborated thoughts but also unmediated and embodied representations; not only voluntary and reasoned engagements but also automatic and obligatory loyalties. This enables the revolutionary event to be placed within the long-term transformations of what Edgar Quinet designated "temperament" when he contrasted the inflexible nature of the religious reformers of the sixteenth century and the more malleable temper of the revolutionaries of the eighteenth century,[10] opening the way to an essential reflection on variations in the structure of personality, or, to use Norbert Elias's terminology, psychic economy.[11] But will this enlargement of perspective

9   Thomas Schleich, *Aufklärung und Revolution. Die Wirkungsgeschichte Gabriel Bonnot de Mablys in Frankreich (1740–1914)* (Stuttgart: Klett-Cotta, 1981), p. 210; Hans Ulrich Gumbrecht and Rolf Reichardt, "Philosophe, Philosophie," in *Handbuch politisch-sozialer Grundbegriffe in Frankreich 1680–1820*, 10 vols., ed. Rolf Reichardt and Eberhard Schmitt (Munich: R. Oldenbourg Verlag, 1985–), 3:7–88. See also Jeremy Popkin, "Recent Western German Work on the French Revolution," *Journal of Modern History* 59 (December 1987): 737–50.
10   Edgar Quinet, *La Révolution* (Paris: A. Lacroix, Verboeckhoven et cie, 1865; reprint, Paris: Belin, Littérature politique, 1987), "Timidité d'esprit des hommes de la Révolution," pp. 185–90, and "Du Tempérament des hommes de la Révolution et de celui des hommes des révolutions religieuses," pp. 513–15.
11   Norbert Elias, *Über den Prozess der Zivilisation. Soziogenetische und psychogenetische Untersuchungen* (1939; Frankfurt-am-Main: Suhrkamp, 1969); available

be enough to avoid the snares of teleological interpretation? "The postulate that 'what actually happened' did so of necessity is a classical retrospective illusion of historical consciousness, which sees the past as a field of possibilities within which 'what actually happened' appears *ex post facto* as the only future for that past," François Furet wrote,[12] putting us on guard against the a posteriori reconstructions that seem to be necessarily implied in any search for origins.

But is this danger avoidable? Must we, inspired by "counterfactual history," behave as if we were unaware of how the 1780s ended? Must we suspend judgment and suppose that the French Revolution never took place? It might be amusing, even profitable, to take up that challenge. But if we did, what question and what principle of intelligibility would we use to organize our interrogation of the many series of discourse and practice that intertwine to make up what is usually designated as the culture of eighteenth-century France? History stripped of all temptation to teleology would risk becoming an endless inventory of disconnected facts abandoned to their teeming incoherence for want of a hypothesis to propose a possible order among them. Whether we like it or not, then, we have to work within the terrain staked out by Mornet (and before him by the revolutionaries themselves) and consider that no approach to a historical problem is possible outside the historiographical discourse that constructed it. The question posed by *Les Origines intellectuelles de la Révolution française* – the question of the relationship of ideas formulated and propagated by the Enlightenment to the occurrence of the Revolution – will serve us as a set of problems that we both accept and place aside, that we receive as a legacy and continue to subject to doubt.

. . .

The Political Culture of the Old Regime

Any attempt to reformulate the question that Mornet posed fifty years ago inevitably leads to taking a fresh look at the categories that he took

in French as *La Civilisation des moeurs* (Paris: Calmann-Lévy, 1973), and *La Dynamique de l'Occident* (Paris: Calmann-Lévy, 1975), and in English as *The Civilizing Process: Sociogenetic and Psychogenetic Investigations*, trans. Edmund Jephcott (Oxford: Basil Blackwell, 1978, 1982; New York: Pantheon Books, 1982).

12   François Furet, *Penser la Révolution française* (Paris: Gallimard, 1978), p. 35, quoted from *Interpreting the French Revolution*, trans. Elborg Forster (Cambridge: Cambridge University Press, Paris: Editions de la Maison des sciences de l'homme, 1981), p. 19.

for granted and to constructing other categories that for him had little pertinence. The notion of "political culture" is one such category. Faithful to Lanson, the entire plan of *Les Origines intellectuelles de la Révolution française* was aimed at discerning the dynamics of a diffusion after 1750, and even more after 1770, that gradually introduced the new ideas into all cultural institutions and social milieux. Thus Mornet was interested in forms of intellectual sociability, in book readership and newspaper circulation, in what was taught in schools, and in the progress of Freemasonry. His book notes the introduction of these institutions, measures participation in them, and remarks on innovations, thus opening up a new field of research that the retrospective cultural sociology of the 1960s took up with greater rigor and urgency. In doing so, however, Mornet's *Origines* created a reductive dichotomy that set "principles and doctrines" against "political realities," thus returning to a bland form of Tocqueville's distinction between general theories and practical experience in public affairs. His scheme left no place for political culture, if that culture is understood as "constituted within a field of discourse, and of political language as elaborated in the course of political action."[13]

To consider the politics of the Old Regime as a set of concurrent discourses within an area unified by identical references and by the constitution of goals accepted by all the protagonists opens two perspectives. On the one hand, it becomes possible to connect the two domains that Tocqueville so clearly – perhaps too clearly – separated: the "government" and "literary politics." To counteract the vision of an all-powerful, inexorable, and seamless administrative centralization, we should stress the importance of the political and "constitutional" conflicts that shook the foundations of the monarchy after 1750. Similarly, to counter the idea of an abstract, homogeneous, unique public policy we need to note the vivacity of rival currents within philosophical discourse that presented contrasting representations of social and political order. It is certain, in any event, that contemporaries were quite aware of the radical transformation of discourse and political debate, starting with the Jansenist crisis and the withdrawal of the sacraments from the priests who had refused to subscribe to the papal bull *Unigenitus*, and with the strengthening of parlementary resistance. Not only did intellectual ferment expose the secret workings of the state, thus depriving,

13　Keith Michael Baker, "On the Problem of the Ideological Origins of the French Revolution," in *Modern European Intellectual History: Reappraisals and New Perspectives*, ed. Dominick LaCapra and Steven L. Kaplan (Ithaca: Cornell University Press, 1982), pp. 197–219, quotation p. 212; Baker, *Inventing the French Revolution: Essays on French Political Culture in the Eighteenth Century* (Cambridge: Cambridge University Press, 1990), pp. 12–27.

it of powers of restraint over people's minds; more important, the discussion that had been launched focused on the very nature of the monarchy and its founding principles.[14]

Furthermore, setting up the politics of the Old Regime as a discrete field of discourse – not to be merged either with philosophical thought or with the exercise of state authority – allows us to reinvest the intellectual sociability of the century with a political content, even though the manifest practices of that sociability seem distant from conflicts over power. There are two ways to portray that politicization. The first identifies the various associations of the eighteenth century (clubs, literary societies, Masonic lodges) as places in which to experiment and elaborate a democratic sociability that found its most complete and explicit form in Jacobinism. The *sociétés de pensée* of the Enlightenment developed individualistic and egalitarian modes of operation that could not be reduced to the representations underlying the society of "orders" and "estates." Set up to produce a necessarily unanimous public opinion, and endowed with a function of representation totally independent of the traditional sources of authority such as the provincial Estates, the parlements, or the sovereign himself, which thought to seize that role, the *sociétés de pensée* have been seen as the matrix of a new political legitimacy incompatible with the hierarchical and corporative legitimacy that the monarchical system demanded. Thus, even while their discourses affirmed respect for authority and adherence to traditional values, in their practices the new forms of intellectual association prefigured revolutionary sociability in its most radical forms.[15]

This first model of politicization, which we might call the Cochin–Furet model, differs from another that could be designated the Kant–Habermas model. The latter sees intellectual sociability in the eighteenth century as founding a new public area in which the use of reason and judgment was exercised without putting limits to critical examination and without obligatory submission to the old authority. The various instances of literary and artistic criticism (in the salons, the cafés, the academies, and the newspapers and periodicals) formed a new, autonomous, free, and sovereign public. To understand the emergence

14   Baker, "On the Problem of the Ideological Origins," pp. 213–16.
15   Augustin Cochin, *Les Sociétés de Pensée et la démocratie moderne* (Paris: Plon-Nourrit et cie, 1921; Paris: Copernic, 1978); Augustin Cochin, *Les Sociétés de Pensée et la Révolution en Bretagne (1787–1788)* (Paris: H. Champion, 1925); François Furet, "Augustin Cochin: la théorie du jacobinisme," in his *Penser la Révolution française*, pp. 212–59, available in English as "Augustin Cochin: The Theory of Jacobinism," in Furet, *Interpreting the French Revolution*, pp. 164–204; Ran Halévi, "L'Idée et l'événement. Sur les origines intellectuelles de la Révolution française," *Le Débat* 38 (1986): 145–63.

of the new political culture is thus to remark the progressive politicization of the public literary sphere and the shift in criticism toward the
domains traditionally prohibited to it – the mysteries of religion and of
the state.[16] Those two perspectives, although not incompatible, nonetheless mark two different ways of understanding the place of political
culture within the forms of intellectual culture: the first localizing it in
the operations automatically implied by the very modalities of voluntary association; the second founding it on the demands and conquests
of public use of critical functions.

What Is Enlightenment?

Rethinking Mornet also necessarily implies questioning the notion of
the "philosophical spirit" equated with the forward progress of enlightenment. The term seems easy to define as long as it is held to be a corpus
of doctrines formulated by the Philosophes, diffused through all classes
of the population, and articulated around several fundamental principles such as criticism of religious fanaticism, the exaltation of
tolerance, confidence in observation and experimentation, critical
examination of all institutions and customs, the definition of a natural
morality, and a reformulation of political and social ties on the basis of
the idea of liberty. Still, faced with this classical picture, doubt arises. Is
it certain that the Enlightenment must be characterized exclusively or
principally as a corpus of self-contained, transparent ideas or as a set of
clear and distinct propositions? Should not the century's novelty be read
elsewhere – in the multiple practices guided by an interest in utility and
service that aimed at the management of spaces and populations and
whose mechanisms (intellectual or institutional) imposed a profound
reorganization of the systems of perception and of the order of the social
world?

   That perspective authorizes a reevaluation of the relationship
between the Enlightenment and the monarchical state, since the state –
the prime target of philosophical discourse – was doubtless the most
vigorous initiator of practical reforms, as Tocqueville noted in book 3,
chapter 6 of *L'Ancien Régime et la Révolution*, which bears the title "How

16   Jürgen Habermas, *Strukturwandel der Öffentlichkeit, Untersuchungen zu einer Kat-
egorie der bürgerlichen Gesellschaft* (Neuwied: Hermann Luchterhand Verlag, 1962),
available in French as *L'Espace public. Archéologie de la publicité comme dimension constitutive de la société bourgeoise*, trans. Marc B. de Launay (Paris: Payot, 1978), and
in English as *The Structural Transformation of the Public Sphere: An Inquiry into a Category of Bourgeois Society*, trans. Thomas Burger and Frederick Lawrence (Cambridge: Polity Press, Cambridge, Mass.: MIT Press, 1989).

certain practices of the central power completed the revolutionary education of the masses." Moreover, to think of the Enlightenment as a web of practices without discourse (or at least without those varieties of discourse traditionally and spontaneously defined as "enlightened") is to give oneself a way to postulate distances and even contradictions between ideological declarations and the "formality of practices" (to make use of one of Michel de Certeau's categories).[17]

To move from the "intellectual" to the "cultural" is thus, to my mind, not only to enlarge an inquiry or change its object. Fundamentally, this movement implies casting doubt on two ideas: first, that practices can be deduced from the discourses that authorize or justify them; second, that it is possible to translate into the terms of an explicit ideology the latent meaning of social mechanisms. Mornet used the second of these two procedures when he attempted to restore the "subconscious of Masonry"; Cochin used it when he designated the implicit ideology of intellectual and social practices of the *sociétés de pensée* as Jacobin. The first procedure, which is typical of all the literature devoted to the Enlightenment, sees the diffusion of philosophical ideas as leading to acts of rupture directed at the established authorities, on the assumption that actions are engendered by thoughts. Against these two procedures (which operate both to reduce and translate) we might postulate a different articulation of the series of discourse and regimes of practice on the basis of which social and intellectual positions are organized in a given society. From the one to the other there is neither continuity nor necessity, as seen, for example, in the contradiction between the liberating ideology of the Enlightenment and the mechanisms that, while they claimed to be based in that ideology, set up multiple restraints and controls.[18] If the Revolution did indeed have cultural origins, they resided not in any harmony (either proclaimed or unacknowledged) that supposedly united annunciatory acts and the ideology governing them, but in the discordances that existed between the (moreover, competing) discourses that in representing the social world proposed its reorganization, and the (moreover, discontinuous) practices that, as they were put into effect, created new differentiations and new divisions.

17   Michel de Certeau, "La Formalité des pratiques. Du système religieux à l'éthique des Lumières (XVIIe–XVIIIe)," in his *L'Ecriture de l'histoire* (Paris: Gallimard, 1975), pp. 153–212, available in English as "The Formality of Practices: From Religious Systems to the Ethics of the Enlightenment (the Seventeenth and Eighteenth Centuries)," in his *The Writing of History*, trans. Tom Conley (New York: Columbia University Press, 1988), pp. 153–212.
18   Michel Foucault, *Surveiller et punir: Naissance de la prison* (Paris: Gallimard, 1975), available in English as *Discipline and Punish: The Birth of the Prison*, trans. Alan Sheridan (New York: Pantheon Books, 1977).

As a study of the propagation of the "philosophical spirit," Mornet's book makes extensive use of the notion of opinion. The fluctuations and evolution of opinion were the measure of the penetration of the new ideas. When those new ideas became "general public opinion" or "public thought," the cause was won for the Enlightenment and the way was thrown open for "intelligence" to give form and expression to political contradictions. Thus Mornet granted to opinion traits that opposed it, term by term, to the production of ideas: opinion was impersonal and anonymous, whereas ideas could be assigned to an individual and advanced in his or her name; opinion was dependent and active, whereas ideas were original and innovative intellectual creations. In Mornet's view, it was inconceivable to think of opinion in other terms, and he handled the notion as if it were a historical invariant, present in all societies, that offers history the sole task of taking note of its diverse and changing contents.

This postulate is no longer satisfactory. First of all, the diffusion of ideas cannot be held to be a simple imposition. Reception always involves appropriation, which transforms, reformulates, and exceeds what it receives. Opinion is in no way a receptacle, nor is it soft wax to be written upon. The circulation of thoughts or cultural models is always a dynamic and creative process. Texts, to invert the question, do not bear within them a stable and univocal meaning, and their migrations within a given society produce interpretations that are mobile, plural, and even contradictory. There is no possible distinction (Mornet to the contrary) between diffusion, grasped as a progressive enlargement of the milieux won over by the new ideas, and the body of doctrines and principles that were the object of that diffusion and that could be identified outside of any appropriation. Moreover, "general public opinion" is not a transhistorical category that only requires particularization. As an idea and as a configuration, it was constructed in a specific historical situation on the basis of discourses and practices that assigned particular characteristics to it. The problem is thus no longer whether opinion was receptive to the philosophical spirit or resistant to it, but to comprehend the conditions that, at any given moment in the eighteenth century, led to the emergence of a new conceptual and social reality: public opinion.

The Public Sphere and Public Opinion

A reading (which necessarily will be an interpretation) of Jürgen Habermas's classic work *Strukturwandel der Öffentlichkeit* (in English translation, *The Structural Transformation of the Public Sphere*) offers a first guide to how the notion of public opinion was constructed in the eighteenth century.[19] Habermas stated his thesis clearly: at the heart of the century (in some places sooner, in others later) there appeared a "political public sphere," which he also called "a public sphere in the political realm" or a "bourgeois public sphere." Politically this sphere defined a space for discussion and exchange removed from the sway of the state (that is, from the "sphere of 'public authority'" or "public power") and critical of the acts or the foundation of state power. Sociologically it was distinct from the court, which belonged within the domain of public power, and from the people, who had no access to critical debate. This is why this sphere could be qualified as "bourgeois."

The Political Public Sphere

Several organizing principles governed the political public sphere, which issued directly from the public literary sphere and was based in the salons and cafés and in periodical literature. Its first definition was as a space in which private persons made public use of their reason: "The bourgeois public sphere may be conceived above all as the sphere of private persons come together as a public."[20] A fundamental link thus existed between the emergence of a new form of "publicness" – which was no longer simply that of the exhibition or celebration of state authority – and the constitution of a domain of the private that included the intimacy of domestic life, the civil society founded upon exchange of merchandise and labor, and the sphere given over to the critical exercise of "public reason."

The process of privatization typical of Western societies between the end of the Middle Ages and the eighteenth century is thus not to be considered merely as a retreat of the individual into the various convivialities (conjugal, domestic, or sociable) that removed him from the demands and surveillance of the state and its administration. Doubtless there was a basic distinction between the private and the public in that the private person did not participate in the exercise of power and took his place in spheres not governed by the monarch's domination. But it was precisely that newly conquered autonomy that made it possible and conceivable to constitute a new "public" founded on the communication established between "private" persons freed of their duties to the ruler.

19   See also Peter Hohendahl, "Jürgen Habermas: 'The Public Sphere' (1964)," *New German Critique* 1, 3 (1974): 45–48, and Jürgen Habermas, "The Public Sphere: An Encyclopedia Article (1964)," *New German Critique* 1, 3 (1974): 49–55.
20   Habermas, *L'Espace public*, p. 38; *The Structural Transformation*, p. 27.

Such a communication postulates that the various participants are by nature equal. The political public sphere thus ignored distinctions of "orders" and "estates" that imposed hierarchy on society. In the exchange of judgments, in the exercise of critical functions, and in the clash of differing opinions an a priori equality was established between individuals that differentiated between them only for the self-evidence and coherence of the arguments they advanced. To the fragmentation of an order organized on the basis of a multiplicity of bodies, the new public sphere opposed homogeneity and uniformity; in place of a distribution of authority strictly modeled on an inherited social scale, it offered a society that accepted only its own principles of differentiation.

The exercise of public reason by private individuals was to be subjected to no limit, and no domain was to be forbidden. The critical exercise of reason was no longer reined in by the respect due to religious or political authority, as the exercise of methodical doubt had been. The new political public sphere brought on the disappearance of the division instituted by Descartes between obligatory credences and obediences, on the one hand, and, on the other, opinions that could legitimately be subjected to doubt. The first of the "maxims" in the "provisional code of morality" with which Descartes armed himself was to "obey the laws and the customs of my country, retaining the religion which I judged best, and in which, by God's grace, I have been brought up since childhood."[21] This led Descartes to a fundamental distinction: "After thus assuring myself of these maxims, and having put them aside with the truths of faith, which have always been most certain to me, I judged that I could proceed freely to reject all my other beliefs."[22] In the public sphere constructed a century later this reservation disappeared, since no domain of thought or action was to be "put aside" and removed from critical judgment.

Such judgment was exercised by the institutions that made the public into a tribunal of aesthetic criticism – the salons, the cafés, the clubs, and the periodicals. The publicity these groups provided, wresting from the traditional authorities in such matters (the court, the official academies, a small circle of connoisseurs) their monopoly on the evaluation of artistic production, involved both an enlargement and an exclusion: an enlargement because the large number of outlets for publicity (peri-

---

21   René Descartes, *Discours de la Méthode*, in his *Oeuvres complètes* (Paris: Gallimard, Bibliothèque de la Pléiade, 1953), pt. 3, p. 141, quoted from *Descartes's Discourse on Method*, trans. Laurence J. Lafleur (Indianapolis: Bobbs-Merrill, Liberal Arts Press, 1960), p. 18.
22   Ibid.: *Discours de la Méthode*, p. 144; *Discourse on Method*, p. 22.

odicals in particular) created a critical community that included "all private people, persons who – insofar as they were readers, listeners, and spectators [supposing they had wealth and culture], could avail themselves via the market of the objects that were subject to discussion";[23] an exclusion because "wealth and culture" were not everyone's lot, and the majority of people were kept out of the political debate that derived from literary criticism because they lacked the special competence that made possible "the public of private persons making use of reason."[24]

It was the process of exclusion that gave full importance to the debates centering on the concept of representation during the eighteenth century. Eliminated from the political public sphere by their "literary" inadequacy, the people needed to make their presence felt in some manner, "represented" by those whose vocation it was to be their mentors or their spokesmen and who expressed thoughts the people were incapable of formulating. This was all the more true since all the various lines of political discourse that founded the sphere of public power developed, each in its own way, a theory of representation. Following Keith Baker, we can distinguish three such theories: the absolutist theory, which made the person of the king the only possible representative of a kingdom divided into orders, estates, and bodies: the judiciary theory, which instituted the parlements as interpreters of the consent or the remonstrances of the nation; and the administrative, or "social," theory, which attributed the rational representation of social interests to municipal or provincial assemblies founded not on privilege but on property.[25] In light of these contrasting and competing definitions (all of which, however, focus on the effective or desired exercise of governmental and state authority), the new public sphere defined an alternative mode of representation that removed the concept from any institutional setting – monarchical, parlementary, or administrative – and that postulated the self-evidence of a unanimity designated by the category "public opinion" and faithfully represented by enlightened men who could give it voice.

23 Habermas, *Structural Transformation*, p. 37.
24 Ibid., p. 51. On the place of women in the public sphere, absolutist or bourgeois, see Joan B. Landes, *Women and the Public Sphere in the Age of the French Revolution* (Ithaca: Cornell University Press, 1988).
25 Keith Michael Baker, "Representation," in *The French Revolution and the Creation of Modern Political Culture*, vol. 1, *The Political Culture of the Old Regime*, ed. Keith Michael Baker (Oxford and New York: Pergamon Press, 1987), pp. 469–92; reprinted as "Representation Redefined," in Baker, *Inventing the French Revolution: Essays on French Political Culture in the Eighteenth Century* (Cambridge: Cambridge University Press, 1990), pp. 224–51.

The Public Use of Reason

Reading Habermas opens an entire field of reflection that leads, first, to questioning the articulation between the concepts of public and private, and, from there, to pausing to consider the text that served Habermas as the matrix for his demonstration: Kant's response to the question "What is Enlightenment?" which appeared as an article in the *Berlinische Monatsschrift* in 1784.[26] Kant discussed the conditions necessary to the progress of Enlightenment, which he defined as humanity's emergence from its nonage. His answer rested on two observations. First, an emancipation of this kind supposes that individuals will take control of the use of their own understanding and will be capable of freeing themselves from "statutes and formulas, those mechanical tools of the rational employment or rather misemployment of . . . natural gifts" that hinder the exercise of the mind. Enlightenment thus requires a rupture with obligatory thought patterns inherited from the past and the duty of all to think for themselves.

But – and this is Kant's second observation – for the majority of men this is not an easy conquest, thanks to the force of ingrained habit, "which has become almost [their] nature," and to the weight of the accepted authority of mentors to whom humanity has entrusted responsibility for doing its thinking: "Therefore, there are few who have succeeded by their own exercise of mind both in freeing themselves from incompetence and in achieving a steady pace." The progress of enlightenment could not result from a reform of understanding embarked on by separate, isolated individuals left to their own devices. "But that the public should enlighten itself is more possible; indeed, if only freedom is granted, enlightenment is almost sure to follow." Thus the progress of enlightenment required the constitution of a community to back up each individual's advances and in which the daring moves of the most forward-looking could be shared.

---

26   Emmanuel Kant, "Beantwortung der Frage: Was Ist Aufklärung?" *Berlinische Monatsschrift* (1784), available in English as *Foundations of the Metaphysics of Morals and What Is Enlightenment*, trans. Lewis White Beck (Indianapolis: Bobbs-Merrill, 1975), pp. 85–92. On this text, see the commentaries of Ernst Cassirer, *Kants Leben und Lehre* (Berlin: Cassirer, 1918), available in English as *Kant's Life and Thought*, trans. Jame Haden (New Haven: Yale University Press, 1981), pp. 227–28, 368; Jürgen Habermas, *Structural Transformation*, pp. 104–7; Michel Foucault, "Afterword: The Subject and the Power," in *Michel Foucault: Beyond Structuralism and Hermeneutics*, ed. Hubert L. Dreyfus and Paul Rabinow (Chicago: University of Chicago Press, 1982), pp. 208–26, especially pp. 215–16; and Michel Foucault, "Un cours inédit," *Le Magazine littéraire* 207 (1984): 35–39. All quotations from Kant in this section are from the Beck translation of "What Is Enlightenment?"

At this point in his argument Kant proposed a distinction between the "public use" and "private use" of reason that, as he formulated it, entails an apparent paradox. Private use of reason is "that which one may make of it in a particular civil post or office which is entrusted to him." Private use of reason is thus associated with the exercise of a charge or an office (Kant offered the examples of the army officer under orders and the pastor teaching his congregation) or with the citizen's duty toward the state (for example, as a taxpayer). The exercise of understanding in such circumstances could legitimately be restrained in the name of "public ends" that guarantee the very existence of the community to which the officer, the pastor, or the taxpayer belong, in what Kant called "the interest of the community." This obligatory obedience, which leaves no room for criticism or personal reasoning, is not prejudicial to enlightenment, because it facilitates avoidance of the disruption of the social body that would necessarily be engendered were discipline refused.

Why, though, should this use of reason, which seems the most "public" sort of reason in terms of the old definitions that identified "public" as partaking in state or religious authority, be designated by Kant as "private," thus inverting the accepted meanings of these terms? Using the example of the churchman teaching the faithful, Kant sketched his reasons for this paradoxical definition: "The use . . . which an appointed teacher makes of his reason before his congregation is merely private, because this congregation is only a domestic one (even if it be a large gathering)." The category "private" thus refers to the nature of the community in which use is made of understanding. An assembly of the faithful, a particular church, an army, even a state, all constitute single, circumscribed, and localized entities. In that they differ radically from the "society of world citizens," which occupies no determined territory and the composition of which is unlimited. Social "families," whatever their size and their nature, are thus so many segments fragmenting the universal community; they must therefore be considered as belonging to the order of the "private," in contrast to a "public" defined not by participation, as agent and subject, in the exercise of any particular authority but by identification with humanity as a whole.

Placed on a universal scale in this manner, the public use of understanding contrasts term for term with the "private" use exerted within a relation of specific and limited domination. "By the public use of one's reason I understand the use which a person makes of it as a scholar before the reading public"; "as a scholar" – that is, as a member of a society without distinctions of rank or social condition; "before the reading public" – that is, addressing oneself to a community not defined by being part of an institution. The "public" necessary for the advent of enlightenment and whose liberty cannot be limited is thus constituted of individuals who have the same rights, who think for themselves and speak in their own names, and who communicate in writing with their peers. No domain should be out of reach of their critical activity – not the arts and sciences nor "religious matters" nor "lawgiving." The enlightened prince (read Frederick II) is enlightened precisely because he allows this public use of reason to develop without constraint or restriction, thus permitting men to reach full maturity. A tolerance of this sort in no way endangers "civil order," which is guaranteed by the limits imposed on the use made of reason in the duties required by social status or profession. Furthermore, tolerance has the merit of providing a striking example: "This spirit of freedom spreads beyond this land, even to those in which it must struggle with external obstacles erected by a government which misunderstands its own interest" (as was the case in the kingdom of France, which Kant perhaps had in mind without saying so).

Kant broke with two traditions in this text. First, he proposed a new articulation of the relation of the public to the private, not only by equating the public exercise of reason with judgments produced and communicated by private individuals acting as scholars or "in their quality as learned men" (as Habermas held), but also by defining the public as the sphere of the universal and the private as the domain of particular and "domestic" interests (which may even be those of a church or a state). Second, Kant shifted the way in which the legitimate limits put on critical activities should be conceived. Such limits, then, no longer lay in the objects of thought themselves, as in Cartesian reasoning, which starts from the postulate that there are domains forbidden to methodical doubt; they lay in the position of the thinking subject legitimately constrained when he was executing the duties of his charge or of his status, necessarily free when he acted as a member of "a society of world citizens."

That society was unified by the circulation of written works that authorized the communication and discussion of thoughts. Kant insisted on this point, systematically associating the "public use of one's reason" with the production or reading of written matter. As an educated person, every citizen must be allowed to "make his comments freely and publicly, i.e., *through writing*, on the erroneous aspects of the present institution" (emphasis added). Here the "public" was not construed on the basis of new forms of intellectual sociability such as clubs, cafés, societies, or lodges, because those groups doubtless retained something of the "domestic congregation" by gathering together a specific, discrete community. Nor was the "public" constituted in reference to the ideal of the city in classical antiquity, which presupposed being able to listen to the spoken word and deliberate in common, and which involved the physical proximity of all members of the body politic. For Kant, only written communication, which permitted exchange in the absence of the author and created an autonomous area for debating ideas, was admissible as a figure for the universal.

Kant's conception of the domain specific to the public use of reason was drawn from the notion and the functions of the *Respublica litteratorum*, a concept that united the lettered and the learned, through correspondence and through print, even before the Enlightenment.[27] Founded on the free engagement of the will, on equality among its interlocutors, and on the absolutely disinterested exercise of the intellect, the Republic of Letters (invented not by the Philosophes but by men of learning in the preceding century) provided a model and a support for free public examination of questions regarding religion or legislation. At the same time, reference to the notion of freely engaged will marks the distance separating the theoretical universality of the concept of public and the actual composition of that body. In Kant's time, the "reading public" was not the whole of society by any means, and the public capable of written production was even smaller. Kant explained the distance that he implicitly recognized between the public and the people as a whole by saying that "as things now stand, much is lacking which prevents men from being, or easily becoming, capable of correctly using their own reason in religious matters with assurance and free from outside direction" (or, we might add, in matters pertaining to the arts, the sciences, or legislation as well). "The whole community" only potentially constituted "a society of world citizens." When those two entities coincided, one could augur the advent of "an enlightened age."

27   Reference to the practices of intellectual life in the seventeenth century, founded, since the age of the learned libertines, on the exchange of correspondence, the communication of manuscripts, books lent or offered as gifts, and, after the 1750s, on learned periodicals; see Robert Mandrou, *Des humanistes aux hommes de science (XVIe et XVIIe siècles)* (Paris: Fayard, 1988), pp. 263–80, available in English as *From Humanism to Science: 1480 to 1700*, trans. Brian Pearce (Harmondsworth and New York: Penguin Books, 1978), pp. 151–53. It coexists in Kant's text with an implicit recognition of the situation in Germany, which, even more than in France, where intellectuals were more concentrated in a capital city, depended on the circulation of written matter. In 1827 Goethe noted this national trait with particular force: "All our men of talent are scattered across the country. One is in Vienna, another in Berlin, another in Königsberg, another in Bonn or Düsseldorf, all separated from each other by fifty or a hundred miles, so that personal contact or a personal exchange of ideas is a rarity" (quoted by Norbert Elias, *Über den Prozess der Zivilisation. Soziogenetische und Psychogenetische Untersuchungen* [1939; Frankfurt-am-Main: Suhrkamp, 1969], 1:33–34, and given here from Elias, *The History of Manners: The Civilizing Process*, vol. 1, trans. Edmund Jephcott [New York: Pantheon Books, 1978], p. 28). See also Paul Dibon, "Communication in *Respublica litteraria* of the 17th Century," *Res Publica Litterarum* 1 (1978): 42–55.

The Public or the People

Kant held the distinction between the public and the popular to be temporary, transitory, and characteristic of a century that was "an age of enlightenment" but not yet "an enlightened age." For other thinkers of the eighteenth century, however, the two constituted an irreconcilable dichotomy. "The public was not a people," Mona Ozouf stated as she showed how, during the last decades of the Old Regime, public opinion was defined in precise contrast to the opinion of the greater number. Lexical contrasts show this particularly forcefully: Condorcet contrasted "opinion" with "populace"; Marmontel opposed "the opinion of men of letters" and "the opinion of the multitude"; d'Alembert spoke of "the truly enlightened public" and "the blind and noisy multitude"; Condorcet, again, set "the opinion of enlightened people which precedes public opinion and ends up by dictating to it" against "the popular opinion."[28] Public opinion, set up as a sovereign authority and a final arbiter, was necessarily stable, unified, and founded on reason. The universality of its judgments and the constraining self-evidence of its decrees derived from that unvarying, dispassionate constancy. It was the reverse of popular opinion, which was multiple, versatile, and inhabited by prejudice and passion.

These writers reveal a strong persistence of older representations of "the people": a negative image of the public to which all opinions must submit. The definition of *people*, which varies little in dictionaries of the French language from Richelet to Furetière and from the *Dictionnaire de l'Académie* to the *Dictionnaire de Trévoux*, emphasizes the fundamental instability attributed to popular opinion throughout the eighteenth century.[29] For example, the 1727 edition of Furetière's *Dictionnaire Universel* gives: "The people is people everywhere; that is, foolish, restless, fond of novelties." Two examples follow: "The people has the habit of hating in others the same qualities that it admires in them (Voiture)," and "There is no happy medium in the humor of the people. If it does not fear it is to be feared, but when it trembles it can be scorned with impunity (d'Ablancourt)." Subject to extremes, inconstant, contradictory, blind, the *people* in eighteenth-century dictionaries remained true to its portrayal in classical tragedy: always quick to change course, from one minute to the next docile or furious, but always manipulable.

28   Mona Ozouf, "L'Opinion publique," in Baker, *The French Revolution*, vol. 1, *The Political Culture of the Old Regime*, pp. 419–34. Quotations are given as per n. 24, pp. 432–33.
29   Elizabeth Fleury, "Le peuple en dictionnaires (fin XVII–XVIIIe siècle)" (Diplôme d'Etudes Approfondies, Paris, Ecole des Hautes Etudes en Sciences Sociales, 1986), typescript.

Burdened with these deep-rooted representations, the people could not easily be seen as a political agent, even when discourse was not deliberately disparaging. The article "Peuple," compiled by Jaucourt for the *Encyclopédie*, stands as proof of this.[30] The article proposes a strictly sociological definition: the people are exclusively "the workers and the plowmen," excluding men of law and men of letters, businessmen, financiers, and even that "species of artisans, or rather, mannered artists who work on luxury items." Considered as forming "always the most numerous and the most necessary part of the nation," this worker and peasant people, pitied and respected, was considered in no way capable of participating in government by counsel and representation but rather as linked with the sovereign in a relationship of fidelity offered in exchange for safeguard, of attachment in return for the assurance of a "better subsistence." The article continues: "Kings have no more faithful subjects and, dare I say, better friends. There is more public love in that order perhaps than in all the others; not because it is poor but because it knows very well, in spite of its ignorance, that the authority and protection of the prince are the only gage of its security and its well-being."

The *Encyclopédie* does not acknowledge the notion of "public opinion." The term *opinion* can be found in it as a logical category ("a judgment of the dubious and uncertain mind," opposed to the self-evidence of science) or, in the plural, as a technical term in the language of justice.[31] The term *public* is used only as a qualifier, as in "the public good" or "the public interest," the safeguarding of which is entrusted "to the sovereign and to the officials who, under his orders, are charged with this responsibility."[32] We need not force the analysis to the extent of contrasting the *Encyclopédie*'s definition of "the people" with a notion of "the public" that did not yet exist in this philosophic *summa* of the eighteenth century (proof, incidentally, of the late affirmation of the newer notion). Nonetheless, when it reiterates the traditional images of the people as either loving or rebelling, the *Encyclopédie* manifests the continuing validity of a representation that considered the harsh demands of the popular condition incompatible with participation in the reasoned conduct of government.

When the power of public opinion did emerge – defined as the superior authority to which all particular opinions must bow, even those of the king and his administration – the distinction between public

---

30 *Encyclopédie, ou Dictionnaire raisonné des sciences, des arts et des métiers*, 36 vols. (Lausanne and Berne: chez les Sociétés typographiques, 1778–81), 25:543–45.
31 Ibid., 23:754–57.
32 Ibid., 27:752–53.

opinion and popular opinion became essential. As Keith Baker has indicated, the concept of public opinion arose in discussions that took place around 1750, first in the controversy over the refusal of the sacraments to the Jansenists, then over the liberalization of the grain trade, and finally over the financial administration of the kingdom.[33] Powerless to forbid public debate, the monarchy itself was forced to enter into it to explain, persuade, and seek to win approval and support.

A new political culture thus took shape, recognized as a novelty by contemporaries in that it transferred the seat of authority from the will of the king alone, who decided without appeal and in secret, to the judgment of an entity embodied in no institution, which debated publicly and was more sovereign than the sovereign. This increased the acuity and the urgency of new questions: How could one distinguish this authority that had devolved on the public from the violent differences between rival factions so detestably illustrated in England? Who were the true spokesmen for the opinion that had become public in this manner: the men of letters who fashioned it, the magistrates of the Parlement who formulated it, or the enlightened administrators who carried it out? Finally, how was one to evaluate the self-evidence of its decrees that was the guarantee of consensus? Although everyone recognized the existence of public opinion and postulated its unity, there was no unanimous answer to these questions because public opinion was both a voice that demanded to be heard and a tribunal that had to be persuaded.

The Tribunal of Opinion

In 1775, in his maiden speech before the Académie française, Chrétien-Guillaume Malesherbes forcefully expressed the idea – by then commonly accepted – that public opinion was to be considered a court of justice more imperious than any other:

> A tribunal has arisen independent of all powers and that all powers respect, that appreciates all talents, that pronounces on all people of merit. And in an enlightened century, in a century in which each citizen can speak to the entire nation by way of print, those who have a talent for instructing men and a gift for moving them – in a word, men of letters

33   Keith Michael Baker, "Politics and Public Opinion under the Old Regime: Some Reflections," in *Press and Politics in Pre-Revolutionary France*, ed. Jack R. Censer and Jeremy D. Popkin (Berkeley: University of California Press, 1987), pp. 204–46; reprinted as "Public Opinion as Political Invention" in Baker, *Inventing the French Revolution*, pp. 167–99.

– are, amid the public dispersed, what the orators of Rome and Athens were in the middle of the public assembled.[34]

There are several arguments contained in this comparison. First, it invested the new judges –"in a word, men of letters" – with an authority that ordinary judges did not have. Their competence knew no bounds and their jurisdiction no limits; their freedom of judgment was guaranteed because they were in no way dependent upon the power of the ruler; their decrees had the force of self-evident propositions. Setting up men of letters as the magistrates of an ideal and supreme tribunal in this manner was to invest them with the fundamentally judiciary legitimacy of all the traditional powers, beginning with those of the king and the Parlement. Thus the power of "men of letters" was no longer exclusively founded – as in the *Système figuré des connaissances humaines* of the *Encyclopédie* – on the submission of the "science of God, or natural Theology, which it has pleased God to correct and to sanctify by Revelation" to a "science of being in general," the first branch of the "philosophy or the science (for these words are synonyms)" that was "the portion of human knowledge which should be related to reason." This subjection permitted the role of guide for humanity to be transferred from the scholastics to the philosophers.[35] With the invention of public opinion, "the enlightened nation of men of letters and the free and disinterested nation of the philosophers" found itself entrusted with a veritable public office.[36]

Reference to the judiciary had another function, however. It aimed at establishing a connection between the universality of judgments and the dispersal of persons, and at constructing a uniform opinion that, unlike that of the ancients, had no physical location in which it could express or experience its unity. As for Kant later, it was the circulation of printed matter that made it possible for Malesherbes, in the remonstrances that he presented in May 1775 in the name of the Cour des Aides, to envisage the constitution of a unified public in a nation in which people were necessarily separated from each other and formed

34   Quoted from Mona Ozouf, "L'Opinion publique," p. 424.
35   Jean Le Rond d'Alembert, *Discours préliminaire de l'Encyclopédie* (Paris: Editions Gonthier, Médiations, 1965), "Explication détaillée du système des connaissances humaines," pp. 155–68, quotations pp. 159–60, quoted from "Detailed Explanation of the System of Human Knowledge," in *Preliminary Discourse to the Encyclopedia of Diderot*, trans. Richard N. Schwab, with Walter E. Rex (Indianapolis: Bobbs-Merrill, Library of Liberal Arts, 1963), pp. 143–57.
36   Ibid., "Dédicace à Monseigneur le comte d'Argenson," pp. 14–15. See also Robert Darnton, "Philosophers Trim the Tree of Knowledge: The Epistemological Strategy of the *Encyclopédie*," in his *The Great Cat Massacre and Other Episodes in French Cultural History* (New York: Basic Books, 1984), pp. 190–213.

their ideas individually: "Knowledge is being extended by Printing, the written Laws are today known by everyone, everyone can comprehend his own affairs. The Jurists have lost the empire that other men's ignorance gave to them. The Judges can themselves be judged by an instructed Public, and that censure is much more severe and more equitable when it can be exercised in a cool, reflective reading than when suffrages are constrained in a tumultuous assembly."[37] By associating the public nature of the written word – vastly increased by the presses (an indispensable resource in combating the "clandestinity" of the administration) – with the supreme authority of the judgments pronounced by opinion binding even on the judges, Malesherbes converted the congeries of particular opinions that emerge from solitary reading into a collective and anonymous conceptual entity that is both abstract and homogeneous.

Condorcet developed the same idea in the opening pages of the eighth "epoch" of his *Esquisse d'un tableau historique des progrès de l'esprithumain*, written in 1793. He launched his argument by contrasting the spoken word, which touches only nearby listeners and excites their emotions, with the printed word, the circulation of which creates the conditions for unlimited and dispassionate communication:

> Men found themselves possessed of the means of communicating with people all over the world. A new sort of tribunal had come into existence in which less lively but deeper impressions were communicated; which no longer allowed the same tyrannical empire to be exercised over men's passions but ensured a more certain and more durable power over their minds; a situation in which the advantages are all on the side of truth, since what the art of communication loses in the power to seduce, it gains in the power to enlighten.

Printing thus made possible the constitution of a public realm that was unreliant on proximity – a community with no visible presence: "The public opinion that was formed in this way was powerful by virtue of its size, and effective because the forces that created it operated with equal strength on all men at the same time, no matter what distances separated them. In a word, we now have a tribunal, independent of all human coercion, which favours reason and justice, a tribunal whose scrutiny it is difficult to elude, and whose verdict it is impossible to evade."[38] That tribunal, in which readers were the judges and authors

---

37   Malesherbes, "Remontrances relatives aux impôts, 6 mai 1775," in *Les "Remontrances" de Malesherbes 1771–1775*, ed. Elisabeth Badinter (Paris: Union Générale d'Editions, 10/18, 1978), pp. 167–284, quotation pp. 272–73.

38   Condorcet, *Esquisse d'un tableau historique des progrès de l'esprit humain* (Paris: Flammarion, GF, 1988), p. 188, quoted from *Sketch for a Historical Picture of the*

the interested parties, was a manifestation of the universal because "all men who speak the same language can become alive to any questions discussed anywhere."[39] Even though Condorcet gave the most "democratic" definition of it, public opinion, ideally universal, had to come to terms with obvious cultural rifts, and it was not an easy matter to make the absolute concept coincide with the realities of the social world: "And so, though there remained a great number of people condemned to ignorance either voluntary or enforced, the boundary between the cultivated and the uncultivated had been almost entirely effaced, leaving an insensible gradation between the two extremes of genius and stupidity."[40] The very terms Condorcet used ("though"; "almost entirely") clearly indicate the persistence of a distance that was, however, considered to have been abolished.

Thus from the seventeenth century to the eighteenth century there had been a radical shift in the manner of conceiving the public. In the age of "baroque" politics the traits that defined the public were the same as those that typified the theater public: heterogeneous, hierarchized, and formed into a public only by the spectacle that they were given to see and to believe. This type of public was potentially composed of men and women from all social levels; it brought together all whose adherence and support were sought – the mighty and the common people, shrewd politicians and the ignorant plebs. It was also a public to be "led by the nose"; to be "seduced and deceived by appearances," according to Naudé, the self-appointed theoretician of a politics in which the most spectacular effects always masked the maneuvers that produced them and the goals they sought.[41] Ensnared, held captive, and manipulated in this manner, the spectators of the *theatrum mundi* in no way constituted a "public opinion" (even if the expression can be found before 1750, for example, in Saint-Simon).

When the concept of "public opinion" did emerge, it effected a dual rupture. It countered the art of pretense, dissimulation, and secrecy by appealing to a transparency that was to ensure the visibility of intentions. Before the tribunal of opinion all causes were to be argued

---

Progress of the Human Mind, trans. June Barraclough (London: Weidenfeld and Nicolson, 1955), p. 100. For a discussion in another context of the connection between the circulation of printed matter and the public sphere, see Michael Warner, *The Letters of the Republic: Publication and the Public Sphere in Eighteenth-Century America* (Cambridge, Mass.: Harvard University Press, 1990).

39   Condorcet, *Esquisse d'un tableau*, p. 189; *Sketch*, p. 101.
40   Condorcet, *Esquisse d'un tableau*, p. 229; *Sketch*, p. 140.
41   Christian Jouhaud, "Propagande et action au temps de la Fronde," in *Culture et idéologie dans la genèse de l'Etat moderne*. Actes de la table ronde organisée par le Centre National de la Recherche Scientifique et l'Ecole française de Rome, Rome, 15–17 October 1984 (Rome: L'Ecole française de Rome, 1985), pp. 337–52; Christian Jouhaud, *Mazarinades. La Fronde des mots* (Paris: Aubier, 1985).

without duplicity: causes that evidently had justice and reason on their side would necessarily triumph. But all citizens were not (or not yet) adept at exercising their judgment in this fashion or at joining together to form enlightened opinion. Thus a second rupture rejected the public that mingled in the theaters, where the inexpensive places in the pit ajoined the boxes and where everyone had his own interpretation – subtle or rough-hewn – of a spectacle destined for all, in favor of the more homogeneous public that served as the tribunal to judge literary or poetic merits and talents. When opinion was thought of as actor rather than as acted upon, it became public and lost its universality, and by that token it excluded many people who lacked the competence to establish the decrees that it proclaimed.

The Constitution of the Public

Constituting the public as an entity whose decrees had more force than those of the established authorities supposed several operations. Two examples should suffice to illustrate them. The first operation, which concerns the memoirs published in great numbers by both lawyers and litigants from 1770 onward, was to take the judicial comparison literally. Malesherbes justified this operation in his remonstrances of 1775, in which he spoke against the criticism of judges who thought that "the public should not be constituted as the judge in the courts": "Basically, the common order of justice in France is that it be rendered publicly. It is to a public hearing that all cases should normally be brought; and when one takes the Public as a witness by means of printed Memoirs, all that does is to augment the public character of the hearing."[42] In all cases, an affair being examined by a normal tribunal should be exposed before opinion. To take a specific case that set private persons against one another and was subjected to the secret procedures of justice and transform it into a public debate charged with letting the truth shine through and, in effect, with shifting the context in which judgment took place necessitated the adoption of several strategies.

The most fundamental strategy consisted in endowing the cause one was defending with general and exemplary value. Lacretelle, a lawyer, said as much: "Any particular affair that leads to general considerations and that is apt to become a major focus of public attention must be considered as a major event in which experience testifies with full authority and public opinion rises up with all its influence." An admiring witness tells us that this was also Lacretelle's practice: "Instead of shut-

42   Malesherbes, "Remontrances," pp. 269–70.

ting himself within the narrow circle of an ordinary subject, he soars above the constitutive laws of the various governments; he sees only major outcomes; each particular case becomes in his hands the program of a question of state." The debt that a court noble refused to pay to his commoner creditors thus became an ideal occasion for denouncing unjust privilege, just as the arbitrary imprisonment of a Breton gentleman was an opportunity to denounce the *lettres de cachet*.[43]

Two other things had to be accomplished before specific cases could be endowed with universal significance. First, the secrecy of judicial procedure had to be broken by mobilizing the potential of the circulation of printed texts on the largest possible scale. This accounted for both the large press runs of judicial memoirs (three thousand copies at the least, often six thousand, and occasionally ten thousand or more) and their low price (when they were not distributed free). Second, a different writing style had to replace the customary legal prose, a style that took its models and references from successful genres and gave narration a dramatic form, or else a style based in first-person narrative that lent veracity to the defendant through an exhibition of the "I," as in the literature of the times. Universalizing the particular, making public what had been secret, and "fictionalizing" discourse were the techniques that lawyers used to appeal to opinion and, in doing so, to proclaim themselves the authorized interpreters of that opinion.

The traditional direct, discreet, and exclusive relationship that bound individuals to the king – the guarantor and guardian of domestic secrets – gave way to a totally different mechanism in the public exposition of private differences.[44] From that point of view, judicial memoirs are the exact inverse of the *lettres de cachet* accorded by the sovereign in

43   Sarah Maza, "Le tribunal de la nation: les mémoires judiciaires et l'opinion publique à la fin de l'Ancien Régime," *Annales E.S.C.* (1987): 73–90. I am indebted to this article for both quotations and ideas concerning the judicial memoirs. See also John Renwick, "Voltaire et Morangiès 1772–1773, ou, Les Lumières l'ont échappé belle." *Studies on Voltaire and the Eighteenth Century* 202 (Oxford: Voltaire Foundation, 1982); Hans-Jürgen Lüsebrink, "L'affaire Créaux (Rouen, 1786–1790). Affrontements idéologiques et tensions institutionnelles autour de la scène judiciaire de la fin du XVIIIe siècle," *Studies on Voltaire and the Eighteenth Century* 191 (1980): 892–900.

44   Arlette Farge, "Familles: l'honneur et le secret," in *Histoire de la vie privée*, ed. Philippe Ariès and Georges Duby (Paris: Editions du Seuil, 1986), vol. 3, *De la Renaissance aux Lumières*, ed. Roger Chartier, pp. 580–617, available in English as "The Honor and Secrecy of Families," in Ariès and Duby, *A History of Private Life* (Cambridge, Mass.: Belknap Press of Harvard University Press, 1989), vol. 3, *Passions of the Renaissance*, ed. Roger Chartier, trans. Arthur Goldhammer (1989), pp. 570–607; Arlette Farge and Michel Foucault, *Le Désordre des familles. Lettres de cachet des Archives de la Bastille* (Paris: Gallimard/Julliard, Collection Archives, 1982).

response to requests from families interested in stifling "disorders" that sullied their honor. The memoirs displayed what the *lettres* concealed; they expected from the judgment of opinion what the *lettres* hoped to gain from the omnipotence of the monarch; they converted into a civil suit the scandals that the *lettres* were charged with burying. The "politicization" of the private sector thus seems to have arisen out of a development that based the very existence of a new public sphere on a process of "privatization" in which individuals gradually conquered autonomy and freedom from state authority.

The second operation, the emergence of the public as a higher court of judgment, is clear in the evolution of artistic criticism. After 1737, when the Salon became a regular and well-frequented institution, its very existence transferred legitimacy in aesthetic appreciation away from the narrow milieux that up to that point had claimed monopoly (the Académie royale de Peinture et Sculpture, aristocratic and ecclesiastical clients, collectors, and the merchants who sold to them) toward the mixed and numerous public who passed judgment on the paintings hung on the walls of the Salon carré of the Louvre. Setting up that throng of visitors as a tribunal of taste was not without its problems. As Thomas Crow wrote, one question was central in the minds of all those who backed the expectations and the tastes of the new spectators against the old authorities:

> What transforms [an] audience into a public, that is, a commonality with a legitimate role to play in justifying artistic practice and setting value on the products of that practice? The audience is the concrete manifestation of the public but never identical with it. . . . A public appears, with a shape and a will, via the various claims made to represent it; and when sufficient numbers of an audience come to believe in one or another of these representations, the public can become an important art-historical actor.[45]

Transforming spectators into a "public" encountered strong resistance from the Académie, the connoisseurs, and even the artists themselves. The move was nonetheless achieved, more or less successfully, by independent critics (often anonymous, on occasion clandestine) whose numbers increased after the 1770s and whose writings circulated discernibly more widely than the comments Denis Diderot reserved for the subscribers to Melchior Grimm's *Correspondance littéraire*. Just like the public that was both invoked and represented by the lawyers who wrote judicial memoirs, the public that was thought to regulate taste in the

45   Thomas E. Crow, *Painters and Public Life in Eighteenth-Century Paris* (New Haven: Yale University Press, 1985), p. 5.

fine arts found its earliest interpreters in the critics who set it up as the aesthetic lawgiver.

Even if, or because, it was defined as a conceptual entity, and not in sociological terms, the notion of public opinion that invaded the discourse of all segments of society – political, administrative, and judicial – in the two or three final decades of the Old Regime operated as a powerful instrument both for division and for social legitimization. In reality, public opinion founded the authority of all who, by affirming that they recognized its decrees alone, set themselves up as mandated to pronounce its judgments. It was in constructing opinion into a unified, enlightened, and sovereign public that men of letters, as Tocqueville wrote, "took the lead in politics." Universal in its essence, the public capable of making critical use of reason was far from universal in its actual composition. The public sphere, emancipated from the domain in which the ruler held sway, thus had nothing in common with the shifting opinions and blind emotions of the multitude. Between the people and the public there was a clear break. From Malesherbes to Kant, the line of demarcation ran between those who could read and produce written matter and those who could not.

4

The Forbidden Best-Sellers of Pre-Revolutionary France

Robert Darnton

Originally appeared as Robert Darnton, *The Forbidden Best-Sellers of Pre-Revolutionary France* (1995) pp. 217–46 (New York: W. W. Norton & Company).

Editor's Introduction

The following selection comprises the two final chapters of Robert Darnton's *Forbidden Best-Sellers of Pre-Revolutionary France*. The chapter entitled "Reader Response" (p. ••) addresses the question of how eighteenth-century French readers responded to what they read. Keith Baker has implicitly criticized both Daniel Mornet and Darnton for supposedly assuming that readers simply believed what they read and proceeded to act upon the ideas with which writers had indoctrinated them.[1] Roger Chartier has similarly imputed a simplistic view of the effects of reading to Mornet and Darnton.[2] In "Public Opinion" (p. ••), Darnton defends his principal thesis: that printed matter, in addition to other "media," played a decisive role in the rupture between the people and the monarchy, thus enabling the French Revolution to take place.

Darnton begins by challenging the theory, developed in the 1970s by German scholars, that a "reading revolution" took place in the eighteenth century. According to this theory, the increasing availability of printed matter changed readers' approaches to their texts from the reverential, *intensive* and repetitive reading of a few books (especially the Bible) to a more skeptical, *extensive* reading of the many texts to which they increasingly had access. Although the "reading revolution" argument was geared toward explaining the allegedly "peculiar" path that Germany took toward modernity, Chartier has applied it to French reading habits in order to

---

1   See chapter 2.
2   See chapter 3.

question the suggestion that "books make revolutions."[3] Darnton, who in fact challenged the "reading revolution" thesis as early as 1984,[4] reiterates his argument here. He admits that very little documentation exists to support claims about how readers responded to texts, yet considers the sources in existence to be instructive. Among those sources are letters from booksellers to a publishing house, privately-circulated manuscript book reviews by *philosophes*, letters from officials in the royal administration, the papers of a lieutenant-general of police in Paris and some published considerations on the power of the printed word by the popular journalist Mercier. Although Darnton concedes that these sources contain biases and cannot tell us exactly how readers interpreted books, they do reveal, in his opinion, that readers were influenced by what they read. In particular, he argues, the forbidden literature of the period, especially the *libelles* (libels) in which the royal family and ministers of state were accused (at times in explicitly pornographic terms) of immoral conduct and indifference to the fate of the people, took its toll: "Years of slander had damaged something fundamental in the people's attachment to the monarchy." He does not presume that readers naïvely believed everything they read, or that they were incapable of forming their own judgments, but nevertheless argues that publications attacking the monarchy played a significant role in the formation of *public opinion*.

Public opinion is the subject of the second part of the excerpt, which corresponds to the final chapter in *Forbidden Best-Sellers*. Again Darnton addresses the work of Chartier and Baker, among others. He directly confronts the possibility that "forbidden books did not affect public opinion at all" but "merely reflected it." Chartier raises this suspicion in his *Cultural Origins*, where he suggests that a "desacralization" of the monarchy began long before the forbidden literature became popular and finds evidence of this process in the casual use of the term "royal" in descriptions of everyday products (e.g. "cakes à la royale"). Darnton counters that the widespread use of such language was only documented long after the first libels against Louis XV, and adds that "familiarity" can just as easily be seen as a sign of affection as of disaffection.

Next Darnton addresses the claim, made by Jacques Revel and Arlette Farge, that Parisians showed "open hostility" to the king from 1750 and perhaps earlier. If this were true, then it would be possible to argue that the libels Darnton has studied in such depth had no independent histor-

3   Chartier cites the "reading revolution" argument in a chapter of his *Cultural Origins of the French Revolution* (not excerpted in this volume) entitled, "Do Books Make Revolutions?"

4   Robert Darnton, "Readers Respond to Rousseau: The Fabrication of Romantic Sensitivity," in *The Great Cat Massacre and Other Episodes in French Cultural History* (New York: Basic Books, 1984; Vintage Books, 1985), 214–56.

ical force, that they were mere effects rather than causes. On the basis of reports by police spies who monitored cafés and other public gathering places for subversive *mauvais propos* or "bad speech," Darnton concedes that Parisians showed considerable disapproval of Louis XV for keeping mistresses and persecuting the Jansenists.[5] Yet he insists that criticism of particular monarchs and ministers was not new in the eighteenth or even the seventeenth century, and that disaffection with a particular government was far from a fundamental break with a belief in the legitimacy of the monarchical form of government itself.

He continues by criticizing historians for setting up a badly posed question in which libels were said either to cause or to be caused by *mauvais propos*. Rather than embarking on a "chicken-and-egg hunt for an original cause," he calls for an attempt to "understand how all the media interacted in the process of forming public opinion." By "media" he means all the instruments by which information was communicated, including word of mouth, songs, manuscripts, prints, as well as the more familiar medium of printed books. By "public opinion" he means a real sociological phenomenon, not the "discourse" that Baker, Chartier, and Mona Ozouf study. He acknowledges that Daniel Mornet distinguished between different types of media. For Mornet books had helped to create a "climate of opinion," whereas only an examination of the content of pamphlets, underground newspapers (*gazettes*) and gossip (as reported by police spies) revealed the more immediately decisive "public opinion." Darnton criticizes Mornet, however, for having failed to establish the relationship between the former and the latter. He observes that a historian reading the sources of "public opinion" during the reign of Louis XVI prior to 1787 would find little discussion of political matters, as though the French had "lapsed into a curious calm before the storm," which, when it "finally broke . . . seemed to come from nowhere."

Darnton attempts to resolve "[t]hese paradoxes" by arguing that *libelles*, although ostensibly about the previous reign, carried a set of coded political meanings relating to contemporary politics. They were "newsworthy" in the sense that, like the *gazettes* and gossip through which "the news" was conveyed, they contained stories about well-known figures; and if many of those figures were from the previous reign (e.g. Louis XV's royal mistresses), they exemplified the themes with which the contemporary French were, in Darnton's view, still preoccupied under Louis XVI. Most important among these were "the decadence and despotism of Versailles." Moreover, unlike the more ephemeral "news" media, *libelles* took the form of books and hence lasted longer, thus granting an extended life to the anti-Versailles "political folklore" found in all eighteenth-century

5   On the Jansenists see chapter 9.

media. Their durability, Darnton argues, ensured that they would perpetuate the damaging stories of decadence and despotism, permitting them to reach a greater number of people and reinforcing the impressions of those who read them more than once.

Finally, Darnton considers the relationship between forbidden literature and the political crisis that began in 1787, when nobles resisted (not for the first time) the crown's proposed changes in the fiscal system and demanded a greater role in government. He argues that the pamphlet literature of 1787 to 1789 (in which contemporary political matters were now explicitly addressed) suggests that contemporaries did not perceive the famous "aristocratic reaction" that historians have posited. According to that long-held thesis, the nobles, particularly those whose privileges stemmed from their seats in the *parlements*, opposed an alliance between the Third Estate and a reforming monarchy dedicated to reducing those very privileges until, at the last moment, the crown yielded to noble pressure and convoked the Estates General, an "archaic body" that seemingly favored their caste. According to Darnton, the pamphlet literature published during this period of crisis reveals that "public opinion," while not always siding with the *parlements*, consistently opposed the "despotism" of the monarchy, especially of its ministers. In this climate, he concludes, the *libelles* of the previous reign acquired a new and especially incendiary meaning.

The Forbidden Best-Sellers of Pre-Revolutionary France

Robert Darnton

Reader Response

Despite some preliminary forays into the history of reading, we know very little about the ways readers responded to books under the Old Regime.[1] We have learned only enough to distrust our own intuition, for whatever the responses might have been, they took place in a mental world so different from our own that we cannot project our experience onto that of French readers confronted with texts two hundred years ago.

I think it valid nonetheless to make a minimal assertion: readers' reactions, though varied, tended to be strong. In an era when television and radio did not challenge the supremacy of the printed word, books aroused emotions and stirred thoughts with a power we can barely imagine today. Richardson, Rousseau, and Goethe did not merely wring tears from their readers; they changed lives. *Pamela* and *La Nouvelle Héloïse* inspired lovers, spouses, and parents to reconsider their most intimate relations and, in some well-documented cases, to modify their behavior. *The Sorrows of Young Werther* drove a few of Goethe's readers to take their own lives, even if the "Werther fever" did not produce a wave of suicides, as some Germans believed.

Those early romantic novels may seem unbearably sentimental today, but to readers in the eighteenth century they had an irresistible ring of authenticity. They established a new rapport between author and reader and between reader and text. Of course, there were many other genres and many different kinds of readers under the Old Regime. Compared with the sparse diet of earlier eras, the reading matter consumed in the eighteenth century seems so enormous that some have associated it with a "reading revolution." According to this thesis, the experience of reading was basically "intensive" until the mid-eighteenth century and "extensive" thereafter. "Intensity" derived from the practice of reading

1   As examples of programmatic essays, see Henri-Jean Martin, "Pour une histoire de la lecture," in Martin, *Le Livre français sous l'Ancien Régime* (Paris, 1987); Roger Chartier, "Du Livre au lire: les pratiques citadines de l'imprimé, 1660–1780," in Chartier, ed., *Lectures et lecteurs dans la France d'Ancien Régime*; and Robert Darnton, "First Steps Toward a History of Reading," in *The Kiss of Lamourette*.

a few works, particularly the Bible, over and over again, usually aloud and in groups. When readers took up "extensive" reading, they raced through a wide variety of printed matter, especially periodicals and light fiction, without considering the same text more than once.

This formula was developed by some German scholars to explain the peculiar course of German history: while France had a political revolution and Britain an industrial revolution, Germany's route to modernity led through a "reading revolution," which opened up a domain of culture peculiar to a nation of *Dichter und Denker* (poets and philosophers). The thesis had a beguiling simplicity, but it rested on little evidence, except in the case of the densely Protestant and commercial regions around cities like Leipzig, Hamburg, and Bremen. Insofar as it could be applied to other parts of Germany and of Europe, it made a useful distinction between an older pattern of culture in which people owned only one or two books and read them repetitively, and a more prosperous and more literate phase in which people read one text after another. But this distinction did not correlate with the more important opposition between "intensive" and "extensive" reading. It ignored evidence that the old-fashioned, repetitive reading was often mechanical or ritualistic rather than intensive, while the new vogue for novels produced a more not a less intensive experience. Many Germans read *The Sorrows of Young Werther* over and over again (Napoleon read it seven times), and some even memorized it.[2]

True, readers turned increasingly to periodicals and other kinds of literature that had been relatively scarce in the seventeenth century. Reading habits no longer conformed to the picture of the paterfamilias declaiming Scripture to his household. But that picture never corresponded closely to practices in France, despite the sentimental evocation of it by Restif de la Bretonne in 1779.[3] In fact, Parisians may have read

2   The main arguments for the "reading revolution" were developed by Rolf Engelsing, especially his "Die Perioden der Lesergeschichte in der Neuzeit. Das statistische Ausmass und die soziokulturelle Bedeutung der Lektüre," *Archiv für Geschichte des Buchwesens*, X (1970), 945–1002, and *Der Bürger als Leser. Lesergeschichte in Deutschland 1500–1800* (Stuttgart, 1974). For contrasting views, see Rudolf Schenda, *Volk ohne Buch. Studien zur Sozialgeschichte der populären Lesestoffe 1770–1910* (Frankfurt-am-Main, 1970), and Erich Schön, *Der Verlust der Sinnlichkeit oder Die Verwandlung des Lesers. Mentalitätswandel um 1800*, especially pp. 298–300. The best and most recent survey of the history of books in Germany treats the notion of a "reading revolution" very skeptically: Reinhard Wittmann, *Geschichte des deutschen Buchhandels. Ein Überblick*, chap. 6. A fairly recent account of the "Werther fever" is Georg Jäger, "Die Wertherwirkung. Ein Rezeptionsästhetischer Modellfall," in Walter Müller-Seidel, ed., *Historizität in Sprach-und Literaturwissenschaft* (Munich, 1974), pp. 389–409.
3   Nicolas-Edmé Restif de la Bretonne, *La Vie de mon père* (Ottawa, 1949; 1st edn., 1779), pp. 216–17.

more ephemera in 1649, when the presses of the Fronde turned out a half dozen pamphlets a day, than they did a century later. The first evidence of new reading habits can be detected around 1750, when catalogues of private libraries and registers of book privileges show a decline in religious works as opposed to fiction, history, scientific and travel literature.[4] But truly "extensive" reading on a mass scale did not predominate until late in the nineteenth century, when cheap paper, steam-powered presses, and greatly increased literacy brought new varieties of popular literature within the range of the general public. Nothing comparable happened in the eighteenth century. The technology of printing, the organization of the book trade, and the education of children did not differ fundamentally from what had existed a hundred years earlier. Although tastes changed and the reading public expanded, the experience of reading was not transformed. It became more secular and more varied, but not less intense. It did not undergo a revolution.[5]

Historians have discovered and dismissed so many hidden revolutions of the past that the "reading revolution" might be safely ignored, except that it has been invoked to explain the possible reaction of readers to the forbidden literature of the Old Regime in France. If reading had been revolutionized and readers had adopted a radically new attitude of casualness and skepticism toward texts, then perhaps they shrugged off the *livres philosophiques* as a trivial form of amusement.[6] This argument employs a hypothetical cause to account for a hypothetical effect, but it deserves to be taken seriously, because it is the only argument that has been advanced to dispute the influence of forbidden books. We cannot submit it to much of a test, however, because we have so little documentation of readers' responses, especially in the clandestine sector of the book trade. Pending further investigation, I can offer only a few scraps of evidence culled from the correspondence of authors, publishers, booksellers, and the book police.

Book reviews, unfortunately, provide little help. Forbidden books could not be discussed in periodicals that circulated in France, and in any case reviewing usually involved little more than publishing extracts or plugging works of allies and attacking those of enemies. But the Parisian literati often reported on scandalous works in newsletters that

4   François Furet, "La 'librairie' du royaume de France au 18e siècle," in Furet, et al., *Livre et société dans la France du XVIIIe siècle* (Paris, 1965), and Michel Marion, *Recherches sur les bibliothèques privées à Paris au milieu du XVIIIe siècle (1750–1759)* (Paris, 1978).

5   The best overview of these questions is Chartier and Martin, eds., *Histoire de l'édition française*, vol. II: *Le Livre triomphant 1660–1830*.

6   Chartier, *Les Origines culturelles de la Révolution française*, pp. 103–15.

they wrote for foreign princes. Although these private gazettes could be even more biased than the official press – the gazeteers frequently reviewed their own books and those of their friends – they were uninhibited enough to contain some clues to the reception of illegal literature in the literary circles of Paris.

The most influential of the newsletters, Grimm's *Correspondance littéraire* (established in 1753 by F. M. Grimm with help from Diderot, Raynal, and others, and continued by J. H. Meister during the 1770s and 1780s), discussed many *livres philosophiques*. Its favorable reviews of atheistic tracts like *Le Christianisme dévoilé* do not prove much, because they were written by the Holbacheans within its own ranks.[7] But its reviews of the *libelles* against Louis XV indicate that sophisticated readers took political slander seriously, even if they disapproved of its vulgarity. Although he could not identify the authors of *Vie privée de Louis XV* and *Anecdotes sur Mme la comtesse du Barry*, Meister showed no sympathy for them: the first wrote like a lackey, he said, and the second like a valet. Nonetheless, the substance of their writing deserved serious attention. By endeavoring to separate fact from fiction, the *Vie privée* provided a fairly balanced account of Louis XV's reign.[8] And the *Anecdotes* deserved high marks for impartiality and verisimilitude if not for style: "His [the anonymous author's] history is neither absolutely false nor absolutely true: although it falls short of the truth, it comes close to it most of the time."[9] Meister had an even higher opinion of *Lettres originales de Mme la comtesse du Barry*, a collection of obviously apocryphal letters that were "all the more true for having been invented." They captured the spirit of Louis XV's reign:

> The very anonymous author of these letters not only seems to be quite well informed about all the minor intrigues that filled the last years of the reign of Louis XV, but he also seems to have an excellent knowledge of the character and turn of mind of most of the personages that he represents. . . . But the first reflection one is tempted to make after reading this extraordinary work is that in all the dazzling social whirl surrounding Mme du Barry during the time of her favor there was no one, truly no one, any more worthy of respect than she was. One sees the greatest dig-

---

7 Maurice Tourneux, ed., *Correspondance littéraire, philosophique et critique par Grimm, Diderot, Raynal, Meister, etc.* (Paris, 1877–1882), 16 vols. In praising *Le Christianisme dévoilé*, the *Correspondance littéraire* claimed that it had an energizing, liberating effect on the reader: "It sweeps one up. . . . One does not learn anything new from it, yet one feels involved, engaged" (V, 368). It condemned *Thérèse philosophe* as a work "without taste, without decency, without spice, without logic, without style" (I, 256).
8 *Correspondance littéraire*, XII, 482.
9 Ibid., XI, 399.

nitaries, the most powerful figures of the kingdom debase themselves at her feet, beg for her credit, exhibit incomparably more greed than she does. They promote general disorder in the hope of profiting from it, alternately seek and betray her trust, undergo the most well deserved humiliations, and merit all the contempt that hatred and envy sought to heap on her.[10]

In short, the folkloric view of du Barry and politics in the court of Louis XV seemed convincing to a sophisticated contemporary in the Parisian intelligentsia.

The letters that have survived in the correspondence of publishers demonstrate the public's fascination with a half dozen authors of illegal books: Voltaire, Rousseau, Raynal, Linguet, and Mercier. But they almost never discuss the readers' responses. A rare exception in the papers of the STN is a letter from a merchant in Nantes named Barre, who sold a few books on the side. Barre had nothing good to say about the book trade in his town: "Merchants hardly think of literature at all."[11] But Raynal's *Histoire philosophique* was an exception:

> The public has received this work with enthusiasm. The author has genius, true knowledge, and an honest heart. He paints things in vivid colors, and in reading him you feel your heart has been set on fire. He has torn away a great deal of the fatal blindfold that covers the eyes of the human race and prevents it from seeing the truth.[12]

The STN received a similar report from Pierre Godeffroy, a merchant in Rouen, who also dabbled in the book trade. He, too, was an enthusiast, but for the more rationalist side of the Enlightenment. He asked the STN to send him a half dozen copies of the *Système de la nature* so that he could supply friends who had developed an appetite for forbidden fruit. Everyone in his circle "venerated" Voltaire, he wrote; and he himself especially admired the rustic liberty of the Swiss, which he contrasted with the slavish spirit in France. While reading a travel book about a journey into the Swiss mountains, he said that he was moved by "the advantages that liberty produces. We need to show as many examples of that as we can to people here, who don't even have an idea of what liberty is."[13]

The professional booksellers did not write personal commentaries of this sort, but their letters provide plenty of testimony about the demand

10   Ibid., XII, 339–40.
11   Barre to STN, the Société Typographique de Neuchâtel, a Swiss publisher of books in French, whose archives provide much of the documentary evidence for Davton's claims about the history of pubishing and reading, Sept. 15, 1781.
12   Barre to STN, Aug. 23, 1782.
13   Godeffroy to STN, June 10, 1771; May 5, 1772; and Feb. 10, 1776.

for *livres philosophiques* – "the philosophical genre, which seems to be this century's favorite," according to Pierre-Joseph Duplain of Lyon.[14] In the course of their shop talk, they offered observations about their customers' interest in particular authors and genres. For example, a peddler named Le Lièvre who operated out of Belfort noted the peculiar "curiosity" concerning bawdy and irreligious works among the officers of the local garrison.[15] In Loudun, Malherbe picked up a strong interest in anti-clericalism: "The new words of M. Voltaire will certainly be in great demand. . . . As to sermons, their sales don't amount to much. Devotional works are common and religious ardor has cooled."[16] Everywhere booksellers sensed a powerful desire for political *libelles* – "critical works," as Petit of Reims called them, or "piquant articles" (Waroquier of Soissons), or "works on current affairs" (Carez of Toul).[17] They always mentioned the same texts, above all, *Anecdotes sur Mme la comtesse du Barry*, *Mémoires authentiques de Mme la comtesse du Barry*, *Journal historique . . . par M. de Maupeou*, *Correspondance secrète et familière de M. de Maupeou*, *Vie privée de Louis XV*, *Mémoires de Louis XV*, *Fastes de Louis XV*, *Mémoires de l'abbé Terray*, *Mémoires secrets*, *L'Espion anglais*. Their letters leave no doubt about the interest in such books; but, alas, they say nothing about how their customers read them.[18]

Of course, the texts themselves contain many clues about the responses anticipated by their authors and publishers. It was assumed, for example, that pornographic books were read for erotic stimulation. Hence Rousseau's famous remark about "books that one reads with one hand,"[19] and the climax of *Thérèse philosophe*, entitled "The Effects of Painting and Reading," where the Count provokes Thérèse to masturbate by plying her with *Histoire de dom B . . .* , *portier des Chartreux*, *Histoire de la tourière des Carmélites*, *L'Académie des dames*, and other pornographic best-sellers. But how can one test such assumptions against the actual experience of readers?

Some indications, especially about the effect of political works, are scattered through the memoranda and letters exchanged within the

14   P.-J. Duplain to STN, Oct. 11, 1772.
15   Le Lièvre to STN, Jan. 3, 1777.
16   Malherbe to STN, Sept. 13, 1775.
17   Petit to STN, August 31, 1783; Waroquier to STN, Jan. 7, 1778; Carez to STN, Feb. 23, 1783.
18   A rare exception was Malherbe's comment that some customers objected that the theological articles of the *Encyclopédie* were written "too much in the taste of the Sorbonne, no doubt in order to favor its circulation in France; but those obstacles to the freedom of thought do not please all the readers": Malherbe to STN, Sept. 14, 1778.
19   Quoted in Jean-Marie Goulemot, *Ces Livres qu'on ne lit que d'une main. Lecture et lecteurs de livres pornographiques au XVIIIe siècle* (Aix-en-Provence, 1991), p. 9. This monograph offers an incisive analysis of how erotic texts orient readers.

Book Trade Department (Direction de la librairie) of the royal adminis-tration. In June 1771, the subdelegate of the intendant of Caen warned the authorities that Normandy was flooded with forbidden books and that the readers took them seriously: "Reading these bad books produces a disturbed spirit among the citizens and provokes them constantly to shake the yoke of submission, of obedience, and of respect."[20] Labadie, a retired bookseller from Valenciennes, advised the police to take strong measures, although they could not expect to turn the tide of public opinion: "Today, everyone wants to think philosophically and to discuss governmental affairs. Everyone discourses on such matters and rushes to get even the most dangerous works that appear on them."[21] Not that the police informants connected this danger with an impending revolu-tion. They perceived voguishness as well as discontent in the rage for "bad" books. Hence an anonymous memoire of 1766, which warned the police that the spread of *livres philosophiques* seemed to be unstoppable:

> Never has one seen so many forbidden works as today. . . . No one is ashamed to be occupied with a bad book. Instead, people take pride in it; it's enough for a book to be known as such for people to desire it all the more. And someone who can hardly spare an hour a day for healthy reading will talk about staying up whole nights with something bad.[22]

The professionals on both sides of the law realized that forbidden books attracted different kinds of readers who read in different ways. In a memo written from the Bastille, the sieur Guy, who peddled *livres philosophiques* while working for the Veuve Duchesne in Paris, described the varieties of readers and reading as follows:

> People are bent on getting them [forbidden books], no matter what the price. And who are these people? Precisely those who by their birth, their position, their knowledge, and their attachment to religion should be the first to condemn them. But on the contrary, if they merely hear some-thing mentioned in a hushed tone about a new work of this kind, they run after it – the courtier for his amusement, the magistrate in order to be kept informed, the clergyman to refute it, and members of the Third Estate in order to say that they have something rare and difficult to get.

20   "Projet pour la police de la librairie de Normandie donné par M. Rodolphe, subdélégué de M. l'intendant à Caen," Bibliothèque Nationale, ms fr. 22123, item 33.
21   Labadie, "Projet d'un mémoire sur la librairie," ibid., item 21.
22   "Mémoire sur le corps des libraires imprimeurs," 1766, unsigned: ibid., item 19.

In short, it's a way of cutting a figure and being fashionable; and a man who doesn't have a six-livre *écu* to pay his cobbler will spend four louis [96 livres] in order to swim with the tide.[23]

To be in fashion, to be informed, to be aroused or moved – readers turned to illegal literature for many reasons and reacted in many ways. No one in the book business expected the reactions to be the same. But everyone treated the forbidden literature as a serious matter, important enough to demand attention from the highest officials in the kingdom and to occupy a whole department of the police.

Of course, police archives have a bias of their own. Inspectors of the book trade could curry favor with the lieutenant general by discovering threats to Church and State, and the lieutenant general could ingratiate himself with his superiors in Versailles by detecting and suppressing slander of "les grands." The papers of Jean-Charles-Pierre Lenoir, the most important lieutenant general of the Parisian police during the pre-Revolutionary years, must be read with particular caution, because Lenoir composed them at different times between 1790 and 1807, when he had fled from the French Revolution. He wanted to defend his administration against the revolutionaries, who had accused him of abusing his power and had run him out of the country. But Lenoir also wanted to understand what had brought about the collapse of the Old Regime. And he knew so much about its inner workings that his observations, scribbled in drafts for memoirs that he never completed, provide valuable information about the attitudes and policies toward forbidden books at the highest levels of the French government.[24]

According to Lenoir, *libelles* did not cause much concern in Versailles during the first years of Louis XVI's reign. The comte de Maurepas, the dominant minister in the government and a veteran of court intrigue, collected slanderous songs and epigrams: "In private gatherings, M. de Maurepas gaily declamed the verse written against him. He said that such things always were and always would be an amusement, something that occupied Parisians who had little to do and who wanted to impress people in high society."[25] But policy changed under the min-

23   "Mémoire sur la librairie de France fait par le sieur Guy pendant qu'il était à la Bastille," Feb. 8, 1767: ibid., item 22.
24   On the character of Lenoir's manuscript memoirs, see Georges Lefebvre, "Les Papiers de Lenoir," *Annales historiques de la Révolution Française* IV (1927), 300, and Robert Darnton, "The Memoirs of Lenoir, Lieutenant de Police of Paris, 1774–1785," *English Historical Review*, LXXXV (1970), 532–59.
25   Papers of Lenoir, Bibliothèque municipale d'Orléans, ms. 1422, "Titre sixième: De l'administration de l'ancienne police concernant les libelles, les mauvaises satires et chansons, leurs auteurs coupables, délinquants, complices ou adhérents."

istries of Necker, Calonne, and Brienne. By 1780, the ministers secretly subsidized writers to undercut one another. *Libelles* that had circulated in manuscript during the stormy last years of Louis XV now appeared in print, attacking the monarch himself. Then the slander turned on Louis XVI, deriding his supposed impotence, and on Marie-Antoinette, deploring her supposed sexual orgies. Defamation of this kind could not be laughed off, not even by Maurepas, who reversed his policy and organized secret missions to cut off the production of *libelles* in foreign countries. The Foreign Minister, the comte de Vergennes, dispatched undercover agents to kidnap *libellistes* in London. The police sent agents to Vienna and Brussels and kept raiding bookstores in Paris. But the slander appeared faster than they could repress it, so "the law was particularly ineffective against anti-government *libelles* during the years before the Revolution."[26]

In retrospect, it seemed to Lenoir that the mud slinging had "caused great harm to domestic tranquility, to the public spirit, and to [the spirit of] submissiveness."[27] The public believed the wildest stories, despite the government's attempts to counter them with accurate reports in propaganda of its own: "Parisians put more faith in wicked rumors and *libelles* that circulated clandestinely than in the facts, which were printed and published by order of the government or with its permission."[28] By 1785, Lenoir had to bribe the crowds to shout "Vive la reine!" when Marie-Antoinette appeared in Paris. But despite great efforts, he managed to produce "only some scattered applause, which everyone knew to be bought."[29] Years of slander had damaged something fundamental in the people's attachment to the monarchy.

Lenoir's remarks can be confirmed by documents in the Ministry of Foreign Affairs and the archives of the Bastille. In 1783, the Foreign Minister spent almost as much time trying to stamp out the London *Libellistes* as he did negotiating the Treaty of Paris, which put an end to the American war. Slander was despicable, he wrote to the French chargé d'affaires in London, but when it struck at crowned heads it could not be ignored: "You know how evil our century is and how easily the most absurd fables are accepted."[30] After a great deal of huggermugger, the police bribed off some of the *libellistes* and lured others to France, where they were clapped up in the Bastille.[31] But soon afterwards, the Diamond Necklace Affair – the scandal involving the queen

26   Ibid.
27   Lenoir Papers, ms 1423, "Résidus."
28   Lenoir Papers, ms 1422, "Sûreté."
29   Lenoir Papers, ms 1423, untitled note.
30   Vergennes to comte d'Adhémar, May 21, 1783, Ministère des Affaires Etrangères, Correspondance politique, Angleterre, ms 542.
31   Bibliothèque de l'Arsenal, ms 12517, ff. 73–78.

and the cardinal de Rohan – produced an even more disastrous wave of pamphleteering, and many Frenchmen went into the Revolution convinced that the king had been cuckolded by a cardinal.

Nowhere in all this material can one find any suggestion that books were simply "machines made to produce effects" and that readers were simply recipients with minds like "soft wax" ready to accept any message stamped on them.[32] Eighteenth-century Frenchmen understood enough about communication to expect readers and readings to be diverse. But they believed that *livres philosophiques* could produce powerful responses and that *libelles* could upset the stability of the state. We have no access to the minds of men and women as they manipulated texts two centuries ago. We can only study them indirectly, through the testimony of authors, publishers, booksellers, government officials, and the occasional reader who left some record of his reaction. But all the evidence points to the same conclusion: readers took forbidden literature seriously. All of it, that is, except one final document.

In his *Tableau de Paris*, Louis-Sébastien Mercier seems to minimize the effects of the *libelles*:

> The more a *libelle* is forbidden, the more it is coveted. But when you have read it and seen that it provides no reward for your audacity, you are ashamed to have run after it. You hardly dare say, "I have read it." It's the froth produced by the lowlife of literature. . . . What *libelle* after two weeks has not been condemned by public opinion and left to its own infamy? . . . An excessive *libelle* is revolting, disgusting, and undercuts itself by its own violence. But if it is more moderate, it sometimes counterbalances an excessive concentration of power; it goes beyond the limits of decency in the same way as the authorities abuse their power. It was often provoked by insolent little despots, and the public perceives the truth between two extremes.[33]

This passage does indeed suggest that the public did not believe everything purveyed by the *libellistes*, but it does not prove that readers refused to take *libelles* seriously. On the contrary, it makes a distinction between exaggerated slander, which could produce a counterreaction, and more moderate attacks on abuses of power, which could turn the public against the despots in the government. In this case, Mercier's description of "the public" seems to apply primarily to people like himself

---

32   This is the position Roger Chartier seems to attribute to those who would argue that forbidden books had a strong effect on the reading public: Chartier, *Les Origines culturelles de la Révolution française*, pp. 104 and 109.
33   Mercier, *Tableau de Paris* (Amsterdam, 1783), VII, 23 and 25. Chartier cites this passage in order to argue that *libelles* had little effect on readers: *Les Origines culturelles de la Révolution française*, pp. 103–4.

– that is, well-informed people, the insiders in the world of publishing and public affairs. In a similar discussion of satirical posters and pamphlets, he noted, "People in high society are amused by them but take them with a grain of salt."[34] Thus, like the booksellers and police agents, Mercier distinguished between sophisticated and ordinary readers. He never defined the latter, although he wrote a suggestive essay on "Monsieur le public" as an "indefinable composite" made up of ill-assorted and incompatible social traits.[35] Nonetheless, he insisted that a public did exist, in the form of a tribunal above the ebb and flow of fashion, which sifted through conflicting opinions and ultimately pronounced the truth.[36] The conviction that the truth would [come] out also shaped Mercier's view of libeling, because he maintained that "a few good truths" in a lowly *libelle* could make a minister quake, and he even argued that the infamous Maupeou ministry was brought down by one of the most popular *libelles* on the best-seller list, *Correspondance secrète et familière de M. de Maupeou*.[37]

But suggestive as it is, Mercier's *Tableau de Paris* cannot be taken literally, as if it were a window into the minds of eighteenth-century Parisians. Like all texts, it has a rhetorical undertow, which carries it in contradictory directions. The contradictions stand out strongest in Mercier's references to reading, because on the one hand he celebrates the printed word as the supreme power in history and on the other he deprecates journalism, hack writers, and *libelles*. Why this aversion to the humbler forms of literary activity? Basically, I believe, because Mercier did not want to be identified with them. He had acquired a reputation as a "Rousseau of the gutter" (*Rousseau du ruisseau*) very much like Restif de la Bretonne, for whom that phrase had been coined. In the literary newsletter of Jean-François de La Harpe, Mercier appears as a failed playwright, vulgar compiler, and bosom companion of Restif.[38] In the *Mémoires secrets* of Bachaumont, he appears as a hack, who threw all sorts of garbage into the *Tableau de Paris* in order to increase the number of volumes and squeeze the maximum return from the market.[39] And in the files of the police, he is

---

34   Mercier, *Tableau de Paris*, VI, 79.
35   Ibid., VI, 268.
36   Ibid., VI, 269.
37   Ibid., I, 176.
38   Jean-François de La Harpe, *Correspondance littéraire adressé à son Altesse Impériale Mgr. le Grand-Duc, aujourd'hui Empereur de Russie, et à M. le Comte André Schowalow, Chamberlain de l'Impératrice Cathérine II, depuis 1774 jusqu'à 1789*, 6 vols. (Paris, 1804–1807), III, 203 and 251.
39   *Mémoires secrets pour servir à l'histoire de la République des lettres en France, depuis 1762 jusqu'à nos jours*, attributed to Louis Petit de Bachaumont and others, 36 vols. (London, 1777–89), entries for Aug. 1, 1781; April 20, 1782; and April 23, 1784.

[a] lawyer, a fierce, bizarre man; he neither pleads in court nor consults. He hasn't been admitted to the bar, but he takes the title of lawyer. He has written the *Tableau de Paris*, in four volumes, and other works. Fearing the Bastille, he left the country, then returned and wants to be attached to the police.[40]

All the reviews concurred on the audacity of Mercier's criticism of the government and the social order. Like *L'An 2440*, the *Tableau de Paris* became a best-selling *livre philosophique*. But was it also a *libelle?* A review of the first, two-volume edition in the *Courrier de l'Europe* said categorically, "This is not a *libelle*; it is the work of a courageous and sensitive citizen." That may sound like praise, but it cut Mercier to the quick. In volume IV of the next edition, Mercier devoted a long, vehement chapter to the *Courier's* remarks, the only review he ever mentioned: "The criticism hardly amounts to an absolution! You who have read me, tell me, can this work conceivably conjure up any notion linked with that odious word *libelle?* Why use it? It oppresses me."[41] Mercier's horror of *libelles* gave vent to his anxiety that his own work could be classified as one, just as his deprecation of hack writing expressed his fear that he might be considered a hack.[42]

Indeed, everything that Mercier published about writers and readers is revealing, not so much about actual practices as about dominant themes in the contemporary discourse on literature. In nearly all his works, he returned obsessively to the same topic: Enlightenment is spreading everywhere; writers are the unacknowledged legislators of the world; the printing press is the most powerful engine of progress; and public opinion is the force that will sweep despotism away. One example should be enough to illustrate his tone:

A great and momentous revolution in our ideas has taken place within the last thirty years. Public opinion has now become a preponderant

40   Lenoir papers, ms 1423, "Extraits de divers rapports secrets faits à la police de Paris dans les années 1781 et suivantes, jusques et compris 1785, concernant des personnes de tout état et condition [ayant] donné dans la Révolution."

41   *Tableau de Paris*, IV, 279. The quotation from the review is taken from Mercier's own reprint of it.

42   Throughout the *Tableau de Paris* and in his other works, notably *De la Littérature et des littéraires* and *Mon Bonnet de nuit*, Mercier tried to distinguish true authors and genuine men of letters from pampered academicians on the one hand and hacks on the other. See, for example, *Tableau de Paris*, II, 103–13; IV, 19–26 and 245–61; VII, 230; X, 26–29 and 154–56; and XI, 181. Did Mercier also castigate *libelles* in order to ingratiate himself with the police, as one might suspect from the remarks in his own police report? I have found no evidence that he acted as an informer or propagandist for the authorities, but the *Tableau de Paris* contains several passages that flatter the lieutenant general of police: see, for example, I, 187–93, and VII, 36.

power in Europe, one that cannot be resisted. In view of the progress that has occurred and will occur, one may hope that enlightened ideas will bring about the greatest good on earth and that tyrants of all kinds will tremble before the universal cry that echoes everywhere, awakening Europe from its slumbers. . . . The influence of writers is such that they may now openly proclaim their power and no longer disguise the legitimate authority they exercise over people's minds.[43]

Reading occupied a central position in this bundle of leitmotifs. Mercier drew on the stock images of early Romanticism to describe its operation: a moral force, as irresistible and invisible as gravity or electricity, was generated by a genius, released from his pen, transmitted through type, and imprinted in the soul of the reader.[44] Hence the chapter on printing in *De la Littérature et des littéraires*, which Mercier reprinted in *Mon Bonnet de nuit:*

> It [printing] is the most beautiful gift of heaven. . . . It soon will change the countenance of the universe. From the compositor's narrow cases in the printing shop great and generous ideas emerge, which man cannot resist. He will adopt them, despite himself; their effect is already visible. Printing was born only a short while ago, and already everything is heading toward perfection. . . . A despot, surrounded by guards, by fortresses, defended by two thousand naked swords, may be deaf to the call of conscience; but he cannot resist a stroke of the pen: this stroke will fell him in the heart of his grandeur.
> . . . Tremble, therefore, tyrants of the world! Tremble before the virtuous writer![45]

Mercier did not allow anything ignoble to spoil this picture. In the Utopian fantasies of *L'An 2440*, he eliminated all unworthy books, filled public spaces with statues of writers, and made reading and writing into solemn spiritual exercises. In his essays, he often protested against overly sophisticated or trivial literature, which undercut the moral purpose of reading.[46] And in his plays and novels, he inserted reading scenes to

43   Mercier, *Tableau de Paris*, IV, 258–59. This passage is a reprint of one Mercier had already published in *De la Littérature et des littéraires* (Yverdon, 1778), pp. 8–9. Mercier blended a great deal of his earlier writing into his multi-volume works, the *Tableau de Paris, L'An 2440*, and *Mon Bonnet de nuit.*
44   On this general theme, see Auguste Viatte, *Les Sources occultes du romantisme: illuminisme-théosophie, 1770–1820* (Paris, 1928), 2 vols.
45   Mercier, *De la Littérature*, 19–20, and Mercier, *Mon Bonnet de nuit*, 4 vols. (Neuchâtel, 1785), I, 112–14. See also the similar remarks in *De la Littérature*, 38–41, and *Tableau de Paris*, V, 168–73; VII, 180; and VIII, 98.
46   See, for example, "Discours sur la lecture," in Mercier's *Eloges et discours philosophiques* (Amsterdam, 1776), which he inserted in parts of *Mon Bonnet de nuit.*

redirect the plot at crucial turning points. For example, *Jezennemours*, a sentimental tale about the triumph of love over religious bigotry, recounts a Jesuit plot to seize control of the hero's soul and to turn him into a priest by force-feeding him with theological and devotional works in a boarding school in Strasbourg. One day, a peddler accosts him in the street and offers him some *livres philosophiques* under the cloak. His curiosity piqued, the hero buys four Voltairean tracts. A preliminary skim through the texts is enough to whet his appetite. He stays up all night, devouring them in his cell. Then the scales fall from his eyes. He abandons the priesthood and escapes to his true love, Suzanne, the "belle luthérienne."

In telling the story, Mercier uses all sorts of concrete details to evoke the sensation of consuming forbidden literature: the ample folds of the peddler's cloak in which the books were hidden; the cheap paper and crude printing of the underground editions; the fascination evoked by the diabolical name of Voltaire; the peddler's assurance that such things sold like hot cakes; the sensation of cutting the first pages with a pocket knife; the excitement of carrying the small volumes under a shirt and in a pocket; and the final immersion in the texts late at night, as the wick of the lantern sputtered and burned down to a stub. The description, narrated in the first person, goes on for two chapters, providing one of the richest accounts of reading as an author of forbidden books liked to imagine it:

> Anyone who had seen me reading would have compared me to a man dying of thirst who was gulping down some fresh, pure water. . . . Lighting my lamp with extraordinary caution, I threw myself hungrily into the reading. An easy eloquence, effortless and animated, carried me from one page to the next without my noticing it. A clock struck off the hours in the silence of the shadows, and I heard nothing. My lamp began to run out of oil and produced only a pale light, but still I read on. I could not even take out time to raise the wick for fear of interrupting my pleasure. How those new ideas rushed into my brain! How my intelligence adopted them![47]

Mercier warned against the danger of excessive reading, especially of ephemeral literature, which could dull one's sensitivity: "Discours sur la lecture," pp. 245–46, 253, 269, 284, and 289–92. In this respect, his remarks could be taken as a reaction against "extensive" reading and a call for a return to an earlier, "intensive" style. But similar complaints about the unmanageable overproduction of books and the vanity of reading ephemera can be found in the sixteenth and seventeenth centuries.

47 Mercier, *Histoire d'une jeune luthérienne* (Neuchâtel, 1785), pp. 142–43. (The first edition, Neuchâtel, 1776, was published under the title *Jezennemours, roman dramatique*.)

Overblown as it is, this description actually corresponds to the experience of many eighteenth-century readers.[48] Of course, it represents an ideal type rather than a common practice. But that is the point: far from providing unambiguous evidence about the diminished power of the printed word and the casualness of readers, Mercier articulated a widespread conviction that reading could move mountains – and remove despots, especially if the books were "philosophical."

How could *livres philosophiques* produce such extraordinary effects? Even Mercier did not invoke simple notions of causality. Like many of his contemporaries, he envisioned an indirect process by which books determined the course of public opinion and public opinion shaped events. But that notion, too, is an ideal construct, expressed in its noblest form by Condorcet in the *Esquisse d'un tableau historique des progrès de l'esprit humain*. Having examined what people thought happened to them and ought to happen to them when they read forbidden books, we now face a final problem: How did *livres philosophiques* contribute to the radicalization of public opinion?

Public Opinion

The question of public opinion cannot be dispatched in a few pages any more easily than the problem of reader response. But a brief discussion of it may help clear the way for further study and also for an answer to a final objection: Perhaps forbidden books did not affect public opinion at all; perhaps they merely reflected it. This thesis rests on two kinds of arguments about the autonomous character of attitudes toward the monarchy among the common people in Paris. According to the first, a

---

48   In this case, Mercier depicted a young man liberating himself from dogmatic Catholicism by reading Voltaire and Fontenelle. In other works, he emphasized the overwhelming effect of reading Rousseau, and his descriptions fit those of Rousseau's actual readers: see Darnton, "Readers Respond to Rousseau: The Fabrication of Romantic Sensitivity," in *The Great Cat Massacre*. For example, in the *Tableau de Paris*, V, 58, Mercier described a girl who furtively bought a copy of *La Nouvelle Héloïse*, despite her mother's prohibition, and then was so moved by reading it that she resolved to dedicate her life to the domesticity exemplified by the novel's heroine. Mercier evoked his own experience in similar language: "Writing! Thy power has not been adequately admired! By what mechanism do words traced on paper, whose influence seems at first to be so slight, make such lasting and profound impressions? . . . There is something astonishing and supernatural about the power of combining ideas rapidly with the help of some simple figures. . . . The words strike the imagination more than things themselves. . . . I open a volume of Rousseau's *Nouvelle Héloïse*: it is still black on white, but all of a sudden I become attentive, heated, aroused; I catch flame, I am moved in a thousand different ways": *Mon Bonnet de nuit*, I, 298 and 302.

"desacralized" view of kingship can be detected from spontaneous, small changes in the daily life of Parisians.[49] According to the second, the Parisians began to express open hostility to the king in the 1750s and perhaps even earlier.[50]

The first argument derives from some other observations about everyday life in the *Tableau de Paris*. Mercier noted that second-hand dealers sold old, wrought-iron signs painted with images of kings and queens and that Parisians thought nothing of buying a picture of Louis XVI or Catherine II to hang outside their taverns and tobacco shops. Nor did they hesitate to purchase "cakes à la royale" and "beef à la royale" in food stores.[51] According to Roger Chartier, this casual use of images and words demonstrates a "symbolic and emotional disinvestment" that desacralized the monarchy, robbing it of all "transcendent significance." Indeed, it explains the success of the *livres philosophiques*, because the desacralization of attitudes came before the publication of the books rather than vice versa.[52] In fact, the chronology does not serve this interpretation very well, because the first edition of the *Tableau de Paris* came out in 1781, long after the first *libelles* against Louis XV, and *libellistes* had been slinging mud at monarchs for two centuries before Mercier noticed the familiarity with royal accoutrements of Parisian shops. More important, casual and even irreverent handling of sacred objects does not provide evidence of desacralization. In the Middle Ages, people chatted with, leaned against, and defecated near holy objects with a familiarity that seems sacrilegious to us but that actually expressed the all-pervading power of their faith. And even today, royal signs outside pubs and labels on toiletries in England proclaiming, "By special appointment from Her Majesty the Queen," do not bespeak any disaffection for the monarchy; quite the contrary.[53]

---

49   Chartier, *Les Origines culturelles de la Révolution française*, pp. 108–10.
50   Arlette Farge and Jacques Revel, *Logiques de la foule. L'affaire des enlèvements d'enfants. Paris 1750* (Paris, 1988), and Arlette Farge, *Dire et mal dire. L'opinion publique au XVIIIe siècle* (Paris, 1992).
51   Mercier, *Tableau de Paris*, V, 109 and 130, and Chartier, *Les Origines culturelles de la Révolution française*, pp. 109–10. In fact, Mercier used his remarks on signs as an occasion for a moral essay on the transitoriness of glory among "les grands." And he discussed the expression "à la royale" as an example of the Parisians' view that everything connected with the king must be elevated and excellent, not as an indication that they had lost respect for the monarchy. In either case, Mercier's comments should be taken as a literary text, not as unmediated street-corner sociology.
52   Chartier, *Les Origines culturelles de la Révolution française*, pp. 108–9.
53   Johan Huizinga, *The Waning of the Middle Ages* (1st edn., 1919; New York, n.d.). Anthropologists have often emphasized the familiarity with the sacred: see, for example, E. E. Evans-Pritchard, *Witchcraft, Oracles and Magic Among the Azande* (Oxford, 1937).

The second argument is more serious; and as it leads directly into the problem of charting public opinion, it must be examined carefully. Like everyone else, the French authorities failed to define "the public," but they knew it had opinions and they took those opinions seriously. The Paris police developed an elaborate network of informers in order to keep track of discussions in cafés, taverns, and other public places. Reports of these *propos* – loose talk about current events – provide a rough index to the state of public opinion in Paris throughout the eighteenth century.

Here, for example, is what was being said in cafés during the late 1720s, according to the police spies. At one point in 1728, the customers in the Café de Foy could hardly believe that N.-P.-B. d'Angervilliers had been appointed Minister of War, because his rival, F.-V.-L. de Breteuil was protected by the queen. Those in the Café Rousseau thought the appointment presaged further changes, probably a new intendant of Paris and perhaps a new lieutenant general of police. Meanwhile, at the Café de l'Enclume, a heated argument broke out between those who condemned d'Angervilliers for his brutal, autocratic manner and those who admired his character. The controller general Philibert Orry won the applause of the regulars at the Café de la Régence, because he had just humiliated the directors of the General Tax Farm (wealthy financiers who contracted with the crown to collect indirect taxes) in a quarrel over a *Te Deum* to be sung by the Jacobins. Talk at the Café Cotton was about maneuvers on the Bourse, at the Café de la Veuve Laurent about the price of bread, at the Café de Poinselet about speculation on grain, at the Café de Basteste about speculation on gold, at the Café du Puits on the pregnancy of the queen, at the Café de Conti on the French sympathies of the king of Spain, at the Café Gradot about the prohibition of a play, at the Café Procope about the poor health of the cardinal de Fleury, at the Café de Moisy about Jansenist agitation, and so on, in stupendous detail, including plenty of remarks about non-political events – a highway robbery, a prison break, a fire in Troyes, and a storm in Champagne that damaged vineyards with hailstones as big as chicken eggs. The reports covered about fifty cafés scattered throughout the city. Other agents informed the police about conversations in working-class taverns, *bons mots* in salons, and general gossip in public gardens. Strategically placed at the center of this vast information system, the lieutenant general of police had a remarkable knowledge of the talk of the town. By means of his weekly reports to the king and the minister of the *maison du roi* (in effect the Ministry of the Interior), the government kept a firm hand on the pulse of the public. It lacked pollsters, but it followed the course of public opinion.[54]

54   Bibliothèque de l'Arsenal, ms. 10 170. This volume contains only undated and unsigned notes, mainly on scraps of paper, and there is no comparable series from

Some of the reports were written in the form of dialogue, so that in reading them, one can imagine eavesdropping on political discussions held 260 years ago. That fantasy should be resisted, however, because the police spies were not stenographers, and their reports, like all historical documents, are just texts, not transparent windows into the past. Nonetheless, the reports reveal enough for one to get a general idea of how Parisians talked about Louis XV early in his reign. Here is an example:

> At the Café de Foy someone said that the king had taken a mistress, that she was named Madame Gontaut, and that she was a beautiful woman, the niece of the duc de Noailles and the comtesse de Toulouse. Others said, "If so, then there could be some big changes." And another replied, "True, a rumor is spreading, but I find it hard to believe, since the cardinal de Fleury is in charge. I don't think the king has any inclination in that direction, because he has always been kept away from women." "Nevertheless," someone else said, "it wouldn't be the greatest evil if he had a mistress." "Well, Messieurs," some others added, "it may not be a passing fancy, either, and a first love could raise some danger on the sexual side and could cause more harm than good. It would be far more desirable if he liked hunting better than that kind of thing."[55]

As always, the royal sex life provided plenty of material for gossip, but the talk tended to be friendly. In 1729, when the queen was about to give birth, the cafés rang with jubilation:

> Truly, everyone is delighted, because they all hope greatly to have a dauphin. . . . One of them said, "*Parbleu*, Messieurs, if God graces us with a dauphin, you will see Paris and the whole river aflame [with fireworks in celebration]." Everyone is praying for that.[56]

Twenty years later, the tone had changed completely. Here are some typical extracts from the archives of the Bastille for 1749:

> Jules-Alexis Bernard, chevalier de Bellerive, esquire, former captain of dragoons: In the shop of the wigmaker Gaujoux, this individual read aloud . . . an attack on the king in which it was said that His Majesty let himself be governed by ignorant and incompetent ministers and had made a shameful, dishonorable peace [the Treaty of Aix-la-Chapelle], which gave up all the fortresses that had been captured . . . that the king, by his affair with the three sisters [the daughters of the marquis de Nesle,

other periods, so we do not have a consistent set of police reports on café gossip covering the entire century.
55   Ibid., ms 10 170, fo. 175. I have added the quotation marks.
56   Ibid., ms 10 170, fo. 176.

whose affairs with Louis XV were commonly considered both incest and adultery] scandalized his people and would bring down all sorts of misfortune on himself if he did not change his conduct; that His Majesty scorned the queen and was an adulterer; that he had not confessed for Easter communion and would bring down the curse of God upon the kingdom and that France would be overwhelmed with disasters.[57]

Fleur de Montagne, defrocked Jesuit . . . Among other things, he said that the king didn't give a fuck about his people, as shown by his enormous expenditures; that he [Louis XV] knew the people were destitute and that he would make them still more miserable by burdening them with a new tax [the *vingtième* proposed by Machault d'Arnouville], as if to thank them for all they had done for him. "The French are crazy to stand for this," he added. He whispered the rest into somebody's ear.[58]

Jean-Louis Leclerc, lawyer in the parlement: Made the following remarks in the Café Procope: that there was never anything as rotten as the court, that the ministers and that whore Pompadour were making the king do unworthy things, which completely disgusted the people.[59]

Despite the imperfections of the sources and the fuzziness surrounding the very idea of public opinion, it seems clear that the public's respect for the monarchy plummeted in the mid-eighteenth century. One can find plenty of reasons for this change: the humiliation in foreign affairs after the War of the Austrian Succession, the fiscal crisis and the controversy over the *vingtième* tax, and the Jansenist agitation, which produced a new round of fierce conflict between the crown and the parlements. Much of the discontent became attached to the king's private life, which fed "public noises" at the very time when the king lost touch with the public and abandoned some of the key rituals of kingship. After 1738, when he began to parade his mistresses at court, Louis XV found it impossible, as an open adulterer, to confess himself and take communion on Easter with the traditional pomp. Having failed to maintain the rites of confession and communion, he then discontinued the rite of touching people afflicted with scrofula. His brush with death at

57   Bibliothèque Nationale, "Personnes qui ont été détenues à la Bastille depuis l'année 1660 jusques et compris l'année 1754": nouvelles acquisitions françaises, ms 1891, fo. 419. Unfortunately, the collections in the Bibliothèque de l'Arsenal do not contain reports from spies in cafés for this period, so one must rely on the dossiers of prisoners in the Bastille. By their very nature, those dossiers contain reports of seditious talk rather than ordinary conversations, so the disparity in the documentation vitiates the comparison. Nonetheless, the *mauvais propos* reported in the Bastille papers from the late 1740s and 1750s are much more extreme and numerous than those from earlier periods.
58   Ibid., fo. 427.
59   Ibid., fo. 431. See also the similar dossier of Victor Hespergues, a wood merchant: ibid., 489.

Metz in 1744 brought a brief period of penance for his notorious love affairs and a brief resurgence of his popularity. But Louis soon took up again with the de Nesle sisters, then with Madame de Pompadour and Madame du Barry – all of them so hated by the Parisians that he finally stopped coming to Paris. By 1750 there were no more ceremonial *entrées* to the city, no more masses graced with the king's presence, no more touching of the sick in the Great Gallery of the Louvre, and no more reaffirmation of God's protection of "the Eldest Son of the Church" at Easter. The king had lost the royal touch, and with it he had lost contact with the common people of Paris.[60]

Sea-changes in attitudes cannot be dated precisely, nor can they be assigned exact causes. But it seems likely that many French people – not salon sophisticates but shopkeepers and artisans – felt that the king's sins had brought down the wrath of God upon his people. Bad harvests and military defeat could be interpreted as signs of the loss of God's favor. And they occurred just when a wave of chiliastic, popular Jansenism swept through the lower classes of Paris and the main provincial cities. By persecuting the Jansenists, Louis seemed to be doing the work of the devil, or even acting as Anti-Christ, a role in which Louis XIV had been cast by the Huguenot pamphlets. Although the government vacillated in its handling of the Jansenist agitation, it generally supported the archbishop of Paris in his campaign to prevent Jansenists, whom he considered as crypto-Protestants, from receiving the last sacraments on their deathbed. In 1750 most Frenchmen still adhered to a highly ritualized, "baroque" variety of Catholicism. For them, the deathbed ritual remained the most important moment in the quest for salvation. By making a "good death," they could repair a lifetime of sinning. But Louis, a sinner himself, seemed to snatch that possibility away from his most saintly subjects, the Jansenist leaders whom the common people revered. It was as if he stood between them and their sacraments, and so condemned their souls to Purgatory.[61]

In short, by tampering with the sacred, in both royal and personal rituals, Louis XV seems to have ruptured the lines of legitimacy that

60   For a scholarly account of Louis's private life, which has given rise to a great deal of rose-colored popular history, see Michel Antoine, *Louis XV*, pp. 457–510.
61   On baroque religiosity and doctrinal quarrels, see Michel Vovelle, *Piété baroque et déchristianisation en Provence au XVIIIe siècle* (Paris, 1973), and Jean Delumeau, *Le Catholicisme entre Luther et Voltaire* (Paris, 1971). On Jansenism – the austere, Augustinian strain within Catholicism identified with Cornelius Jansenius, bishop of Ypres – see Edmond Préclin, *Les Jansénistes du XVIIIe siècle et la constitution civile du clergé; le développement du richérisme, sa propagation dans le bas clergé, 1713–91* (Paris, 1929); René Taveneaux, *Jansénisme et politique* (Paris, 1965); and Dale Van Kley, *The Damiens Affair and the Unraveling of the Ancien Regime* (Princeton, 1984).

bound the people to the crown. The monarch himself may have done more to desacralize the monarchy than any *libelliste*. And the damage took place in midcentury, at least twenty years before the publication of the most important books attacking him. Does it follow that the *libelles* had little impact on public opinion, that they should be understood more as an effect than as a cause of the public's disaffection with the monarchy?

At this point, it seems appropriate to issue a warning about the bag of tricks that historians play on the dead. I have spliced some police reports with a narrative about popular Jansenism, ordering the chronology and adding ethnographic comments in a way to make the years around 1750 appear as a crucial breaking point in the history of the French monarchy. I have done so in good faith. But I have offered an argument, nothing more, and I cannot pretend to know what really makes a value system rupture. Certainly it seems extravagant to think that the French could have read some smutty accounts of the kings' private lives and then suddenly, as a consequence of their reading, lost their faith in kingship. The shattering of belief probably occurs at a more fundamental level, one involving sacred rituals on the one hand and patterns of everyday behavior on the other.

Yet it also seems exaggerated to claim that something, at this visceral level of belief, snapped circa 1750, permanently severing the people from their sovereign. The sound, the pain of the wound do not appear in the documents. I can locate a change of tone in the gossip of cafés and pick up echoes in a few contemporary diaries, but is that enough to support a major claim about the collapse of legitimacy in an ancient political system? One can find plenty of angry talk about kings and queens before 1750. According to Arlette Farge, an expert on police archives and the history of the Parisian poor, the bad-mouthing of sovereigns extends far back into the eighteenth century.[62] I would argue that it contributed to all the political explosions in early modern Paris – especially the great crises of 1648–52, 1614–17, and 1588–94, which made the troubles of the mid-eighteenth century look mild in comparison. Instead of positing a scission that severed the people's attachment to the crown in 1750, I think it more reasonable to envisage a series of shocks and a long-term process of erosion. The mid-century crisis was important, but so were the earlier traumas and the supreme crises of 1770–74 and 1787–88. At every critical juncture, *libelles* and *mauvais propos* appeared together, marking off phases in the emergence of public opinion as an ingredient in the political system of the Old Regime.

Cause or effect? Slander by word of mouth or by print? The questions have a misleading, either / or quality. The *libelles* and the *mauvais propos*

62   Farge, *Dire et mal dire*, pp. 187–240.

existed simultaneously, reflecting and reinforcing one another as they evolved over a long span of time. They both shaped and expressed public opinion as it, too, changed form and gathered force across the centuries. To attach priority to one element or the other would be to lose one's way in a chicken-and-egg hunt for an original cause. The point, as I see it, is not to determine what came first or what caused what, but rather to understand how all the media interacted in the process of forming public opinion.

"The media" conjures up notions of television, radio, and daily newspapers. France had none of those (the first French daily, the *Journal de Paris*, began publication in 1777, but it contained little that we would recognize as "news"), yet the French received a great deal of information through the communication systems peculiar to the Old Regime. Word spread through gossip, songs, letters, prints, posters, books, pamphlets, manuscript gazettes, and newspapers of sorts – foreign periodicals and the official, heavily censored French press. How did these modes of communication – oral, visual, written, and printed – insert themselves into contemporary consciousness, articulating and directing that mysterious force called "public opinion"? No one knows. In fact, no one has even raised the question, because public opinion has rarely been taken seriously as an ingredient of Old Regime politics. Insofar as historians have studied it at all, they have generally treated public opinion as an idea debated by philosophers rather than a force shaping events. I cannot dispense with the subject in what remains of this chapter, but I would like to try to dispel some of the confusion surrounding it by discussing the importance of libel literature in the 1780s.[63]

On the face of it, books would seem to have little influence on events. According to diffusion studies like Mornet's *Origines intellectuelles de la Révolution française*, they contribute to the formation of a climate of opinion – a general outlook or set of attitudes – which provides the background of events. They do not determine public opinion, which occupies the foreground and can best be studied by consulting pamphlets, gazettes, and gossip. But the relation between these phenomena remains unclear. How does a climate of opinion turn into public opinion, or background connect with foreground? Not simply by the popularization in journals of ideas developed in books. Journals convey news. So did

63   I do not mean to deprecate the importance of understanding the contemporary conceptions of public opinion, nor to minimize the contribution of research on journalism and pamphleteering. For examples of excellent scholarship on those subjects, see the works by Keith Baker, Mona Ozouf, Jean Sgard, Pierre Rétat, Jack Censer, and Jeremy Popkin cited above. My point is rather that scholars have not addressed the problem of how different media, working through the peculiar communication systems of the Old Regime, actually influenced public opinion, and how public opinion actually influenced events.

café gossips and clandestine gazeteers, two varieties of *nouvellistes* who spread the news through oral and written circuits of communication. To follow the flow of public opinion, one must consult the work of these premodern newsmen. But the historian who sifts through such sources looking for signs of the oncoming Revolution is bound to be disappointed. Let us say he reads all the available police reports on *mauvais propos* (regrettably thin for the 1780s), all the issues of the *Journal de Paris* (the heavily censored Parisian daily), all of the *Courrier de l'Europe* (a French periodical produced twice a week in London and Boulogne-sur-Mer and tolerated by the French government), and every entry in the *Mémoires secrets pour servir à l'histoire de la république des lettres* (a highly illegal, printed version of a manuscript gazette): he will get the impression that the French were interested in little more than balloon flights, the miraculous cures of Dr. Mesmer, and American rebels. Public opinion in the late 1770s and the 1780s seems to have been oblivious to domestic politics. True, it heated up during the turbulent ministries of Turgot and Necker. But between Necker's fall (1781) and the so-called pre-Revolution (1787–88), political news virtually disappears from all the sources. The French seem to have lapsed into a curious calm before the storm. And when the storm finally broke, it seemed to come from nowhere – neither from a "climate of opinion" produced by books, nor from a public opinion whipped up by journals and seditious talk.

These paradoxes look less puzzling if one considers the nature of news. It is, I believe, a cultural construct: not what happened, but stories about what happened, stories produced by specialists who share conventions about what a story is and how it should be told. Those conventions vary over time; so the news of one century can look bewildering to readers in another, and it can differ greatly from the restrospective stories constructed by historians. We know little about what made stories compelling to eighteenth-century readers; but whatever it was, we may get it wrong if we assume too great a divergence between the narratives of books and the narratives of news. Perhaps *libelles* were newsworthy after all.

They certainly made news immediately after Louis XV's death in 1774. At that time the reading public was hungry for the inside story about the "king's secrets" during the previous reign. But the secrets made such good stories that they continued to fascinate the French for the next fifteen years, as they were recounted over and over again, sometimes in the form of epistolary exchanges, sometimes as reports of an English spy, or as what-the-butler-saw, or as memoirs, biography, *chronique scandaleuse*, or contemporary history. The *libelle* literature kept changing form and growing, until it composed a corpus of enormous proportions and dominated the best-seller list throughout the 1780s. Thus, as Lenoir observed, the slandering of Louis XV did most damage long after his death. In fact, it helped to bring down Louis XVI.

Perhaps the interest in royal sex remains strong enough today for us to appreciate the appeal of this literature, but we need to understand how that appeal operated. It involved three basic rhetorical strategies, each of which had affinities with contemporary journalism. First, as in the notion that "names make news," it gave readers a specious sense of familiarity with "les grands." The *libellistes* used devices perfected by Bussy-Rabutin – precise physical descriptions, dialogue, and excerpts from letters – to build up the illusion of witnessing the inner life of the court from the perspective of an invisible voyeur. Second, the *libellistes* crystalized general themes in anecdotes, which seemed to convey the flavor of life at the summit of society. They borrowed this material from the gossip of cafés and the vignettes of the underground gazettes. In fact, as we have seen, the *Anecdotes sur Mme la comtesse du Barry* interrupted its narrative so often with quotes from the gazettes and tidbits from the *nouvellistes* that it reads in places like a news sheet. But its anecdotes always illustrated a general point: the decadence and despotism of Versailles.

Third, unlike non-print media such as gossip and handwritten news sheets, the *libelles* embedded these stories permanently in books, making them available for multiple readings by a multitude of readers. And unlike other print media such as the short pamphlet and the *chronique scandaleuse*, they did not simply recount brief anecdotes or string them out in endless, formless series. Instead, they worked them into complex narratives, amplifying and diversifying their meanings. In *Anecdotes sur Mme la comtesse du Barry*, the anecdotes fit inside a bawdy Cinderella story, which could also be read as a political biography and a contemporary history of France. Moreover, the story belonged to a whole corpus of similar narratives. Together they constituted a repertory of related tales, using stock characters (evil ministers, conniving courtiers, libidinal royal mistresses) in stock plots (sexual success stories, rags to riches, *jeux de l'amour et du hasard*). Taken altogether as it evolved over the centuries, this literature expressed what I have called a political folklore. But segments of it, particular *libelles* published at a propitious moment, could also be news – revelations of hitherto unsuspected scandal in the secret recesses of Versailles.

News of this kind was hardly new. The skeletons, as they came out of the closet, looked remarkably alike and illustrated the same master theme: Following the excesses of Louis Quatorzean absolutism, decadence had set in, and the monarchy had degenerated into a despotism. But the material was lurid enough to engage the attention of the reading public during the quiet years of Louis XVI's reign, when direct discussions of political issues had relatively little appeal. Political messages in the 1780s often became attached to ostensibly apolitical subjects such as foreign affairs, spectacular court cases, and scandals on the Bourse. The private life of Louis XV served them best of all – until the fiscal catastrophe forced the king to summon the Assembly of Notables in 1787, and the Old Regime entered into the last and greatest of its political crises. At that point, the vast corpus of *libelle* literature acquired a new meaning, one that became embedded in the events themselves.

Without attempting to relate the events, I think it fair to contrast two general views of them: one favored by most historians, and another held by most of the Frenchmen who followed them as they happened. Ever since Albert Mathiez launched the idea in 1922, historians have usually begun their accounts of the Revolution with an "aristocratic revolt" that broke out in 1787. This notion fits a general view of eighteenth-century political history, which pits a reforming monarchy allied with a rising bourgeoisie against a reactionary nobility protected by the parlements. Thus, at the climactic moment in February 1787, when the controller general, Charles Alexandre de Calonne, presented the Assembly of Notables with a progressive tax plan that would solve the crown's financial problems, the aristocratic Notables revolted, forced Calonne out of office, and precipitated the Revolution. This "pre-Revolution," or first stage of the overall Revolution, lasted until August 1788, when the king dismissed Calonne's successor, Loménie de Brienne, and summoned the Estates General. Brienne had adopted the main ingredients of Calonne's reform program, while the resistance to it passed from the Notables to the parlements. In a desperate effort to crush the parlements, Brienne reorganized the entire judicial system, repeating in essence the Maupeou "coup" of 1771. But the public refused to support him, and the fiscal pressure remained so intense that the king finally surrendered to the aristocracy, convoking an archaic body, the Estates General, which the privileged orders expected to dominate.

Although some historians have challenged this view,[64] the great majority have adopted it, whether they belong to the Left, like Mathiez, Georges Lefebvre, Albert Soboul, and Michel Vovelle, or to the moderate

---

64   The key challenge, though muted, came from Jean Egret, whose work has still not been assimilated adequately in general histories of the Revolution. See especially Egret, *La Pré-Révolution française (1787–1788)* (Paris, 1962). The most extensive reworking of Egret's position is William Doyle, *Origins of the French Revolution* (Oxford, 1980). To make my own position clear, I should say that I have been a non-believer in the "aristocratic revolt" since I first read Egret and tried to apply his insights in my doctoral dissertation, *Trends in Radical Propaganda on the Eve of the French Revolution (1782–1788)*.

Left and Center-Right, like Alfred Cobban, Robert Palmer, Crane Brinton, and François Furet. The "aristocratic revolt" provided them with an interpretation that made sense of the whole course of early modern French history, while explaining the immediate cause and the first stage of the Revolution. It also helped to sort out the roles played by individuals. It made the leaders of the Notables and the parlements look like self-interested reactionaries, and cast Calonne and Brienne as progressive reformers. In one supremely anachronistic version, the reform program even appeared as "Calonne's New Deal."[65]

To contemporary Frenchmen, the world looked completely different. They did not perceive the "aristocratic revolt" that supposedly broke out under their noses. Most of them despised Calonne and applauded the Notables' resistance to him. When Brienne tried to force Calonne's taxes through the parlements, the public took the parlements' side. And when he tried to destroy the parlements, it took to the streets. Ordinary Frenchmen did not necessarily support the parlementary cause, but they did not want to pay more taxes. Instead of seeing the ministers' program as a war against tax privileges, they saw it as ministerial despotism. Calonne and Brienne seemed to repeat the authoritarian measures of Maupeou, and 1787–88 looked like a replay of 1771–74 or even of the Fronde.

Never has the historians' version of events and the contemporary perception of them diverged so greatly. This disparity can be explained in several ways, but ultimately it comes down to a dilemma: Either the historians have badly misinterpreted the causes of the Revolution, or the contemporaries suffered from a colossal case of false consciousness. For my part, I believe the historians are wrong, not simply because they see little more than class interest in the stand taken by the Notables and parlements, but also because they fail to see what the contemporaries saw – that is, they do not take adequate account of public opinion. The contemporary view of events was as important as the events themselves; in fact, it cannot be separated from them. It gave them meaning, and in so doing it determined the way people took sides when a truly revolutionary situation came into existence.

We are back to where we started, with the problems of determining public opinion, analyzing discourse, and developing a history of meaning.

I realize, of course, that I may have created a false dilemma, which can easily be resolved by locating the difficulty elsewhere – not with the historians, but with me. How do I, a fellow historian, dare speak for the

65   Wilma J. Pugh, "Calonne's New Deal," *Journal of Modern History*, IX (1939), 289–312.

consciousness of Frenchmen who died two centuries ago? To make my case, I will have to go over the "pre-Revolution" event by event, showing both what happened and how contemporaries construed those happenings. That is the subject of another book. In this one, I can only confess that the argument remains unproven, although I have read enough of the evidence (every pamphlet published between February 1787 and August 1788 in the Bibliothèque Nationale and the British Library) to be convinced of its correctness. I raise the issue here because it bears on the general problem of assessing the impact of forbidden literature.

By 1787, the reading public was saturated with illegal books of all kinds, which attacked the orthodox values of the Old Regime on every front. But the political *libelles* had particular resonance, because they fitted the events of 1787–88 in a specific way. As the crisis broke, lines were drawn and people took sides – informed people, that is, the "public" that constituted public opinion. In April 1787, everyone in this broad segment of society felt compelled to take a stand for or against Calonne. In July 1788, everyone rallied for or against the parlements. Seen through the historical literature, the situation looks hideously complex; and indeed it was – a bewildering mixture of rising expectations and rising bread prices, destitution among the poor and bankruptcy among the rich, impenetrable procedures by royal bureaucrats and uncon-scionable vexations by semi-public, semi-private tax collectors, all of it ostensibly directed by a government so eaten away by vested interests and special privileges that one can hardly locate power, much less see who was in charge. The more one learns about the Old Regime, the more inscrutable it appears. But in considering public opinion, which com-plicates things further by adding another dimension to them, I would push the argument in the opposite direction: from complication to simplification.

Instead of splitting the issues into hundreds of fragments, the pam-phlets of 1787–88 simplified them. They presented the situation as a radical choice: for or against the government, for or against the par-lements. They provoked the drawing of lines; they helped to polarize public opinion – and they also expressed it, because the formation of public opinion and the agitation of pamphleteers reinforced one another, functioning simultaneously as cause and effect. The complex-ities of tax reform hardly appear in the pamphlets. The vexed question of privileges was rarely raised, at least not before the convocation of the Estates General transformed the situation by posing the question of who would dominate the new constitutional order. Instead of analyzing the issues, the pamphlets heaped scorn on the government. Of course Calonne and Brienne had their defenders, who produced propaganda on

the government's side. But the great majority of the pamphlet literature
– and as much of the *propos* and "public noises" as one can trace
through manuscript sources – reduced the issues to a single theme:
despotism.

Or, more precisely, ministerial despotism. Few of the pamphlets
attacked Louis XVI. After the Diamond Necklace Affair, he appeared
more as an object of derision than as a threat to life and liberty. Instead,
the pamphlets vilified Calonne and Brienne, making them look like mon-
sters, depraved, debauched, and ready to fling any honest citizen into
the Bastille. So much abuse was heaped on Calonne that it acquired
a generic name: "Calonniana," the counterpart to the "Maupeouana"
of the 1770s. The pamphlets, too, were *libelles* – shorter, sharper, and
more up-to-date versions of the stories that had circulated in book form
for the last fifteen years.

In this way, the libel literature from the end of Louis XV's reign
became devastatingly pertinent at the end of the reign of Louis XVI. It
fitted the events of 1787–88, providing a general frame for a fresh
supply of anecdotes and *propos*. It helped contemporaries make sense of
things by furnishing them with a master narrative, which went far back
in time, beyond Louis XVI and Louis XV to Louis XIV, Mazarin, Marie de
Médicis, and Henri III. A literary genre had grown from obscure verbal
jousting in the Renaissance court to a full corpus of best-selling books.
As it grew, it provided a running commentary on more than two centuries of political history. It assimilated new material and new rhetorical techniques into a body of tales, a political folklore, organized around
a central theme with a single moral: The monarchy had degenerated
into despotism. Instead of providing space for serious discussion of state
affairs, this literature closed off debate, polarized views, and isolated
the government. It operated on the principle of radical simplification,
an effective tactic at a time of crisis, when the drawing of lines forced
the public to take sides and see issues as absolutes: either/or, black
or white, them or us. That the Bastille was nearly empty and that
Louis XVI desired nothing more than the welfare of his subjects did not
matter in 1787 and 1788. The regime stood condemned. It had lost the
final round in the long struggle to control public opinion. It had lost its
legitimacy.

5

The Great Chain of Buying: Medical Advertisement, the Bourgeois Public Sphere, and the Origins of the French Revolution

Colin Jones

Originally appeared as Colin Jones, "The Great Chain of Buying: Medical Advertisement, the Bourgeois Public Sphere, and the Origins of the French Revolution," *American Historical Review* 101:1 (1996) pp. 13–40.

Editor's Introduction

The title of the following article is a pun on *The Great Chain of Being*, a book by the intellectual historian Arthur Lovejoy (1873–1963) tracing the history of the idea that all things, including people, are connected in a continuous hierarchy or "chain" running from the lowest forms of existence at the bottom to God at the top. This concept had long been used to justify both monarchy (with the king at the top of the earthly chain) and the privileges of the upper ranks in society. Yet Colin Jones argues that toward the end of the Old Regime French society resembled not a vertical chain but a horizontal one in which human beings were connected in a "relatively egalitarian social organization." It was commerce, according to Jones, that provided the links between individuals, hence the image of the "Great Chain of Buying."

Moreover, Jones argues that the Great Chain of Buying is important for an understanding of the origins of the French Revolution. The claim that the Revolution had economic origins is not new. Indeed, from the 1920s to the 1970s French historians typically explained the Revolution as the product of the transformation from feudalism to capitalism and from a society dominated by nobles to one led by the *bourgeoisie*. Yet since François Furet's "revisionist" challenge and the decline of Marxism more generally, this class-based explanation has fallen out of favor. Jones's article, therefore, attempts to restore some credibility to an approach that emphasizes economics and stresses the role of the bourgeoisie in particular.

Yet Jones does not merely resuscitate the old economic interpretation. Invoking the German social theorist Jürgen Habermas (1929–), he suggests that the capitalist mode of production supported the growth of a "bourgeois public sphere" made up of autonomous individuals who submitted state policies to rational critique. It was from this sphere, he argues, that political and indeed revolutionary action emerged. As we have seen, Chartier borrows from Habermas as well[1] and similarly views the public sphere as an important precondition of the Revolution. Yet Jones faults Chartier and others for "cut[ting]" him "off at the knees" by omitting his argument that the public sphere was the consequence of capitalism. He aims, by contrast, to refute "the 'de-economized' version of Habermasian theory currently in fashion," to demonstrate that the creation of the public sphere had "both economic and cultural dimensions," and "to provide a way of looking at Old Regime France that brings the bourgeoisie back into the picture."

In order to make his case, Jones examines the provincial newspapers known as *Affiches*. Unlike the news-bearing *gazettes*, which historians have studied carefully, the relatively neglected Affiches specialized in advertisement but also carried news and commentary to a significant degree. On the basis of the number of different Affiches and their circulation figures, Jones challenges those historians who have assumed the weakness of the provincial press and instead argues for its vitality. His point is not simply to revise the claims of historians of the press. The existence of the Affiches seems to confirm the presence of Habermas's public sphere. The audience to whom the Affiches were directed – primarily "merchants, traders, businessmen, and the middling professions" in medium-sized to large provincial cities – suggests that this public sphere was indeed *bourgeois*. Insofar as women, artisans and peasants were envisaged as potential readers (or, when illiterate or only partially literate, as auditors), they were treated as potential consumers of the advertised products, thus further attesting, in Jones's view, to the commercialization of late Old Regime France. Jones argues that the Affiches contained an ideology, either implicitly through advertisements, or explicitly through editorial commentary, of optimistic capitalism or the belief that commerce would lead inevitably to a higher

---

1 See chapter 3.

level of civilization and a greater degree of human happiness. The implication is that capitalism, the famed ideology of the bourgeoisie, was behind
the cultural and intellectual transformations of the late eighteenth century.
Furthermore, Jones suggests, since the editors of the Affiches carefully
avoided anything that would displease their readers, the ideology they
propagated was identical with "public opinion." He argues against "Keith
Baker and others" who have suggested that public opinion was primarily
a *discourse*, a political battle cry meant to legitimate specific claims, and
insists that it was a real sociological phenomenon.[2] Yet he avoids the
dilemma that Darnton, Mornet, and "diffusionist" intellectual historians
have had of proving that printed matter had an *impact* on public opinion,
since the Affiches, in his view, merely echoed what their readers already
believed.

Jones focuses on medical advertisements in the Affiches as a means of
proving three things. First, he holds that the multitude of ads for medical
products and services "testified to growing medical entrepreneurialism."
Whereas previous historians have tended to see medical professionals in
late eighteenth-century France as stagnant, Jones sees a growing, adapt-
able and self-confident profession. The implications of this claim extend
far beyond the history of medicine, however, since Jones suggests that
other "bourgeois" professions were similarly vibrant, as was the bourgeoisie more generally. Secondly, he maintains that the medical advertisements "highlighted the strength of the demand for medical goods and
services." In other words, they attest to the existence of a consumer
society and of a bourgeoisie that was willing and able to spend money.
Third and finally, he suggests that the preoccupation with the health of
the body indicated by the advertisements had important political implications, and that in this respect the Affiches had political meaning despite
their editors' claims to non-partisanship. In particular, they reveal " a newly
emergent politics of the body" according to which matters (such as marriage and sexuality) once thought to be personal became public, and which
provided a metaphorical language enabling critics of the political system
to use medical terms ("regime," "constitution," "circulation," "blockages,"
etc.) as a means of justifying their claims. In this last respect, Jones has
adapted the type of discourse analysis favored by Baker to his own needs,
though his emphasis is on the connections between discourse and its
"plausible social referent," i.e. the bourgeoisie.

2   See chapters 2, 3 and 4.

The Great Chain of Buying: Medical Advertisement, the Bourgeois Public Sphere, and the Origins of the French Revolution

Colin Jones

Q.: What is the only thing which connects all classes?
A.: The post.

Beffroy de Reigny

On February 15, 1772, Antoine Clesse, surgeon-herniotomist at Metz, placed an advertisement in his local newspaper, the *Affiches des Trois-Evêchés*. He announced he had "bandages and trusses for all sorts of descents and ruptures." He was in addition, he noted, a qualified dentist and could clean, polish, and level teeth on request.[1]

This is a fairly typical example of a medical advertisement drawn from France's provincial press in the last half-century of the *ancien régime*. It may appear a long and tortuous way from such a trivial notation on herniary trusses to a problem that has long held a place of affection in the historical imagination, namely, the origins of the French Revolution. But it is my ambition in this article to try to make that link. In this quest, I have taken heart, derived a metaphor, and devised a pun from Arthur O. Lovejoy's classic *The Great Chain of Being*, with its emphasis on the continuity of forms from the very lowest to the highest.[2]

When we think of *ancien régime* society and chains, we may think, for example, of Jean-Jacques Rousseau and man born free but in chains. We may think of Jean-Paul Marat's *Chains of Slavery*. Or we may recall the famous remonstrance made before the Paris Parlement in 1776 by royal Advocate-General Séguier:

> The clergy, the nobility, the sovereign courts, the subaltern courts, the officers attached to these courts, the universities, the academies, the finance bodies, the trade companies, all present, in all parts of the state, existing bodies that may be regarded as links in a great chain, the first

---

1 *Affiches des Trois-Evêchés*, February 15, 1772.
2 Arthur O. Lovejoy, *The Great Chain of Being* (Cambridge, Mass., 1936).

link of which is in the hands of Your Majesty, as head and sovereign administrator of everything that composes the body of the nation.[3]

In all these cases, the chains linking the body of society together are seen as vertically disposed, underpinning a hierarchical society. The "Chain of Buying" is, by contrast, horizontally disposed: grounded in human sociability and exchange, it posits an open and relatively egalitarian social organization and undergirds a commercial society.

To make my case, I need to drive a coach and horses through the existing historiographical consensus in three areas: the medical professions, the provincial press, and the origins of the French Revolution. Medical practitioners are, first of all, normally represented – as is the case with most of the *ancien régime* professions – as a staid, deferential, and backward-looking group. Their social ambitions, it is held, were limited: like other members of the bourgeoisie, they lived "humdrum, unexciting lives" and sought, above all, incorporation into a nobility whose social ascendancy they respected rather than contested.[4] The tripartite, corporative, and hierarchical division of medical practitioners into physicians, surgeons, and apothecaries was being contested in some respects by 1789 – notably by the dynamic group of elite surgeons – but it stayed in place.[5] Even though historians have detected the processes of professionalization at work, these are usually viewed as taking place under the aegis of the state. The Royal Society of Medicine, chartered by the crown in 1778, for example, launched a ferocious attack on all varieties of informal and unlicensed medicine, which it branded charlatanism, and endeavored to use the power of the state to develop medical policing over society as a whole.[6]

If medical practitioners are viewed as essentially undynamic, the same is often said, second, of the provincial press. In a 1985 article com-

3   Cited in Emile Lousse, *La société d'ancien régime: Organisation et représentation corporatives* (Louvain, 1952), 133.
4   William Doyle, *The Oxford History of the French Revolution* (Oxford, 1989) – an authoritative distillation of existing historiographical consensuses: see p. 25 for the humdrum lives. For a fuller account of the historiography of the medical profession – and a revision of it – see Laurence W. B. Brockliss and Colin Jones, *The Medical World of Early Modern France* (Oxford, 1997).
5   See especially Toby Gelfand, *Professionalizing Modern Medicine: Paris Surgeons and Medical Science and Institutions in the Eighteenth Century* (Westport, Conn., 1980); and Matthew Ramsey, *Professional and Popular Medicine in France, 1770–1830: The Social World of Medical Practice* (Cambridge, 1988).
6   Caroline Hannaway, "Medicine, Public Welfare and the State in Eighteenth-Century France: The Société Royale de Médecine" (PhD dissertation, Johns Hopkins University, 1974); Jean-Pierre Desaive, et al., *Médecins, climat et épidémies à la fin du XVIIIᵉ siècle* (Paris, 1972); Charles C. Gillispie, *Science and Polity in Old Regime France* (Princeton, N.J., 1980).

paring the French and the English press during the eighteenth century, for example, Jack Censer and others concluded that while England's press was a faithful reflection of a dynamic commercial society, France's bore the hallmarks of a traditionalist and hidebound society still riven by the corporative distinctions and the hierarchy of taste characteristic of a society of orders. The main state-backed journal, the *Gazette de France*, cut a pale, ponderous, pathetic, and apolitical figure when set against *The Spectator* or the *North Briton*. The authors thus sacrificed the French provincial press on the altar of France's alleged social and economic backwardness.[7] More recently, it is true, Jack Censer has revised this view somewhat: his recent synthesis provides a balanced view of the entire array of press outlets in *ancien régime* France. Yet if one sees here in embryo something of the vitality that the works of Jeremy Popkin and others have located in the revolutionary press, Censer has still to swim against the historiographical stream, which, as he admits, has tended to view provincial newspapers as unpolitical or "literary," totally separate from the analysis of the *ancien régime*, and contributing, on balance, little to the destabilization of the French monarchy.[8]

Third, there also has been a shift of the historiographical consensus away from the search for social or economic origins of the French Revolution, toward a highlighting of cultural and ideological forces.[9] Symptomatic of the issues involved has been the use made of Jürgen Habermas's book *The Structural Transformation of the Public Sphere*.[10] His

7 Stephen Botein, Jack Censer, and Harriert Ritvo, "La presse périodique et la société anglaise et française au XVIIIᵉ siècle: Une approche comparative," *Revue d'histoire moderne et contemporaine*, 32 (1985).

8 Jack R. Censer, *The French Press in the Age of Enlightenment* (London, 1994), see chap. 2 for an analysis of the provincial press consonant in some respects with the analysis offered here. For general disparagement of pre-1789 French periodicals, from an otherwise authoritative source, see the comments on the provincial press in Bellanger, *Histoire générale de la presse*, 329: "sécheresse de ton, . . . style académique, . . . prudence," etc. For post-1789 developments, compare Jeremy Popkin, *Revolutionary News: The Press in France, 1789–99* (Durham, N.C., 1990); and for the Francophone press, Popkin, *News and Politics in the Age of Revolution: Jean Luzac's "Gazette de Leyde"* (Ithaca, N.Y., 1989) (see the comment on the Affiches on p. 47). It is noticeable that the essays in Jack Censer and Jeremy Popkin, eds., *Press and Politics in Pre-Revolutionary France* (Berkeley, Calif., 1987), which present a fine and nuanced account of the contribution of the press to the burgeoning political culture, totally neglect the Affiches that are the focus of the present article.

9 Most prominently in Roger Chartier, *The Cultural Origins of the French Revolution* (Durham, N.C., 1991); and Keith Michael Baker, *Inventing the French Revolution: Essays on French Political Culture in the Eighteenth Century* (Cambridge, 1990).

10 Jürgen Habermas, *The Structural Transformation of the Public Sphere: An Inquiry into a Category of Bourgeois Society*, Thomas Burger, trans. (Cambridge, Mass., 1989).

notion of a sphere of open, rational debate and discussion between private individuals, developing within the interstices of the absolute state, remains an attractive one for scholars, who have retained Habermas's "bourgeois public sphere" and his stress on the importance of public opinion in the late Enlightenment. But they have effectively cut the German scholar off at the knees by denying the validity of his attempts to link these developments to the growth of capitalist relations of production. This rejection chimes with the wider views of "revisionist" scholars of the French Revolution, in free flight from the allegedly Marxist economic interpretation of the eighteenth century, which in their eyes accorded too much dynamism to the bourgeoisie, now held to be composed of "zombies" (Simon Schama) or "indeterminate social mutants" (Colin Lucas). Robert Darnton speaks for most when he declares that Habermas "cannot be taken as a guide to eighteenth-century France." The result has been widespread use of the notion of the "bourgeois public sphere," in the context of a belief in the weakness before 1789 of the French bourgeoisie, especially the professions.[11]

I would like to contest these established viewpoints. To do this, I will be drawing on a corpus of newspaper materials – the provincial Affiches – that historians have largely neglected. If, like most scholars of the eighteenth century at the moment, I draw on Habermas, it will be in the spirit (if not always according to the letter)[12] of his attempt to encompass both economic and cultural dimensions in the formation of the bourgeois public sphere, and I will reject the "de-economized" version of Habermasian theory currently in fashion. By focusing on the kind of newspaper advertiser in which herniotomist Clesse appeared and trying

11   Robert Darnton, *New York Review of Books* (October 24, 1991): 34. Good introductions to the value scholars have derived from Habermas include Keith Michael Baker, "Defining the Public Sphere in Eighteenth-Century France: Variations on a Theme by Habermas," in Craig Calhoun, ed., *Habermas and the Public Sphere* (Cambridge, Mass., 1992); and Dena Goodman, "Public Sphere and Private Life: Towards a Synthesis of Recent Historiographical Approaches to the Old Regime," *History and Theory*, 31 (1992). I have attempted to revive the search for social and economic origins of the French Revolution, in the spirit of the present article; see Colin Jones, "Bourgeois Revolution Revivified: 1789 and Social Change," Colin Lucas, ed., *Rewriting the French Revolution* (Oxford, 1991). (See 72 n. for the "mutants" and "zombies.") For a recent discussion of issues involved, see the round table in *French Historical Studies*, 17 (1992), devoted to "The Public Sphere in the Eighteenth Century" (contributions by David Bell, Daniel Gordon, and Sarah Maza).

12   Habermas says little about the newspapers in question, and his comment on Old Regime advertisers generally (p. 22) does not fit the schema here proposed. As I note later, the forces of aggressive commercialism only enter the Habermasian schema fairly late, from the 1820s: see *Structural Transformation*, chap. 20. I have not thought it worthwhile being systematic about references to Habermas. This is an article about the public sphere, not Habermas.

to identify some of the links in the chain between a herniary truss and, say, the overthrow of French monarchy, I hope to provide a way of looking at Old Regime France that brings the bourgeoisie back into the picture – back, indeed, into the bourgeois public sphere.

The Affiches, which developed from the middle of the eighteenth century onward, were essentially and primarily advertisers. They had a variety of titles but tended to have the phrase "Annonces, affiches et avis divers" in their headings, although this was often shortened, either officially or informally, to the word Affiches plus the name of their place of publication (thus *Affiches de Lyon*, *Affiches de Poitou*, etc.). They normally appeared weekly and were based on subscription purchase rather than bookshop sale. Their annual cost was usually between 6 livres and 7 livres, 10 sols – a little less than a week's wages for an urban artisan – and most were four or eight-page issues whose double-columned pages were packed full of small ads. As time went on, however, they came to devote increasing space to letters, articles, and sundry news items.

Such newspapers constituted an armchair version of earlier types of advertisement. The word *affiche* denotes a wall poster, and many of the types of information contained within the Affiches had previously taken this form – and indeed continued to do so in many locations. There had been previous attempts to establish advertiser newssheets – notably by Théophraste Renaudot, credited as the founder of France's first newspaper, the *Gazette*, in 1631, and creator of the *Bureau d'adresse*, an institution that was a precocious version of a labor exchange and market for services. The *Bureau d'adresse* failed, however, as did similar projects in 1703 and 1716–1717. The *Gazette* and other national newspapers carried advertisements successfully.[13] The Affiches emerged from the early 1750s out of a move to take the advertising arm of the *Gazette* and make it a separate enterprise, with outlets throughout France.[14] The arrangement was based on the strict understanding that the *Gazette* would have a monopoly on all political matters, which would be beyond the purview of the Affiches. There were initial difficulties in establishing a network, and for a while the most prosperous such newssheets were the two produced in Paris, both (infuriatingly) with the same title – *Annonces, affiches et avis divers* – but distinguishable by their formats:

13   Todd, "French Advertising," esp. 523–6.
14   For these operations, see esp. Feyel, "La presse provinciale" (1984 and 1987 versions); Gilles Feyel, *La gazette en province à travers ses réimpressions (1631–1752)* (Amsterdam, 1982); and Feyel, "La 'gazette' au début de la guerre de sept ans: Son administration, sa diffusion (1751–8)," in *La diffusion et la lecture des journaux de langue fraçaise sous l'ancien régime* (Amsterdam, 1987). See also, for the Paris operations, *DJ*, nos. 47–9, 57.

while the *Affiches de Paris*, aimed at an essentially metropolitan audience, rarely surpassed the small-ad form, the so-called *Affiches de province* served a more regional readership and developed a strong literary and cultural dimension. By 1775, roughly a score of provincial Affiches were in existence, and by 1789, forty-four towns could boast one. At that time, they formed over half the newspaper titles whose production was based in France. Indeed, to a considerable degree, they *were* the French provincial press prior to 1789. Their existence allows the French press to be compared – myths of English superiority notwithstanding – with England, which in the late eighteenth century could boast roughly fifty provincial titles.[15]

The heartland of the Affiches was France's exceptionally dense urban network. Although moderately sized towns (Sens, Auxerre) might boast one, the newspaper was most firmly based in big and medium-sized cities: roughly two-thirds of France's fifty biggest cities had one, and the papers were present in all but four of the thirty-two of France's administrative units (*généralités*). They were earliest and most firmly rooted in the big commercial cities of France's booming periphery – notably Rouen, Marseille, Bordeaux, and Lyon – where a wealthy mercantile patriciate dominated local society: 70 percent of the towns with an Affiches also had a chamber of commerce or a mercantile magistracy. They were also located in towns that had strong administrative functions and that contained a large number of bourgeois and noble *rentiers* with private incomes. Characteristically, they did better in business cities than in parlementary ones, for their appeal seemed less obvious to the high Robe and Sword nobility than to those not inhabiting the peaks of the social landscape.[16]

We lack hard data on subscription lists, but it would seem that the circulation of most of the Affiches hovered between 200 and 750. The network as a whole – forty-odd papers – may thus have produced between 8,000 and 30,000 subscribers.[17] To achieve even an approxi-

15   Compare Jeremy Black, " 'Calculated upon a Very Extensive and Useful Plan': The English Provincial Press in the Eighteenth Century," in J. Isaac, ed., *Six Centuries of the Provincial Book Trade in Britain* (Winchester, 1990), 63; thirty-five existed in the 1770s, around fifty in 1782. See, too, Jonathan Barry, "The Press and the Politics of Culture in Bristol, 1660–1775," in Jeremy Black and Jeremy Gregory, eds., *Culture, Politics and Society in Britain, 1660–1800* (Manchester, 1991).

16   For all details on the network, see Feyel, "La presse provinciale" (1984, 1987).

17   Sgard, "La presse provinciale," 64, plumps for a total provincial subscription of 30,000. See, for example, Censer, *French Press*, 218. We lack figures for the biggest of the provincial Affiches, which hobbles our estimates. The Paris-based *Affiches de province* enjoyed a readership of around 3,000 in 1780, according to D. A. Azam, "Le ministre des affaires étrangères et la presse à la fin de l'ancien régime," *Cahiers de la presse*, 1 (1938).

mation of a figure for readership, we need to apply a multiplier, to take into account reading within families, in reading rooms, coffee-houses, and the like. As the editor of the *Affiches de la Franche-Comté* ruefully noted in 1769, his product was more widely read than subscribed to.[18] Jeremy Popkin has proposed a multiplier of ten for newspapers produced in the revolutionary decade; the only *ancien régime* newssheet to venture an opinion – the *Journal de Champagne* in 1784 – suggested four readers to every copy. If we use these two figures as markers, it does not seem implausible to hypothesize a readership of between 50,000 and 200,000, and maybe many more.[19]

Readers appear to have come from the most solid groups within the urban milieu. The physician Baumès in 1802 recalled how in the 1780s he and his friends in Nîmes would read and discuss the local Affiches: he characterized this group as enjoying "a happy mediocrity – that is to say [it consisted of] young lawyers and physicians and merchants of the second rank."[20] This may well be fairly typical: the social constituency of the Affiches was probably not so much the "notables," who formed the backbone of the provincial academies analyzed by Daniel Roche and on whom historians have concentrated so much attention in recent years. The realm of "happy mediocrity" in which the consumerism of the Affiches flourished was composed, rather, of merchants, traders, businessmen, and the middling professions – much the kind of social constituency characterized in England as "the middling sort."[21]

This did not, of course, mean that other groups were excluded. The Affiches were emphatically not house magazines for a handful of cognoscenti, and inclusivity was fundamental to their operations. Artisans and shopkeepers used the Affiches to increase the number of their clients, and many advertisements were targeted at domestic servants. At

---

18   M. Vogne, *La presse périodique en Franche-Comté des origines à 1870*, 3 vols. (Besançon, 1977–78), 1: 18 (*DJ*, no. 25).
19   Popkin, *Revolutionary News*, 84; *Journal de Champagne* (*DJ*, no. 71), "Prospectus," 1784. For other circulation figures, compare Popkin, *Revolutionary News*, 19, 83–5, 87–8, and following; Sgard, *DJ*, passim.
20   Jean-Baptiste-Théodore Baumès, cited in J. Chevalier Lavaure, *Les journaux à Nîmes à la fin de l'ancien régime* (Nîmes, 1980), 14.
21   For the "notables," see Daniel Roche, *Le siècle des lumières en province: Académies et académiciens provinciaux* (Paris, 1978). Roche's most recent synthesis – *La France des lumières* (Paris, 1993) – is, however, particularly strong on the "middling sort" as well as the "middle man," and it provides a useful context for the present article. (See my review, "The Postmaster as Hero," *Times Literary Supplement*, March 31, 1995.) For England, see Jonathan Barry, "Identité urbaine et classes moyennes dans l'Angleterre moderne," *Annales: Economies, sociétés, civilisations*, 48 (1993); and Barry and Christopher Brooks, *The Middling Sort of People: Culture, Society and Politics in England, 1550–1800* (Basingstoke, 1994).

the other end of the spectrum, nobles *were* among the newspapers' patrons – as indeed one would expect of individuals among the most zealous adepts of Enlightenment consumerism. Issues contained advertisements for heraldry, and coverage of genealogy and high-class fashion was a staple item.[22]

To a considerable degree, however, social rank based on the status hierarchies of the *ancien régime* was immaterial to the Affiches, whose cultural and economic functions revolved around the consumer, assumed a unitary economic subject, and predicated a hierarchy of wealth and taste, not birth or privilege. One suspects that much of the invocation of the nobility in the Affiches was less a reference to actual readers than a marketing strategy aimed at lending tone to the mundane nature of their columns. Those who took a subscription to the Affiches were buying into a world of consumption, not corporative status. The comment of Beffroy de Reigny, journalist of the bizarre and eccentric, cited epigraphically at the beginning of this article, stresses the cross-class orientation of subscriber newssheets. "Swift and inexpensive means of communications," noted the editor of the *Journal de Languedoc*, "newspapers ceaselessly circulate among all classes of society."[23]

The market-oriented, bourgeois status of the readership of the Affiches is borne out by the flavor of their contents. Without even thinking about it, the Affiches talked business. The *Affiches de Toulouse* prided itself on carrying "all notices that can influence trade and interest businessmen." "Everything that concerns trade and that bears the traits of utility will be gratefully received," announced the editor of the *Affiches de Lyon*.[24] Merchants and manufacturers would doubtless have wel-

---

22   *Journal de Languedoc*, "Prospectus," January 1787 (*DJ*, no. 660). Consumerism is a growth area in eighteenth-century French studies. The pioneering Daniel Roche, *The People of Paris: An Essay in Popular Culture in the Eighteenth Century* (Berkeley, Calif., 1987), has been followed in particular by Annik Pardailhé-Galabrun, *The Birth of Intimacy: Privacy and Domestic Life in Early Modern Paris* (London, 1991); and Roche's *La France des lumières* and *The Culture of Clothing: Dress and Fashion in the Ancien Régime* (Cambridge, 1994). See, too, Cissie Fairchilds, "The Production and Marketing of Populuxe Goods in Eighteenth-Century Paris," in John Brewer and Roy Porter, eds., *Consumption and the World of Goods* (London, 1993); Jennifer M. Jones, "'The Taste for Fashion and Frivolity': Gender, Clothing and the Commercial Culture of the Old Régime" (PhD dissertation, Princeton University, 1991); and C. Jones, "Bourgeois Revolution revivified," esp. 88–93.
23   Louis-Abel Beffroy de Reigny is cited in Michel Gilot and Marie-Françoise Luna, "Mots-forces, mots-problèmes: L'ambiguité de 1788," in Rétat, *La révolution du journal*, 67; *Journal de Languedoc*, "Prospectus," 1787.
24   M. T. Blanc-Rouquette, *La presse et l'information à Toulouse des origines à 1789* (Toulouse, 1969), 136–7 (for Toulouse); Bellanger, *La presse*, 367 (for Lyon). See *DJ*, nos. 66–7 (Toulouse) and 34 (Lyon).

comed the large number of consumers that the *Affiches* allowed them to reach. They would also appreciate, as a means of reducing business risk, the hard economic and international information that, as we shall see, the newssheets provided.[25] Characteristically, the *Annales de la Franche-Comté* placed a "Poem in Praise of Trade" on the first page of its first issue. "The fatherland [*la patrie*]," declared the editor of the *Affiches du Beauvaisis*, "owes a great deal to trade, and the rank of merchant is one of the noblest, because it is one of the most useful." "We write mainly for merchants and farmers," announced the editors of the *Annales de Picardie*; while the editor of the *Affiches de Toulouse* invoked the aid of "famous lawyers, generous defenders of the fatherland [soldiers], magnificent merchants, savants, writers, artists of every sort, industrious and watchful farmers, and tender mothers."[26] Most editors did in fact hail from these backgrounds, as did many regular contributors.[27] The bulk of the obituaries the *Affiches* carried were dedicated to these bourgeois groups, too: for every high noble in the obituary section of the *Affiches de Paris*, for example, there were three artisans or shopkeepers and six merchants, *rentiers*, and members of the professions.[28]

The principle of inclusiveness on which the *Affiches* were based extended to women, who lacked a French-based newspaper specifically aimed at them through most of the period in which the *Affiches* boomed, following the closure of the *Journal des dames* in 1778. The "tender mothers" evoked by the *Affiches de Toulouse* would doubtless be a target for the huge amount of commodities aimed at children (clothes, toys, books). A good deal of advertisement for domestic commodities of all sorts, as well as books and cosmetics, was similarly oriented around what was assumed to be female taste. Some editors evinced a slight anxiety lest female readership might lessen the seriousness of their enterprise: the editor of the *Affiches de Beauvaisis* claimed that the *Poésies fugitives* he often included were destined for "the Ladies"; others justified

25   This point is highlighted, for England, in John Brewer, "Commercialization and Politics," in Neil McKendrick, et al., *The Birth of a Consumer Society: The Commercialization of Eighteenth-Century England* (London, 1982). Compare Hilton Root, "Institutions, Interest Groups and Authority in Ancien Régime France," *French History*, 6 (1992).

26   Vogne, *La presse périodique*, 1: 16; *Affiches du Beauvaisis* (*DJ*, no. 15), July 27, 1788; *Affiches de Picardie* (*DJ*, no. 54), "Prospectus," January 1774; Blanc-Rouquette, *La presse*, 151 (*Affiches de Toulouse* [*DJ*, nos. 66–7]; the tender mothers were those who breastfed their babies).

27   See *DJ*, passim, for editors. Local *Affiches* could rely on the sterling services of local savants in providing copy: for instance, the surgeon Claude-Nicolas Le Cat in Rouen and the physician Nicolas in Grenoble.

28   Botein, et al., "La presse périodique," 230.

quizzes, anagrams, and light verse on much the same grounds.[29] Such embarrassment and their requisite domesticity notwithstanding, the Affiches comprised one sector of the bourgeois public sphere in which women were firmly planted.

Their common origins imprinted on the Affiches a roughly similar format and set of advertising headings, the latter often laid out in the same sequence.[30] Most Affiches began with small ads for property sales and leases – a popular section. They went on to examine the sale of offices within the state bureaucracy, which offered career opportunities and means of social ascent to the aspiring social climber. This was a regional but sometimes a national market, too: the Normandy Affiches, for example, carried an advertisement for the sale of the (ennobling) post of municipal alderman (*capitoul*) in Toulouse.[31] There were many ads, too, under the heading of movable property, an enormous profusion of consumer objects to be found: jewelry, gold, silver, furniture, decorations, carriages, horses, fashionable clothing, and everything that polite society might seem to require, as well as much that it probably did not but that reached required levels of novelty and modishness: tame monkeys, stain removers, razor strops, billiard tables, indoor fireworks, waterproof shoes, hot-water bottles, water closets, bidets, and (a great deal of) horse manure.[32]

High culture as well as domestic artifacts were here in abundance, too: under the heading "Variétés" were details of local plays, concerts, and other artistic spectacles. Items of local news were profuse: local marriages, obituary notices, ceremonials and great funerals, public municipal meetings and signal events, philanthropic gestures, historical anecdotes, and archaeological finds relating to the region. Books were here in abundance: new titles were announced and sometimes

29 *Affiches de Beauvaisis*, January 1, 1786; Nina Rattner Gelbart, *Feminine and Opposition Journalism in Old Regime France: "Le Journal des Dames"* (Berkeley, Calif., 1987); and, more generally, Evelyne Sullerot, *Histoire de la presse féminine en France des origines à 1848* (Paris, 1966).

30 More flexibility appeared toward the end of the Old Regime, as many Affiches accepted literary and cultural material. Small ads were sometimes confined to a supplement. It seems that bound copies in libraries today are often shorn of this advertising material. For this problem, see Feyel, "La presse provinciale" (1987), 110, n. 23.

31 *Annonces affiches et avis divers de la Haute et Basse Normandie*, 1762 (*DJ*, no. 45). Similarly in 1770, the *Affiches de Bordeaux* in a single year contained advertisements for the sale of the post of *secrétaire du roi* based in Metz (March 22, 1770) and Rennes (December 29, 1770) (*DJ*, no. 16).

32 See, among others, by way of sampling: *Affiches des Trois-Evêchés*, July 20, 1771 (*DJ*, nos. 69–70) (razor strops); November 9, 1771 (waterproof shoes); *Affiches de la Haute et Basse Normandie*, December 19, 1763 (hot-water bottles); *Affiches de Provence* (*DJ*, no. 57), February 15, 1778 (horse manure).

reviewed or excerpted – advertisements often went on to mention that all titles were available from a local bookseller (who invariably was the editor of the local Affiches). Details of legal proceedings were also included: select royal decrees, edicts of local parlements, court reporting. Some Affiches even carried special legal supplements, highlighting titillating details of recent causes célèbres.[33]

There was economic information here, too. A regular feature was the announcement of up-to-the-minute details on the price of grain in local markets, share and other prices, building contracts available, the arrival of shipping (in major ports), sales and auctions. Bringing up the rear in this section was a booming market in lost-and-found objects. The local Affiches was the place to look, had you been careless enough to misplace, say, a parrot, an umbrella, or a Negro slave: fifteen lost umbrellas surfaced in the Affiches de Normandie in 1773 alone, while the Affiches de Bordeaux in 1771 carried details of the escaped Congolese slave doubtless wandering through claret country – readers would recognize him from the fact that he was branded Vincent (the name of the master, not the slave).[34]

Michael Sonenscher has justly characterized the world of work in the late eighteenth century as a "bazaar economy,"[35] and to scan the headings of the Affiches is to suspect that these newspapers formed a dynamic outpost of that world. The lost-and-found columns tailed into the section of the papers containing small ads relating to personal quests, notably employment. Some advertisers looked for traveling companions, and there were the occasional offers of marriage.[36] Masters seeking workers tried the Affiches. More numerous were individuals seeking work: domestic servants from the higher echelons, teach-

33   The *Affiches des Trois-Evêchés* and the *Affiches de Toulouse* both contained these supplements. See, too, R. Gérard, *Un journal de province sous la Révolution: Le Journal de Marseille de Ferréol de Beaugeard (1781–97)* (Paris, 1964), esp. 9. Unfortunately, the Bibliothèque Nationale holdings of the Affiches invariably do not contain these legal supplements. On the cause célèbre, see Sarah Maza, *Private Lives and Public Affairs: The "Causes Célèbres" of Prerevolutionary France* (Berkeley, Calif., 1993); and Lindsay B. Wilson, *Women and Medicine in the French Enlightenment: The Debate over "Maladies des Femmes"* (Baltimore, Md., 1993), esp. chap. 3. It should be noted that the existence of a medium of diffusion of causes célèbres through the Affiches, not mentioned by Maza, considerably strengthens her claim about the wide circulation of the *mémoire judiciaire*.
34   *Affiches de la Haute et Basse Normandie*, 1773 (umbrellas); *Affiches de Bordeaux* (DJ, no. 16), February 14, 1771 (escaped slave). For the parrot, Gérard, *Un journal de province*, 76.
35   Michael Sonenscher, *Work and Wages: Natural Law, Politics and the Eighteenth-Century French Trades* (Cambridge, 1989), 22–7.
36   For an example of a marriage offer, which seems to be a joke: *Affiches de l'Orléanais* (DJ, no. 46), December 7, 1764. One in the *Affiches de province*, May 22, 1771, was formally censored.

ers, and skilled workers. The foothills of the professions were also represented: priests seeking a lowly benefice, feudal lawyers, and specialists in heraldic research seeking clients. (Expertise in "feudal reaction" was a marketable commodity.)[37]

As time went on, the Affiches came to contain more article-length pieces on matters of literary or wider cultural importance. Anything smacking of politics remained formally beyond their purview, and editors often fell over themselves in their determination not to appear contentious. "I would like, if it is at all possible," commented the editor of the *Affiches de Bourges*, with all the pluckiness of a defiant doormat, "not to displease anyone."[38] The *Gazette* remained the locus for, in Habermasian language, the "representational" rituals of absolute monarchy (that is, courtly behavior affirming status through show and display before an admiring audience); the sonorous relation of official "fact" contrasted strikingly with the pluralistic, stereophonic anonymity of the Affiches' million small ads. Editors were increasingly keen to use their newspapers to combine "the pleasing" (*l'agréable*) with "the useful" (*l'utile*). Although social utility had the edge ("the useful," noted the *Affiches de Lyon*, "must always prevail over the pleasing"), the pleasing played an important role in widening horizons and stimulating imaginations.[39] Culture and trade thus came commodified and textualized, in ad-sized pieces. The combination of social utility with cultural interests, modeled on contemporary "commercial nations" such as England and Holland, was destined to "open a more certain channel so as to allow my compatriots" – this is the editor of the *Affiches de la Haute Normandie* speaking – " to communicate reciprocally among themselves their needs and their thoughts."[40]

The initial forum for such aspirations may have been the locality in which the Affiches was centered. This often showed that the spirit of the Affiches was to a large extent the spirit of the parish pump. From what we know about their business history, parochialism was an endless problem: lack of capital, shortages of copy, consumer suspicion – even

37   The domestic servants were the most numerous. For other examples, see *Affiches de Toulouse*, June 18, 1788 (priest); *Affiches de l'Orléanais*, December 20, 1782 (feudal lawyer); *Affiches du Dauphiné* (*DJ*, no. 21), December 12, 1786 (heraldic expert).
38   Cited in *DJ*, no. 17.
39   M. Gasc, "La naissance de la presse périodique à Lyon: Les Affiches de Lyon, annonces et avis divers," in *Etudes sur la presse*, 67 (compare *DJ*, no. 34). For the "representational" dimension of court rituals, see Habermas's discussion in *Structural Transformation*, 6–8.
40   A. Dubuc, "Les 'Annonces, affiches et avis divers de la Haute et Basse Normandie': Premier journal normand (1762–84)," *Actes du 81ᵉ Congrès National des sociétés savantes [Caen 1956]: Section d'histoire moderne et contemporaine* (Paris, 1956), 243–4.

resistance – squabbles with the censors, petty local rivalries, fights over status precedence, and ruinous lawsuits.[41] Nevertheless, to flip through the pages of these newspapers is to gain a sense not of closed, introverted communities but rather of a localism abutting onto something much broader. Editors viewed themselves as engaged in a kind of *mission civilisatrice*, culturally and commercially reaching out into parts of the region – *le pays* – hitherto cut off from the mainstream. The editor of the *Affiches de l'Orléanais*, recalling that poster *affiches* could only be seen in one place at one time, noted their vast inferiority to his newspaper, whose aim was "in some sense to make of this province a single town."[42]

Changes in title expressed this growing aspiration: though named initially after a town or city, many Affiches altered their title to include their surrounding region. Thus the *Affiches de Toulouse* became the *Affiches de Toulouse et du Haut-Languedoc*; the *Affiches de Metz* (after a number of changes), the *Affiches des Evêchés et Lorraine*; while in the nation's capital from 1779, the *Affiches de Paris* assumed the title *Journal général de France*. Indeed, in the 1780s, a great many of the papers dropped the title "Affiches" altogether for the more respectable, literary-sounding "Journal" (which they, moreover, increasingly resembled). In order to live up to this aspiration, the most successful papers created a network of distribution centers around their provinces. Subscriptions and sales were organized through neighboring small-town outlets – which often doubled as local post offices or else served as distribution centers for tobacco, salt, or proprietary medicines. Editors also aimed to secure among their subscribers rural notables – seigneurs and seigneuresses, parish priests – to relay their efforts.[43]

The local and regional patriotism of the Affiches was only a link in an even grander chain. Theirs was not the obscurantist regionalism of feudal law, historical prescription, and topological privilege but rather what we might call a "neo-provincialism," saturated in Enlightenment values of openness and transparency. The editor of the *Journal de Langue-*

---

41 Monographic treatments of individual newspapers give a good flavor of the problems: see esp. Dubuc, "Les 'Annonces, affiches et avis divers de la Haute et Basse Normandie,' " 249; Gérard, *Un journal de province, passim*; and Blanc-Rouquette, *La presse*, esp. 147–9.

42 *Affiches de l'Orléanais*, "Prospectus," January 1764. (This phrase was in fact much cited in other Affiches.)

43 For example, the *Affiches de l'Orléanais* in 1764 had distribution points in nine locations, directed by five booksellers, two notaries, and a postmaster; the *Affiches du Beauvaisis* (*DJ*, no. 15) in 1787 was in ten localities (six booksellers, one librarian's, one lawyer's, one surgeon's, one apothecary's); and the *Affiches du Dauphiné* in 1774 was available from postmasters in seventeen localities. For the latter newspaper, see René Favier, "Les 'Affiches' et la diffusion de l'innovation en Dauphiné à la fin du XVIIIᵉ siècle (1774–89)," *Annales du Midi*, 97 (1985).

doc in 1787 invoked "the reciprocal commerce" that his newspaper represented "between Languedoc and the other provinces of the kingdom and also foreign countries." Although the good of all humanity was seen as being at stake, particular concern focused on the regional, then national, frameworks. For the Affiches, there was no clash of interest between town, region, and nation: all were harmonious links in the grand design of – as the *Affiches de l'Orléanais* put it – "communication and commerce of minds."[44] The great interest editors showed in improved means of material communication – postal services, canals, stagecoach routes and schedules, engineering ventures, ballooning – highlighted the metaphysic of mobility at the heart of the Affiches project. Any of the journals, however humble it might be, was therefore engaged in "exciting emulation and contributing to the happiness that derives from commerce, arts and letters." This made the newssheet "the depository of some of the fruits of the activity and genius of the French nation," a "rich storehouse" of the nation's genius.[45]

France was viewed as being composed not, as the legists would have it, of a vertically arranged assemblage of myriad corporative bodies but rather of the fraternal, horizontally disposed ranks of fellow citizens (*concitoyens*) and compatriots (*compatriotes*), forming up in "neo-provincialist" battalions. In the wondrous economy of fulfilled reciprocal needs, which the Affiches prided themselves on engendering, getting and gaining extended to the goods and services of writers, artists, and the liberal professions. The choice products of merchants and manufacturers – France's capitalist bourgeoisie, if one wants to call them that – were here, but so were the intellectual offshoots and the skills and expertise of writers, middlemen, and professionals. Revisionist historians have often tended to separate France's capitalist bourgeoisie from the other groups within the bourgeoisie, many of whom also maintained a foot in the market. Yet it is clear that from the vantage point of the Affiches, such a division makes little sense. Where historians have tended to see disjuncture and conflict, the Affiches register linkages, overlaps of interests, and languages of mutual reinforcement: thus the *Affiches de province* compared the Republic of Letters to "a major trading city [in which] all writers . . . enjoy civic rights."[46] Commerce in words

44   *Journal de l'Orléanais*, "Discours préliminaire," January 1783. Compare the fine article by Claude Labrosse, "La région dans la presse régionale," in Sgard, *La presse provinciale*.
45   *Journal de l'Orléanais*, "Avertissement," January 6, 1769; Blanc-Rouquette, *La presse*, 145 (*Affiches de Toulouse*).
46   *Affiches de province*, "Avertissement," 1761. The analytical disaggregation of the bourgeoisie into "capitalist" and "intellectual" wings has been a *topos* in revisionist scholarship since the appearance of its Ur-text, Alfred Cobban, *The Social Interpretation of the French Revolution* (Cambridge, 1964).

as well as things was a defining characteristic of the Affiches. They over-looked their profit-oriented organization to conceive of themselves playing an altruistic role in the diffusion of Enlightened ideas and in the infusion of opinion with Enlightenment values. By means of publicity, they acted as relays for the book trade, other press outlets, the world of academies, and even masonic lodges, reaching parts of the French nation that these institutions could not reach by themselves and that lay beyond the normal constituency of other, more literary, and more respectable press organs. They constituted, as the editor of the *Affiches de Limoges* rather grandiloquently put it, "a kind of confraternity, a sort of academy spread out throughout the kingdom."[47]

The Affiches thus prided themselves on a uniquely efficacious capillarity within the bourgeois public sphere. Their nurturing of "a reciprocal commerce in enlightenment" ("un commerce réciproque de lumières")[48] tied in closely with their belief in the enlightening and civilizing powers of trade: *la lumière du commerce* and *le commerce des lumières* were two sides of the same coin. By holding the savant, the expert, and the consumer in the same altruistic basket, they aimed to produce satisfaction for the needs of all. Exchange was viewed as bring-ing both profit and pleasure, as well as bringing into being reciprocal relations of interdependence. Citizen was linked to citizen by "a mutual communication of enlightenment and assistance."[49] Happiness fostered profits, just as profits facilitated happiness: the development of national wealth and the accumulation of collective felicity formed part of the same grand design. The *Affiches de Picardie* spoke warmly of "a com-merce of friendship between citizens, [made] by bringing them recipro-cal benefits." The *Affiches de Poitou* evoked "a kind of correspondence of services and feelings: [the Affiches] is the means of communication between citizens that is the most swift, the most general and the least costly: it instructs at the same time as those who wish to buy and those who wish to sell find their wherewithal."[50] Through the Affiches, there-fore, a novel and cogent cultural circuitry was being assembled, a "Great Chain of Buying" (and selling) was being forged, which valorized even as it helped to create a commercial society.[51]

In the "Great Chain of Buying," the market held few terrors. Editors were happy marketeers to a man. In their pages, the market was presented as anodyne, socially desirable, even lovable; within it, spec-

47   Cited in Feyel, "La presse provinciale," 40 (*DJ*, no. 460).
48   *Journal du Languedoc*, "Prospectus," January 1787.
49   Blanc-Rouquette, *La presse*, 171 (citation from 1777).
50   Bellanger, *Histoire de la presse*, 399–400 (citing the *Affiches de Picardie* [*DJ*, no. 54]); Jean Sgard, "La presse provinciale et les Lumières," in Sgard, *La presse provin-ciale*, 55 (citing the *Affiches du Poitou*, 1772 [*DJ*, no. 55]).
51   Compare Sgard, "La presse provinciale et les Lumières," 53.

ulation, famine, greed, and want seemed to find no place. It answered human needs without pain or neurosis and in so doing celebrated new conceptions of virtue and happiness. The hidden hand of this market even wrote itself: there is little "writerliness" in the Affiches, which proclaimed a kind of degree zero of literarity. The writer was depreciated. Editors prided themselves on being merely the amanuenses of anonymous and transcendent forces, and, as "simple secretaries," they wrote as if under dictation from those forces.[52] "We only point with our finger," noted the editor of the Affiches de l'Orléanais, "what others are doing."[53]

The methods by which copy was obtained underscored this editorial rather than authorial function. The Affiches relied on their subscribers for most of their copy. These included local officials of the government. The provincial intendants were among the most assiduous of readers of the Affiches; they were, after all, their censors. They also utilized the Affiches to publish government measures, pet schemes to animate the local economy, or other faits divers: the government, the editor of the Affiches des Trois-Evêchés announced in 1781, drew to the reader's attention . . . the start of horse racing at Vincennes.[54] In addition, the establishment contract of each Affiches required it to send a copy of each issue to all the other Affiches throughout France. This practice supplied members of the network with an endless supply of potential copy. Wholesale lifting of material was an accepted way of putting a number together: roughly one-third of the contents of the Affiches du Dauphiné derived from this source.[55] Each Affiches was thus to a certain extent the press office of all the others – and indeed of all their sundry contributors. "You never SAY anything," commented a critic of the Courrier d'Avignon irately, "You only repeat."[56] Precisely. By this echo-chamber mechanism, the parish pump spoke to the world, and the world to the parish pump – and public opinion was formed.

The role of the notion of "public opinion" in the formation of the bourgeois public sphere has been underlined in recent years by Keith Baker and others. Yet the tendency has been to view this essentially as a discursive construct lacking a plausible social referent. The Affiches

---

52　Blanc-Rouquette, La presse, 144 ("simple secretaries"). Compare Jack Censer, "La presse vue par elle-même: Le prospectus et le lecteur révolutionnaire," in Rétat, La révolution du journal, 121.

53　Affiches de l'Orléanais, "Avertissement," February 1, 1765.

54　Affiches des Trois-Evêchés, March 1, 1781. For the enlightened intendant, see Roche, La France des lumières, 205–13.

55　Gérard, Un journal de province, 48–9.

56　Cited by René Moulinas, L'imprimerie, la librairie et la presse à Avignon au XVIIIe siècle (Grenoble, 1974), 368 (DJ, nos. 261–3).

provide a rather different – and perhaps more authentically Habermasian – perspective. The anonymity, aliterarity, stereophony, and the very "innocence" of the genre notwithstanding, we see within the Affiches public opinion being formed as if by drip-feed and the simultaneous construction of a new community of citizen-consumers. The Affiches was an organ, noted the editor of the *Affiches de province*, "formed, so to speak, by those who read it." The public discursively invoked in the Affiches was identical to their largely bourgeois – both male and female – readership, rooted in the ranks of "happy mediocrity." The open-endedness and interactiveness that characterized the genre made it at once a laboratory for experiments in individual subjectivity – and in collective class consciousness.[57]

By bringing producers and consumers of goods and services together in mutually beneficial markets and exchanges, by encouraging information flows regarding market decisions, and by establishing new links that transcended geographical localism, social particularism, gender exclusivity, and occupational restrictiveness, the Affiches played a considerable role as agents of the commercialization of *ancien régime* society.[58] They activated and simultaneously legitimated market exchange; they both boosted demand and fashioned the reader as a consumer. The Great Chain of Buying was grounded in the social and cultural capillarity of the small ad, which conjoined the private and the public, the economic and the cultural, the macro economy with the micro level of individual wants and needs.

But what of the place of our herniotomist in this Great Chain of Buying?

So far, I have endeavored to keep medicine and health out of my discussion of this neglected network of newspapers. This has been difficult, for they lie at the very heart of the commercializing, publicizing project of the Affiches. The common task of these newspapers – the service of utility, the making of happiness, the fostering of national spirit, and the nurturing of citizenship – reserved a significant role for medicine, medical personnel, and health issues. The editor of the *Affiches de la Haute Normandie*, for instance, wished his newspaper "to stimulate the intellectual curiosity of the public, and to involve at the same time its health, its wealth and its economic needs."[59] If, as Saint-Just was later

---

57 *Affiches de province*, January 7, 1761. Compare Habermas, *Structural Transformation*, 49. Keith Baker's *Inventing the French Revolution* is a key text at issue here.
58 I do not have space to outline the potential importance of the Affiches for the current rewriting of the economic history of the *ancien régime*. For introductions to this topic, see Jones, "Bourgeois Revolution Revivified"; and Colin Heywood, *The Development of the French Economy, 1750–1914* (London, 1992).
59 *Affiches de la Haute et Basse Normandie*, "Prospectus," January 1762.

to claim, happiness was "a new idea" in eighteenth-century Europe, much the same could be said of good health, one of the buzzwords of Enlightenment optimism.[60]

Health and medicine played a visible role at each of the different levels at which the Affiches operated. The metaphors through which editors conceptualized their activities often had a strong medical hue. As one might expect from journalists with an eye for metaphor, "circulation" was a perennial concern: editors not only sought to ensure a more dynamic "circulation" in their own product, they wished to see it matched in the body of French society generally. Their aim was sometimes a "fermentation," an "effervescence," an "exaltation" of the French nation. Some hoped to "electrify" or to "regenerate" – one or two even to "mesmerize." The body that lay at the center of the culture of the Affiches was thus not the sacral body of the king, "sovereign administrator" of his hierarchical realm, but rather the healthy organism of the assiduous reader – or else, more broadly, the body social, requiring fluidity and energy in the articulation of its parts.[61]

Scientific and medical life is found under most of the conventional headings of the Affiches. Much publicity was given, for example, to medical and scientific courses: practical anatomy classes, major operations (Caesarean sections, removal of cataracts or kidney stones), midwifery courses, and botanical rambles led by academics. Great medical interventions – quasi-miraculous cures, brilliant surgical strokes, and the like – merged imperceptibly into the more sensationalist wing of Affiches reporting: thus accounts of a bewitched woman in Picardy giving birth to six frogs; thus, too, stories of five-footed calves, tongueless women talking, extraordinarily hirsute toddlers, numerate horses, the eccentric hybrid born of a cat and a duck, and 150-year-old geriatrics.[62] Other, more formal medical aspects of public life were also given coverage; medical items were prominent among those pieces conjoining the local with the national. Health bulletins on ailing members

60   Compare Jean Sgard, "La presse provinciale et les Lumières," in Sgard, *La presse provinciale*, 62 and following; and, more generally, Robert Mauzi, *L'idée du bonheur dans la littérature française au XVIIIe siècle* (Paris, 1960), esp. 300–14. For further discussion on this point, see Brockliss and Jones, *Medical World*.
61   See esp. Gilot and Luna, "Mots-forces, mots-problèmes," for an excellent discussion. The Affiches were one of the most significant mediums spreading interest in mesmerism.
62   For medical publicity, see *Affiches du Dauphiné*, July 6, 1787 (Caesarian operations); *Affiches de Picardie*, September 3, 1774 (midwifery courses); *Affiches d'Austrasie* (*DJ*, no. 9), February 13, 1766 (rambles). For sensationalism, see Bellanger, *La presse*, 385 (calves); *Affiches de Picardie*, November 27, 1773 (frogs); *Affiches de Rouen*, December 23, 1763 (tongueless woman); *Affiches de Provence*, June 14, 1778 (duck-cat); *Affiches d'Austrasie*, May 15, 1776 (geriatric).

of the royal family were a specialty. Reports of meetings of academies and learned societies were legion, as were their prize essay competitions. The Royal Society of Medicine was one of the most visible of such societies: its secretary, Vicq d'Azyr, whom historians conventionally represent as a white knight of scientific altruism, proved astonishingly alert to the uses of publicity.[63] Public health measures also attracted much attention: smallpox inoculation, hospital reform, cemetery relocation, medical intervention in epidemics. The Affiches were a prime site of the "eighteenth-century campaign to avoid disease."[64]

Medicine thus lay close to the heart of the public sphere that the Affiches helped to construct. Making the public world more open and rational was matched by a desire – often ascribed to women readers – to render the reader's home cleaner, purer, more comfortable, less smelly, more secure, fire-insured, and vermin-free.[65] The significant role attributed to the maintenance of private and domestic health in the achievement of happiness was endlessly demonstrated by the way in which medicine was used as a selling point for a vast array of commodities and services that had little or nothing obvious to do with health. The phrase "de santé" resounded like a marketing mantra in some unusual places. Private infirmaries were dubbed "maisons de santé," but proprietors of public baths also proudly offered the public "bains médicinaux" and "bains de santé"; caterers, "thé de santé," "thé balsamique et stomachique des Alpes," and "café de santé"; and boilermakers, a "poêle hydraulique et de santé."[66] Furniture manufacturers advertised "tables de santé" (for keeping medicines warm) and touted the charms of "lits mécaniques pour le soulagement des malades," or else air beds, vaunted for "comfort, economy, voluptuousness," and "la santé."[67] Vinegar makers announced a "moutarde de santé," while chocolatiers

63 For the royal family, see, for example, publicity relating to the royal family's smallpox inoculation (*Affiches du Dauphiné*, August 26, 1774) and the birth of the dauphin (*Affiches de Toulouse*, October 7, 1781). Reports of the affairs of the Royal Society of Medicine are extremely widespread in all the major Affiches. For Vicq, see Gillispie, *Science and Polity*, 196–203.

64 James C. Riley, *The Eighteenth-Century Campaign to Avoid Disease* (London, 1987). These endeavors were sometimes placed under the heading of "Patriotisme" or "Bienfaisance."

65 On this theme, see Robert Favre and Pierre Rétat, "L'amélioration de la vie quotidienne," in Sgard, *La presse*, 65 and following.

66 *Affiches de province*, August 15, 1759 ("maisons de santé"); *Affiches des Trois-Evêchés*, November 23, 1771, and *Affiches de Toulouse*, May 13, 1787 (baths); *Affiches de province*, March 5, 1785 ("thé de santé"); *Affiches de Toulouse*, February 13, 1772 (café); *Affiches des Trois-Evêchés*, December 5, 1772 (boilers).

67 *Affiches de Toulouse*, October 9, 1787 (tables); *Gazette de santé*, February 8, 1776 (air bed).

displayed a "chocolat homogène, stomachique et pectoral" and a "chocolat de santé." (Medical critics pointed out that this last was manufactured so poorly it should be renamed "chocolat de maladie.") On a related tack, hairdressers preened their haircutting skills by disparaging wigs, which were invariably, they claimed, composed of hair cropped from the skulls of syphilitic corpses, while dancing masters advertised their skills in "the art of preventing and correcting bodily deformities." Little wonder that doctors and surgeons were already beginning to refer to themselves as "officiers de santé" – a phrase to have a distinguished history in the revolutionary decade and beyond.[68]

Science and medicine tended to serve the pursuit of domestic comfort while also anaesthetizing readers to many of the inequalities and injustices of commercial society. Food, for example, present in cornucopian variety and Rabelaisian volume, was seen as an integral part of citizens' material well-being rather than – as was the case in court gazettes – the occasion for ceremonial ritual and public display. Remedies were earnestly offered for those who ate too much; gout (countered by "sympathetic garters"), hemorrhoids, and indigestion were targeted ailments. As for those who were faced with hunger and want, there were healthy, homey recipes for *soupes économiques* and bread made from potato flour (referred to, significantly enough, as "farine de santé") – the latter particularly recommendable in that any excess might be utilized as wallpaper paste. (Starving peasants, please note!) Here, as so often, the Affiches had an answer, and it was a soothing one.[69]

A staunch and touching optimism obtained, too, in much relating to the body, which was – and is – a special focus for medical consumerism, and which, again, often targeted female readers. Personal appearances were to be endlessly sanitized, endlessly prettified. Creams promised to remove wrinkles and restore hair (occasionally at the same time). Teeth should be clean, pure, white, odor-free, and could, thanks to the Affiches, be worn false. The Rousseauesque, back-to-nature angle of some of the advertising highlighted rude and primitive health: thus the

68   Maille the mustard-maker was an inveterate user of the columns of the Affiches. See also *Gazette de santé* (DJ, no. 544), September 16, 1773 ("chocolat de maladie"); *Affiches des Trois-Evêchés* (chocolate); Blanc-Rouquette, *La presse*, 185 (hairdressers); *Affiches de Toulouse*, November 24, 1787 (dancing master). For the "officier de santé," see Dora B. Weiner, *The Citizen-Patient in Revolutionary and Imperial Paris* (Baltimore, Md., 1993).

69   Excellent discussions of food in the press are in Jean-Claude Bonnet, "La presse et le problème alimentaire," in *Le journalisme*; and Bonnet, "Les problèmes alimentaires dans la presse de 1768," in Jean Varloot and Paule Jansen, eds., *L'année 1768 à travers la presse traitée par ordinateur* (Paris, 1981). For sympathetic garters, see *Affiches de Bordeaux*, August 9, 1770; for hemorrhoidal creams, *Affiches des Trois-Evêchés*, January 18, 1772.

best herb teas were cut on the higher slopes of the Alps; thus the virtues of a "poudre onctueuse" were vaunted on the grounds that it "derived from the most innocent [sic] plants"; thus, too, Louisiana bear grease – "préparé sans feu par les sauvages" – was a well-attested way of overcoming baldness.[70]

Medical books formed a staple market among the wide variety of medical consumer products advertised in the Affiches: one-quarter of the books mentioned in the *Affiches de Lyon* were scientific works – the figure for the *Affiches de province* was close to 40 percent – and roughly a quarter of these were medical works.[71] There were medical engravings, too: Frère Côme, the famous lithotomist, was the subject of one portrait offered for sale (although the same newspaper also offered engravings of the famous charlatan Count Alessandro di Cagliostro).[72] The supply of medical bric-à-brac spilled out beyond the world of print. There were all sorts of anatomical objects on the market: anatomical dolls, upholstered female pelvises for acquiring obstetrical legerdemain, skulls, skeletons, glass eyes. One advertiser offered table-top models of "the genital parts of the two sexes" (along with "300 engravings, most of which show *des sujets galants*").[73] There were medical appliances of a stomach-churningly baroque fantasy, which await their hardened archaeologist: herniary trusses of every shape, size, price, and consistency; scalpels, saws, knives, probes, and cutting edges of every description; tourniquets, catheters, and surgical boots; false teeth, artificial limbs, ear trumpets; electrical contraptions ("one can electrify several patients at the same time"); neck collars and body harnesses; do-it-yourself tooth extractors, portable urinals. The list is endless.[74]

It would be foolish to attempt more than the most elementary inventory of the wide array of drugs and medicines advertised in the Affiches,

70 *Affiches de province*, September 4, 1771 (alpine plants); *Affiches de Bordeaux*, March 12, 1778 ("poudre onctueuse"); *Affiches de province*, April 5, 1777 (bear grease). Dentists were champions of false teeth. Morag Martin is preparing a PhD dissertation for the University of California, Irvine, on cosmetics, drawing on the Affiches.
71 Michel Marion, "Dix années des 'Affiches, annonces et avis divers' (1752–61)," in Jacques Godechot, ed., *Regards sur l'histoire de la presse et de l'information: Mélanges offerts à Jan Prinet* (Paris, 1980), 31.
72 *Affiches de Toulouse*, August 1, 1782 (Côme); June 23, 1782 (Cagliostro).
73 *Affiches de Toulouse*, July 30, 1761 (anatomical dolls); *Affiches des Evêchés et Lorraine* (DJ, no. 69), July 20, 1780, and *Affiches de l'Orléanais*, April 19, 1782 (skulls, etc.); *Affiches de Toulouse*, September 19, 1781 (engravings, etc.).
74 For example, *Affiches des Pays-Bas* (DJ, nos. 50–1), December 5, 1763, and *Affiches de Toulouse*, August 19, 1781 (artificial limbs). Advertisements for herniary trusses and impedimenta are extraordinarily widespread. For the electrical machine, see *Affiches du Beauvaisis*, February 26, 1786.

offering aid to an extraordinarily rich ensemble of ailments and ill-
nesses. The very profusion of the medicines offered may indeed baffle
and perplex the historian who, taking as a guide to the state of the
pharmaceutical art the most recent writings on medicine in the late
eighteenth century, might have expected an altogether more anodyne,
stately, and well-regulated world of medical remedy. The orthodox, corporative medical community had always vigorously opposed unlicensed
practice, and, from the late 1770s, the Royal Society of Medicine led a
renewed charge against medical "charlatanism," performing systematic
chemical and clinical analyses on proprietary medicines and ruthlessly
weeding out those that seemed useless or harmful. The idea of secrecy
involved in "remèdes secrets" seemed at odds with late Enlightenment
themes of transparency, authenticity, and humanitarianism: medical
compounds that could serve humanity should be known to all. The
Society of Medicine outlawed the retailing of a great many medicines
and later claimed, as Matthew Ramsey has noted, that only four medical
compounds ever secured its full endorsement.[75]

In theory at least, the Affiches followed this lead. Editors mouthed
a routine detestation of charlatans living off the health and well-being
of the population – "smugglers in health," "starving vultures," "vam-
pires" whose prey was invariably the unlettered peasant. The *Affiches du
Dauphiné* joined Grenoble surgeons in berating one of their number for
keeping his expertise a charlatanesque secret rather than sharing it in
the public interest with his colleagues.[76] Some Affiches carried the full
list of remedies authorized or proscribed by the Royal Society of Medicine, and they showed caution in the publicizing of unauthorized
medicines. "It is prudent to consult trained physicians," the *Affiches du
Dauphiné* recorded after a dispute over the efficacy of a particular medicine in 1779. "We know," noted the *Affiches de Poitou*, "how much cir-
cumspection is necessary in advertising remedies." Yet in the event, the
Affiches de Poitou went on to give a remedy for quartian fever that lacked
any medical or state endorsement whatsoever.[77] This was in fact fairly
characteristic: while the Affiches saluted the flag of the Royal Society of
Medicine, they failed to toe its line.

75   See esp. Matthew Ramsey, "Traditional Medicine and Medical Enlightenment:
The Regulation of Secret Remedies in the Ancien Régime," in Jean-Pierre Goubert,
ed., *La médicalisation de la société française, 1770–1830* (Waterloo, Ont., 1982).
Ramsey points out that the Royal Society's estimates were woefully below the mark.
Yet his work has had a powerful impact in giving the impression of effectiveness in
medical policing: see Roy Porter, *Health for Sale: Quackery in England, 1660–1830*
(Manchester, 1989), citing Ramsey's work, 22, 27, and following.
76   *Affiches du Dauphiné*, May 28, 1783. Compare November 4, 1774.
77   *Affiches du Dauphiné*, March 19, 1779; *Affiches de Poitou*, October 25, 1781.

The *de facto* tolerance of unlicensed medicines, which makes the pages of the Affiches a rich repository of medical compounds and treatments of every description, had a number of causes. First, the editors were insufficiently vigilant to prevent crackpot remedies from finding their way into their columns (and they must sometimes have welcomed the copy). The *Courrier d'Avignon*, for example, carried advertisements for "reason pills" (*pilules raisonnables*), to be ingested by those suffering from folly, madness, vapors, and nervous attacks; the *Affiches de la Haute Normandie* commended *eau orviétale essencifiée* (Orviétan, habitually peddled by itinerant mountebanks, was the most charlatanesque of all secret remedies); while the *Affiches de Provence* recommended rubbing salt into the navel as a preservative against smallpox.[78]

Tolerance of advertisements for unauthorized medicines is not explained simply by lack of editorial vigilance. The back-to-nature angle that frequently surfaced in advertising copy found an echo in folkloric remedies rescued from obscurity and placed at the disposal of the public. Even as they railed against medical charlatanism, editors celebrated the chthonic, health-giving properties of remedies sent in – "in the name of humanity" – by well-intentioned readers. After recounting a remedy against warts, which involved placing the ailing digit into the mouth of a live frog, the editor of the *Affiches de Poitou* reflected that there were probably "many other remedies against different common ailments that are equally effective and yet are kept as family secrets," before going on to urge readers, "in the interests of humanity," to send them in.[79]

The uncertainty over the legal status of different medicines was a further reason why such a profusion of remedies appeared in the pages of the Affiches. Despite its grandiloquent claims, the Royal Society of Medicine was not the only medical authorizing body, so manufacturers of remedies were able to use legal inconsistencies to get their advertisements published. Sales patter and marketing strategy made a great deal of the principle of endorsement. Medical entrepreneurs came bearing certificates, recommendations, and authorizations – obscure faculties, foreign dignitaries, anonymous recommendations were all grist to a fantastical mill. The increasingly sophisticated paraphernalia of quality control similarly implied legitimacy as well as altruistic concern for public health: entrepreneurs stressed that their product came in sealed and stamped bottles, jars, or packets, so as to forewarn the public against potential counterfeiters.

The plethora of advertisements for medicines testified to growing medical entrepreneurialism, but it also, finally, highlighted the strength

78 Todd, "French Advertising," 536; *Affiches de la Haute et Basse Normandie*, September 6, 1771; and *Affiches de Provence*, March 1, 1778.
79 Example cited in Feyel, "Médecins, empiriques et charlatans," 80.

of the demand for medical goods and services in late eighteenth-century France. The Affiches allowed this demand to be met and – one suspects – created. When combined with the development of sophisticated national distribution networks, proprietary medicines probably reached a larger audience than ever before. The patriotic aura that floated around the name of "the public" in the Affiches, moreover, meant that, for many readers, public opinion had displaced status or acceptance within the corporative medical community as the touchstone of legitimacy. By providing their readers with a wide array of drugs and medicines of every description, editors were to a certain extent only "giving the public what it wanted."

The late eighteenth century saw some remarkable medical entrepreneurs, many of them completely lacking in medical training, who took advantage of the growing demand for health services. Venereal diseases were an elective home for such individuals, whom we occasionally glimpse flitting in and out of the pages of the Affiches. The anti-syphilitic *Poudre médicamenteuse du Chevalier Goderneau*, for example, was advertised in any number of Affiches, along with alleged endorsements by military hospitals, the Paris medical faculty, and the Academy of Sciences. But it had a history of disasters behind it: in the Orléanais, it was held responsible for poisoning hundreds of victims, and it was eventually outlawed by the Royal Society of Medicine.[80]

Colorful though such cases are, it would be erroneous to imagine that the pages of the Affiches housed only the crook, the quack, and the crackpot. By the end of the Old Regime, the publicist techniques of the "charlatan" were also available to the medical practitioner solidly ensconced within the establishment. This had not always been the case. In 1759, for example, a Dr. Arrazat placed a notice in the *Affiches de Toulouse*, stating that he had just arrived in the city and would welcome any patients. A week later, the Toulouse Faculty of Medicine inserted a furious note in the paper condemning this action: it was utterly wrong, they stated, that a physician "in order to make himself known, should use the means of small ads [*annonces*] and such other channels normally the preserve of charlatans and empirics."[81]

Such a ringing condemnation, grounded in the traditional corporative ethic of the medical world, would not have carried far two or three decades later. Well before the end of the Old Regime, all types of medical

---

80   See, for example, *Affiches du Dauphiné*, December 15, 1780; *Journal de l'Orléanais*, March 9, July 30, September 10, and October 1, 1784; and, in amended form, *Journal de Troyes* in 1783 and *Journal Général de France* 1784, *passim*.

81   *Affiches de Toulouse*, November 18 to December 19, 1759. Compare, for similar cases, September 2, 1760; and *Gazette d'Epidaure* (*DJ*, no. 539), 1761, 196 (the Academy of Surgery wanting to expel a member for unseemly advertising).

practitioners were availing themselves of the Affiches. This was at once a compliment to the acceptability of the Affiches and a symptom of a growing interest in publicity and commercialism evident in the medical community. The newssheets were certainly the home of a Darntonesque "Quack Street" of jobbing medics and shameless adventurers, but they were also a forum for individuals firmly embedded within establishment practice, just looking for a job or drumming up custom. Thus, from the *Annonces de Picardie*:

> A physician of mature years, well-versed in chemistry and pharmacy . . . wishes to find an establishment in the countryside or in the employ of a seigneur . . . He will be content with an honorarium that will ensure him a modest comfort appropriate to his station.[82]

Comparatively few medical practitioners sold themselves as blatantly on the strength of their persons. The more normal practice was to hover behind some special commodity, facility, or skill. This might be a proprietary medicine: the renowned Montpellier professor Fizes, for example, backed the "Ratafia purgatif" of his apothecary and fellow townsman, Carquet. It might also take the form of puffery in book reviewing, characterized by one editor as "a type of advertisement to proclaim the author's medical reputation and existence." The Royal Society of Medicine's Vicq d'Azyr was good at this kind of (self) promotion – he also advertised his anatomy courses in the press.[83] In addition, a surprisingly large number of medical advertisements offered treatment in the home of the practitioner. We know, of course, about the emergence of private madhouses in Paris in this period: Jacques Belhomme, Philippe Pinel's early employer, advertised in the *Affiches de Paris*. The city also contained centers for the treatment of venereal diseases. These ads in the Affiches suggest that home-based practice was a new and growing area of enterprise in these and other branches of medicine. A Paris optician took in the blind; a surgeon admitted persons wishing to be inoculated against smallpox; a physician took in the aged; an upwardly mobile midwife ("accoucheuse"), pregnant women for their travails; an herbalist, individuals wanting herbal treatment for ailments of various kinds.[84]

82   *Affiches de Picardie*, September 11, 1773. For other similar appeals, *Affiches de l'Orléanais*, July 4, 1776 (physician); *Affiches de Picardie*, September 11, 1773 (physician); *Affiches de Provence*, May 31, 1778 (surgeon).
83   For Fizes, *Affiches de Bordeaux*, August 1, 1765; for Vicq, see especially *Gazette de santé*, July 1777, and *Journal général de France*, October 18, 1785.
84   For madhouses, Michel Foucault, *Folie et déraison: Histoire de la folie à l'age classique* (Paris, 1961), 657–8; for Belhomme, *Affiches de Paris*, June 3, 1776 (and for a similar institution run by Esquiros, September 18, 1775). For Paris VD clinics, Pierre Delaunay, *Le monde médical parisien au XVIIIe siècle* (Paris, 1906), remains an unsur-

The word "charlatanism" was becoming too blunt a term to be of much help in outlining what was going on in the world of medical practice. A pejorative discursive category, it increasingly lacked a clearly defined social referent. The division between the incorporated medical community and unlicensed practitioners – a division that was the basis of the medical campaign against charlatanism – was being progressively overlaid by a rather fuzzier distinction between commercial and publicist medicine on the one hand and more conventional, noncommercial medicine on the other. The Affiches provide an excellent entrée into this world, for they constituted a site in which the publicity-minded academician could rub shoulders with the denizens of "Quack Street." One issue of the *Affiches du Dauphiné* in 1781, for example, contained both an account of a meeting of the Royal Society of Medicine and the adventures in Strasbourg of the medico-spiritualist Cagliostro.[85] The Affiches demonstrated that the division between "orthodox" medicine and "charlatanism" was becoming increasingly artificial. This shift is highlighted by itinerant specialists with a particular skill. Itinerant specialists, who were assiduous users of the Affiches, included dentists (who often doubled up, like friend Antoine Clesse, with a sideline in herniotomy) and opticians. Cataract-cutter extraordinaire "Chevalier" John Taylor was among the latter, as well as "Chevalier" Tadini (petty noble status was clearly infectious among opticians) and the Toulouse-based Nizet de Varennes, who was a particularly loquacious publicist. Taylor was viewed as a charlatan by some, but he treated the crowned heads of Europe and won a scientific reputation. Tadini also claimed to be advancing medical science – but was not infrequently harassed on his travels for being an unlicensed showman and quack.[86] For such figures, the Affiches offered both an orthodox literary platform, where before

passed vade mecum; and for the provinces, see *Affiches de Toulouse*, March 25, 1760. For other cases, *Affiches du Dauphiné*, December 24, 1779 (optician); *Affiches des Trois-Evêchés*, January 19, 1771, and *Affiches de la Haute et Basse Normandie*, May 24, 1771 ("maison d'inoculation"); *Affiches des Evêchés et Lorraine*, August 2, 1781 (aged); August 25, 1785 ("accoucheuse"). Compare other cases, involving midwives and surgeons, such as *Affiches de l'Orléanais*, May 1, 1768, and *Affiches des Trois-Evêchés*, October 28, 1780; *Affiches de Bordeaux*, July 9, 1786 (herbalist).
85   *Affiches du Dauphiné*, May 2, 1781.
86   For example, *Affiches de Bordeaux*, October 3, 1765, and *Affiches de l'Orléanais*, February to June 1766 (Taylor); *Affiches de la Haute et Basse Normandie*, March 12, 1773, *Affiches de province*, January 17, 1778, *Affiches de l'Orléanais*, March 1, 1782, *Affiches des Evêchés et Lorraine*, May 19, 1785, and following issues (Tadini). For Nizet de Varennes, *Affiches de Toulouse*, *passim*, in the 1770s and 1780s. For Taylor's career in England, see Porter, *Health for Sale*, esp. 66–80. Another good example of the fuzziness of categorization is Laffecteur, the progenitor of a *rob antisyphilitique* that was widely berated as outright quackery but that lasted on the French Codex until the twentieth century. See Brockliss and Jones, *Medical World*.

they had only a soapbox, and a launching pad for projection into the ranks of establishment practitioners.

The case of the Austrian proponent of "animal magnetism," Franz-Anton Mesmer, also highlights the complexities of this medical world in flux. As Robert Darnton has shown, mesmerism, with its rococo mixture of fantasy, commercial salesmanship, and Rousseauian purity, divided the medical community. While those in established positions decried the immorality and trickery of Mesmer and his followers, many other physicians and medical men of every stripe rallied to his cause. Questions regarding the politicization of health seemed to have priority over the alleged scientific status of orthodox medical knowledge. In the Affiches, moreover, where the mesmerist debate was followed very closely, this form of health care was figured both as a form of medical charlatanism and as virtuous, even patriotic, medicine. The medical practitioner who tailored his wares to the needs of the public was the quintessential patriot.[87]

The dynamism in the medical world during the last decades of the *ancien régime* – the inroads of commercialism, the progress of health consumerism, the avatars of medical entrepreneurialism – could, I believe, be extended to other professions. It would be possible to track commercial and more overtly publicist reflexes among lawyers, accountants, engineers – maybe even priests, too.[88] The Affiches open a window onto an increasingly materialistic, consumerist world, inhabited by increasingly entrepreneurial and publicity-minded professional groupings too easily written off as traditionalist or deferential. In addition, the newssheets provided a place in which an enlarged volume of commercial operations could be transacted. They propagated an ideology of commercialism, preaching but also engaging in the "commerce des lumières." We see in action close links between the practices of commercial capitalism and the formation of the bourgeois public sphere.

There was, moreover, a political upshot to the activities of the Affiches – although recent work on them has largely failed to acknowledge it. Current historiography makes a strong contrast between allegedly

87 Robert Darnton, *Mesmerism and the End of the Enlightenment in France* (Cambridge, Mass., 1968). An excellent discussion of the phenomenon appears in Gillispie, *Science and Polity*, 261–89. There is a great deal of scope for following the mesmerist debate in the provinces through the pages of the Affiches.
88 See Jones, "Bourgeois Revolution Revivified," for broader consideration of these points. All groups, including priests, are found offering their services in the pages of the Affiches. The legal profession is starting to attract attention: besides Maza, *Private Lives and Public Affairs*, see David A. Bell, *Lawyers and Citizens: The Making of a Political Elite in Old Regime France* (Oxford, 1994).

"literary," infra-political journals and newspapers of the Enlightenment with the ultra-political stance of the press in the revolutionary
decade. Habermas, too, seems to consider the commercialization taking
place in the Affiches a phenomenon that started under the Restoration
and the July Monarchy rather than the *ancien régime*.[89] In this final
section, I will question these assumptions and highlight some of the
political stakes in play in the seemingly sunny world of the Affiches.

Political news was – as several editors put it – the "ark of the
covenant," and officially it was beyond the scope of their operations even
to consider it. More prosaically, it was, first, specifically excluded from
the original franchise contract by which editors undertook publication;
the *Gazette*, from whose loins they had sprung, continued to have a
monopoly on hard news. Second, that agreement was carefully policed
at the local level. Many Affiches depended heavily on the local state
official, the *intendant*, to circumvent the problems of establishing a
newspaper in a sometimes difficult environment. The *intendant* not only
censored copy, he often also required editors to exercise self-censorship
– an even more potent means of enforcing political prudence.[90]

Making a few examples served as a deterrent. The copies of the
Affiches de province in the Bibliothèque Nationale for the early 1770s are
the editor's proofs before and after censorship, and so show the censor
in action. The issues he targeted for excision are extraordinarily petty,
and they highlight the extreme caution necessary regarding news
about public life or news affecting the honor of persons.[91] To court the
intervention of higher authority was to risk administrative hassles,
suspension of publication, and thus loss of readers. The *Affiches des
Trois-Evêchés* told its readers in 1773 that "superior orders" had obliged
it to withdraw from supplying any political news, and its successor, the
Affiches des Evêchés et Lorraine, had its publication suspended by the
intendant from April to July 1782.[92] The editor of the *Affiches de la Haute*

---

89   In addition to the works cited above, notes 1, 7, 8, see Harvey Chisick, ed., *The
Press in the French Revolution* (Oxford, 1991), esp. "Introduction." Censer, *French
Press*, wavers between acknowledging and denying political import to the Affiches.
Compare Habermas, *Structural Transformation*, chap. 20.
90   Monographs on individual journals are most insightful on the plight of the
editor: see especially Blanc-Rouquette, *La presse*; Dubuc, "Les 'Annonces, affiches et
avis divers de la Haute et Basse Normandie' "; Gérard, *Un journal de province*; Vogne,
La presse périodique. Compare, too, Moulinas, *L'imprimerie*, esp. 376–7; A.
Demougeot, "Les origines de la presse à Nice," *Nice historique*, 62 (1959), esp. 103.
For the "ark of the covenant" (a much-used phrase), see *Affiches des Evêchés et
Lorraine*, January 6, 1780.
91   *Affiches de province*, 1771–3.
92   It is difficult to follow the issue through to see the stakes involved. See *Affiches
des Evêchés et Lorraine*, August 30, 1781, January 3, 1782, and July 18, 1782.
Compare *Affiches des Trois-Evêchés*, December 18, 1773.

Normandie was firmly admonished for an article that allegedly impugned the honor of the local chamber of commerce, and, following an anodyne article on Voltaire, he was instructed that he should keep a full register of all the journal's subscribers and letter writers. Pressure from local legal and administrative bodies, notably the Parlement, led the editor of the *Affiches de Toulouse* to resign in disgust in 1777. Other Affiches that started to carry news judged too political – the *Affiches de Nantes* from 1759 to 1761, for example – were soon cowed back into line.[93]

It thus behooved editors to explore the contours of the forbidden only with the greatest caution. Beneath a morass of prudent conformism and loyalist yea-saying, it is remarkable that many chose to explore at all. A kind of subterranean, anti-authority journalism evolved, in which editors often took a leaf from the book of their English colleagues by loudly trumpeting their putatively nonpolitical, nonpartisan positions even as they adopted postures of contention and critique.[94] The *Affiches de la Haute Normandie* daringly tracked the political crisis involving the local court in the early 1760s. The *Affiches de Bordeaux* provided cautious updates on the Calas Affair in 1765 and even carried an advertisement for an engraving of the widow Calas. Some foreign policy news in the late 1760s and early 1770s – notably relating to events in Poland and the Polish Partition and to English diplomacy – appears to have been given the green light. The Affiches also came to play an important role in spreading knowledge of and support for the American Revolution. In the early 1780s, the *Affiches de Toulouse* began to publish accounts of the meetings of the local Protestant synod, well ahead of this body's legalization within the state. A number of newspapers also mentioned – and sometimes provided a book review of – Jacques Necker's *Compte-rendu au roi* in 1781, the minister's account of the state's finances (and one of the main reasons for his dismissal).[95]

The book review – as in the case of Necker – highlighted one consequence of the state prohibition on the Affiches carrying overtly political news: namely, the displacement of politics into other, more overtly licit news activities within its pages. If the book notice or review was one

---

93 Dubuc, "Les 'Annonces, affiches et avis divers de la Haute et Basse Normandie,'" 249 and following (*Affiches de la Haute Normandie*); Blanc-Rouquette, *La presse*, 149–51 (*Affiches de Toulouse*); *DJ*, no. 43 (*Affiches de Nantes*).

94 "Frondeur journalism" is the expression Nina Gelbart, in her *Feminine and Opposition Journalism*, 11–16, uses to describe vociferous reformism in journals and pamphlets. For England, compare Barry, "Press and the Politics of Culture," 70–1.

95 Compare *Affiches de Bordeaux*, August 22, 1765; *Affiches de Toulouse*, 1782, *passim*; *Affiches des Trois-Evêchés et Lorraine*, March 15, 1781 (see March 29, 1781, for an obituary of another reforming minister, Turgot).

such niche,[96] legal and diplomatic supplements constituted another. The *Journal de Lyon* in 1774 carried a lengthy, six-page account of the "Speech of the King of Sweden to the Estates Held on 21 August 1772, and Proposals Made to Them for a New Form of Government" – a pretty cheeky item, even if no additional comment was given, in the context of the imminent coronation of Louis XVI.[97] A section that a great many Affiches carried by the 1780s, "Patriotism and Beneficence" (*bienfaisance*), provided another site for coded politics. The telling of tales of beneficence within France allowed the recounting of social and economic ills, as well as providing endorsement for a new "patriotic" ethic of fraternal citizenship.[98] Recording acts of philanthropy performed by other crowned heads (Frederick the Great was a favorite) could be seen as an implicit reproach to the French monarch.

Insidious polarization such as this was a favored technique for at least riffling the fringes of the "ark of the covenant." The development of the notion of civic benevolence, or *bienfaisance*, was grounded in a contrast with the allegedly selfish, sectionalist Christian charity preached by the established Catholic church. Similarly, the *Affiches du Beauvaisis* painted its picture of the "obscure citizen," in whom it saw "a model of virtue, humanity and *bienfaisance*" precisely by contrasting him (*sic*) point by point with the haughty aristocrat.[99] This kind of "politics by implicit contrast" also came out in debates on luxury. Most editors followed the middle line adopted by Denis Diderot, who had contrasted a *luxe d'ostentation* with a *luxe de commodité*: the former was usually figured as the preserve of the courtier and the aristocrat (and was therefore bad), the latter was the kind of good bourgeois luxury one would expect in a reader of the Affiches.[100] After all, one needed to have some margin of wealth, if only to be dutifully *bienfaisant*. There was an important gender element in these processes of polarization: the idle, disordered world of the court was made to contrast with the "natural" gender roles of solidly bourgeois domesticity. Though for all intents and purposes, women, like

96   On a similar tack, the *Affiches de Provence* brought its readers' attention in 1778 to the *Babillard*, the radical newspaper opened by Chevalier Rutledge in Paris.
97   *Journal de Lyon, ou Annonces et variétés littéraires* (*DJ*, no. 668), July 7, 1774.
98   On *bienfaisance*, see esp. Sgard, "La presse provinciale et les Lumières," 55 and following; Colin Jones, *Charity and Bienfaisance: The Treatment of the Poor in the Montpellier Region, 1740–1815* (Cambridge, 1982), esp. 1–8; and Catherine Duprat, *"Pour l'amour de l'humanité": Le temps des philanthropes; La philanthropie parisienne des Lumières à la monarchie de Juillet, Tome I* (Paris, 1993), esp. chap. 1.
99   *Affiches du Beauvaisis*, January 1, 1786; "Prospectus," January 1, 1787. This heading in the *Affiches de Toulouse* began "Traits of beneficence and patriotism, which encourage virtue"; see January 2, 1782.
100   *Encyclopédie, ou Dictionnaire raisonné des sciences, arts et métiers*, 17 vols. (Paris, 1751–65), 9 (1765): art. "luxe." Compare Roche, *La France des lumières*, 513–14.

men, had been formed as citizen-consumers in the pages of the *Affiches*, women were viewed primarily as "citizens who [will] train future citizens."[101]

In such ways, the *Affiches* were not only fashioning (and gendering) the citizen who would come into his own in 1789, they were also constructing the portrait of one of the revolutionaries' principal adversaries. This exercise in socio-political demonization may not have had the lurid colors of other forms of political critique, such as anti-court pornography. But that made it all the easier to digest, and its anodyne coloration allowed it a wider and, seemingly, more receptive audience as 1789 approached.[102] On the eve of the revolution, columns on "Patriotism and Beneficence" continued to tell tales of misery highlighting both grim social conditions and the call for reform. Literary debates on luxury and speculation were given extra acuity. The *Journal de Normandie* carried book reviews on "The Causes of Public Disorder, by a True Citizen" and "Plan for the Useful Organization of the Grain Trade," while the *Affiches du Dauphiné* reviewed "Remarks on the Nobility" (and highlighted how recently many nobles had acquired their status). The *Affiches d'Angers* launched attacks on the 1786 Anglo-French Trade Treaty.[103] The terms "citizen," "nation," and "public opinion" were carrying increasingly heavy political baggage. The political spirit even reached the medical advertisements: in the *Affiches de Toulouse*, the former military apothecary Garnaus offered patriotic cough drops – *véritables pastilles à la Neckre* (*sic*) – "for the public good."[104]

---

101   *Affiches d'Angers* (1777), according to Sgard, "La presse provinciale," 61. Anxiety about the political aspirations of female readers comes out quite strongly in some Affiches. See, for example, the detabe on a potential female "academy" in *Affiches de Troyes* in 1783. This is a footnote to a much larger question of female involvement in the late Enlightenment; see Joan Landes, *Women and the Public Sphere in the Age of the French Revolution* (Ithaca, N.Y., 1988); and Dena Goodman, *The Republic of Letters: A Cultural History of the French Enlightenment* (Ithaca, 1994).

102   See especially Lynn A. Hunt, *The Family Romance of the French Revolution* (London, 1992), chap. 4; Maza, *Private Lives and Public Affairs*, chap. 4.

103   A. Dubuc, "Le 'Journal de Normandie' avant et durant les Etats Généraux," *Actes du 92ᵉ Congrès National des sociétés savantes: Section d'histoire moderne et contemporaine* (Paris, 1964), 391; *Affiches du Dauphiné*, November 9, 1787; François Lebrun, "Une source de l'histoire sociale: La presse provinciale à la fin de l'Ancien Régime: Les 'Affiches d'Angers' (1773–89)," *Le mouvement social* (1962): 59 (compare *DJ*, no. 7). For examples in 1787, see the *Affiches d'Artois* (*DJ*, no. 8), *Affiches du Dauphiné, Affiches de Toulouse*, and *Affiches de la Haute Normandie* on the Assembly of Notables; and the *Affiches du Beauvaisis* for provincial assemblies. For 1788, again by way of example, the *Affiches du Beauvaisis* was talking about the meeting of the Estates General, while the *Affiches d'Artois* gave the full text of local cahiers in early 1789.

104   *Affiches de Toulouse*, December 3, 1788.

By that time, the Affiches had become more straightforward in their attitudes toward political reporting, especially following the relaxation of censorship from late 1787. The Assembly of Notables in 1787 received a great deal of coverage, as did the operations of the new provincial assemblies. The Revolution of 1789 took things even further. Indeed, politics replaced material goods as the most fashionable of commodities offered in the newspapers: some 14 percent of the *Affiches de Toulouse* had been given over to politics in early 1789; by late 1789, it was up to 56 percent and was soon heading for 80 and 90 percent.[105] Such cases were fairly representative. Some newspapers failed to adapt – as the Estates General opened in May 1789, the *Journal du Hainaut* was running a story on the origin of Easter Eggs – and paid the price. But a great many Affiches revamped and prospered, while a good number of their editors made a career out of revolutionary journalism.[106]

Although the Affiches had an increasing role in reporting and commenting on political life from the late 1780s, perhaps their most important legacy to the French Revolution was more than biographical or institutional; it concerned a newly emergent politics of the body. To a certain degree, politics under the Old Regime had always been the politics of the body, but only the body of the king, emblematically and metaphorically inflated to cover the whole of the polity, had been at issue. As Séguier remarked in the extract at the beginning of this article, the chains of which the body of the state were made were under the personal control of the "sovereign administrator." In the late Enlightenment, however, conceptions of the body politic were being transformed. As Sarah Maza has elegantly demonstrated, the legal brief (*mémoire judiciaire*) for causes célèbres became both the site and the generator of a cultural politics grounded in melodramatic narratives and metaphorical transferences. The depiction of a bad father in a lawsuit could be read as a critique of the monarch/"father of his people."[107] What was true for the *mémoire judiciaire* was true for the far more anodyne and apparently conformist pages of the Affiches. The consumer of the Affiches, the decrypter of the small ad, was well used to such allegorical styles of reading. Furthermore, the master metaphors

105   M. Taillefer, "Les journaux toulousains au début de la Révolution, 1789–93," in *Les pratiques politiques en province à l'époque de la Révolution française* (Montpellier, 1988), 165.
106   Hugh Gough, "Continuité ou rupture? Les transformations structurelles de la presse provinciale, 1789–99," *Annales historiques de la Révolution française*, 273 (1988); Gough, "La transformation de la presse provinciale en 1789," in Rétat, *La révolution du journal*. See, too, *Journal du Hainaut* (*DJ*, no. 719).
107   Maza, *Private Lives and Public Affairs*. Compare Hunt, *Family Romance of the French Revolution*.

in which the Affiches had conceptualized their activities – the body social and the bourgeois body both requiring improved "circulation" and energy – lent themselves very well to the new political scripts in gestation. Just as bodily health (and the Affiches themselves) demanded a free flow, a regular circulation, so the body social required the removal of social forces obstructing that circulation.

The Affiches were, therefore, a site in which Enlightenment France recast its views on what politics was all about. Their stock-in-trade – the private, the domestic, the quotidian, the personal – may have been disdained by those before 1789 who regarded politics as located in courts and councils. Under the prism of the Affiches, however, courts and councils could be represented as removable blockages on the vivifying forces of commerce and exchange within the body social. The body of the state was being de-composed, before being re-composed as the body of the Nation. The latter was, moreover, a bourgeois body, for the Affiches had allowed readers to re-make the body of French society in their own, bourgeois, image. It emerged as altogether more amorphous, more decentered, more depersonalized than the absolutist body of the king. Rather than being controlled from the top, it was a self-activating (or perhaps interactive) vitalist organism. Choices were to be made not from the "head" but from within, in the interests of organic harmony.

By 1789, moreover, the nation – which had, as we have seen, been fashioned from the accumulation of civically minded consumers within a commercial society – was used to making choices. The Affiches could claim to embody as well as represent that "public opinion" whose importance recent historians have not been slow to emphasize. In the revolution, we might hypothesize, citizen-voters were presented with a series of political consumer choices and were called on to evaluate the quality and the utility of the political commodities offered. It thus seems possible to argue – against both a Habermas who underrates the forces of commercialism in *ancien régime* society and the most flagrantly "de-economizing" of the revisionist and post-revisionist analysts of the causes of the French Revolution – for the need to place the discourses of revolution in their social and economic context. The Affiches allow us to grasp something of the processes by which the post-1789 citizen had been fashioned in the marketplace constructed by the prerevolutionary world of print.

It is perhaps little wonder, therefore, that the languages of the body that the Affiches had helped to disseminate became so influential in political discourse after 1789. One could start, for example, with medical terms such as "regime" and "constitution," passing through "degeneration," "crisis," and "convulsions," and taking in attacks on a wide range of "charlatans," before we reached "purge" – the bottom line of Terror. Anti-monarchical sentiment would be fanned by the activities alleged to have taken place (or not) in the bedchambers of the king and queen. And, fittingly enough – to bring this article full circle – the infant "Louis XVII" would end up in prison in the mid-1790s clad in a herniary truss, required, it was said, because of the strenuousness of his alleged incestuous activities with his mother, Marie-Antoinette.[108] One way or another, the personal, which was the stock-in-trade of the prerevolutionary Affiches, would be the foundation of revolutionary politics and morality.

108   Maza, *Private Lives and Public Affairs*, esp. chap. 4; Lynn A. Hunt, "The Many Bodies of Marie-Antoinette: Political Pornography and the Problem of the Feminine in the French Revolution," in Hunt, ed., *Eroticism and the Body Politic* (Berkeley, Calif., 1992). For Louis XVII, see "Mémoire de blanchissage du linge et racomodage de Charles Capet . . . du 13 jour du 2e mois de la 2e année . . . : . . . 2 suspensoire . . . " (cited in M. A. de Beauchesne, *Louis XVII*, 2 vols. [Paris, 1853]).

6

Luxury, Morality, and Social Change: Why There Was No Middle-Class Consciousness in Pre-Revolutionary France

Sarah Maza

Originally appeared as Sarah Maza, "Luxury, Morality, and Social Change: Why There Was No Middle-Class Consciousness in Pre-Revolutionary France," *The Journal of Modern History* 69 (1997), pp. 199–229 (Chicago: University of Chicago Press).

Editor's Introduction

Like Colin Jones in the previously excerpted article, Sarah Maza addresses the old but until recently dormant question of whether a bourgeoisie or middle class(es) played a decisive role in the origins of the French Revolution. In contrast to Jones, however, Maza answers in the negative. She concedes that eighteenth-century France saw dramatic economic growth, an increasing standard of living, and indeed a "consumer revolution" that enriched merchants and provided a wide array of goods to a larger segment of the (moreover, growing) French population. She supports Jones's claim (from an article not excerpted in this volume) that France just before the Revolution was "characterized as much by circulation, mobility, and innovation" as by the stagnation that some anti-Marxist "revisionists" have seen throughout the country. Yet Maza argues that posing the question of a rising middle class "in conventional economic-determinist terms" can lead to anachronistic explanations of social change. Instead she calls for discourse analysis, an approach that we have seen Keith Baker advocate as a means of reconstructing contemporary perceptions.[1]

1   See chapter 2.

In particular, Maza claims that contemporaries, or at least the literate elite who have left records of their perceptions, "did not single out a middle class either as a problem or as a solution – indeed, they almost never identified such a class at all." She admits that many eighteenth-century French writers saw the condition and status of the nobility as a problem, but argues that anti-noble polemics did not entail the promotion of a middle class. In some cases the peasantry was lauded for its proximity to "nature," its supposed moral superiority and economic productivity, though it was possible to argue for a restoration of the nobility to its purportedly traditional activities of agricultural production and military service, or to call for its entry into "useful" commercial activities. It was also possible, as the writings examined in this article indicate, to omit class from the discussion and simply to divide society into such categories of people as useful and useless, productive and "sterile." Insofar as contemporaries used the term *bourgeois*, Maza argues, they referred either to the legal privileges of certain city-dwellers or to a kind of behavior (vulgar, selfish, grasping) rather than a class in the modern sense.

When imagining the problems their society faced, Maza maintains, French writers tended to focus on the alleged moral effects of commerce. While some Enlightenment thinkers praised commerce as a guarantor of civilization and happiness, the second half of the century saw a denunciation of trade and the selfish mentality it was thought to encourage. The key word in these polemics was *luxe*, a term that literally meant "luxury" but conjured images of socially disruptive moral decay. Yet the decay was not the fault of a single class; rather it stemmed from the "confusion of ranks and estate" that the availability of consumer products facilitated. The fear of social decomposition became all the more prevalent, Maza writes, when a series of mid-century crises destroyed the traditional belief that the king was "linchpin of society." Social critics feared that the French would go the way of England, the commercial nation *par excellence*, which in the early Enlightenment had served as a model of tolerance and liberty but following mid-century became an example of selfishness, factionalism, and revolution. Thus Maza's picture of eighteenth-century perceptions of economic life could not be more different from that of Jones, who reports a cheerful attitude toward capitalism among editors and readers of the provincial press.

Having described the problems of commercial growth as viewed by contemporaries, Maza proceeds to examine the proposed solutions. Implicitly ruled out was a class of people defined by its income level, since wealth, after all, was the *problem* that needed to be solved. Instead late eighteenth-century French writers emphasized *les moeurs*, which in this article is translated as "social morality." With the decline of traditional religion (among elite writers, at least), Maza observes a tendency among social commentators to replace the old religion with a secularized ethos. At the level of the family, *moeurs* were seen in filial piety, marital fidelity, love of parents for their children and affection of brothers and sisters for one another. At the more general level of the community, they expressed themselves in an *esprit social* or "sense of human kinship expressed in spontaneous acts of kindness and compassion." Finally, moralists envisaged this attitude extending to all of France, that is, to the *patrie* or Fatherland, which was not coincidentally described in familial language, and, by implication, to all of humankind. Maza sees the conflict between the ideal of *moeurs* and the facts of a divisive commercial society in the *drame bourgeois*, a theatrical genre in which virtue is tested by confrontations with the sordid reality of society, particularly the class divisions or "conditions" within it. *Moeurs* always triumphed at the end of the play, thus the playwrights and their audiences confirmed the power of human kindness to repair the damage that *luxe* and "conditions" had done to society.

Maza concludes with reflections on the specificity of the French experience, or at least its difference from that of England. Whereas the English happily recognized the competing interests and class division of their society and confided their fate to a moneyed and landed elite, she argues, the French saw interest and distinctions of class as harmful and "sought answers . . . in the moralistic universalism conveyed by concepts such as family, *moeurs*, or *patrie*." She attributes this difference to "long-term cultural trends particular to France," including a tradition of "contempt for trade," a "Catholic universalism" that removed morality from class status, and two factors that suggest a debt to Alexis de Tocqueville (1805–59).[2] The first of these is a hatred of "privilege," which Tocqueville explained as the consequence of the absolute monarchy's strategy of removing the nobles from government, thus leaving them only with apparently superfluous privileges. The second is the "leveling tradition within monarchical absolutism," which Tocqueville similarly associated with the monarchy's disenfranchisement of the nobility and saw as decisive in producing the egalitarian ideology of the revolutionaries. Although she does not explicitly make these "particular features of French sociopolitical culture" responsible for the Revolution, Maza does suggest that the tendency to imagine the polity or state in terms of a social unit, i.e. the family, had revolutionary consequences. These consequences, moreover, were not limited to the Revolution itself, but extended into the nineteenth century, when family and *moeurs*-based discourses competed with new, post-revolutionary ideologies based on class.

2 See chapters 1 and 2 for discussions of Tocqueville.

Luxury, Morality, and Social Change: Why There Was No Middle-Class Consciousness in Pre-Revolutionary France

Sarah Maza

Was there a rising middle class in eighteenth-century France, and did it contribute decisively to the upheaval that began in 1789? Right now that question is murkier than ever for having been mostly abandoned in recent years. In the past two decades in the historiography of pre-revolutionary France the spotlight has moved away from social issues; while excellent monographs dealing with society continue to appear each year, the central debate on the causes and nature of the French Revolution has focused lately on political life.[1] Amid the flurry of pathbreaking recent publications on political culture, print culture, and political ideologies, of debates on gender, sexuality, and the public and private spheres, we seem to have lost sight of the old question of the middle class.

How important, dynamic, and central to society and to historical change were the urban professional and commercial middle classes in eighteenth-century France? "Very," argued the now defunct orthodox interpretation, which in the Marxist tradition viewed the Revolution as the result of early capitalist development; "Not at all," answered the revisionists in the 1970s and 1980s, pointing to the lack of significant social and economic change in France prior to 1789. In recent years assessments of France's pre-revolutionary development have become, if anything, more confusing. There are in fact two revisionist positions. One anti-Marxist argument sees the eighteenth-century French economy as, on balance, stagnant and traditionalist.[2] Other revisionists

---

1 Some of the landmark contributions to these trends include Mona Ozouf, *La fête révolutionnaire, 1789–1799* (Paris, 1976); François Furet, *Penser la Révolution française* (Paris, 1978); Lynn Hunt, *Politics, Culture and Class in the French Revolution* (Berkeley and Los Angeles, 1984), and *The Family Romance of the French Revolution* (Berkeley and Los Angeles, 1992); Joan Landes, *Women and the Public Sphere in the Age of the French Revolution* (Ithaca, N.Y., 1988); Keith Baker, *Inventing the French Revolution* (Cambridge, 1990); and Keith Baker, ed., *The French Revolution and the Creation of Modern Political Culture*, 3 vols. (Oxford, 1987–94).
2 See William Doyle's influential syntheses, *Origins of the French Revolution* (Oxford, 1980), esp. pp. 30–4, and *The Oxford History of the French Revolution*

acknowledge expansion, modernization, and social mobility but maintain that these changes happened in the absence of significant social antagonism: with a booming economy in the hands of liberal nobles and their non-noble associates, France had no need for social or economic upheaval.[3] Further complicating the picture is an important recent article by the neo-Marxist Colin Jones in which he aptly points out that a whole array of recent work in the field has produced evidence of considerable socioeconomic dynamism and change before the Revolution: the figures lined up by economic historians and the evidence unearthed by historians of consumption all point to steady economic growth, commercial expansion, and what can only be called a consumer revolution. Is it not time, Jones asks, to return to some version of the idea of a "bourgeois revolution"?[4]

None of this work has brought about any real consensus on the matter of social change in general and the status of the middle class(es) in particular. The reason for this is, I would argue, that historians continue to address this question in conventional economic-determinist terms: questions about social values and social change are still considered subordinate to the "hard evidence" about prices, trade, or industrial concentration. That evidence is, however, particularly ambiguous. By all accounts, in the century before the Revolution all sectors of the French economy showed a pattern of slow, steady, cumulative growth (with the exception of overseas trade, which grew much faster). At the same time the country's deep structures remained unchanged – there was no rapid urbanization, no dramatic concentration of the industrial sector. As a result, historians have been able to see the glass as either half-empty or half-full. Some have pointed to all the signs of growing wealth and commerce in order to assert the presence of a dynamic middle class, while others have highlighted the equally solid evidence of socioeconomic traditionalism in order to argue the reverse.

The solution I will propose for this deadlock is to bring current developments in historical method to bear on the question of the middle class. In recent years postmodern theory and practice have led us to question many of the categories we take for granted in organizing our identities

(Oxford, 1989), esp. chaps. 1 and 17; or see the well-documented synthesis by T. C. W. Blanning, *The French Revolution: Aristocrats versus Bourgeois* (Atlantic Highlands, N.J., 1987).

3   Simon Schama, e.g. forcefully argues the revisionist thesis that the Revolution was the unfortunate result of a series of political contingencies, while stressing the dynamism of the Old Regime, particularly in the area of "capitalist" enterprise; see *Citizens: A Chronicle of the French Revolution* (New York, 1989), pp. 183–99.

4   Colin Jones, "Bourgeois Revolution Revivified: 1789 and Social Change," in *Rewriting the French Revolution*, ed. Colin Lucas (Oxford, 1991), pp. 69–118.

and experiences – gender, sexuality, race, ethnicity, and nationhood – and to explore the ways in which these are socially constructed. It has taken longer for historians (or anyone else) to attack social class with the solvent of postmodernism, however – no doubt because it was easier, in coming to terms with the "social" construction of gender or nationhood, to continue to take that "social" for granted.

In the field of modern British history, where issues of class have traditionally taken pride of place, creative challenges to the "given-ness" of "class" and "society" have begun to appear in recent years. Gareth Stedman Jones blazed the trail in the seventies and eighties with his essays on the languages of class, and more recently Patrick Joyce has become the most eloquent advocate of the position that class should be approached as "an imagined form, not something given in a 'real' world beyond this form."[5]

The middle class is the prime candidate for this sort of shake-up, since it is the most obviously artificial among familiar social groupings. Unlike both aristocracies, whose existence usually rests on a combination of legal distinctions and kinship patterns, and rural and urban working classes, which are united by common forms and objects of labor, the middle class exists by definition only in relation to other social groups. Dror Wahrman has most clearly articulated this methodological point in his recent work on the "invention" of the British middle class between 1790 and 1830. "It is my contention," he writes, "that the existence of a 'middle class' in a fairly complex society lies primarily in the eye of the beholder. . . . The 'middle class' can be seen or not seen depending on the scheme one chooses to employ, and this choice is highly political, carrying political implications at any given juncture."[6]

Most societies have harbored groups we would call "middle class," although the boundaries of such groupings are usually subject to dispute. The importance of "middle class–ness" is certainly related to

5   Gareth Stedman Jones, *Languages of Class: Studies in English Working-Class History, 1832–1932* (Cambridge, 1983); Patrick Joyce, *Democratic Subjects: The Self and the Social in Nineteenth-Century England* (Cambridge, 1994), quote on p. 1. See also Patrick Joyce's *Visions of the People: Industrial England and the Question of Class, 1840–1914* (Cambridge, 1991). William Reddy has also argued that the concept of class is currently in crisis and should be rethought, although his conclusions are different from Joyce's; see his *Money and Liberty in Modern Europe: A Critique of Historical Understanding* (Cambridge, 1987), esp. chap. 1, and "The Concept of Class" in *Social Orders and Social Classes in Europe since 1500: Studies in Social Stratification*, ed. Michael Bush (London, 1992), pp. 13–25.

6   Dror Wahrman, "Virtual Representation: Parliamentary Reporting and Languages of Class in the 1790s," *Past and Present*, no. 136 (August 1992), p. 111, and *Imagining the Middle Class: The Political Representation of Class in Britain, c. 1780–1840* (Cambridge, 1996).

such objective factors as industrialization, urbanization, and overall wealth; but I want to argue here that a decisive factor in determining the presence and role of a middle class is the discourse about it – whether and how it is named and invested with social, political, moral, or historical importance.

To ask whether the idea of a "rising middle class" existed in the discourse of the pre-revolutionary educated elites amounts to asking several distinct but related questions: Did contemporaries discern a unified social "middle" in their society, as opposed to a constellation of different groups we might call middling? Or did they entertain the notion of a distinct upper-middle-class non-noble elite, similar to the English gentry or the post-revolutionary *notables*? If they did discern one or the other group, did they consider it to be central to society as it then existed, or to the nation's future? This article answers these questions mostly in the negative and offers an analysis of the ways in which the educated elites did perceive both society and social change. For the sake of clarity, I will use the term "middle class(es)" rather than "bourgeoisie" to refer to the group I discuss: in Old Regime France the term "bourgeoisie" had a precise set of meanings that I will discuss below.

I hope it is already clear that my focus on linguistic and cultural categories should not be read as dismissive of the abundant evidence we possess on social experience in eighteenth-century France. Like many historians today, I believe that social experience and consciousness are mutually constitutive, that the concrete aspects of experience both shape and are shaped by the language through which they are apprehended; I choose to concentrate here on discourse because, unlike the facts of social and economic life, it has so far been neglected in the controversy about the existence and importance of the pre-revolutionary middle class(es).

I will argue here that French writers of the later eighteenth century, in describing their society and its problems did not single out a middle class either as a problem or as a solution – indeed, they almost never identified such a class at all. My sources are the published works of French writers of all persuasions, ranging from the very well known (Diderot, d'Holbach, Turgot) to the utterly obscure. These writings cover three sorts of issues: descriptions and analyses of society in general; commentaries on perceived economic and social change; and discussions of positive social norms and values, such as marital and family life. I have read as many texts as possible in order to discover the commonplaces and banalities, the ideas and themes that recurred insistently in eighteenth-century discussions of society. I am not claiming that the idiom of educated writers represents the only possible discourse on social class at the time: the poor and barely literate no doubt had different views of the social world than did the writers featured here. Nonetheless, what follows represents, I believe, a description of the views common among educated and articulate French people in the second half of the eighteenth century.

In most contexts descriptions of the social order are a matter of dispute, and this was especially true of eighteenth-century France, where it would have been hard to find two people who agreed on what their society looked like, either in theory or in practice. Any number of people, however, would have agreed on what it did not look like – namely, the official three orders of clergy, nobility, and Third Estate, a tripartite division that was blithely dismissed or ignored in most discussions of what society was really about. When a meeting of the Estates-General was announced in 1788 for the first time in nearly two centuries, the division of deputies into those three orders provoked such a rush of definition, redefinition, and general outrage that it is hardly an exaggeration to say that the irrelevance of those categories was an immediate cause of the French Revolution.

There is no surer symptom of the bankruptcy of the official ordering of society than the mounting criticism in the eighteenth century directed at the nobility's traditional functions and prerogatives. Such criticism was not new, of course; in the sixteenth and seventeenth centuries there were plenty of non-noble writers like the jurist Charles Loyseau ready to denounce the old nobility as fatuous *traisneurs d'épée* (sword draggers).[7] The cultural climate of the eighteenth century was, however, increasingly and irrevocably hostile to a group identity based on bloodlines, martial prowess, court culture, and legal privilege. The clearest language of class in eighteenth-century France was anti-noble: philosophers, including those of noble descent, denigrated the nobility's uselessness and vanity; historians and legal scholars chronicled the origins of what they called "feudalism" in medieval land grants that became breeding grounds for violence and tyranny; lawyers portrayed aristocrats as bullies, cheats, and sexual predators in printed trial briefs that reached many thousands of readers.[8] The most telling sign of how well this sort of criticism hit its mark is that nobles themselves, or at least some of the most prominent and articulate among

7   George Huppert, *Les Bourgeois Gentilhommes: An Essay on the Definition of Elites in Renaissance France* (Chicago, 1977), p. 11 and passim.
8   Henri Carré, *La noblesse de France et l'opinion publique au XVIIIe siècle* (Paris, 1920); J. Q. C. Mackrell, *The Attack on "Feudalism" in Eighteenth-Century France* (London, 1973); Sarah Maza, *Private Lives and Public Affairs: The Causes Célèbres of Prerevolutionary France* (Berkeley and Los Angeles, 1993); Patrice Higonnet, *Class, Ideology and the Rights of Nobles during the French Revolution* (Oxford, 1981).

them, rushed to redefine the nature and functions of their order. In the second half of the century especially, propagandists for the nobility insisted that the raison d'être of their class was not race and honor but "capacity," "merit," and "virtue" -- even if these were sometimes inherited.[9]

Since the nineteenth century, the strong antinoble bias that appeared everywhere from legal scholarship to street doggerel in pre-revolutionary France has been interpreted as evidence of middle-class consciousness – as if the only possible obverse of nobility were mid-dlingness. It has been considerably harder, however, to locate the other side of the coin, to find in pre-revolutionary culture explicit endorse-ments or even mere acknowledgments of a middle class (or classes) as a central feature of society.

In the middle of the eighteenth century two main idioms for describ-ing society prevailed among intellectuals, each in a different way build-ing a bridge between ancient and newer sets of beliefs. Many writers still clung to the traditional division of the social world into a hierarchy of multiple "estates." By the 1750s, however, few commentators professed to believe in the intrinsic, hereditary superiority of the higher orders; the argument that was inevitably made, following Montesquieu, had to do with the connection between a society of orders and France's "mod-erate" monarchical constitution. The gentle slope of multiple social "degrees" guaranteed sociopolitical stability, it was maintained, by con-necting the monarch to the full range of his subjects.[10] Alongside this updating of the language of orders, the burgeoning science of political economy was already producing different sorts of classifications based not on history and social dignity but on productivity. These, however, usually wound up glorifying the most traditional groups in society, landowners and agricultural workers.

The conflict between these two visions was played out in the course of the famous debate initiated in 1756 by the Abbé Gabriel Coyer with the publication of his pamphlet *La noblesse commerçante*.[11] Coyer's provocatively utilitarian argument for allowing French nobles to engage in commerce like their English counterparts (the law of *dérogeance* forbade them most forms of trade) prompted a number of heated responses, the most famous of which was penned by an aristocratic officer, the chevalier d'Arcq. In *La noblesse militaire*, d'Arcq seized upon

9   Guy Chaussinand-Nogaret, *La noblesse au XVIIIe siècle: De la féodalité aux lumières* (Paris, 1976), chaps. 1, 2.
10   Elie Carcassonne, *Montesquieu et le problème de la constitution française au XVIIIe siècle* (Paris, 1927; Geneva, 1970), chap. 5.
11   Abbé Gabriel Coyer, *La noblesse commerçante* (Paris, 1756). For an overview of the debate between Coyer and his adversaries, see Chaussinand-Nogaret, chap. 5.

the political implications of Coyer's suggestion, reminding his readers of the demonstrable link between commerce and republicanism – were Holland and England not proof of this?[12]

The debate prompted d'Arcq to restate the official tripartite ordering of society, although he subdivided each order in two so as to bring the ancient divisions more up to date: upper and lower clergy, upper and lower nobility, bourgeoisie and populace. Each of these orders pursued its designated function, and he insisted that any proposal to shift functions between classes would threaten the whole carefully balanced edifice.[13] Since a monarchical state was dependent on the existence of a long chain of mediated connections between the monarch and each of his subjects, any confusion of ranks could bring down the whole card-castle of society, causing the monarchy to dissolve into either "despotism" or "republicanism."

D'Arcq's polemic and the publicity around the debate pushed Coyer into a more aggressive stance. In his response, he drew upon history to point out that the hallowed three orders had not always been there: the Franks knew only a single class, the Gauls were their serfs, and it took centuries for the orders to emerge. If things had changed in the past, they certainly could do so in the present and future.[14] Coyer argued vigorously against social inequality and bluntly described the nation as divided into two classes, producers and parasites: the first was made up of all the working and commercial classes, the second of "the regular and secular clergy, the military, men of law and finance, rentiers, lackeys, beggars, wastrels, and *grands seigneurs*."[15]

Each of the two most prominent participants in the debate laid claim to one of the social idioms, d'Arcq waving the banner of a "monarchical" ordered society, Coyer proudly wearing the colors of political economy and productivity. But other participants in the controversy could invoke both languages within the same text. This happens in one of the most interesting contributions to the Coyer debate, a piece by a woman named Octavie Guichard, dame Belot, entitled *Observations sur la noblesse et le tiers-état*.[16]

---

12   Philippe Auguste de Sainte-Foy, chevalier d'Arcq, *La noblesse militaire ou le patriote françois* (Amsterdam, 1756), pp. 7–13.
13   Ibid., pp. 16–19.
14   Abbé Gabriel Coyer, *Développement et défense du système de la noblesse commerçante* (Paris, 1758), pp. 47–8.
15   Ibid., p. 20.
16   Octavie Guichard, dame Belot, *Observations sur la noblesse et le tiers-état* (Amsterdam, 1758).

Belot follows d'Arcq in arguing against noble commerce on the grounds that this will create too wide a gulf in society, leaving "no middling estate [*état mitoyen*] between the artisan and the nobleman, an interval hitherto filled by commerce."[17] Belot also echoes d'Arcq's political concerns, explaining in a striking passage that Coyer's proposal would make "the throne too steep" and the ruler appear as "a colossus" by removing the nobility that "step by step levels, in the eyes of the weak, the steep incline which exists between the sovereign and his subjects."[18] In many respects, then, Belot's view of society is quite traditional: she sees middling estates as necessary not because they are inherently better than the upper or lower estates but because mediation and gradualism are indispensable to the stability of an ordered monarchical society.

At the same time, the author declares her opposition to hereditary nobility and offers the model she would adopt if she were planning a state "as metaphysically as did Plato." At the top of society would be agriculturalists, its strongest and most useful members; second would come warriors, who deserve support on account of their sacrifices for the nation; and in last place would be those who engage in commerce and craft – they are the least deserving, as they face neither hard labor nor danger and give their fellow men neither sweat nor blood.[19] Belot thus moved back and forth between a defense of the traditional sociopolitical order and a model of a pastoral and warlike utopia.

Even when eighteenth-century writers based their social analyses on concepts of labor and productivity, they rarely came up with orderings of society that prefigured the advent of a recognizable modern class system. The best examples of this can be found in the writings of the physiocrats and their followers. Physiocracy was the school of economic thought that developed in France around the middle of the eighteenth century, defining itself in opposition to traditional mercantilist economic theories. Where mercantilism encouraged the production and foreign sale of luxury goods, the physiocrats built their systems around the primacy of agriculture and population as the source of all riches and campaigned for the freedom of domestic markets from internal tariffs and guild regulations.

In the work that is sometimes considered the founding text of physiocracy, *L'ami des hommes* (1756), the Marquis de Mirabeau sketched out a mostly traditional hierarchy of occupations in the state. The monarch

17   Ibid., p. 13.
18   Ibid., pp. 104–5.
19   Ibid., pp. 30–40.

is aided by the three *ordres consultans*: the clergy, the military, and the magistrates. These are "the absolute essence of the constitution of the political edifice" and are followed by all those occupations whose function is to assist and adorn them: sciences, the fine arts, and the liberal and mechanical arts.[20] Agriculture, however, occupies a special, preeminent, almost suprasocial place: "Agriculture is in a word the universal art, the art of innocence and virtue, the art of all men and all ranks." And commerce is but its complement, "not a separate estate but only the brother of agriculture."[21] As Elizabeth Fox-Genovese points out, the founders of physiocracy faced a dilemma: their faith in the laws of economics led them to repudiate an ordering of society based on transcendent principles, yet they feared the void thus created and the dangerously dissolvent effects of the very freedom of trade they advocated. Singing the praises of agriculture was a way of trying to recreate community by valorizing a pursuit that in their eyes was closest to nature and transcended social divisions – especially since this had the practical result of leaving the traditional upper classes (landed proprietors) safely at the helm.[22]

There was virtually no room for an urban middle class in the social schemes, whether analytical or prescriptive, drawn up by the physiocrats and their many followers. Theirs was an ideology obsessed with "production," by which they meant agrarian and demographic fertility. The closer one stood, by work or ownership, to the bountiful earth, the higher one's spiritual and social ranking. The social class that was idealized in the eighteenth century was the peasantry – never any of the urban middling groups. In his *Réflexions sur la formation et la distribution des richesses* of 1766, for instance, the economist and statesman Turgot described the principal fault line in society as that dividing "salaried" workers, who earn only enough to live on and create neither employment nor surplus wealth, from "productive" workers – that is, rural *laboureurs* – who produce as much as the earth will yield, thereby generating excess wealth for their society. Historical evolution results in the most deserving rural "producers" increasing the size of their property, with the result that society is now divided into three classes: productive (rural) workers, salaried artisans (also called the "sterile" class), and a class of (rural) proprietors whose wealth frees them to engage in other occupations useful to society such as warfare or the administration of

20   Victor de Riquetti, marquis de Mirabeau, *L'ami des hommes ou traité de la population*, 4 vols. (Avignon, 1756; reprint, Aalen, 1970), 1:141.
21   Ibid., 1:142.
22   Elizabeth Fox-Genovese, *The Origins of Physiocracy: Economic Revolution and Social Order in Eighteenth-Century France* (Ithaca, N.Y., 1976), pp. 210–20.

justice.[23] Some fifteen years later an author inspired by the physiocrats, Charles de Butré, came up with a very similar classification. Society, he wrote, falls "naturally" into three classes: a productive class of agricultural entrepreneurs, a class of rural property owners whose position allows them to "improve" the land, and a "sterile" class of salaried workers. Butré calls these the "natural laws" of the social order.[24]

Eighteenth-century writers came up with a variety of schemes for describing the society they lived in or the one they wished to inhabit. But one classification they never proposed was the one that seems commonsensical to the average inhabitant of the twentieth century: a division into upper, middle, and lower classes determined mostly on the basis of wealth and income.[25] This was unlikely to occur to a denizen of eighteenth-century France because wealth alone could not be imagined as a basis for explaining society, let alone running it; everyone knew that the effects of money were disjunctive rather than conjunctive, and a community would need some other principle to give it meaning.

Visions of society in the later eighteenth century coalesced around two competing principles: there were those who began to understand "society" as an autonomous concept, on the one hand, and those who clung to the belief that the (ordered) form of French society was inseparable from the political principle of a tempered monarchy, on the other. The latter continued to produce updated visions of France as a constellation of vertically ordered estates binding each subject to the sovereign and through him to God: in such a scheme the important social groups were at the top of the ladder, not in the middle.

23 Anne-Robert Turgot, *Oeuvres de Turgot et documents le concernant*, ed. Gustave Schelle, 5 vols. (Paris, 1913–23), 2:536–42.
24 Charles de Butré, *Loix naturelles de l'agriculture et de l'ordre social* (Neuchâtel, 1781), pp. 89–97.
25 A conspicuous exception among well-known social commentaries of the period is the description of the city of Montpellier in 1768 by an anonymous observer, the subject of a widely read essay by Robert Darnton ("Etat et description de la ville de Montpellier, fait en 1768," in *Montpellier en 1768 et 1836 d'après deux manuscrits inédits*, ed. Joseph Berthelé [Montpellier, 1909], pp. 9–174), in his *The Great Cat Massacre and Other Episodes in French Cultural History* (New York, 1984, pp. 107–43. The manuscript's author certainly extols the "second" or "bourgeois" estate, made up of businessmen, merchants, professionals, and rentiers as "the most useful, the most important, and the wealthiest" (p. 67). But Montpellier, as the chronicler himself indicates, was unusual in its strong commercial vocation and in the small number of noble families it harbored – the "bourgeoisie" celebrated in this text is the oligarchy of an ancient trading center. Furthermore, Darnton's analysis of the "Description" does not suggest an unproblematic "bourgeois" point of view but stresses in the end the confusion of sociological idioms running through this complex account (pp. 139–40).

As Daniel Gordon has shown, the idea that "society" rather than the afterlife was the framework for human existence, and hence that social life could be independent from the polity, was one that grew steadily in importance and influence in the writings of the philosophes and their followers. But Gordon also demonstrates how closely linked the idea of *société* remained to aristocratic, or at least elitist, ideals of *sociabilité*. The French Enlightenment's nascent concept of society was equally indebted to universalistic natural law theories and to the aristocratic culture of *politesse*.[26] Intellectuals influenced by physiocracy were among those who first understood and discussed "society" as an autonomous entity; but because they wanted to root society in "nature" they most often looked to the rural world of the landed gentry and the peasantry as a source of meaning and community. Neither in the older language of monarchy and orders nor in the newer one of nature and productivity did middling urban groups take on any special meaning or importance.

The reason why all attempts to locate and describe a middle class or (in the modern sense) bourgeoisie in eighteenth-century France have failed is that such efforts always amount to forcing nineteenth- and twentieth-century categories onto a society that would not have recognized them.[27] It is high time for us to stop trying to squeeze eighteenth-century French society into the procrustean bed of modern sociology.

It could be objected, however, that Old Regime France did include a prominent urban group called the bourgeoisie, that the term "bourgeois" was widely used to describe certain types of behavior and culture, and that this is where one might reasonably expect to find the core of an eighteenth-century middle class. As every textbook on Old Regime society explains, "bourgeois" was a title distinguishing a member of a legally privileged, non-noble urban upper class; it was an appellation first granted in the eleventh and twelfth centuries by the Capetian kings to the free men dwelling in new towns.[28] Over time, the status of "bour-

26   Daniel Gordon, *Citizens without Sovereignty: Equality and Sociability in French Thought, 1670–1789* (Princeton, N.J., 1994), introduction and chap. 2.

27   For a typical example of this, see Elinor Barber, *The Bourgeoisie in Eighteenth-Century France* (Princeton, N.J., 1973), which explicity relies on twentieth-century sociology to define an eighteenth-century group. Barber arbitrarily draws the lower line of the bourgeoisie just above those who worked with their hands (which excludes master artisans, whom their workers called *le bourgeois*) and the upper limit just short of the robe nobility. She acknowledges but then ignores the association of *bourgeoisie* with idleness, and the class she defines, principally "business and the professions," reflects a nineteenth- or twentieth-century view of which occupational groups were/are central to the "middle class": see esp. pp. 15–20.

28   See Régine Pernoud, *Histoire de la bourgeoisie en France*, 2 vols. (Paris, 1960–62), vol. 1. chaps. 1–3; Adhémar de Cardevaque, "Essai sur la bourgeoisie

geois" developed into a variable set of obligations and privileges. In earlier times, when the category was more socially mixed and the bourgeois were still masters of their towns, it meant heavy local fiscal and military obligations such as contributing to the upkeep of town walls and serving in the militia.[29] With the consolidation of the royal state and the divide-and-rule impulses of the French kings, the category "bourgeois" became more clearly a matter of privilege with respect to royal taxes.

By the eighteenth century, while the precise rights and responsibilities of legally defined bourgeois varied significantly from place to place, the status had become strongly associated with an expectation of de jure or de facto idleness. In Paris, different statutes regulating the title of *bourgeois de Paris* forbade persons of that status to work with their hands, to sell anything but fruit from their properties, and to do anything "derogating" from their status of bourgeois – strictures that were very similar to those imposed on nobles. In return the bourgeois of Paris enjoyed an array of fiscal and honorific privileges – not as many as nobles, but identical ones in kind.[30] In short, the legally defined bourgeoisie of Paris looked very much like a lesser version of the nobility. In Paris, the legal title of "bourgeois" was hereditary; in a provincial town like Chartres it was not, but it usually sanctioned the sort of financial success that meant one could live off one's income without working and thus become, to use the confusing terminology of the tax rolls, a *bourgeois vivant noblement*, a bourgeois living nobly.[31] Thus, although the legally defined bourgeoisie was an intermediate group, modern historians in quest of the middle class have been loath to consider it on its own, routinely saddling it with commercial and professional affiliations: the *bourgeoisie d'ancien régime*, a privileged group abolished under the Revolution, defies our association of middlingness with purposeful professional activity.

It is true that the noun "bourgeois," and especially the adjective, were frequently used in a looser way to describe a certain kind of person or

d'Arras avant la Révolution de 1789," *Mémoire de l'Académie des Sciences, Lettres et Arts d'Arras*, IIe série (1888), pp. 195–225; Joseph di Corcia, "Bourg, Bourgeois, Bourgeois de Paris from the Eleventh to the Eighteenth Century," *Journal of Modern History* 50 (June 1978): 207–331.

29   Pernoud, vol. 1, chaps. 2, 3; di Corcia, pp. 213–19; E. Ducéré, "La Bourgeoisie Bayonnaise sous l'ancien régime (moeurs, usages et costumes)," *Bulletin de la Société des Arts Lettres et Sciences de Pau* 18 (1888–89): 87–255.

30   Di Corcia, pp. 224–31.

31   Michel Vovelle and Daniel Roche, "Bourgeois, Rentiers, Propriétaires: Eléments pour la définition d'une catégorie sociale à la fin du XVIIIe siècle," *Actes du 77e Congrès des Sociétés Savantes* 84 (1959): 419–52.

style involving prosperity with connotations of stodginess. The casual use of the word "bourgeois" to designate well-to-do townspeople (it occurs repeatedly, e.g., in Sébastien Mercier's *Tableau de Paris*) is the closest we will get in eighteenth-century French culture to a recognition of something like a modern middle class. Eighteenth-century dictionaries, however, reveal that "bourgeois" was an odd term. From the late seventeenth century to the 1790s, standard French dictionaries all gave variations of the same set of definitions (they copied one another liberally). The first definition was the etymological one of "town dweller" (in the examples, always a *gros bourgeois* or a *riche bourgeois*), followed sometimes by an indication that the word was used to designate all members of the Third Estate, those in society who enjoyed no privileges. As the 1704 edition of the Trévoux dictionary put it: "One says in this sense, so-and-so is a gentleman, while this other person is only *bourgeois*. Such a woman is a lady; this other one only a simple *bourgeoise*."[32]

Two definitions are at the heart of the entry "bourgeois" in all of the dictionaries. First, "bourgeois" or "bourgeoise" is what workers call the person they work for (the example was always about cheating or not cheating the bourgeois). Second (although the order was sometimes reversed), "bourgeois" is the term that courtiers and other worldly types use to designate someone who is socially uncouth: "not polite enough, too familiar, not respectful enough" was how the Richelet dictionary put it. "It is said in a derogatory way in opposition to a man of the court to mean a man with little gallantry or wit, who lives and reasons in the manner of the lowly populace" was Antoine Furetière's version in 1690; and the hallowed dictionary of the Académie Française suggested (and went on doing so into the 1830s) that one could crush a man with contempt by describing his manners, conversation, or general demeanor as bourgeois.[33]

It will come as no surprise to anyone who has tried to define the word, or to locate its social referent, that in the eighteenth century "bourgeois" was an extremely slippery term: it meant that you were *not* something (a gentleman, a lady, a worker, a courtier), that you failed to behave in certain ways. It was a term defined by absence and negation. And as a social archetype, the bourgeois drew an inordinate amount of hostility. Most people are familiar with the type's most famous literary incarnation, Molière's Monsieur Jourdain, the draper's son who takes crash

32 *Dictionnaire Universel François et Latin*, 2 vols. (Trévoux, 1704), vol. 1; and the very similar article "Bourgeois" in Antoine Furetière, *Dictionnaire Universel*, 3 vols. (Paris, 1690; reprint, Paris, 1978), vol. 1.
33 César Pierre Richelet, *Dictionnaire François*, 2 vols. (Geneva, 1680; reprint, Geneva, 1970); Furetière; *Dictionnaire Universel François et Latin*; and the 1694, 1765, 1798, and 1835 editions of the *Dictionnaire de l'Académie Française*.

courses in minuet dancing; *Le bourgeois gentilhomme* is but the best known of dozens of plays and novels written under the Old Regime that lampooned the bourgeois as social climber.[34] It is usually assumed that Monsieur Jourdain gets his comeuppance because, although his family is moving upward in the accepted way, he is breaking the rules by trying to go too fast.

Although this is no doubt true, there are surely other reasons for the hostility so often evinced by the word "bourgeois" throughout the Old Regime – reasons reflected, I would suggest, in the odd dictionary definitions of the bourgeois as a creature always apprehended from above or from below. The acknowledged function of bourgeoisie in the society of Old Regime France was that of a sort of holding category: it was where you parked your family for a couple of generations before, ideally, moving into the aristocracy. We are so used to associating the concept of bourgeoisie or middle class with stability and conservatism that it may be hard to apprehend just how unstable the term, and the social experience it suggested, really were: the bourgeois was, above all, a social mutant. The writer Marivaux put his finger on this when he wrote in 1717: "The bourgeois of Paris, Madame, is a mixed animal, who takes after the great lord and the people. When he has a grandeur in his manners he is always an ape; when he is petty he is natural: thus he is noble by imitation, and plebeian by character."[35] These are exactly the words used repeatedly in the eighteenth century to denigrate domestic servants, another socially ambiguous and much reviled group.[36]

The concept of bourgeoisie in this society was fraught with problems. The group of people officially designated as bourgeois were in effect a non-noble aristocracy; by definition they belonged to a world of corporate particularism and privilege that was becoming increasingly controversial. (Montesquieu wrote in *The Spirit of the Laws*: "If you abolish the prerogatives of the lords, clergy, nobility, and towns in a monarchy, you will soon have a popular state or else a despotic state."[37] The Old Regime bourgeois were the incarnation of the towns' "prerogative.") At a time when even nobles were devising arguments for the social usefulness of their class, a group such as the bourgeoisie defined by law or

---

34   Jean Alter, *Les origines de la satire antibourgeoise en France*, 2 vols. (Geneva, 1970), 2:78–81.
35   Pierre Carlet de Marivaux, *Journaux et oeuvres diverses* (Paris, 1969), p. 14.
36   See Mary Douglas, *Purity and Danger: An Analysis of Concepts of Pollution and Taboo* (London, 1966); Victor Turner, *The Ritual Process: Structure and Anti-Structure* (Ithaca, N.Y., 1969); Sarah Maza, *Servants and Masters in Eighteenth-Century France: The Uses of Loyalty* (Princeton, N.J., 1983), chap. 3.
37   Charles de Secondat, baron Montesquieu, *The Spirit of the Laws*, trans. and ed. Anne Cohler, Basia Miller, and Harold Stone (Cambridge, 1989), p. 18.

convention as both privileged and "nobly" idle was unlikely to elicit much admiration.

Yet even in its broader senses the notion of bourgeoisie was problematic, since it seems to have retained strong connotations of ambiguity and instability. To be bourgeois was to be in transit, uncomfortable about your social identity, with workers muttering against you and noblemen sneering at your manners. The writings of most social commentators in the later eighteenth century strongly suggest a perception that society was in crisis and that new sources of order and cohesion had to be sought. For that project, the bourgeoisie in either its narrow or wider senses would have been a most unlikely place to start.

I have argued that social observers and commentators in the later eighteenth century, while acknowledging the existence of what we would call the urban middle classes, did not view such groups as unified, important, or especially praiseworthy. To those who clung to updated versions of a social "chain of being," commercial, industrial, and professional groups were just some of the many rungs in the long ladder between king and pauper. As for those who held more "modern" views, physiocrats and others interested in political economy, they invariably sang the praises of agriculture. Writers who called for change in society typically believed that the nobility, the traditional elite, should take on new roles. Coyer and his partisans thought that nobles should be allowed to make commercial fortunes, while the physiocrats wanted them to take the lead in improving the land. Commoners still wanted to become nobles, and nobles now wanted to become useful; nobody thought, or at least nobody wrote, that the torch of leadership should be passed to a new social class.

This is all the more surprising in light of the fact that the society and economy of France changed significantly in the eighteenth century and that those changes were especially conspicuous in the decades after 1750. The consensus among economic historians nowadays is that French economic growth in the eighteenth century was remarkable. The country's foreign trade quintupled during that period, and its share of European (but not American) markets grew faster than England's. Economists Don Leet and John Shaw have calculated that France saw a sevenfold increase in its industrial output over the course of the century.[38] Historians still quarrel over whether or not there was an

---

38   Early and important contributions to this argument were Jan Marczewski, "The Take-Off and French Experience," in *The Economics of Take-Off into Sustained Growth*, ed. Walt Rostow (New York, 1963); and François Crouzet, "Angleterre et France au XVIIIe Siècle: Essai d'Analyse Comparée de deux croissances

"agrarian revolution" in eighteenth-century France, but unquestionably some striking improvement occurred: famines abated in the century before the Revolution, and the population grew from 20 to 27 million.[39] Recent work by social historians also shows us that eighteenth-century France was a society on the move. To begin with, many more people lived in towns. Although the urban population only grew between 16 and 19 percent in the sixty years before the Revolution, given the overall demographic surge this meant an increase of 1.5 million. Most large towns saw their populations swell – on average by close to 48 percent – chiefly as a result of immigration.[40] And a succession of distinguished studies have demonstrated that France became, in the age of Enlightenment, a much more commercial society. Jean-Claude Perrot's classic study of Caen, for instance, shows the Norman town transformed from a local textile center to a hub for national and international commerce, its population growing with an influx of immigrants after 1740, increasing numbers of whom found jobs in the expanding service sector.[41]

Even areas of rural France were affected, we now know, by increased commercialism. Jonathan Dewald's remarkable study of the seigneury of Pont-Saint-Pierre over four centuries allows us to follow in one rural area the concentration of property, the monetarization of village

économiques," *Annales: Économies, sociétés, civilisations* 21 (1966): 254–91, translated in *The Causes of the Industrial Revolution*, ed. R. M. Hartwell (London, 1967). In the 1970s and 1980s a new generation of economic historians of France built the evidence of eighteenth-century growth into a revisionist argument: France's pace and pattern of industrial growth in the eighteenth and nineteenth centuries should not be seen as a failure to follow the English model but as an entirely different, and perhaps less socially traumatic, form of transition to a modern economy. Salient works in this vein include Richard Roehl, "French Industrialization: A Reconsideration," *Explorations in Economic History* 13 (1978): 233–81; Patrick O'Brien and Caglar Keyder, *Economic Growth in Britain and France, 1780–1914: Two Paths to the Twentieth Century* (London, 1978); Don Leet and John Shaw, "French Economic Stagnation, 1700–1960: Old Economic History Revisited," *Journal of Interdisciplinary History* 8 (Winter 1978): 531–44; Rondo Cameron and Charles E. Freedman, "French Economic Growth: A Radical Revision," *Social Science History* 7 (Winter 1983): 3–30; Nicholas Crafts, "Economic Growth in France and Britain, 1830–1910: A Review of the Evidence," *Journal of Economic History* 44 (March 1984): 49–67; and Robert Aldrich, "Late Comer or Early Starter? New Views on French Economic History," *Journal of European Economic History* 16 (1987): 89–100.
39   Leet and Shaw, pp. 536–7; Cameron and Freedman, pp. 16–17; François Crouzet, *De la supériorité de l'Angleterre sur la France: L'économique et l'imaginaire, XVIIe–XVIIIe siècles* (Paris, 1985).
40   Georges Duby et al., *Histoire de la France urbaine*, 4 vols. (Paris, 1981), 3:295–8.
41   Jean-Claude Perrot, *Genèse d'une ville moderne: Caen au XVIIIe siècle*, 2 vols. (Paris, 1975).

economies, the expansion of rural markets, and the rise, by the eighteenth century, of what the author calls "rural capitalism."[42] Nobody would deny that many areas of France remained isolated and tradition bound; but there is on balance increasing reason to accept Colin Jones's description of France at the end of the Old Regime as "a society characterized as much by circulation, mobility, and innovation as by . . . traditionalism, subsistence farming and cultural stagnation."[43]

If this was the case, how did contemporaries perceive and react to these changes? How did large-scale, abstract developments like "urbanization" and "commercialization" translate into lived experience for, say, the inhabitants of eighteenth-century French towns? One answer to that question is becoming increasingly clear: at least for town dwellers living above subsistence level, the century brought profound changes in the material world and in people's relationships to objects, the result of what can only be called a consumer revolution. Thanks to the pioneering work of Daniel Roche, Cissie Fairchilds, and Annick Pardailhé-Galabrun on after-death inventories, and of Colin Jones on local advertising, we are beginning to understand how the eighteenth-century surge in commercial activity and overall wealth made a difference to the daily lives of people of all stations.[44]

In Paris the interior of even modest dwellings began to change in the early decades of the century. Apartments were larger, and because

---

42 Jonathan Dewald, *Pont-Saint-Pierre, 1398–1789: Lordship, Community, and Capitalism in Early Modern France* (Berkeley and Los Angeles, 1987).

43 Colin Jones, "Bourgeois Revolution Revivified" (n. 4 above), p. 87.

44 Daniel Roche, *The People of Paris: An Essay on Popular Culture in the Eighteenth Century*, trans. Marie Evans and Gwynne Lewis (Berkeley and Los Angeles, 1987), and *The Culture of Clothing: Dress and Fashion in the Ancien Régime*, trans. Jean Birrell (Cambridge, 1994); Cissie Fairchilds, "The Production and Marketing of Populuxe Goods in Eighteenth-Century Paris," in *Consumption and the World of Goods*, ed. John Brewer and Roy Porter (London, 1993), pp. 228–48; Annick Pardailhé-Galabrun, *La naissance de l'intime: 3000 foyers parisiens, XVIIe–XVIIIe siècles* (Paris, 1988); Colin Jones, "The Great Chain of Buying: Medical Advertisement, the Bourgeois Public Sphere, and the Origins of the French Revolution," *American Historical Review* 101 (February 1996): 13–40. Colin Jones's article makes another case for putting the bourgeoisie back into the center of pre-revolutionary history on the basis of abundant evidence of commercialism in the local advertising newspapers known as *affiches*; this piece appeared too late for me to integrate it centrally into my argument here. Jones's image of an inclusive, horizontal "chain of buying," which he sees as a concrete instance of Jürgen Habermas's bourgeois public sphere, is richly suggestive, as is the abundant empirical evidence he presents. But I remain unconvinced that the *affiches* tell us anything decisive about the existence of a middle class. Jones's argument about the consumers of the *affiches* is circular: those who engaged in this form of buying and selling are presumed bourgeois (see pp. 18–19, 24); therefore, these newspapers document the existence of a bourgeois public sphere.

smaller and more numerous fireplaces were built into them families occupied different rooms instead of crowding around one enormous hearth in the common *salle*.[45] Brightly colored or patterned wallpapers and fabrics began to replace heavy drab tapestries on the walls. Mirrors, clocks, paintings, and statuettes, once a mark of significant wealth, became widespread, as did a range of utilitarian objects such as umbrellas, fans, snuffboxes, watches, and books. More and more families ate from matching sets of decorated earthenware instead of tin or pewter plates.[46]

The most conspicuous changes occurred in the volatile and symbolically charged area of clothing. The value of wardrobes in the Parisian working population multiplied over the course of the century: for women of the upper working classes it increased six-fold, for domestics four-fold, for professionals and their wives three- or four-fold.[47] As with furnishings, garments became more varied and cheerful: cotton and silk supplemented wool and broadcloth; bright colors and pastels gained ground; stripes, checks, and patterns proliferated.[48] Everyone above the poorest level of society owned more clothes, women especially (it was in the eighteenth century that fashion became decisively associated with femininity). The function of clothing evolved over the course of the century: where garments had once primarily marked a person's status, they became increasingly (for women especially) a sign of taste and fashion.[49] All of these changes provoked criticism of lower-class sartorial hubris and complaints that it was becoming difficult to tell a person's rank from her or his clothing.

For all but the very poor, then, the material world changed dramatically in French towns from the 1730s to the eve of the Revolution, as more and more people in the middling and lower ranks of society had access to garments and furnishings once available only to the elites. As Colin Jones has pointed out, the evidence unearthed by recent studies of commercialism and consumerism seems to be bringing us back to the discarded paradigm of the "rise of the middle class." If commerce was on the rise, towns were growing, and the country's increasing wealth allowed middling and poorer groups access to consumer goods, does this not necessarily mean that France was becoming more middle class? The

---

45 Pardailhé-Galabrun, chap. 6; Roche, *The People of Paris*, chap. 4.
46 Pardailhé-Galabrun, pp. 306–14, 368–429; Roche, *The People of Paris*, pp. 141–53; Fairchilds, pp. 228–48.
47 Roche, *The People of Paris*, chap. 6, and *The Culture of Clothing*, pp. 108–16.
48 Roche, *The Culture of Clothing*, pp. 134–45, and *The People of Paris*, pp. 167–75.
49 Jennifer Jones, "The Taste for Fashion and Frivolity: Gender, Clothing, and the Commercial Culture of the Old Regime" (Ph.D. diss., Princeton University, 1991), and "Repackaging Rousseau: Femininity and Fashion in Old Regime France," *French Historical Studies* 18 (Fall 1994): 939–67.

major problem with such a conclusion lies in the realm of consciousness: while the occasional text in praise of roturiers can be dug up, nowhere in the culture of pre-Revolutionary France can one find a substantial, conspicuous body of literature arguing for the separate merits, rights, or historical identity of a middle class or bourgeoisie.[50] Social observers certainly noted the country's marked increase in wealth and the effect it was having on behavior and identities, in towns especially. There does exist a large corpus of works commenting on, and mostly bemoaning, the drastic changes rocking this society, but in these works neither the problem nor the proposed solutions to it had anything to do with the middle classes.

In the later eighteenth century, many educated French men and women shared the views expressed by Turgot in 1775 when he wrote to Louis XVI of his sense that society was falling apart: "This is a society composed of a variety of ill-connected orders, a people whose members have very few social bonds with one another, where as a result each man looks only to his particular and exclusive interest, and almost no one is at pains to fulfill his duties or recognize his links to others."[51] In general, the concept used to describe this sense of social dissolution was the old, multifaceted notion of luxury. What John Sekora says of eighteenth-century England appears to have been true of France as well – that "luxury probably was the greatest single social issue and the greatest commonplace."[52] Luxury, as commentators have pointed out, was a singularly protean concept. In eighteenth-century France it brought together such different concerns as the state of Christian values, worries about aristocratic profligacy, the effects of commerce and consumerism on society, and the condition of the countryside; in sum, it was a convenient code for all of society's perceived problems.[53]

Concerns about luxury can be traced back to the beginnings of recorded Western history. From Genesis via Plato to Augustine and the church fathers, right into the early nineteenth century, this "chameleon of a concept" adapted to many cultural environments while retaining

50 The few texts that appear to do so, such as [Abbé] Jaubert, *Éloge de la roture dédié aux roturiers* (London, 1766), are remarkable precisely because they are unusual; and Jaubert defines *roture* in the traditional sense of Third Estate – all commoners, regardless of status or income.
51 Anne-Robert Turgot, "Mémoire sur les municipalités" (1775), in *Oeuvres de Turgot et documents le concernant* (n. 23 above), 4:576.
52 John Sekora, *Luxury: The Concept in Western Thought, Eden to Smollett* (Baltimore, 1977), p. 74.
53 Keith Baker, *Condorcet: From Natural Philosophy to Social Mathematics* (Chicago, 1975), p. 19.

its primary dual connotations: greed for the superfluous, and social chaos.[54] Periodically, in certain times and places, "luxury" became a focus of intense concern and comment, and France in the last two-thirds of the eighteenth century was one of the last and most acute instances of this. The resurgence of the theme in France starting in the 1730s is often labeled the "debate on luxury," but that is something of a misnomer. Defenses of luxury, spin-offs of Newtonian optimism, were few and penned mostly in the 1730s and 1740s: they include primarily Voltaire's famous paean to luxury in *Le mondain*; the writings of France's leading Mandevillian, Jean-François Melon; and some passages in Montesquieu. Condemnations of luxury are more typical of the second half of the century, especially the years after 1770, and they are far more numerous than defenses.[55] (It is no accident, of course, that the rebirth of polemics about luxury from the 1730s on coincided with the beginnings of France's commercial boom and consumer revolution.)

Jeremiads against luxury in the second half of the eighteenth century were so numerous and formulaic that their themes are well known to most students of the period. *Le luxe* was described as an active agent of destruction, cascading down the social scale from the princes and grandees to the lowest orders. Its concrete manifestations were seen as social anarchy and usurpation – the lower and middling orders were adopting the manners, trappings, and especially the clothing of the elites, thereby perilously confusing the social landscape. Such tirades always called up the same characterization of luxury as *mollesse* – flaccidity, enervation, impotence. *Le luxe* caused sterility in different ways, either directly, by tempting urban dwellers into hedonistic singlehood (contraceptive practices were hinted at), or indirectly, by drawing country folk into towns where unmarried lackeys crowded the antechambers of the rich while the good earth they had left lay untended. Luxury thus caused or threatened depopulation, food scarcity, social confusion, physical impotence, and moral rot.

If it is easy to enumerate the themes of this literature, nailing down its meanings is a far more difficult matter. That the fear of "luxury" signaled aversion to change is obvious; in premodern Europe "luxury" was one of the few ideological tools available for making sense of change in a world where stasis was considered normal and desirable.[56] Because

---

54 Sekora, pp. 1–47.

55 Ellen Ross, "The Debate on Luxury in Eighteenth-Century France: A Study in the Language of Opposition to Change" (Ph.D. diss., University of Chicago, 1975); Harvey Chisick, *The Limits of Reform: Attitudes towards the Education of the Lower Classes in Eighteenth-Century France* (Princeton, N.J., 1981), chap. 4; Pierre Rétat, "Luxe," *Dix-Huitième Siècle* 26 (1994): 79–88.

56 Sekora, p. 68.

they included so much criticism of growing wealth and consumerism, denunciations of luxury in eighteenth-century France have sometimes been interpreted as an aristocratic, conservative reaction to the rise of new commercial money, along the lines of what was happening in England at the time.[57]

That is certainly the impression one gets from some of the contributions to this literature, such as the strident *Lettres critiques sur le luxe* published in 1771 by a man named François Béliard, who singles out the bourgeoisie for rebuke. The bourgeois, writes the author, are now as given to "magnificence" as great lords; worse still are their "impertinent" wives, who insist on having their own carriages and lackeys, smear their faces with powder and rouge, and talk down to everyone. Merchants, he continues, have gotten swollen heads from writings in praise of their occupation and now consider themselves society's most useful members, when in fact they traffic in useless frivolities that create artificial needs.[58]

The author, however, identifies himself as born and raised in the bourgeoisie (which is why, he says, he can be critical), and, furthermore, he asserts that he is a follower of Rousseau.[59] Unquestionably, Rousseau's fulminations against the culture of his time did much to inspire and shape the arguments against luxury of the second half of the eighteenth century. Other contributors to the literature on luxury from the 1750s on included many of the leading physiocrats, such as the Marquis de Mirabeau and the Abbé Baudeau, the Encyclopedists, and some of the more radical philosophes like d'Holbach and Helvétius. Keeping in mind the fact that denunciations of *le luxe* continued to draw on traditional Christian motifs, one can only conclude that this ubiquitous theme transcended both social and ideological divisions. That, indeed, was its power.

The essence of *le luxe* was the confusion of rank and estate, a theme that lies at the heart of every discussion of the problem. Luxury was, one could say, the negative image of the Great Chain of Being: if social harmony lay in a precise gradation of ranks, then, conversely, moral rot would spread through the social fabric "by degrees" as each class sought to emulate and displace the one above it. Normally, the force that guaranteed both hierarchy and cohesion was the monarch; in traditional

57   This is the main line of interpretation in Renato Galliani, *Rousseau, le luxe et l'idéologie nobiliaire*, Studies on Voltaire and the Eighteenth Century, no. 268 (Oxford, 1989), esp. chap. 6. For England, see Sekora, chap. 2.

58   François Béliard, *Lettres critiques sur le luxe et les moeurs de ce siècle* (Amsterdam, 1771), pp. 18, 25–9, 60–1, 101–2.

59   Ibid., pp. xxi–xxii, and see pp. 47 ff., his stated admiration for Rousseau and long digression in praise of maternal breast-feeding; Ross, p. 137.

absolutist theory it was the royal will that balanced the interests of different members of the body politic. The king acted as mediator between disparate interests so that, as Keith Baker puts it, "Frenchmen related to one another indirectly, as subjects of the crown."[60]

In the middle and late decades of the century, the monarch's position as linchpin of society and his credibility as ultimate arbiter were undermined by an array of political and ideological developments. The misfortunes of the Seven Years' War, the destabilizing effects of conflicts around Jansenism and the Enlightenment, recurrent grain shortages, and above all, the crown's protracted power struggle with its own courts of high justice, the Parlements, all contributed to what historians have called the "desacralization" of the French monarchy.[61] Panic and outrage about *le luxe* reflected, I believe, the combined effects of these developments and the unprecedented access of segments of the population to wealth and consumer goods. Many French people felt dangerously adrift in a world devoid of both its traditional sacred center and of recognizable markers of social rank. The result, as reflected in the voluminous literature of luxury, was an acute sense of moral void and social dissolution.[62]

Increased wealth and consumerism – central components of what is usually described as the rise of the middle class – were perceived as the core of the problem, and therefore could be no part of any solution. Social critics professed horror at the thought of what money was doing to human relationships: "Money will level all ranks, wash away all stains on birth, money will erase all crimes, money will stand in for talents, virtues, and services, and everything, including love, will be for sale," was how Antoine Polier de Saint-Germain imagined the near future, with the rich increasingly proud and hard-hearted and the poor increasingly servile.[63] In contemporary England, moreover, French writers saw mostly an illustration of the dangers of wealth and venality; they regarded the English constitution, with its balancing of interests and parties, as a source of factionalism and violence.[64]

60   Baker, *Condorcet*, pp. 203–4.
61   Dale Van Kley, *The Damiens Affair and the Unraveling of the Ancien Régime, 1750–1770* (Princeton, N.J., 1984); Jeffrey Merrick, *The Desacralization of the French Monarchy in the Eighteenth Century* (Baton Rouge, La., 1990); Arlette Farge and Jacques Revel, *The Vanishing Children of Paris: Rumor and Politics before the French Revolution*, trans. Claudia Mieville (Cambridge, Mass., 1991).
62   Chisick, pp. 185–205.
63   Antoine Polier de Saint-Germain, *Du gouvernement des moeurs* (Lausanne, 1784), p. 58; see also Béliard, p. 113.
64   Keith Baker, "Politics and Public Opinion under the Old Regime," in *Press and Politics in Prerevolutionary France*, ed. Jack Censer and Jeremy Popkin (Berkeley and Los Angeles, 1987), pp. 208–13. See also Baker, *Inventing the French Revolution* (n. 1 above), chap. 8.

While writers of the early Enlightenment, most famously Voltaire and Montesquieu, looked to England as a model, by the second half of the century anglophobia was more common than anglophilia among French intellectuals.[65] The example of England was naturally invoked during the debate on nobility and commerce in the 1750s, and it was not infrequently dismissed. Albion was financially the prey of trading companies and mercenary soldiers, politically torn apart by factions and parties: there, wrote Octavie Belot, were the effects of commerce.[66] The use of England as a negative model was not limited to intellectual elites: in Caen in the 1770s and 1780s college teachers had their students write essays deploring the corruption of "merchant nations" such as England and Holland or the moral decline of "anglicized" (i.e., commercialized) French towns.[67]

Money, wrote d'Holbach in his *Système social* (1773), was what corrupted the English political (and by implication social) system. Arguing against Montesquieu's anglophilia, d'Holbach dismissed the idea that English representative government should be admired for balancing the interests of different segments of society. "Interest" was precisely the problem: the Peers would always throw in their lot with the monarchy against the people, and the Commons were dependent on securing through bribes the votes of an indigent populace.[68] "What felicity, what security can there be," he wrote, "for a people who can at any moment be thrust into useless wars by the scheming, the disorder, the sordid self-interest of a few rapacious merchants? . . . Peoples of Albion . . . hear the true cause of your fears and afflictions: never did the love of gold make for good citizens."[69] Self-interest, commercial values, and class-based politics as practiced in England appeared clearly to breed all manner of corruption and strife – why else were the English so prone to revolution and regicide?

England, which Voltaire had extolled in the 1730s as a land of religious and social tolerance and healthy business activity, became in the second half of the century a negative model for many writers. One can only speculate about the causes of the shift from predominant

---

65   Frances Acomb, *Anglophobia in France, 1763–1789: An Essay in the History of Constitutionalism and Nationalism* (Durham, N.C., 1950). See also Josephine Grieder, *Anglomania in France, 1740–1789: Fact, Fiction, and Political Discourse* (Geneva, 1985).
66   Belot (n. 16 above), pp. 86–7.
67   Perrot (n. 41 above), 1:298–9.
68   Paul Henri Thiry, baron d'Holbach, *Système social ou principes naturels de la morale et de la politique*, 3 vols. (London, 1773), 2:67–70 (hereafter cited as *Système social*).
69   Ibid., 2:72–4.

anglophilia to anglophobia, but the waning of classic Parlementaire ideology in the tradition of Montesquieu and the devastating effects of the Seven Years' War on the national psyche would undoubtedly rank among the main causes. England presented to many French writers the image of a country run on the principle of division and competition; at a time when French social commentators perceived their country as threatened by all manner of centrifugal forces, English "freedom" looked more like a threat than a promise. In the last decades of the eighteenth century, writers ranging from luminaries to obscure scribblers obsessively promoted ideals of deep social unity. Under the rubric of what they called *les moeurs*, they proposed a system of social morality that negated class difference and sought to bring the French together in a moral community called *patrie*, which was itself a sentimental family writ large.

Like *le luxe*, the concept of *les moeurs* (which I translate as "social morality") is easier to describe than to explain.[70] The theme of *moeurs* was even more ubiquitous than that of *luxe*, and to the student of eighteenth-century French culture evokes the set of images that accompanied it with dreadful predictability – nursing mothers, venerable fathers, chaste peasant girls, agrarian utopias, and swooning families in the manner of Greuze. *Moeurs* could be described as a virtuous predisposition that in any given individual would be manifest in three guises: as family love, as a more generalized *esprit social* or sense of human kinship expressed in spontaneous acts of kindness and compassion, and at the most abstract level as the selfless community spirit known as *patriotisme*.

Clearly, this system of social morality was intended as a substitute for religion. D'Holbach wrote that the problem began with the state's relinquishing morality to the church, which, given the (implied) failure of the latter, had resulted in an immoral society and polity (hence, luxury).[71] The cult of *les moeurs* was an attempt to promote new forms of spiritual fulfillment in one's sense of connectedness to a community of fellow human beings. The family occupied a towering place in this ideological system. As the natural incarnation of a feeling rooted in nature, it was both the origin of one's moral sensibility and a model for

---

70   *Moeurs* is conventionally translated either as "morals" or as "manners." In his translation of Rousseau's "Letter to d'Alembert," Allan Bloom opts for the awkward solution of translating the French term as "morals [manners]" (Jean-Jacques Rousseau, *Politics and the Arts: Letter to M. d'Alembert on the Theater*, trans. Allan Bloom [Ithaca, N.Y., 1960]). Some translators use either English term depending on context, but to my mind this betrays a central feature of the French meaning, which is precisely the overlapping of inner and outer norms of behavior.
71   D'Holbach, *Système social*, 3:87–9.

all other social connections. The passage on this subject in Gabriel Bonnot de Mably's popular *Entretiens de Phocion sur le rapport de la morale avec la politique* (1763) is a typical example: "It is in the bosom of their families that loving and prudent fathers offered the first model for the laws of society. . . . It is only through the practice of domestic virtues that a people prepares itself for the practice of public virtues. . . . Domestic morality determines, in the end, public morality."[72] D'Holbach, like many others, explained why this should be the case: "Any political society is but an assemblage of particular societies; many families make up that bigger one called the *Nation*."[73]

A society in which *les moeurs* were heeded would be one in which each person would have for any other human being the same (presumably positive) feelings naturally harbored toward family members. This was the assumption behind the vogue for "humanity" and sentimental benevolence characteristic of the period from the 1760s through the 1780s. In those decades, periodicals like the *Journal encyclopédique* began retailing anecdotes about acts of compassion and loyalty, prompting readers to send in money in aid of the virtuous but impoverished. Such stories were equally successful when gathered and sold in anthologies with titles like *Tableau de l'humanité* or *Annales de la bienfaisance*.[74] The ubiquitous celebration of country life in the last decades of the Old Regime sprang from the fanciful assumption that remote villages and farms were places where such natural feelings of human community survived.

Political considerations were deeply embedded in this promotion of social morality. D'Holbach put it most pointedly in his *Système social* when he contrasted this *esprit social* with the *esprit de corps*, the division of society into corporate interests promoted by despotic governments. Tyranny, he explained elsewhere, thrives on the division of the population into separate groups, although he argued, against Montesquieu, that monarchies as well as republics could be based on virtue.[75] The political manifestation of "social spirit" was what eighteenth-century writers called *patriotisme*, devotion to the community on the highest and most abstract level. *Patrie* was the third tip of a triangle whose other two points were family and humanity.

As Harvey Chisick suggest, eighteenth-century "patriotism" should not be confused with later forms of nationalism. Patriotism was not

---

72 Gabriel Bonnot de Mably, *Entretiens de Phocion sur le rapport de la morale avec la politique* (Amsterdam, 1763), p. 45.
73 D'Holbach, *Système social*, p. 137.
74 Chisick (n. 55 above), pp. 225–36.
75 D'Holbach, *Système social*, p. 156, and *Ethocratie ou le gouvernement fondé sur la morale* (Amsterdam, 1776), pp. 7, 12–13 (hereafter cited as *Ethocratie*).

exclusive but universalist. It was described as a commitment that transcended a narrow love of country; the opposite of patriotism was not cosmopolitanism but selfishness.[76] James Rutlidge, an Anglo-Irish expatriate, described "patriotism" as "a virtue which leads us to find our own happiness in that of every member of the community." He saw patriotism as directly linked to a happy family life, for it was doubtful that a man without the capacity to cherish those closest to him could feel love and devotion for that more remote entity, his *patrie*.[77]

Family, humanity, and *patrie* were thus closely overlapping categories in the discourse of social morality of the late eighteenth century. The classification most obviously missing from this discussion is that of rank or class. Everyone deplored selfish corporate interests, and while some writers mentioned in passing that good *moeurs* would mean a happy and harmonious acceptance of the social hierarchy, the more radical critics, like Helvétius and d'Holbach, argued that gross inequalities of wealth were a breeding ground for moral corruption and that a certain leveling of fortunes would speed up the promotion of morality.[78] What is most remarkable, however, about the discourse of *moeurs* is the way in which it ignores distinctions of social class; the triumph of social morality would not so much overcome social divisions as make them irrelevant. The ideal promoted in these ideological commonplaces is one of emotional fusion and bonding, the submersion of social divisions in the warm milk of family feeling.

Eighteenth-century France went through social and economic changes that were, to many observers, alarming and incomprehensible and yet widely understood as irreversible: there could be no going back to an antiquated corporate social world. New wealth and new social divisions were deeply troubling to eighteenth-century observers, who could not yet imagine, as did their nineteenth-century descendants, a resolution through the dynamics of historical change. Instead, a culture that worshipped "nature" promoted the most "natural" human arrangement, the family, as the panacea for society's ills.

---

76 Chisick, pp. 215–25.

77 James Rutlidge, *Essai sur le caractère et les moeurs des françois comparés à celles des anglois* (London, 1776), pp. 182–4. The work was originally published in English as *An Account of the Character and Manners of the French* (London, 1770).

78 Polier ([n. 63 above], p. 26) writes that in a society governed by *moeurs*, "chacun s'y tiendroit naturellement à sa place"; Jaubert ([n. 50 above], p. 45) says that in such a society "la subordination, loin de paroitre gênante, fait naître l'admiration et le respect." Compare with d'Holbach's argument about great inequalities of wealth not being conducive to "patriotic" feeling, in *Ethocratie*, pp. 117–20; and Claude-Adrien Helvétius's suggestions about leveling wealth in *De l'homme: De l'esprit et de L'homme*, ed. Albert Keim (Paris, 1909), pp. 235–43.

The idealization of family relations (as opposed to family lineage) in the culture of the later eighteenth century has usually been interpreted as a glorification of a "bourgeois" or middle-class ethos, and indeed one can find in this culture plenty of portrayals of domestic bliss among people of "mediocre" condition. The association of middlingness and domestic happiness is, however, purely accidental (why should the middle of society care more about family life than either end?) yet so common both then and now that it has come to seem inevitable. A final look at the literary genre most commonly associated with the middle class in eighteenth-century France, the so-called *drame bourgeois*, will offer an illustration of the proposition that representations of family in this culture were not a vehicle of class consciousness but a substitute for it.

The *drame* has a precise birthdate, 1757, when Diderot published a dialogue that was a critical commentary on his new play, *Le fils naturel* (The illegitimate son). The themes of the *Entretiens sur le fils naturel* are well known to students of eighteenth-century literature: Diderot announced the need for a new genre situated between existing tragedy and comedy, one that would put onstage the experiences of ordinary people rather than kings and heroes and would show them in everyday settings, wearing ordinary clothes and speaking prose instead of spewing alexandrine verse. In style these new plays were to be expressive, even histrionic: Diderot stressed the importance of gestures such as weeping or falling to one's knees, which he called "pantomime" and which he valued more highly than vocal utterances. The subjects of these dramas would reverse the traditional primacy of character on the French stage. Instead of Molièresque plots revolving around an embodiment of pride, greed, or misanthropy, Diderot wanted a drama propelled by the tensions between different "conditions," by which he meant both social conditions (involving persons of different status and occupation) and family relations.[79]

Diderot's prescriptions for the contemporary stage included a call to "create domestic and bourgeois tragedy,"[80] and since the nineteenth century the genre he helped popularize has often been called *drame bourgeois* (although contemporaries most often referred to it as *genre sérieux* or simply *drame*). In this light it may seem odd that Diderot's two major plays in this genre, *Le fils naturel* (1757) and *Le père de famille* (1758), are set in what seems to be a very upper-class milieu and that the pro-

---

79   Denis Diderot, *Paradoxe sur le comédien précédé des entretiens sur le fils naturel* (Paris, 1967), see the discussion of "conditions," pp. 96–7 (hereafter cited as *Paradoxe*).
80   Ibid., p. 109.

tagonists, who do not appear to work for a living, bear "aristocratic" stage names like Dorval, Clairville, Saint-Albin, and Germeuil. And this was not the case only for Diderot. Social characterizations in what was perhaps the most successful play in this genre, Sedaine's *Le philosophe sans le savoir* (1765), further illustrate the ambiguity of the *drame*'s social allegiances.

The hero of the play is a wealthy merchant, Monsieur Vanderck, who apparently embodies the dignity and usefulness of his occupation. It turns out, however, that he was born a nobleman but took on, out of gratitude, the name and business of his late adoptive father, a Dutchman. In the course of a scene in which Vanderck lectures his son about the merits of trade, he mentions that he knows only two occupations he values more highly: that of the magistrate and that of the warrior – the traditional noble callings.[81] The play ends, after the requisite crises, with the marriage of Vanderck's daughter to a young noble of the robe in the presence of the Vandercks' new friends, a baron and his son. This is not to say that the *drame* was pro-noble; in good middle-of-the-road enlightened fashion these plays engaged in plenty of debunking of aristocratic vanities and abuses. And a later, more radical practitioner of the genre, Sébastien Mercier, featured a wide spectrum of social types among his protagonists, including the very poor. Questions of wealth and status do loom large in many plots, and quite a few feature celebratory portrayals of merchants and professionals. But on the whole their story lines and characters hardly support the traditional claim that these plays were written primarily for and about the "middle class."

What all of them do share is the cult of family: just about all of their plots include the portrayal of a highly emotional, expressive love between parents and children, brothers and sisters. (Such is the power of the association between family love and the social middle that this is no doubt the main reason why these dramas were tagged "bourgeois.") This celebration of family bonds often reaches a climax in the very last scene of the play, with the disclosure of previously unknown kinship between some of the characters. Obviously, the resolution of a crisis by the revelation of a foundling or lost child's true identity is not unique to this genre or even to this century. What is notable is how often this device is used in the *drame* to resolve tensions created by social differences.

The crisis in Diderot's *Le père de famille* is triggered by the infatuation of young Saint-Albin with a poor woman named Sophie – a love his good father tries gently to talk him out of, and his authoritarian uncle, the

---

81   Michel-Jean Sedaine, "Le philosophe sans le savoir," in *Four French Comedies of the Eighteenth Century*, ed. Casimir Zdanowicz (New York, 1933), p. 279.

Commandeur (the bad father figure) attempts to forbid by force. All is resolved with the discovery that Sophie is the Commandeur's niece and Saint-Albin's cousin, and the play ends with the double betrothal of Saint-Albin to Sophie and of his sister Cécile to Germeuil, a young man raised in the household as their "brother"; in the last scene the good father blesses the merging of the four quasi-siblings into a family.

Mercier's most famous *drames* offer variations on this sort of plot. *Le juge* is about the dilemma of a highly moral judge whose conscience tells him to rule in a dispute over land in favor of a poor peasant family and against the local count who has been his protector and surrogate father. Although the furious count at first threatens to ruin the judge, he is ultimately moved, at the sight of the pathetic peasant family and of the judge with his delightful wife and daughter, to reveal that the magistrate is in fact his son from an early and clandestine marriage. The dispute over land involving three social strata thus vanishes when the count acknowledges and joins his real family.

As a final example we can take Mercier's *L'indigent*, in which a family of destitute spinners, old Rémi and his children, Charlotte and Joseph, inhabit a basement in the house of a callous young nobleman named De Lys. A crisis is provoked by De Lys's attempt to seduce Charlotte, first with money and then by proposing marriage. It turns out that Charlotte is not Rémi's daughter after all, but De Lys's lost sister whom he had been trying to disinherit. Charlotte is now a wealthy noblewoman, but she chooses to marry her ex-brother, Joseph, whom she has always loved. De Lys is promptly sucked into the family love between Charlotte, Joseph, and Rémi and has time before the curtain falls to realize that familial embraces are better than any other kind. Typically, what strikes the modern reader as an alarmingly incestuous triangle (Charlotte's eroticized relationship with both of her "brothers") is presented by Mercier as an ideal, moving instance of the deepest human connections.

What distinguishes the *drame* from, say, classical tragedy is that the crises at the heart of these plays are brought on by disparities of status, wealth, power, and prejudice. This was probably what Diderot had in mind when he argued that "conditions" should form "the basis of the plots and morals of our plays."[82] As Julie Hayes has suggested, what these plays illustrate above all is the proposition that human beings are social creatures, involved for better or worse in a network of human connections. "The good man lives in society; only the evil live alone," says a character in *Le fils naturel*, and many of these plays illustrate the point.[83] The Commandeur, De Lys, the count in *Le juge* – all are wealthy,

82 Diderot, *Paradoxe*, p. 96.
83 Julie Hayes, "A Theater of Situations: Representation of the Self in the Bourgeois Drama of La Chaussée and Diderot," in *The Many Forms of Drama*, ed. Karelisa

isolated, and unhappy, saved (in most cases) by the news that they have an authentic human connection in their new families.

These dramas are almost never performed today, because modern spectators would find their hyperbolic sentimentalism – the weeping, collapsing, exclaiming, and pontificating – at best comic, and more likely, tedious and embarrassing. But critics have recently been drawing attention to the *sensible* style as a collection of signs that, like the plots of these plays, served to convey the message that "virtuous" feelings of compassion can and should transcend and negate differences of social status. If, as most educated people believed, identity was built on a succession of individual sensations and experiences, how could this serve as a basis for building a human community? The language of sensibility, David Denby argues, was a system of signs aimed at connecting individual sensation and collective existence by making inner experience visible and insisting on its universal character.[84]

This is why gesture (in its theatrical guise, pantomime) was even more important to Diderot and his successors than verbal language: the deepest emotions were ineffable and could only be "spoken" by the body.[85] A famous passage in Diderot's *Entretiens* illustrates the way in which the verbal and bodily languages of sensibility act as a solvent for class differences. It concerns a peasant woman whom the narrator happens upon just as she has discovered the body of her husband, murdered by a kinsman. The haggard woman has dropped to the ground by the corpse; she is clutching her husband's feet and sobbing that she never thought those feet would lead him to his death. Diderot comments that the same situation would have drawn the same words and "pathetic" gestures from a woman of any social rank: "What the artist must find is what anyone would say in a situation like this, what no one will hear without recognizing it in himself."[86]

The *drame* is emblematic of social attitudes among the educated public of pre-revolutionary France. These plays promoted the ideal of a community that transcended social divisions, for which the metaphor of choice was the family. The *drame*'s dual, almost paradoxical, outlook is very much that of its time. Playwrights like Diderot and Mercier broke with classical theater through their assertion that the drama of human

---

Hartigan (Lanham, Md., 1985), pp. 69–77; Denis Diderot, *Le fils naturel ou les épreuves de la vertu* (Amsterdam, 1757; reprint, Bordeaux, 1965), p. 97. In *La religieuse*, Denis Diderot makes similar statements to the effect that isolation from society of the sort practiced in convents and monasteries leads to evil and misery ([Paris, 1968], pp. 153–4).

84   David Denby, *Sentimental Narrative and the Social Order in France, 1760–1820* (Cambridge, 1994), esp. pp. 21–47.

85   Ibid., pp. 83–4.

86   Diderot, *Paradoxe*, p. 47.

existence is not governed by transcendent forces but by day-to-day confrontations in the social world, the world of "conditions." But that social world was alarmingly devoid of coherence and a prey to the raw forces of money and power: the *drame* dealt with this potential threat by offering the family as the solution to dangerous social tensions.

The argument proposed in this article highlights, I believe, some of the particular features of French sociopolitical culture, features that have been obscured in the past by the imposition of Anglo-American or Marxian categories upon a cultural landscape they do not really fit. I have sought to describe the ways in which the educated elite of eighteenth-century France understood, and came to terms with, the effects of commercialization and increased social mobility. While the language of *moeurs* and the promotion of the sentimental family cannot be equated with class-consciousness, they are nonetheless socially *located* discourses, reflecting anxiety in the upper levels of society. The *drame*'s preoccupation with "conditions" as the motor of dramatic action undoubtedly points, as does the discourse on *le luxe*, to deep misgivings in the face of a rapidly changing social and material world. In response to such concerns, the educated classes of pre-revolutionary France sought answers not in the leadership of a middle class or gentry but in the moralistic universalism conveyed by concepts such as family, *moeurs*, or *patrie*.

Why did the French adopt moralistic and universalistic discourses rather than, for instance, placing their hopes in an explicit redefinition of the nation's elite? At this stage the reasons can only be suggested; many of them probably involve long-term cultural trends particular to France. To explain why no new class was singled out to lead the nation, one can invoke the long-standing contempt of trade and "bourgeois" status, the growing critique of corporate society, and the collapse of traditional aristocratic preeminence – the fear of recreating any sort of "privilege" no doubt contributed greatly to the rhetoric of classlessness described above. To understand why the answer to the age's problems was couched in a language of moralistic holism, one can point to the enduring influence of both absolutist and Catholic universalism.

Various "enlightened" discourses, building upon a leveling tradition within monarchical absolutism, came increasingly to define the pursuit of particular or private interests as pernicious to the community. The formation of a new language of class was thus precluded, I would argue, even as legal privilege and the corporate idiom were cast aside. While the new idea of a "society" distinct from the polity did emerge in eighteenth-century France, it retained features strongly reminiscent of the absolutist synthesis.[87] The French persisted in their suspicion – and most often condemnation – of "English"-style definitions of society as an arena in which opposing groups played out their conflicts, balanced interests, and reached compromises. In contrast, French views of society remained highly functional, emphasizing the harmonious integration of various social groups into a transcendent whole. This was as true of the physiocratic or the sentimental-familial models as it had been of corporate and "ordered" ones.[88]

Dror Wahrman has recently argued that political language is the most common source of discourses about society – that competing interests within the polity will invoke the support of social groups that they themselves define to legitimate their claims.[89] I would like to suggest, in conclusion, that discursive influences can work both ways – that ideas about society can define the polity as well. The conception of the *patrie* as an expression of unmediated social bonds, rather than an arena in which social antagonisms are resolved, shaped a definition of the state reflected in a recent statement by a French politician: "The Republic does not recognize groups; it recognizes only individuals."[90] This, in turn, explains a great deal about the precarious status of the French bourgeoisie even when it did emerge, seemingly triumphant, in the nineteenth century.

87   On the emergence of "society," see Gordon (n. 26 above).
88   I wish to thank David Bell for stressing and clarifying this idea in response to an earlier draft of this article.
89   See Wahrman, *Imagining the Middle Class* (n. 6 above), pp. 9–10 and passim. I have also argued this in *Private Lives and Public Affairs* (n. 8 above), chap. 1.
90   Cited by Stanley Hoffman at a meeting of the French Historical Studies Association, Boston, March 22, 1996.

7

French Feminists and the Rights of "Man": Olympe de Gouges's Declarations

Joan Wallach Scott

Originally appeared as Joan Wallach Scott, "French Feminists and the Rights of 'Man': Olympe de Gouges's Declarations," *History Workshop Journal* 28 (Autumn 1989), pp. 1–21.

Editor's Introduction

The following article explores a fundamental paradox in the political theory espoused by most French revolutionaries. On the one hand, this theory, which Joan Scott and others have designated a form of *liberalism*, presumes that all individuals bear the right to play an active role in the making of the laws by which they are governed. This theory is *abstract* and *universal* because specific or particular characteristics, what distinguishes one such participant in lawmaking (otherwise known as a *citizen*) from the next, are deemed irrelevant. The principle of *equality*, upon which it rests, suggested that you were a citizen if (and because) you were a human being. On the other hand, French revolutionary liberalism simultaneously (and in a contradictory fashion) assumed that only certain kinds of human beings could be citizens, and, moreover, that the marks or signs according to which they were to be classified were typically physical or *bodily* distinctions. (This is what Scott means by the revolutionary idea of the citizen as *embodied*.) The poor and domestic servants were seen by many as lacking control over their persons (i.e. bodies) and hence ineligible for citizenship. Blacks and other people of color were more obvious candidates for distinction on the basis of physical difference, and only received acknowledgment of their equality for a brief period following a successful slave insurrection in the Caribbean colony of Saint-Domingue (today Haiti). The group most consistently excluded from citizenship on the basis of physical difference was that of women, and it is on the challenge that one woman, Olympe de Gouges, posed to this exclusion, that Scott focuses in this article.

Scott has chosen de Gouges not because she was representative of French women or even of the small and largely ineffective feminist contingent at the time of the Revolution. Rather she examines de Gouges's writings because they best reveal, in her opinion, the contradictionary nature of the revolutionaries' liberal ideology. Paradoxically, Scott attempts to achieve this goal by pointing to the contradictions in de Gouges's own political claims. In particular, she observes that de Gouges supported the liberal notion of citizenship as universal, abstract, hence equally applicable to women and men. At the same time, Scott notes, the revolutionary feminist expressed the belief that women should be citizens because they exemplified characteristics (e.g. beauty, selflessness, the capacity to bear children) that were considered specific to their sex. Thus she invoked *difference* to declare *equality*. In her *Declaration of the Rights of Woman and Citizen*, moreover, de Gouges pointed to the violation of universalist principles in the *Declaration of the Rights of Man and Citizen* by adding women to the "men" whose rights the prior Declaration had proclaimed. Yet she also justified the inclusion of women on the basis of their particular physical condition. Thus freedom of speech was essential to women primarily because it authorized them to name the father(s) of their children. Scott finds other contradictions in de Gouges's writings as well. Specifically, de Gouges pointed to *nature* as the source of rights, thus emphasizing the fact that women and blacks (for whose equality she also petitioned) shared with white men the fundamental physical characteristics of human beings. At the same time, however, she invoked the principle of *justice* as a corrective to the brute facts of natural life whereby the strong dominated the weak.

Taking her cue from the technique of literary analysis known as *deconstruction*, whereby the critic systematically reveals the contradictions in a particular text, Scott has deconstructed de Gouges's writings. Yet her point in revealing these contradictions is not to criticize de Gouges. Rather her aim is to show the contradictions inherent in the *discourse* of revolutionary liberalism. Like Keith Baker, Roger Chartier and Sarah Maza,[1] Scott borrows the concept of discourse, or a set of linguistic practices (especially naming or defining) determining power relations in any given society, from Michel Foucault (1926–84). Like Foucault, moreover, she assumes that discourses have the tendency to define the terms of debate in such a way that even opponents of the powerful are constrained to make their claims by using the very vocabulary that excluded them in the first place.

1   See chapters 2, 3 and 6.

Thus de Gouges's tendency to further the rights of women by pointing to their special, particular status and the allegedly crucial differences between their bodies and those of men undermined her claims because the discourse in which she had to make them had already defined "particularism" as subordinate to *universal* considerations and designated women as fundamentally *particular* on the basis of their physical difference. Her critique, in turn, sheds light on the character of revolutionary liberalism, suggesting that it made citizenship dependent upon particular, bodily characteristics despite its pretensions to universalism.

Implicit in Scott's analysis of the revolutionary discourse illuminated by de Gouges's critique is the claim that liberal feminism is ultimately ineffective precisely because liberalism stacked the deck against women by marking them as "particular," and that other self-described universalist ideologies performed the same type of exclusion. Thus "the recurrence since the Revolution of feminist critiques reminds us not only that the democratic promise of liberal (and socialist and republican) political theory is as yet unfulfilled, but also that it may be impossible of fulfilment in the terms in which it has so far been conceived." In other words, Scott argues, feminism must invent new terms for its political program, terms that have not been defined by discourses that exclude women.

French Feminists and the Rights of "Man": Olympe de Gouges's Declarations

Joan Wallach Scott

'In my writings, I am a student of nature; I might be, like her, irregular, bizarre even, yet also always true, always simple.'

For women, the legacy of the French Revolution was contradictory: a universal, abstract, rights-bearing individual as the unit of national sovereignty, embodied, however, as a man. The abstraction of a genderless political subject made it possible for women to claim the political rights of active citizens and, when denied them in practice, to protest against exclusion as unjust, a violation of the founding principles of the republic. The equally abstract gesture of embodiment – the attribution of citizenship to (white) male subjects – complicated enormously the project . of claiming equal rights, for it suggested either that rights themselves, or at least how and where they were exercised, depended on the physical characteristics of human bodies.

There is no denying the presence of bodies – of the physical traits of sex and skin colour – in the political debates of the French Revolution. Whether we take the conflicting opinions expressed during the writing of constitutions, the arguments about slave, mulatto or women's civic rights propounded by Barnave, Brissot, Condorcet or Robespierre, the contrasting reflections of Edmund Burke and Mary Wollstonecraft, or the minutes of section meetings in Paris, we find interpretations that assume that bodies and rights alike could be thought of as 'natural' and that this 'naturalness' provided a connection between them. Rights were often referred to as being inscribed on bodies, inalienably attached to them, indelibly imprinted on human minds or hearts.[1] But the

---

[1]   Thus Robespierre's evocation of 'the reign of that eternal justice, the laws of which are graven, not on marble or stone, but in the hearts of men, even in the heart of the slave who has forgotten them, and in that of the tyrant who disowns them'. Maximilien Robespierre, *Report upon the Principles of Political Morality which are to Form the Basis of the Administration of the Interior Concerns of the Republic* (Philadelphia, 1794), reprinted in *History of Western Civilization: Selected Readings* Topic VIII (Chicago, The University of Chicago Press, 1964), pp. 73–4.

connection between 'natural' bodies and 'natural' rights was neither transparent nor straightforward. The meanings of nature, rights, and bodies, as well as the relationships between them, were at issue in the revolutionary debates and these contests about meanings were contests about power.

There were many different contests about bodies and rights in the course of the Revolution and few were definitively resolved. Under the first constitution, passive citizens were distinguished from active according to levels of property ownership and wealth; the distinction disappeared with the monarchy and reappeared in different language under the Directory. 'Men of colour' were initially excluded from and then included in the category of citizen. Slaves were denied and then granted the rights of free men, only to lose them again under Napoleon. Women were systematically barred from formal political rights; but were granted rights to divorce and some control of marital property in 1792, only to have them restricted under the Code Napoléon and revoked by the Restoration. Each of these instances was characterized by different kinds of arguments; each has a complicated, contextual explanation – the abolition of slavery, for example, took place as the French sought to repel a British conquest of Santo Domingo by enlisting all male inhabitants of the island in the army.[2] What they have in common, however, is the persistent question of the relationship of specific, marked groups to the embodied universal: how could the rights of the poor, of mulattos, blacks, or women be figured as the rights of Man?

The general answer is: with difficulty. There was no simple way either to expand the category of Man to take in all his Others or to disembody the abstract individual so that literally anyone could represent him. Specific contests about the rights of excluded groups did not resolve this paradox, but exposed it; the terms of debate and the strategies of the contenders show equality to be a more elusive ideal in both its formulation and achievement than was ever acknowledged by the Revolution's most visionary architects or, for that matter, by many of its historians. Women are a case in point.

---

2   David Brion Davis, *The Problem of Slavery in the Age of Revolution* (Ithaca, N.Y., Cornell University Press, 1975), pp. 137–48, 328; C. L. R. James, *The Black Jacobins: Toussaint l'Ouverture and the San Domingo Revolution*, second edition (N.Y., Vintage, 1963); Georges Lefebvre, *The French Revolution: From its Origins to 1793* (N.Y., Columbia University Press, 1962) translated by Elizabeth M. Evanson, pp. 151, 172–3; Lefebvre, *The French Revolution: 1793–99* (N.Y., Columbia University Press), p. 358. See also, Nancy Leys Stepan, 'Race and Gender: The Role of Analogy in Science', *ISIS* 77 (1986), pp. 261–77.

I

From the outset of the Revolution, there were scattered demands for women's rights. These were most often passed over in revolutionary legislation until 1793 (several days after the execution of Marie-Antoinette), when the question of women's political role was directly addressed. Using the occasion of a street disturbance between market women and members of the Society of Revolutionary Republican Women, the National Convention outlawed all women's clubs and popular societies, invoking Rousseauist themes to deny women the exercise of political rights and to end, some hoped definitively, persistent feminist agitation.[3] 'Should women exercise political rights and meddle in the affairs of government?' asked André Amar, the representative of the Committee of General Security. 'In general, we can answer, no.' He went on to consider whether women could meet in political associations and again answered negatively:

> because they would be obliged to sacrifice the more important cares to which nature calls them. The private functions for which women are destined by their very nature are related to the general order of society; this social order results from the differences between man and woman. Each sex is called to the kind of occupation which is fitting for it; its action is

3   On the history of women and feminism (two different topics) in the French Revolution see Maïté Albistur and Daniel Armogathe, *Histoire du féminisme français*, Vol. I (Paris, Des Femmes, 1977); Paule-Marie Duhet, *Les Femmes et la Révolution 1789–1794*, (Paris, Julliard, 1971); Jane Abray, 'Feminism in the French Revolution', *American Historical Review* 80 (1975), pp. 43–62; Jeanne Bouvier, *Les Femmes pendant la Révolution* (Paris, 1931); Olwen Hufton, 'Women in the French Revolution', *Past and Present* 53 (1971), pp. 90–108; Hufton, 'The Reconstruction of a Church, 1796–1801', in Gwynne Lewis and Colin Lucas (eds), *Beyond the Terror: Essays in French Regional and Social History, 1794–1815* (Cambridge, Cambridge University Press, 1983), pp. 21–52; Scott Lytle, 'The Second Sex' (September 1793), *Journal of Modern History* 26 (1955), pp. 14–26; Jules Michelet, *Les Femmes de la Révolution* (Paris, 1854); R. B. Rose, 'Women and the French Revolution: The Political Activity of Parisian Women, 1789–94', University of Tasmania Occasional Paper 5 (1976); David Williams, 'The Politics of Feminism in the French Enlightenment', in P. Hughes and D. Williams (eds), *The Varied Pattern: Studies in the Eighteenth Century* (Toronto, A. M. Hakkert, 1971); Darline Gay Levy, Harriet Branson Applewhite and Mary Durham Johnson (eds), *Women in Revolutionary Paris, 1789–1795* (Urbana, University of Illinois Press, 1979). See also Dorinda Outram, 'Le langage mâle de la Vertu: Women and the discourse of the French Revolution', in Peter Burke and Roy Porter (eds), *The Social History of Language* (Cambridge, Cambridge University Press, 1987), pp. 120–35; and Lynn Hunt, 'The Many Bodies of Marie-Antoinette: Political Pornography and the Problem of the Feminine in the French Revolution' (unpublished paper, 1988).

circumscribed within this circle which it cannot break through, because nature, which has imposed these limits on man, commands imperiously and receives no law.[4]

An even more explicit articulation of these so-called natural facts came from Pierre-Gaspard Chaumette, a radical hébertist and member of the Paris Commune. On behalf of the Commune he indignantly rejected an appeal for support from female petitioners protesting the Convention's decree:

> Since when is it permitted to give up one's sex? Since when is it decent to see women abandoning the pious cares of their households, the cribs of their children, to come to public places, to harangues in the galleries, at the bar of the senate? Is it to men that nature confided domestic cares? Has she given us breasts to feed our children?[5]

Less brilliantly than Rousseau, but no less clearly, the Jacobin politicians set forth the terms of their new social order. Their invocation of nature as the origin of both liberty and sexual difference drew on certain prominent (but by no means uncontested) views of political theory and medicine. These views treated nature and the body as synonymous; in the body one could discern the truths upon which social and political organization ought to rest. Constantin Volney, representative for the Third Estate of Anjou at the meetings of the Estates General in 1788–9, argued firmly in his catechism of 1793 that virtue and vice 'are always ultimately referable to . . . the destruction or preservation of the body'.[6] For Volney, questions of health were questions of state; 'civic responsibility [was] health-seeking behaviour'.[7] Individual illness signified social deterioration; the failure of a mother to breast-feed her infant constituted a refusal of nature's corporeal design, hence a profoundly anti-social act.[8] The misuse of the body incurred not only individual costs, but social consequences since the body politic was, for Volney, not a metaphor but a literal description.

The body, of course, was not considered in these writings a singular object; sexual difference was taken as a founding principle of the

4   Levy, Applewhite and Johnson, p. 215.
5   Levy, Applewhite and Johnson, p. 219.
6   Ludmilla J. Jordanova, 'Guarding the Body Politic: Volney's Catechism of 1793', in Francis Barker, et al. (eds), *1789: Reading, Writing Revolution* (University of Essex, 1982), p. 15.
7   'Guarding the Body Politic', p. 15.
8   Ludmilla J. Jordanova, 'Naturalizing the Family: Literature and the Bio-Medical Sciences in the Late Eighteenth Century', in Jordanova (ed.), *Languages of Nature* (London, Free Association Books, 1986), p. 115.

natural, hence the social and political order. Tom Laqueur has shown that ideas of sexual difference are not fixed; their long and variable history demonstrates that sexual meanings are not transparently attached to or immanent in sexed bodies. Laqueur argues instead that a new biology emerged in the eighteenth century which replaced an earlier 'metaphysics of hierarchy' with 'the anatomy and physiology of incommensurability'.[9] Moreover, genital differences made all the difference; masculinity or femininity constituted the entire identity of biological males or females. One of the differences between them, in fact, had to do with how completely sex defined their beings. A Dr Moreau offered, as his own, Rousseau's explanation for the commonly accepted notion that women were (in Denise Riley's words) 'thoroughly saturated with their sex'.[10] He maintained that the location of the genital organs, inside in women, outside in men, determined the extent of their influence: 'the internal influence continually recalls women to their sex . . . the male is male only at certain moments, but the female is female throughout her life'.[11]

In the intersecting discourses of biology and politics, theories of complementarity resolved the potentially disruptive effects of sexual difference. Species reproduction and social order were said to depend on the union of the opposite elements, male and female, on a functional division of labour that granted nature her due. Although it was logically possible to present complementarity as an egalitarian doctrine, in fact it served in the predominant political rhetoric of this period to justify an asymmetrical relationship between men and women. The goals of the revolution, after all, were liberty, sovereignty, moral choice informed by reason, and active involvement in the formation of just laws. All of these were firmly designated male prerogatives, defined in contrast to the female. The constrasting elements were:

9   Thomas Laqueur, 'Orgasm, Generation, and the Politics of Reproductive Biology', *Representations* 14 (1986), p. 3.

10   Denise Riley, 'Does a sex have a history? "Women" and feminism', *New Formations* 1 (Spring 1987), pp. 39–40.

11   Yvonne Knibiehler, 'Les Médecins et la "Nature Féminine" au temps du Code Civil', *Annales, E.S.C.* 31 (1976), p. 835. The original version can be found in J-J. Rousseau's *Emile*, and is cited in Denise Riley, *'Am I That Name?' Feminism and the Category of 'Women' in History* (London, Macmillan, 1988), note 57, p. 37. See also, D. G. Charlton, *New Images of the Natural in France* (Cambridge, Cambridge University Press, 1984); Jean Borie, 'Une gynécologie passionée', in J-P. Aron (ed.), *Misérable et Glorieuse: La Femme du XIXe siècle* (Paris, Fayard, 1980), pp. 153–89; and M. Le Doeuff, 'Pierre Roussel's Chiasmas: From Imaginary Knowledge to the Learned Imagination', *Ideology and Consciousness* 9 (1981–2), pp. 39–70.

active	passive
liberty	duty
individual sovereignty	dependency
public	private
political	domestic
reason	modesty
speech	silence
education	maternal nurture
universal	particular
male	female[12]

The second column served not only to define the first, but provided the possibility for its existence. 'Natural' sexual difference permitted a resolution of some of the knotty and persistent problems of inequalities of power in political theory by locating individual freedom in male subjects and associating social cohesion with females. Maternal nurture awakened or instilled human empathy (pity) and love of virtue, the qualities that tempered selfish individualism; modesty at once equipped women to perform their roles and served as a corrective to their inability otherwise to restrain (sexual) desire. Women's modesty was, furthermore, a precondition for the successful exercise of male reason in restraint of desire.[13] The dependency of the domestic sphere elicited from men the fulfilment of their social duty; indeed duty denoted here not women's obligations but their position as the objects of male obligation. The active/passive distinction, in fact, resting as it did on contrasting theories of natural rights, summed up the differences: those who enjoyed active rights were individual agents, making moral choices, exercising liberty, acting (speaking) on their own behalf. They were, by definition, political subjects. Those who enjoyed passive rights had the 'right to be given or allowed something by someone else'.[14] Their status as political subjects was ambiguous, if not wholly in doubt.

12   On education and maternal nurture, see, Mona Ozouf, 'La Révolution Française et l'idée de l'homme nouveau', unpublished paper, 1987, p. 15. Ozoof reworked this paper in her book of essays, *L'homme régénéré: Essais sur la Révolution française* (Paris: Gallimard, 1989). She made the same point about the role of mothers in the education of children on p. 142. For a critique of binary constructions of liberal politics, especially the antinomy between reason and desire, see Roberto Mangabeira Unger, *Knowledge and Politics* (N.Y., Free Press, 1975).
13   My discussion here is based on Jacques Derrida, *Of Grammatology* (translated by Gayatri Chakravorty Spivak) (Baltimore, Johns Hopkins University Press, 1974), part II, chapter 3, pp. 165–95.
14   Richard Tuck, *Natural Rights Theories: Their Origin and Development* (Cambridge, Cambridge University Press, 1979), pp. 5–6.

Historians of natural rights theories rightly describe active and passive rights as antithetical paradigms; but they often also imply that these logically conflicting notions could not prevail simultaneously. Political regimes, they suggest, have been premised historically on one or another of these theories; from this perspective, the age of democratic revolutions was quintessentially the age of liberty and active rights. These characterizations reckon, however, neither with the ingenuity of the French revolutionaries who, in their first effort at constitution-making in 1791, reconciled their fear of democracy and their commitment to liberty by establishing two categories of citizen – the active and the passive – nor with the operations of gender within the universal languages of political theory.

In the constitution of 1791, active citizens were men over 25 who were independent (they could not be domestic servants) and who possessed measurable wealth (they had to pay a direct tax equivalent to three days of labour). The prerequisite was property – in land or money and the self. After the fall of the monarchy in 1792, citizenship was granted to all men who were over 21 and self-supporting. The means test was dropped, leaving as the operative concept property in the self. But, I would argue, the active/passive distinction did not disappear, even if it was no longer explicitly articulated in official political documents. Instead, it was employed to differentiate between the rights of those with and without autonomy or agency, and these were largely, though not exclusively, men and women. Unlike distinctions of wealth, those of sex were considered natural; they were therefore taken for granted, treated as axiomatic, assumed to be unalterable rules of 'imperious' nature, hence left outside the legislative arena. Constitutions and legal decrees dealt, for the most part, with the rules of (active) political participation and so dropped reference to those whose rights were taken care of for them by others. Invisibility, however, did not mean absence. The terms *citoyen* and *citoyenne* often carried the active/passive contrast, and from time to time it was clearly invoked – by the exasperated Chaumette, for example, in October 1793: 'Impudent women who want to become men,' (I imagine) he shouted, 'aren't you well enough provided for? What else do you need?'[15]

This rather crude form of political theorizing sums up the outlook I have been describing and brings me to the real beginning of this paper. I do not want to spend any more time discussing how women were constructed in revolutionary political discourse; rather I want to look at how some women criticized these constructions. For from the outset, there were feminist critics of these theories, women and men who

15   Levy, Applewhite and Johnson, p. 220.

argued for genuine equality of political rights. There were also, of course, women who paid no heed to the arguments and whose participation in the events of the Revolution has offered social historians ample evidence both for insisting that women were active historical subjects and for rejecting the importance of political theory in the practice of 'real' politics. The presence of women in crowds, their centrality in the march to Versailles, their membership in clubs (and the prominence of figures like Pauline Léon and Claire Lacombe among the Jacobins), their proposals to the various legislatures, their actions on behalf of and in opposition to the Revolution, all support the claim made by Camille Desmoulins in 1791 that action established agency: 'The active citizens,' he reminded his colleagues, 'are those who took the Bastille.'[16]

Yet action by women was insufficient, either during the Revolution or long after it, to secure formal recognition of this point. Some of the explanation for the legal disempowerment of women and their invisibility in the historical record must come from analyses of the discourses that established and justified exclusion. Sometimes feminists provided those analyses; more often their formulations furnish material from which such analyses can be fashioned. In their search for ways out of the paradox of an embodied equality, feminists show us the dead-ends, the limits of certain paths, and the complexity of others – all effects of the paradox itself. It is for that reason, and not because of their prominence or the size of their following (never very large in this period), that they interest me.

My primary interest in these feminists has to do with *how* they articulated their dissent, *how*, in the face of powerful beliefs to the contrary, they asserted that women deserved political rights. I want to address, with material from the French Revolution, the thoughtful and provocative questions raised by the British historian Barbara Taylor. She asks:

> What does it mean when [feminists] engage with a theory of the subject in which the reasoning speaker – that is the person who displays possession of natural rights and a place in the civic sphere *through* . . . speech – is actually constituted on the male side of the sexual axis? And where does that take us with egalitarianism?[17]

Taylor's questions assume that asymmetrical representations of rights are not easily corrected by universalist or pluralist arguments and that such arguments can never be formulated entirely outside the discourses they challenge. I would add that feminism's inherently political aspect

16   M. J. Sydenham, *The French Revolution* (N.Y., Capricorn Books, 1966), p. 67.
17   Barbara Taylor, commenting on Geneviève Fraisse, 'The Forms of Historical Feminism', *m/f* 10 (1985), p. 17.

comes from its critical engagement with prevailing theories and practices; it does not stand as an independent philosophical movement with a definable content and a coherent legacy of its own.[18] It must be read, therefore, in its concrete manifestations, and then not only for its programmatic recommendations. Tests of logical consistency or philosophical purity, like categorizations of feminist 'schools' of equality or difference, entirely miss the point. The historical and theoretical interest of modern feminism (which I take to date from the seventeenth century) lies in its exposure of the ambiguities and repressions, the contradictions and silences in liberal political systems that present themselves as coherent, comprehensive, rational, or just, because resting on natural, scientific, or universal principles. This suggests that feminism must not only be read in its historical contexts, but also that it cannot be detached from those contexts as evidence either for some transcendent Woman's identity or for the teleology of women's emancipation. The meaning of any feminism instead lies in the historical specificity of a recurring critical operation.

II

My interest in this essay is in the ways feminists addressed the issue of equality during the French Revolution. How did they formulate their claims for political rights? How did they create the political subject they claimed already to represent? How did they demand citizenship when such public status for women was taken as a contradiction of nature's functional design for social order? How did they attempt to refute or confound what was assumed to be the indisputable evidence of the body? How did they understand the influence of nature on the definition of their rights?

A full scale study of all the manifestations of feminism in the French Revolution is beyond the scope of this paper. I will instead concentrate

18   Geneviève Fraisse has completed a major study of these questions which I have not yet read, since it arrived as I was sending off this paper to *History Workshop*. It is called *Muse de la Raison: La démocratie exclusive et la différence des sexes* (Paris, Alinea, 1989). I have drawn on the following of Fraisse's work for this piece: 'The Forms of Historical Feminism', *m/f* 10 (1985), pp. 4–19; 'Natural Law and the Origins of Nineteenth-century Feminist Thought in France', in Judith Friedlander *et al.*, *Women in Culture and Politics* (Bloomington: Indiana University Press, 1986), pp. 318–29; 'Singularité féministe: Historiographie critique de l'histoire du féminisme en France', in Michelle Perrot (ed.), *Une Histoire des Femmes est-elle possible?* (Paris, Rivages, 1984), pp. 189–204; 'Du bon usage de l'individu féministe', *Vingtième Siècle* 14 (avril–juin 1987), pp. 45–54. See also Denise Riley, *'Am I That Name?' Feminism and the Category of 'Women' in History*, and Cora Kaplan, *Sea Changes: Culture and Feminism* (London, Verso, 1986), pp. 49, 166–7, 226.

on one figure – Olympe de Gouges (1748–93). I take de Gouges neither as a typical feminist nor an exemplary heroine, but because she provides a site where cultural contests and political contradictions can be examined in some detail. I chose Olympe de Gouges because she left behind a fairly substantial corpus of writings – political pamphlets, speeches, and plays – which constantly engaged the political issues of the day. Her most famous text was the *Declaration of the Rights of Woman and Citizen*, written as the constitution was being debated in 1791. Read alongside the 1789 *Declaration of the Rights of Man and Citizen* (as it was meant to be read) it at once adds to and supplants that document. Indeed, the *Declaration of the Rights of Woman* is, like many of de Gouges's efforts, a supplementary document for the revolution. It constitutes a supplement in the double and contradictory sense that Jacques Derrida points out is attached to the term *suppléer* in French. It was both an addition and a replacement, something superfluous, but also absolutely necessary for completion.[19] De Gouges's declarations were offered in this double and contradictory sense: as an additional comment on the meaning of universal rights (and in that sense 'only' extraneous) and as a necessary replacement for official edicts which lacked universality because they were incomplete. This 'undecidable' aspect of the 'logic of the supplement' gives de Gouges's work both its ambiguity and its critical force.

Olympe de Gouges! This name always calls forth smiles from those who hear it for the first time, bemused recognition from veterans of women's history courses. Its pretention and inauthenticity seem to produce a comic effect, comic because satirical or transgressive. The name Olympe de Gouges was not, indeed, the one recognized in law for this woman; rather it was one she crafted for herself. Born Marie Gouzes, daughter of a butcher and former servant in Montauban, she was married at age 16 to a man much older than herself. Shortly after the birth of her son, her husband Louis Yves Aubry died, but Marie refused to use the customary designation, Veuve Aubry. Instead she took her mother's middle name, Olympe, added a 'de' and changed her father's surname to Gouges. She vowed never again to marry, although she had at least one long-standing heterosexual liaison. She later suggested that the butcher hadn't been her father at all, but that she was the illegitimate offspring of a romance between her mother and a local notable,

19 Jacques Derrida, *Positions* (translated by Alan Bass) (Chicago, University of Chicago Press, 1981), especially p. 43; Derrida, *Of Grammatolgy*, pp. 141–64. For a concise explication of the concept of the supplement, see Barbara Johnson's Introduction to her translation of Derrida's *Disseminations* (Chicago, University of Chicago Press, 1981), p. xiii.

the marquis Le Franc de Pompignan.[20] This lineage added intrigue and status to her life and (since the marquis had won a reputation as a man of letters) provided a genealogy for her own literary aspirations. It also, of course, made a mockery of the rules of patrilineal origin and naming. (The theme of naming and renaming the father reappears, albeit with inconsistent and varied usage, throughout de Gouges's life and work.) No one has ever proven de Gouges's story of her birth, but that is less important than her repeated assertions of its veracity. These assertions, like her self renaming, constituted her identity: tentative, ambiguous, and never fully secured.[21]

De Gouges was always involved in a process of self-construction. She fought valiantly, for example, for recognition as a playwright and vastly exaggerated her standing when she did succeed in having several of her plays accepted (and even performed) by the Comédie Française. Writing was an important, indeed primary, aspect of her self-representation, although she wrote with great difficulty, dictating most of her texts. Speaking came more easily; she was apparently eloquent and inspired in her verbal displays; but these she considered an insufficient measure of her talents.[22] When the Revolution came, she claimed status as an active citizen by rushing into the fray, writing and speaking on behalf of a number of causes: freedom from bondage for slaves, the creation of a national theater, clean streets, provision of maternity hospitals, divorce, and the recognition of the rights of illegitimate children and unmarried mothers. In order more fully to follow the deliberations of the various political assemblies, de Gouges rented lodgings adjacent to their headquarters, in this way literally attaching herself to these august bodies. She was a familiar figure in the galleries and at the podium and her proclamations often covered the walls of the city of Paris. It was as if only her continuing physical presence could assert her status as a political subject; and even then, of course, this was a

20   For biographical treatment, see Olivier Blanc, *Olympe de Gouges* (Paris, Syros, 1981); and the Introduction to *Olympe de Gouges: Oeuvres* by Benoîte Groult (Paris, Mercure de France, 1986). See also, Léopold Lacour, *Les origines du féminisme contemporain. Trois Femmes de la Révolution: Olympe de Gouges, Théroigne de Méricourt, Rose Lacombe* (Paris, 1900).

21   De Gouges's actions were not unique or specific to women in this period. The article 'de' was often added to the names of aspiring young men; during the Revolution 'new men' displayed their regeneration or rebirth by rebaptising themselves often with heroic classical names. De Gouges's self is, in this sense, revealing of a process not confined to one gender, and can be taken as emblematic of the process of self-construction more generally.

22   Chantal Thomas, 'Féminisme et Révolution: les causes perdues d'Olympe de Gouges', in *La Carmagnole des Muses: L'homme de lettres et l'artiste dans la Révolution* (Paris, Armand Colin, 1988), p. 309.

vulnerable, contested identity at best, one whose terms she could never fully control.

Along with her proposals usually came a sometimes playful, sometimes disturbing reminder of the fact that a woman was speaking. De Gouges at once stressed her identity with the universal human individual and her difference. Indeed, her formulations demonstrate the difficulty for a woman of unambivalently securing status as an abstract individual in the face of its masculine embodiment. In order to claim the general status of 'human' for women, she insisted on their particular qualifications; in the process of insisting on equality, she constantly pointed out and acknowledged difference. 'It is a woman who dares to show herself so strong and so courageous for her King and her country. ...'[23] 'They can exclude women from all National Assemblies, but my beneficent genius brings me to the center of this assembly.'[24] 'Oh people, unhappy citizens, listen to the voice of a just and feeling woman.'[25] The title of one of her brochures was 'Le cri du sage: par une femme.'[26] When she put herself forward to defend Louis XVI during his trial she suggested both that sex ought not to be a consideration ('leave aside my sex') and that it should be ('heroism and generosity are also women's portion and the Revolution offers more than one example of it').[27]

De Gouges never escaped the ambiguity of feminine identity in its relationship to universal 'Man' and she often exploited it. On the one hand, she attacked women as they were – indulgent, frivolous, seductive, intriguing and duplicitous[28] – insisting they could choose to act otherwise (like men); on the other hand, she appealed to women to unite to defend their special interests, and to the legislature to recognize its duty to protect mothers. If she asserted that their worst characteristics had been constructed for women by unjust social organization, she none the less appealed to her sex to unite (around her leadership) regardless of rank, in order to exert political power in the common interest.[29] And, while she maintained that equality, and not special privilege, was the only ground on which woman could stand, she none the less (unsuccessfully) sought special advantage by claiming that she was pregnant

23   De Gouges, 'Remarques Patriotiques: par la citoyenne, Auteur de la lettre au Peuple, 1788', in *Oeuvres*, p. 73.
24   De Gouges, 'Le cri du sage: par une femme, 1789', in *Oeuvres*, p. 91.
25   De Gouges, 'Lettre au people ou projet d'une caisse patriotique par une citoyenne, 1788', in *Oeuvres*, p. 69.
26   In *Oeuvres*, pp. 88–92.
27   Groult, 'Introduction', *Oeuvres*, p. 47.
28   Groult, 'Introduction', *Oeuvres*, p. 28, and de Gouges, 'Lettre au peuple ou projet d'une caisse patriotique par une citoyenne, 1788', in *Oeuvres*, p. 72.
29   De Gouges, 'Préface pour les dames, ou le portrait des femmes, 1791', in *Oeuvres*, pp. 115–19.

in order to avoid (or at least postpone) the death sentence conferred on her by the Jacobins in 1793.

The *Declaration of the Rights of Woman and Citizen* contains the same ambiguous invocation of stereotypes of femininity and of claims to equality which deny those stereotypes. For the most part, its articles parallel those of the *Declaration* of 1789, extending to women the rights of 'Man'. Woman and Man are usually both invoked, for in her effort to produce the complete declaration de Gouges most often simply pluralized the concept of citizenship. But she also addressed her declaration to Marie-Antoinette, first woman of the realm, with the coy remark that if the Queen were 'less educated . . . I would fear that your special interests would prevail over those of your sex'.[30] And her preamble to the document, after echoing phrases about how ignorance, forgetfulness or contempt of (women's) rights had been 'the sole causes of public unhappiness and the corruption of governments', concluded with the stunning assertion that 'the sex superior in beauty as in courage during childbirth, recognizes and declares, in the presence and under the auspices of the Supreme Being, the following rights of woman and citizen'.[31] The very difference of women, this formulation suggests, as well as their exclusion, requires a separate discussion of their rights.[32]

In the declaration itself, article XI, on the right of free speech, stands out for the attention it draws to the distinctive needs of women:

> The free communication of ideas and opinions is one of the most precious rights of woman, since this liberty guarantees that fathers will recognize their children. Any Citizen (citoyenne) can thus say freely: I am the mother of your child, without being forced by barbarous prejudice to hide the truth.[33]

30   De Gouges, 'Déclaration des droits de la Femme, dédiée à la reine, 1791', in *Oeuvres*, p. 100.
31   De Gouges, 'Déclaration', in *Oeuvres*, p. 102.
32   Like much of de Gouges's writing, the *Declaration of the Rights of Woman* has an excessive quality. It strains within its chosen format. Surrounding the 17 articles which list women's rights there is, first a long dedication to Marie Antoinette, then a preamble more than twice the length of the one for the *Declaration of the Rights of Man*. At the end there is a postamble, followed by a model 'marriage' contract, followed by a rambling discussion that touches on ancient marriage customs, the rights of men of colour in the colonies, and the role of the legislative and executive power in the French nation. It is as if the statement of women's rights cannot stand without explanations. It must correct all that upon which the *Declaration of the Rights of Man* rests in order to make its point. This sense of strain, the excessive quality of the writing, is an attempt to deal, I would argue, with contradiction, with the paradoxical operations of the logic of the supplement.
33   De Gouges, 'Déclaration', in *Oeuvres*, p. 104.

What is striking about this statement is the particularity (even peculiarity) of its interpretation. De Gouges could not stay with the abstract universal language she used in most of the other articles of her proclamation; simply adding Woman to the *Declaration of the Rights of Man* did not suffice at this point. Why? Clearly the right to speech was, for her, *the* expression of liberty and so most important to discuss at length. In article X, in fact (which dealt with freedom of opinion), de Gouges added a phrase that belonged more properly in article XI: 'woman has the right to mount the scaffold, she ought equally to have the right to mount to the rostrum'.[34] (De Gouges here plays with the notion of 'right'. She turns being subject to the coercive power of the state into a recognition of individual rights, insisting on the literal terms of the social contract.) In this phrase and in article XI it is the right to speech that is at issue. But in both places, representing women as speaking subjects seems to have required more than expanding or pluralizing the category of citizen. It called for refutation of sexuality and maternity as grounds for silencing women, for disqualifying them as subjects, for leaving them out of the *Declaration of the Rights of Man*.

In de Gouges's article XI the unstated grounds of exclusion became the explicit reasons for inclusion. The sexual contract that established the social contract was here (and in the appendix to the *Declaration*) made visible.[35] De Gouges contradicted, with a concrete example, the revolutionaries' endorsement of oppositions between active and passive, liberty and duty, individual and social. Naming the father acknowledged the power of law and exposed the transgressions of the powerful. Without the right to speak, she insisted, women were powerless to enforce paternal duty, to call men back to their obligations, the obligations on which social cohesion and individual liberty depended. Naming the father was both a claim on paternal obligation and an exposure of the abuses of patriarchal power; it also arrogated to women a masculine prerogative. (The repeated appearance of this theme suggests that de Gouges incorporated into her political 'imaginary' elements of contemporary political discussions about the relations between King and people, family and state.)[36]

From one perspective de Gouges's article XI was an argument for equality that gained force and persuasive power from its use of specific detail. At the same time, however, its very specificity weakened its objec-

34   De Gouges, 'Déclaration', in *Oeuvres*, p. 104.
35   Carole Pateman, *The Sexual Contract* (Stanford, Stanford University Press, 1988).
36   A useful discussion of the relationship between social identity and the psychological imaginary is in Peter Stallybrass and Allon White, *The Politics and Poetics of Transgression* (Ithaca, N.Y., Cornell University Press, 1986).

tive. The abstract clauses of the *Declaration of the Rights of Man* never indulge in this level of specific and particularized detail, which by contrast seems to lack seriousness and generalizability. At the most crucial point in the argument – the demand for liberty to speak – the specificity of Woman marks her difference from the universality of Man. But the addition of Woman also implies the need to think differently about the whole question of rights.

There is another even more troubling ambiguity in de Gouges's argument. For it is precisely in the area of pregnancy that a woman's speech is simultaneously most authoritative and most open to doubt. Only a woman is in a position to know the truth and so designate paternity (only she can say 'I am the mother of your child' or 'you are the father of my child'). But precisely because that is the case – because a man can't know the truth, he must take the woman's word and she may be lying. The terms by which de Gouges claims the rights of speech for women, then, raise the spectre of the unreliable feminine, the devious and calculating opponent of rational, truth-speaking man, and so they are literally fraught with uncertainty.[37]

If de Gouges unwittingly evoked prevailing views of women, she also sought explicitly to counter them. Her analysis of women's artifice and unreliability stressed their lack of education and power. She particularly attacked marriage, 'the tomb of trust and love', for its institutionalization of inequality. Through it men imposed 'perpetual tyranny' on women, in contradistinction to the harmonious cooperation evident, she insisted, in nature.[38] The prevailing inequality had important personal effects for it forced women to resort to manipulative ploys in their dealings with men and it had negative political effects as well, since a just social order depended on granting all parties to the social contract the same interest in its preservation. For this reason de Gouges recommended replacing the marriage contract with a social contract. She appended to the *Declaration of the Rights of Woman* a 'social contract for Man and Woman' and she defined the Nation as 'the union of Woman and Man'. By this she meant to equate marriage and society, both

37   I am grateful to Ruth Leys for suggesting this point.
38   Here we find her playing with versions of Rousseau's distinctions between artifice and nature, between man in civilization and man in nature. See Maurizio Viroli, *Jean-Jacques Rousseau and the 'Well-Ordered Society'* (Cambridge, Cambridge University Press, 1988), chapter 2. See also the discussion of the ways republican thinkers linked artifice with the feminine and with aristocracy in Joan Landes, *Women and the Public Sphere in the Age of the French Revolution* (Ithaca, N.Y., Cornell University Press, 1988). One of de Gouges's strategies here is to attempt to disentangle the feminine from its prevalent association with artifice and aristocracy and to identify it instead with the public virtues of a republic.

voluntary unions, entered either for life or 'for the duration of our mutual inclinations' by rights-bearing individuals. These were unions, moreover, in which neither partner had any legal advantage. Property was to be held in common and divided according to parental discretion among children 'from whatever bed they come'. Moreover, the children 'have the right to bear the name of the fathers and mothers who have acknowledged them'; the father's name having no special status in the family.[39]

De Gouges used examples about marriage to counter notions of fixed social hierarchies, pointing out as the Estates General debated the question of how to represent the three orders of the nation, that fixed divisions between these groups did not exist and hence were absurd to maintain since marriage had already mingled the blood of members of nobility and the Third Estate.[40] The very last line of her *Declaration of the Rights of Woman* improbably took up the question of the separation of powers under the new constitution. There de Gouges argued for a reconciliation of the executive and legislative powers (aligning herself with the supporters of constitutional monarchy): 'I consider these two powers to be like a man and a woman, who ought to be united, but equal in power and virtue, in order to establish a good household.'[41] In these discussions, many of which read like *non sequiturs*, women's rights were not separable from, but integral to all considerations of politics. The union of man and woman replaced the single figure of the universal individual, in an attempt at resolving the difficulty of arguing about rights in univocal terms. But de Gouges's notion of this union was ambiguous. It could be read as an endorsement of functional complementarity based on sex, but also as an attempt to dissolve or transcend the categories of sexual difference. De Gouges tried to deny the possibility of any meaningful opposition between public and private, political and domestic, while at the same time working with a notion of marital or sexual union conceived in terms of those very oppositions.

In the past, de Gouges reminded her readers, the exclusion of women from politics had led to the corruption associated with 'the nocturnal administration of women', when seduction displaced reason and crime prevailed over virtue.[42] These ruses of the weak would disappear in the future, when women were granted full political rights, equal access to property and public employment. Here de Gouges seemed to acknowledge implicitly an often expressed fear of female sexuality, but she

39   Levy, Applewhite and Johnson, pp. 94–5.
40   De Gouges, 'Le cri du sage', in *Oeuvres*, p. 91.
41   De Gouges, 'Déclaration', in *Oeuvres*, p. 112.
42   De Gouges, 'Déclaration', pp. 109–11.

attributed it to faulty institutions. Inherently, desire was polyvalent; social usage gave it its meaning and value. For this reason de Gouges urged, in another context, that women be mobilized to 'incit[e] young men to fly to the defence of the Fatherland', promising the 'hand of your mistress' for those who were brave, rejection for cowards. 'The art we possess to move the souls of men would produce the salutary effect of enflaming all spirits. Nothing can resist our seductive organ.'[43] Deployed in defence of the nation, as an exercise in active citizenship, female sexuality might secure, not destabilize, the social order. Yet the appeal to this kind of femininity also carried the risk of unleashing a desire already defined as antithetical to rational politics. The ambiguity of woman seems always to haunt de Gouges's most creative arguments.

De Gouges's statements about sexuality, rights, and the possibilities for men and women referred for legitimation, like the arguments she criticized, to 'Nature'. This reference was at once ingenious and limiting; it allowed her to reinterpret the meaning of the ground for arguments about rights, but not ultimately to contest the usefulness of 'natural' justifications for human political arrangements. (It allows us to ponder the question of whether and how it is ever possible to exceed the constitutive terms of political discourse, whether redefinition and refiguration are the best means available, or whether this depends on specific context, finite historical moments.)

De Gouges refused the differentiation of bodies into fixed binary categories, insisting instead on multiplicity, variety, ranges of difference, spectra of colours and functions, confusion of roles – the ultimate undecidability and indeterminacy of the social significance of physical bodies. Running through many of her writings are examples and observations meant to elucidate (what was for her) a primary truth: (she didn't put it this way, but she might have) Nature abhors binary categorization. Appealing to the prevailing rules of science, de Gouges reported her observations and what she saw, she said, confirmed her own experience, her perception of the distance between her 'self' and the social category of woman. 'In my writings, I am a student of nature; I might be (je dois être), like her, irregular, bizarre even, yet also always true, always simple.'[44]

In one of her autobiographical pieces, de Gouges explained that the sexes were differentiated only for the purposes of reproduction; otherwise 'nature' had endowed all members of a species with similar, but not necessarily identical, faculties.[45] Physical difference, however, was not

---

43   Levy, Applewhite and Johnson, p. 170.
44   De Gouges, 'Départ de M. Necker et de Madame de Gouges, ou, Les Adieux de Madame de Gouges aux Français et à M. Necker (avril 1790)', in *Oeuvres*, p. 96.
45   De Gouges, 'Autobiographie', in *Oeuvres*, p. 226.

the key to other differences; for there was no system to nature's variations. De Gouges accepted the prevailing belief in the originary status of nature, and then she redescribed it, drawing new implications for human social organization. Systems, she argued, were man-made and she implied that all systems interfered with natural (hence desirable) anarchic confusions. The *Declaration of the Rights of Woman* began by contrasting men's tyrannical oppression of women with the harmonious confusions of the natural world:

> look, search, and then distinguish if you can, the sexes in the administration of nature. Everywhere you will find them mixed up (confondus), everywhere they cooperate harmoniously together in this immortal masterpiece.[46]

Like distinctions of sex, distinctions of colour defied clear categorization. Only the cupidity and greed of white men could explain for de Gouges the enslavement of blacks; only blind prejudice could lead to commerce in human beings and to the denial of a common humanity between black and white. This was the theme of a play she wrote in 1785 first called *Zamore et Mirza* and then renamed *L'Esclavage des Nègres*. Its performance in 1789 by the *Comédie Française* won praise from the small Association of the Friends of Blacks and angry denunciation from an organized club of colonists and their supporters in Paris. The cast, too, refused de Gouges's instruction that the actors wear blackface, a gesture she denounced as intolerable because it undermined the dramatic and political effects she sought. The play was closed after only three performances. The Mayor of Paris was reported to have said that he feared its 'incendiary' aspect would 'provoke insurrection in the colonies'.[47] The year before its appearance (when she was still negotiating with the Comédie Française about producing it), de Gouges issued a brochure that contained her 'Reflections on Black Men'. In it she insisted that 'nature had no part' in the 'commerce d'hommes'. 'The unjust and powerful interests of the whites did it all,' she maintained, suggesting that here particular interests, masquerading as universal, had usurped human rights. She then pondered the question of colour, asking where the lines could be drawn absolutely to differentiate whites, mulattos, blacks, and whether any hierarchy could be established on the basis of these differences:

> Man's colour is nuanced, like all the animals that nature has produced, as well as the plants and minerals. Why doesn't the night rival the day,

46   De Gouges, 'Déclaration', in *Oeuvres*, p. 101.
47   Groult, 'Introduction', *Oeuvres*, p. 27.

the sun the moon, and the stars the firmament? All is varied and that is the beauty of nature. Why then destroy her work?[48]

Underneath the visible variety of nature, de Gouges detected a fundamental physical identity. Distinctions of colour were not only indeterminate, but superficial, she insisted, for the same blood flowed in the veins of masters and slaves. They were, in fact, 'fathers and brothers', but 'deaf to the cries of blood, they stifle all its charms'.[49] This comment, placed as it was near the end of the *Declaration of the Rights of Woman*, raises the issue of how de Gouges understood the relationship between the situation of women and blacks. There was more than an analogy between two groups deprived of liberty. Rather they partook of the same question: the status in nature, and so in politics, of observable physical difference. If undecidability was the answer in nature, decisions became human actions for which people could be held accountable; they were necessarily relative and open to reasonable debate and interpretation. The legitimation for laws could lie only in 'common utility' (article I of both declarations stated that 'social distinctions could only be based on common utility') and that was inevitably decided through political processes. Justice, not nature, required the participation in these processes by everyone affected. The body – or more precisely, structural physical difference – was an irrelevant factor in one sense, for the meanings of these differences were the products not the prerequisites of politics. In another sense, bodies provided the universal ground of human identity, in the identical blood that animated them all and as the site of natural rights. For de Gouges, at least, rights were embodied and universal at the same time and this conception required not denying the existence of physical differences, but recognizing them as at once essential and irrelevant to the meaning of equality.

De Gouges's invocations of nature were always ambiguous. On the one hand, she insisted (in opposition to her Jacobin adversaries) on undecidability and thus on human responsibility for the imposition of categories; on the other, she accepted the orginary 'truth' of nature and so left in place the notion that social arrangements could be referred to natural truths. This, in turn, could focus the argument on what *was* in nature rather than on what should be in politics. And de Gouges could always be open to the charge that, untutored in scientific observation, she had simply misread the facts of the physical world.

None the less, the destabilizing implications of her redefinition of nature were undeniable; if nature was 'irregular, bizarre even', it could

48 De Gouges, 'Réflexions sur les hommes nègres, février 1788', in *Oeuvres*, p. 85.
49 De Gouges, 'Déclaration', in *Oeuvres*, p. 112.

not provide, in her terms (it might in ours), a reliable guide for politics. Rather than being a matter of science, justice had to be understood as a mediation of power.

III

It is possible to read Olympe de Gouges and other feminists, male and female, during the French Revolution, in the context solely of established categories of political debate. Implicit in her critique was an interpretation of liberal political theory that countered the authoritarianism of Rousseauian doctrines of the general will with more conflictual (some might say Madisonian) notions of politics. Her alliances with the Gironde faction in the Convention bear this out; she was finally sent to the guillotine in 1793 not for her feminism, but for plastering the walls of Paris with posters urging that a federalist system replace Jacobin centralized rule. Indeed, the moment of Jacobin centralization was accompanied by ruthlessly masculine political assertions and by the expulsion of prominent women from the Jacobin club. The association between bourgeois democracy and feminism in France goes beyond de Gouges; it is Condorcet, after all, also a Girondist, who is usually cited as the preeminent feminist of the Revolution.[50]

This kind of reading, while acceptable, would be insufficient, I think, on both empirical and philosophical grounds. First, Girondist politicians were not unanimous on the issue of women's rights; most accepted the 'natural' version of the sexual division of labour, and these included prominent women such as Madame Roland. Long after the Revolution, the anti-authoritarian current of French liberalism shared with other political tendencies an aversion to feminism; sexual difference, as explained by science and medicine, seemed to offer a non-political (hence natural) justification for the assignment to women of passive, not active rights. Moreover, in succeeding generations, feminism was as often associated with socialism as with liberalism; indeed it is frequently argued that the real start of a feminist tradition in France began not with the Revolution, but with the utopians – the St Simonian and Fourierist movements of the 1830s and 1840s.[51]

Second, to treat feminism within the received categories of revolutionary politics ignores the most powerful aspects of its critique and

50   Condorcet, 'On the Admission of Women to the Rights of Citizenship (1790)', in *Selected Writings*, K. M. Baker (Indianapolis, 1976).
51   On this history see, Claire Goldberg Moses, *French Feminism in the Nineteenth Century* (Albany, SUNY Press, 1984).

leaves apart many questions, among them the question of how references to the 'natural' legitimated political theory and practice and complicated any critique of them. I forsake the opportunity to examine the interconnections among discourses as well as the contradictions within any one of them; it accepts at face value the terms within which most revolutionaries viewed politics rather than subjecting those terms (as well as the specific programmes advocated) to critical scrutiny. The dichotomies that defined those politics are then perpetuated in our histories as so many natural or functional 'realities', thus obscuring not only their relative meanings but all contests about them. Indeed the most fundamental contests, those about first premises, become most marginal for these histories because they are categorized as concerning non-political matters. The protests of feminists are heard as cries from the sidelines about the exclusion of particular interests, as superfluous utterances rather than as fundamental (and central) critiques of the notion of different categories of rights based on physical difference. And the existence of particularized critiques of universality becomes a way of confirming rather than questioning the very notion of the universal. Its embodiment as a white male is explained as a temporary historical contingency with no overtones of power, for to associate the concept of the universal with relationships of power – of domination, subordination and exclusion – would be to contradict the meaning of the universal, at least as it was offered in liberal theories of political rights. It is precisely that contradiction – expressed through its supplementarity – that the feminine already embodied in those theories and that feminists pointed out again and again, though with different arguments and in different terms.

The recurrence of feminist critiques raises the question of their success or failure, and thus of their depth and significance as political movements. If feminism cannot be subsumed into politics as we have known it (as the conflict of parties and interests in the public realm: Gironde versus Jacobin, republican versus socialist) can it be given a political status of its own?

Certainly Olympe de Gouges (like her feminist contemporaries) cannot be considered successful in the usual terms of political evaluation. She did not win acceptance of her proposals for women's rights; her refiguration of marriage, women, and nature was generally dismissed by those in power (in the government and in various political groupings) as outrageous rather than taken seriously. Within a few days of her death (in November 1793) Chaumette set the terms of her historical reputation. He warned republican women who dared to question their roles of the fate of others who had broken the rules:

> Remember that virago, that woman-man (*cette femme-homme*), the impudent Olympe de Gouges, who abandoned all the cares of her household because she wanted to engage in politics and commit crimes. . . . This forgetfulness of the virtues of her sex led her to the scaffold.[52]

Although her *Declaration of the Rights of Woman* inspired feminist challenges to successive governments throughout the nineteenth and the first half of the twentieth centuries, formal histories either excluded her entirely or classed her with the 'furies' of the Revolution, those women who caused and expressed the excesses of unrestrained passion.[53] In 1904, a Dr Guillois analysed de Gouges as a case of revolutionary hysteria. Her abnormal sexuality (caused by excessive menstrual flow), her narcissicism (evinced by a predeliction for daily baths), and her entire lack of moral sense (proven by her repeated refusal to remarry) constituted the definitive signs of her mental pathology. A defective femininity, in short, had led to her unfortunate interest in politics.[54] The implications of this diagnosis for Guillois's contemporaries was unmistakable: demands for women's rights (as well as all reforming zeal) could not be taken seriously as politics, but must be treated as illness.

These references to de Gouges are misleading, however, for they exaggerate the attention paid to her by historians. The most characteristic treatment of her (as of feminists generally) has been massive silence. I do not in any way want to argue for her rehabilitation as a heroine, although there are some historians who would insist that that is the only way to grant her agency, the only justification for attending to her. Rather, I want to suggest that de Gouges's practice – her writings and speeches – offers a useful perspective for reading the history of politics and political theory in the French Revolution and for considering questions about contemporary feminist politics. What was the legacy of the French Revolution for women? What did feminism reveal about that legacy? What was/is the status of feminism as a politics?

In a way I've already answered most of these questions but I will restate what I've said: if by political we mean a contest about power, feminism was a political movement poised in critical opposition to liberal political theory, constructed within and yet defined out of serious consideration by the terms of that theory. By those terms, political was synonymous with rational, public, and universal, with the free agency of autonomous subjects. Woman, by a set of definitions attributed to nature, was construed as having antithetical traits, hence being outside

---

52   Cited in Groult, 'Introduction', *Oeuvres*, p. 59.
53   Groult, 'Introduction', *Oeuvres*, pp. 60–2. See also Neil Hertz, 'Medusa's Head: Male Hysteria under Political Pressure', *Representations* 4 (Fall 1983), pp. 27–54.
54   Cited in Groult, 'Introduction', *Oeuvres*, pp. 61–2.

politics. In order to formulate a critique of this theory, feminists like de Gouges contested its definitions, and sometimes also its legitimating premises, but at the same time they used the prevailing terminology of the day. This produced an ambiguous discourse which both confirmed and challenged prevailing views, and which exposes to us a fundamental paradox of the political theory of the Revolution: the relative and highly particularized aspect, the undeniable embodiment, of its claim to universality.

The ambiguity of de Gouges's feminism is not a measure of its inadequacy as philosophy and politics; rather it is an effect of the exclusions and contradictions of the political theory within and against which it was articulated. The same can be said of subsequent feminisms in the nineteenth and twentieth centuries. Indeed, the recurrence since the Revolution of feminist critiques reminds us not only that the democratic promise of liberal (and socialist and republican) political theory is as yet unfulfilled, but also that it may be impossible of fulfilment in the terms in which it has so far been conceived.

8

The Band of Brothers

Lynn Hunt

Originally appeared as Lynn Hunt, "The Band of Brothers,"
chapter 3 of *The Family Romance of the French Revolution* (1992)
pp. 53–71, 73–88 (Berkeley: University of California Press).

Editor's Introduction

Like Joan Scott's article,[1] the following excerpt from Lynn Hunt's book, *The Family Romance of the French Revolution*, addresses the importance of bodies and gender in the mental world of the French revolutionaries. Yet whereas Scott limits her analysis to the gendered and embodied discourse of revolutionary politicians (and Olympe de Gouges's attempts at a feminist critique of that discourse), Hunt examines a wide array of sources – including prints, novels, paintings and descriptions of festivals, along with the declarations of politicians – in order to probe the unconscious feelings and impulses of the revolutionaries. In order to shed light on this otherwise hidden landscape, Hunt has recourse to sociological, psychological, and anthropological theory.

From the French sociologist Emile Durkheim (1858–1917) Hunt takes the hypothesis (unstated in this piece but implicit in the argument and explicitly articulated elsewhere in her work[2]) that even ostensibly secular societies depend upon a shared belief in the *sacrality* or sacred nature of certain things, which in turn are identified and articulated through *symbols*. These assumptions explain Hunt's interest in the symbolic aspects of the French Revolution, an interest which has defined much of her earlier scholarship and which underlies the subject of this excerpt: the symbolic meaning of brothers or fraternity to the revolutionaries.

1 See chapter 7.
2 See esp. Lynn Hunt, "The Sacred and the French Revolution," in Jeffrey C. Alexander, ed., *Durkheimian Sociology: Cultural Studies* (Cambridge: Cambridge University Press, 1988), 25–43.

If Durkheim furnishes Hunt with a model of sacred symbolism, Sigmund Freud (1856–1939) enables her to explain the content of revolutionary thought and behavior in greater detail. In particular, Hunt adapts to the revolutionary situation Freud's concept of the "family romance," the fantasy by which children supposedly replace their real parents with more desirable forebears. This idea informs her argument that the revolutionaries, after going through a phase of imagining their king as a "bad father," depicted themselves as a "band of brothers" without parents. Hunt argues that the image of the band of brothers was especially desirable after the arrest and execution of the king, the traditional father figure, because it provided a means of erasing the guilt associated with that act of "parricide." Here she draws on another of Freud's theories (elaborated in his *Totem and Taboo*), according to which religion, morality, and the law emerged historically as the consequence of an original act of parricide. She suggests that the killing of the king was a similarly crucial event in the revolutionaries' attempt to build a new political and social order, though she is careful to note differences between Freud's model and the actual revolutionary experience.

Finally, to give a fuller picture of the relationship between the symbolic parricide and the attempt at establishing a new regime, Hunt invokes the work of René Girard (1923–), the French scholar who has studied, among other things, the tendency of societies to defuse violent urges by channeling them toward symbolic sacrificial victims.[3] Hunt observes that the revolutionaries aimed at just such a solution when they executed Louis XVI, yet she implicitly challenges Girard's theory by noting the many thousands of victims killed after the king's death.

The passage excerpted here focuses on the period between September 1792, when monarchy was abolished (a month after the king's arrest), and the summer of 1794, when Robespierre was overthrown and the Reign of Terror ended. Hunt argues that beginning with the king's trial in December 1792 and January 1793 the traditional image of the king as father disappeared; she suggests that this symbolic revolution enabled those responsible for judging their former sovereign to declare him guilty of treason. In the aftermath of the execution, she observes, many revolutionaries showed signs of guilt and called on their compatriots to forget the momentous event. Those more radical revolutionaries who exulted in the execution, moreover, depicted it as a sacred ceremonial act reminiscent, in Hunt's view, of the sacrificial violence described by Girard. In this way, she suggests, they transferred the sacrality of Old Regime kingship to

---

3 René Girard, *Violence and the Sacred*, trans. Patrick Gregory (Baltimore: Johns Hopkins University Press, 1977).

the new republican polity – thus conforming to Durkheim's belief that all societies, secular or otherwise, require sacred symbols.

Hunt continues with an account of the relationship between the symbolic attack on fatherhood and state policy toward real fathers. She maintains that the mistrust of paternal authority found its legal expression in an attack on what were long considered the rights of fathers. Thus, for example, laws required them to divide their estates equally among all their children, whether the heirs were legitimate or born out of wedlock. Hunt claims that if the aim of such legislation was to establish liberty and equality in hitherto "tyrannical" families, the effect was paradoxically to make families subordinate to "society and the state," i.e. to replace the powerful father with an even more powerful *patrie* or Fatherland.

Next Hunt describes the anti-patriarchal "family romance" in which revolutionaries imagined themselves as a "band of brothers." Through an examination of prints, ceremonies, paintings and revolutionary newspaper articles, she shows how revolutionaries eliminated father-imagery from their self-representations. In contrast to the Freudian model of rebellious sons venerating the most heroic among them as a new father figure, and unlike the American revolutionaries, who followed this "script" by singling out George Washington as "father" of their country, the French revolutionaries as described by Hunt only elevated selected *dead* men to paternal status and otherwise made a cult of young men.

The place of women in this symbolic configuration was entirely different, Hunt shows, and in this respect her work complements that of Joan Scott by revealing the *gendered* character of revolutionary culture. Whereas men occupied a primary place in visual and verbal depictions of the Revolution, women were either entirely absent or played a purely allegorical role – that is, they stood for abstract ideas such as liberty, with the tacit understanding that real women would not enjoy actual political liberty. Hunt goes on to analyze works of literature and painting, noting that female characters in both art forms declined in prominence and that the men who appeared in them were normally depicted as brothers, either literally or figuratively. Finally, she concludes that the various symbolic attempts to create fraternity, including the execution of the father/king, failed to contain the violence that the revolutionaries themselves had unleashed.

The Band of Brothers
Lynn Hunt

Kingship was officially abolished on 21 September 1792. Deputy Henri Grégoire explained, "It is necessary to destroy this word *king*, which is still a talisman whose magical force can serve to stupefy many men."[1] In January 1793 the man Louis Capet himself was executed. The killing of the political father enacted a ritual sacrifice and opened the way to the band of brothers. Between 1792 and the middle of 1794, radical iconography instantiated a new family romance of fraternity: brothers and sisters appeared frequently in this iconographic outpouring, mothers rarely, and fathers almost never. The literal effacement of the political father was the subject of a systematic, official campaign in which images of the kings of France, as well as images of royalty, aristocracy, and feudalism, were destroyed. Local and national officials took steps in this direction immediately after 10 August 1792 and then accelerated their activities in the summer of 1793.

The killing of the king may seem predetermined in hindsight, but the deputies of the newly elected National Convention only backed into it step by hesitant step. The Convention was elected after the uprising against the monarchy on 10 August 1792, and the deputies first met on 21 September 1792 to begin deliberations about a new form for French government. The abolition of the monarchy was quickly accomplished; disposing of the former king, who had been "sacred and inviolable" under the constitution of 1791, raised difficult questions.[2] Could he be tried at all, given his protected status under the constitution of 1791? Would he be tried as king or as an ordinary citizen? Who would try him? How would a verdict be reached?

In the weeks that followed the opening of the National Convention, the Jacobins opposed a trial and argued for a military-style execution. The young deputy and future member of the Committee of Public Safety, Louis-Antoine Saint-Just, argued, "This man must reign or die." Since "no man can reign innocently," and since the king "had no part in the contract which united the French people," he should be treated simply

---

1   *Moniteur universel*, no. 266, 22 September 1792, recounting the session of the National Convention on 21 September 1792.
2   The indispensable guide is David P. Jordan, *The King's Trial: The French Revolution vs. Louis XVI* (Berkeley, 1979).

as a "rebel," a "usurper," and "an enemy alien."[3] The Jacobin view did not carry the day, however, and on 3 December 1792 the Convention decided to try Louis, with the Convention itself sitting as his court of judgment. A simple majority was required for a verdict.

During the trial in December and January, the deputies never referred to the king as father of his people. The commission named to draw up an act of accusation against the former king charged him as "a tyrant who constantly applied himself to obstructing or retarding the progress of liberty, and even to annihilating it by persistently sustained and renewed assaults."[4] This sounds more like a distant and perverse tyrant than like a good father gone wrong. The deputies apparently felt the need to distance themselves from Louis in order to make judging him more palatable.

At the same time, they insisted on treating him like an ordinary accused man. The back and forth of the trial helped push even further the desacralization of the monarchy. Louis appeared in person before his judges, the elected representatives of the nation; and unlike Charles I of England, he chose to respond to his accusers by denying any intention of criminal wrongdoing. To each charge, he responded with "I had no intention of spilling blood," "I do not remember what happened at that time," "I know nothing about it."[5] All sense of majesty was fast disappearing.

In the minds of the deputies, there was no doubt that the king was guilty of betraying the nation. Not one deputy voted "no" in the roll call on the king's guilt. Yet they did disagree about his punishment: should he be killed or banished or imprisoned? Should the people be consulted first? Should a reprieve be offered? By a narrow majority they voted on 16 and 17 January 1793 to execute him. On 19 and 20 January they voted by a larger majority to reject a reprieve. The execution was ordered for the next day, 21 January 1793.

At the scaffold, Louis tried to speak in terms of sacrifice: "I pardon my enemies and I hope that my blood will be useful to the French, that it will appease God's anger." At that point, he was interrupted by the

---

3 From his speech of 13 November 1792, in Michael Walzer, ed., *Regicide and Revolution: Speeches at the Trial of Louis XVI* (Cambridge, 1974), pp. 120–7. In his analysis of the trial and execution, Walzer argues that "revolution marks the end of political fatherhood. No great commitment to psychoanalytic theory is required to describe it as the successful struggle of the 'brethren' against the father, and after it is over, the brethren are alone, without a political father" (p. 26).

4 *Moniteur universel*, no. 348, 13 December 1792, recounting the session of the National Convention on 10 December 1792.

5 Ibid., session of 11 December 1792.

rolling of drums, and the executioners quickly strapped him down and slid him through the window of the guillotine. Once the guillotine had done its work, the crowd responded to the sight of the severed royal head held high by the executioner with cries of "Long live the Republic! Long live Liberty! Long live Equality!"[6]

The momentous event was greeted by remarkably restrained commentary in revolutionary France.[7] On the day of the execution, one of the regicide deputies spoke on the occasion in the Jacobin Club of Paris. He said simply, "Today he [Louis] has paid his debt; let us speak of it no longer, let us be human; all of our resentment must expire with him." Then he and the rest of the club members turned instead to a discussion of the assassination of Deputy Michel Lepeletier by a royalist.[8] In the Convention, discussion on the day of the execution concerned the assassination of Lepeletier and rumors of plots against other deputies. Danton echoed the sentiments of many deputies when he suggested, "Now that the tyrant is no longer, let us turn all of our energy, all of our excitement, toward the war."[9]

The press could not ignore the execution, of course, but in Paris and the provinces the reports on it were very much the same. Many papers simply reproduced official proclamations and reports under the usual rubric of "news from Paris," "city of Paris," and the like.[10] The *Moniteur universel* called for leaving Louis under his shroud: "A victim of the law has something sacred about him for the moral and sensitive man; it is toward the future that all of the good citizens must turn their wishes."[11] The persistent sense that the French should turn away from the killing toward something else permeated all these reactions. They seem to support the contention of René Girard that the sacrificial process

6   Jordan, *The King's Trial*, p. 220.

7   A preliminary version of some of the ideas presented in these pages can be found in my essay, "The Sacred and the French Revolution," in Jeffrey Alexander, ed., *Durkheimian Sociology* (Cambridge, 1988), pp. 25–43.

8   Deputy Bourdon, in F. A. Aulard, ed., *La Société des Jacobins: Recueil de documents pour l'histoire du club des Jacobins de Paris*, vol. 4, *Juin 1792 à janvier 1793* (Paris, 1892), p. 689.

9   *Moniteur universel*, no. 25, 25 January 1793, reporting on the session of the National Convention on 21 January 1793.

10   I base this observation on my reading of the *Journal du département de l'Oise, Abréviateur universel, Courrier de Strasbourg*, and *Journal de Paris national*, among others. Not surprisingly, the Girondin papers were particularly reticent; see, for example, *Chronique de Paris*. See also Alphonse Aulard, "L'Exécution de Louis XVI et la presse française," *La Révolution française* 82 (1929): 65–76. Aulard does not remark on the formulaic qualities of most reports.

11   *Moniteur universel*, no. 23, 23 January 1793.

requires a certain degree of misunderstanding: as Girard argues, "the celebrants do not and must not comprehend the true role of the sacrificial act."[12]

Only the most radical newspaper editors provided any extended commentary on the meaning of the king's death. Marat, who editorialized freely on every subject, gave a rather solemn account: "The head of the tyrant has just fallen under the blade of the law; the same stroke has overturned the foundations of monarchy among us; I believe finally in the republic." Marat went on to compare the execution to a "religious festival" animated by feelings of fraternity: "One would have said that [the people] had just attended a religious festival; delivered from the burden of oppression that weighed on them for such a long time and pierced by the sentiment of fraternity, all hearts gave themselves over to the hope of a happier future." The final punishment of Louis was a world-historical event, in Marat's view, an event which would have a "prodigious" influence on the other despots of Europe and on the peoples who had not yet broken the irons of slavery. It would "terrorize" the Revolution's enemies both within and outside France. It would energize the nation. Marat then cited with approval the statement of another deputy: "We have finally landed on the island of liberty, and we have burned the boat that brought us to it." The monarchy could take the nation only so far, and then they had to destroy it in order to proceed further.[13]

In subsequent days, Marat celebrated again the enormity of the event. That Monday was a day forever memorable: "Goodbye then to the splendor of thrones, the prestige of worldly grandeurs, the talisman of celestial powers; goodbye to all human respect for constituted authorities themselves, when they do not command by virtue, when they displease the people, when they assert any tendency to elevate themselves above the common level." Only a great stroke could have accomplished all this. A monarchy of thirteen centuries was proscribed in a day; a monarch adored for fifteen years was punished as a tyrant. Who could have predicted this outcome? Marat asked. In his analysis, he expressed the radicals' hope that the execution would desacralize power itself and thus make power more accessible to the people. The execution of one of Europe's leading kings had destroyed the magical powers of thrones, but it had also served as a warning to every kind of authority; you had to please the people from now on, and you could not appear to be superior to them.[14]

---

12   René Girard, *Violence and the Sacred*, trans. Patrick Gregory (Baltimore, 1977), p. 7.
13   *Journal de la République française* (one of the many variations on *L'Ami du peuple*), 23 January 1793.
14   Ibid., 26 January and 27 January 1793.

Like Marat, Louis Prudhomme of the paper *Révolutions de Paris* saw the religious and ritual aspects of the killing. The king had to be desacralized in order for the nation to be resacralized as a republic; the king had to be the greatest of all criminals in order to take on himself all the guilt of the nation. "For more than thirteen centuries the first nation of Europe has been the most servile," declared Prudhomme. He regretted that the execution did not take place on the national altar first used in the Festival of Federation, for such an act required a large audience: "The vast expanse of the field would have permitted an even greater number of witnesses to be present at this memorable event, which could not have too many witnesses."[15] In Freud's interpretation of the murder of the father, the sense of guilt felt by the band of brothers "can only be allayed by the solidarity of all the participants."[16] Although Prudhomme would never have subscribed to any feelings of guilt about executing the king (on the contrary, it erased the guilt of willing servitude), his wish for more participation inadvertently bears out Freud's remark.

When describing the scene at the scaffold after the execution and the benediction of the "brothers" with the king's blood, Prudhomme recounted the complaint of a witness, who feared the assimilation of the scene with cannibalism: 'My friends, what are we doing? All of this is going to be reported; they are going to paint us abroad as a ferocious and bloodthirsty mob." A defiant voice responded:

Yes, thirsty for the blood of a despot; let them go retell it, if you like, to everyone on earth; for too long the French people have given proof of their patience; it is the weakness of a nation that emboldens the tyrants. . . . The day of justice is shining finally; it must be as terrible as the crimes have been serious.[17]

In his defense of the act, Prudhomme found himself constantly reverting to the imagery of sacrifice; the king was being metaphorically devoured (the people were "thirsty for the blood of a despot") in order to transform the French from servile slaves of tyranny into brave republicans. The killing was not cannibalism because it was ritualized. The act of terrible communion was with the victim of sacrifice himself. Only by killing him could they overcome their own

15   "Mort de Louis XVI, dernier roi de France." *Révolutions de Paris*, no. 185, 19–26 January 1793. This is by far the longest commentary in a newspaper on the killing of the king; it extends over thirty pages.
16   *Totem and Taboo*, in vol. 13 of *The Standard Edition of the Complete Psychological Works of Sigmund Freud*, trans. James Strachey (London, 1958), p. 147.
17   "Mort de Louis XVI."

weaknesses; only by eliminating a great criminal could they purify the community; only by eating the king could the people become sovereign themselves.

Republicans were divided between the desire to celebrate the act and to forget it. Yet even the radicals who wanted to keep the memory of the deed alive harped on the theme of the king's own guilt rather than the consequences of the act for themselves. Jacques-René Hébert wrote in his newspaper *Le Père Duchesne*, as if in response to the deputy who had advised letting go of all feeling of resentment toward the king, "I would not say like certain dawdlers, 'Let us speak of it no longer' [the exact words of the deputy]. On the contrary, let us talk about it in order to remind ourselves of all of his crimes and to inspire in all men the horror that they ought to have for kings."[18]

The radical insistence on keeping alive the memory of the event was echoed in a few pamphlets and engravings published immediately after the execution. The twenty-three-page pamphlet titled *The Arrival of Louis Capet in Hell* included an engraving of Louis holding his head at his judgment in hell. The mythological figures in hell discuss eating a quarter of "roasted pope" ("pape à la broche"). At the end of his trial in hell, Louis is condemned to have his heart torn to pieces by a vulture, and to perpetuate his agony, his heart will be reborn each day.[19] The most radical writers and engravers thus did not shy away from the most terrifying aspect of the execution – the sight of the king's severed head with its connotations of cannibalism – and they insisted precisely on its capacity to terrify. The best known of the engravings that celebrated the execution was Villeneuve's rendition of the severed head. The reproduction of the king's severed head must have aroused ambivalent reactions in many quarters. The decapitation was supposed to serve as a warning to other kings, but it also had a larger resonance of murder of the father, cannibalism, and potential anarchy.[20]

In fact, however, very few engravings of the execution were published in France immediately after the event. Most representations of the execution were printed outside France and were meant to serve the cause of counterrevolution. During 1793 and 1794 no commemorative medals of the execution were struck in France, though this was a

18   "Oraison funèbre de Louis Capet, dernier roi des Français, prononcé par le père Duchesne . . . ," *Le Père Duchesne*, no. 212.

19   *Arrivée de Louis Capet aux Enfers* (Paris, 1793). Attributed to Villeneuve by Maurice Tourneux, *Bibliographie de l'histoire de Paris pendant la Révolution française* (Paris, 1890), vol. 1, p. 337.

20   For a Freudian analysis of this engraving which relates it to the Medusa's head and threats of castration, see Neil Hertz, "Medusa's Head: Male Hysteria under Political Pressure," *Representations* 4 (1983): 27–54, especially pp. 47–8.

very common way to memorialize important revolutionary events.[21] One of the few engravings of the execution printed immediately afterward accompanied an eight-page pamphlet which admitted that many of the spectators present at the execution had questioned the wisdom of killing the king. Many people said that the former king "being sacred, men had no right to touch him."

The author of the pamphlet claimed in response that the act was desired by all those who understood the "price of liberty." The execution was the revenge of the entire human race.[22] The radicals could only reject the sacredness of the king by killing him and taking on that sacredness for the people as a whole. Ritual sacrifice and the metaphorical eating of the king's body were the essential means of effecting this transformation. The radicals wanted to commemorate the event in order to remind the people of their necessary complicity in the act.

Five years later, one of the deputies who had voted against the death penalty gave his own version of the execution. Louis-Sébastien Mercier insisted that Paris had not been reduced to silent stupefaction by the deed. He also underlined the ritual aspects of the killing. When Louis's blood began to run, the eighty thousand armed men present cried out with joy. Several observers ran forward

> to dip their fingers, pens, or pieces of paper into the blood; one tasted it and said, "it is horribly salty!" At the edge of the scaffold, an executioner was selling little packets of his hair . . . everyone tried to take away a small fragment of his clothing or a bloody reminder of this tragic scene. I saw all the people marching arm in arm, laughing, talking familiarly, as if they were coming back from a festival.

Mercier went on to claim, however, that as the days passed, "further reflection and a kind of anxious fear about the future cast a cloud over every social gathering." The deputies who had voted the death of the king began to feel afraid: "They were feeling a kind of interior dread which in some cases resembled repentance."[23] In his view, many of the deputies definitely felt guilt.

The tension between forgetting and commemorating, between feeling guilty and rejecting guilt, would continue as the Revolution proceeded. Most remarkable in this regard was the first anniversary of the killing of the king, in January 1794. No plans for any kind of celebration were

21 See Michel Hennin, *Histoire numismatique de la Révolution française,* 2 vols. (Paris, 1826).
22 *Décret définitif de la Convention nationale, qui condamne Louis Capet, le Traître, le Patricide, à la peine de mort . . . suivi des réflexions d'un Républicain* (Paris, n.d.).
23 Louis-Sébastien Mercier, *Le Nouveau Paris* (Paris, an VII [1799]), vol. 3, pp. 4–7.

made until the meeting of the Jacobin Club of Paris on 20 January 1794. The fact that no plans had been made ahead of time shows how ambivalent the deputies were about remembering their deed. One club member proposed a solution of typical displacement: a public reading of the Declaration of the Rights of Man and a memorial reading of the story of Lepeletier's assassination. A more zealous member asked for a parade of the effigies of all the kings currently at war with France, followed by their symbolic beheading. Finally, the club voted to present itself en masse to the Convention the next day to congratulate the deputies on the courage that they had shown in the trial of the king.[24] On the day of the anniversary itself, in response to the visit from the Jacobins, the Convention voted to hold an improvised festival and left as a group for the Place de la Révolution, site of the execution of the king. There they found themselves, to the distress of many, witnessing the day's executions.

The same deputy who had encouraged the Jacobins a year earlier to speak no longer of the king now complained bitterly in the Convention about the masquerade to which the deputies had been subjected. Why were four criminals taken to be executed at the same time as the visit of the deputies? he asked. Why were the deputies polluted with their blood? This was a conspiracy to make the deputies look like "cannibals": "We were going to celebrate the death of a king, the punishment of an eater of men; but we did not want to defile our attention with such a disgusting and hideous spectacle."[25] The deputies did not want to become like the king they had denounced as a "mangeur d'hommes." The violence of the Revolution threatened to undo the ritual sacrifice itself. If the situation could not be controlled, the sacrificial crisis would not end, and cannibalism and anarchy would menace the community's continuing existence.

Popular reactions to the "festival" varied from glee to disinterest. One police agent reported that women in a cabaret expressed particular satisfaction at the sight of the guillotine in operation during the festivities: "If the guillotine had not been in action, the festival would not have been so beautiful." Another agent reported, however, that people were revolted at the sight of deputies attending an ordinary execution. Some people blamed this on the city government of Paris, which was rumored to have arranged the coincidence of the four executions taking place as the deputies came to the square to celebrate the death of Louis XVI. At the central market, several people were seen carrying figures made of

24   Aulard, ed., *La Société des Jacobins*, vol. 5, pp. 615–66.
25   *Moniteur universel*, no. 23, 4 pluviôse an II (23 January 1794), reporting on the session of the National Convention of 3 pluviôse (22 January 1794) and the speech by Bourdon.

straw without heads as reminders of the fate of Louis. One of the other agents reported that people thought the very idea of a celebration was inappropriate because the French ought to forget the king altogether.[26]

In other parts of France, hastily organized, carnivalesque festivals picked up on the theme of the straw men without heads. Many people, and especially the popular classes, apparently wanted tangible reminders for their celebrations. In Grenoble, figures of Louis, the pope, and the nobility were smashed by two men dressed as Hercules. In Lyon, a carnival king dressed in a tiger skin sat on a throne, attended by the nobility in the guise of a wolf and the clergy in that of a fox. A dragon then set the scene on fire. As news of such celebrations spread, other towns and cities rushed to set up their own festivals. Performances of revolutionary plays, illuminations of private and public buildings, vaudevilles, popular banquets, and speeches denouncing Louis's crimes were all brought out to give the anniversary some moment.[27]

The deputies wanted no repeat of these impromptu celebrations, so they instituted a regular festival for the future, the Anniversary of the Death of the Last King of the French. The festival held in Paris in 1799 was quite typical of these organized, official celebrations. There were no manikins, no parodies, no literal representations of violence. At 10 a.m. an artillery salute inaugurated the festivities. At 11:30 a.m. the deputies gathered in their legislative costumes and, with palm leaves in hand, marched into their meeting hall to the sound of trumpets. On the tribune sat the book of the law ornamented with civic laurels. The law had presumably replaced the father-king as the emblem of authority. Central to the ceremony were speeches and oaths to hate both royalty and anarchy (the oaths varied from year to year depending on the political situation). The speech by the president of the Council of Ancients was characteristically didactic. The deputies were not there, he proclaimed, to show joy at the memory of a scaffold and punishment, but to engrave in all souls the immortal truths that had issued from that eternally memorable day. Most of the speech consisted of a capsule history of the Revolution up to Louis's death and a review of the evidence against him (again!). Thus, throughout the remainder of the

26 Pierre Caron, ed., *Rapports des agents secrets du ministre de l'Intérieur*, vol. 3, *28 nivôse an II – 20 pluviôse an II; 17 janvier 1794–8 février 1794* (Paris, 1943), pp. 67–99; the quotation is from p. 67.
27 Auguste Prudhomme, *Histoire de Grenoble* (Grenoble, 1888), pp. 640–1; Joseph Mathieu, *Célébration du 21 janvier depuis 1793 jusqu'à nos jours* (Marseille, 1865), pp. 54–5; *Discours prononcé dans le temple de la Raison, à Strasbourg, le décadi 20 pluviôse, 2e année de la République françoise, une et indivisible; jour auquel on a célébré l'anniversaire de la mort du tyran Capet* (n.p., n.d.); *Abréviateur universel*, no. 397, 13 pluviôse an II (1 February 1794), report on the festival in Rouen on 8 pluviôse.

revolutionary decade, officials were constantly trying to displace, contain, and dissipate violence even as they recognized the need to remember the violence which had given birth to republican history.[28]

After the death of the king, the deputies carried forward the attack on paternal prerogatives. Many deputies now went beyond the vague condemnation of the tyranny of parents to a more precise indictment of paternal authority, especially the control of fathers over their grown children. Jean-Jacques Cambacérès explained in his proposal for a civil code in August 1793, "The imperious voice of reason has made itself heard; it says, no more paternal power; it is deceiving nature to establish its rights by compulsion."[29]

The revolutionaries wanted liberty and equality to rule in the family just as they ruled in the state, though just what was meant by liberty and equality within the context of the family remained subject to continual redefinition. Revolutionary legislators were clearest about what they opposed: tyrannical power within the family. Deputy Berlier explained, "Excessive power leads to tyranny, tyranny embitters, and too often, instead of a tender father and a grateful son, there is seen only a barbarous master and a slave in revolt." In place of this tyranny, the deputies hoped to establish what Berlier aptly called "this gentle correlation of duties," "this authority of affection that the laws cannot command," in other words, friendship and mutual recognition of rights and obligations.[30] Liberty would guarantee individual autonomy, and love would provide familial solidarity.

The effort to establish a new equilibrium between parents and children always included a paradox, however; revolutionary legislation took power away from the father (and from the church) and ultimately vested a large portion of it in the state.[31] Legislators wanted to ensure the

28   Corps législatif, Conseil des Anciens, commission des inspecteurs de la salle, *Programme de la fête qui aura lieu le 2 pluviôse de l'an 7, dans l'intérieur du Palais des Anciens, à raison de l'anniversaire de la juste punition du dernier tyran des Français*; Corps législatif, Conseil des Anciens, *Discours prononcé par Garat, Président du Conseil des Anciens, le 2 pluviôse an 7, anniversaire du 21 janvier 1792* [sic], *et du serment de haine à la royauté et à l'anarchie*. The speech included a long comparison between the case of Louis XVI and that of Charles I.

29   Emile Masson, *La Puissance paternelle et la famille sous la Révolution* (Paris, 1910), p. 227.

30   *Discours et project de loi, sur les rapports qui doivent subsister entre les enfans et les auteurs de leurs jours, en remplacement des droits connus sous le titre usurpé de puissance paternelle, par Berlier, député de la Côte-d'Or* (Paris, 1793), pp. 4, 6.

31   On the new equilibrium, see Pierre Murat, "La Puissance paternelle et la Révolution française: Essai de régénération de l'autorité des pères," in Irène Théry and Christian Biet, eds., *La Famille, la loi, l'état de la Révolution au Code civil* (Paris, 1989),

freedom of individuals, but in order to accomplish this they had to
on state powers to curb tyrannical fathers. The Convention was 1
active in the area of property law, and it took earlier legislation several
steps further. On 7 March 1793 the deputies declared the equality of all
inheritance in the direct line of succession, thereby extending the earlier
law on intestate successions. On 5 brumaire an II (26 October 1793),
equality was extended to all inheritance in collateral lines as well and
made retroactive to 14 July 1789 (though owners of property could still
dispose of one-tenth of their property in direct successions and one-
sixth in collateral successions).

A week later, on 2 November 1793, the Convention enacted one of
its most controversial laws: it granted illegitimate children equal rights
of inheritance upon proof of paternity and made the provisions retroactive to 14 July 1789.[32] An exception was made for children of adulter-
ous unions, who gained the right to only one-third of a regular portion
of the inheritance. The law authorized legal proceedings by illegitimate
children for establishment of paternity or maternity against parents
unwilling to admit the relationship. Equality of inheritance within the
family was even more rigorously enforced by the law of 17 nivôse an II
(6 January 1794), which provided that the disposable portion of property had to go to someone outside of either the direct or the collateral
line of succession. In essence, then, the Convention was enforcing
through the law the equality within the band of brothers.

Society and the state were now asserting the superiority of their
claims over the family. The attempts to give equal status to illegitimate
children and the severe constraints on testamentary freedom of action
have led some legal scholars to conclude that the revolutionary legislatures disorganized and nearly ruined the family.[33] The deputies in the
Convention certainly did not want to ruin the family, but they did distrust it, and they were most likely to favor the rights of children over
either the individual right to dispose of property or the family's right to
defend its own longterm interests. The deputies defended the new law
on the rights of illegitimate children, for instance, by claiming that it
would help eliminate infanticide and the double standard of sexual
morality: "Sound morals will have an enemy the less, and passion a

pp. 390–411. For a view that deemphasizes the paradoxical aspects of revolutionary legislation, see Philippe Sagnac, *La Législation civile de la Révolution française,
1789–1804* (Paris, 1898).
32   The many complications of this law are discussed in Marcel Garaud and
Romuald Szramkiewicz, *La Révolution française et la famille* (Paris, 1978), pp.
116–30. For an even fuller treatment, see Crane Brinton, *French Revolutionary
Legislation on Illegitimacy, 1789–1804* (Cambridge, Mass., 1936).
33   Masson, *La Puissance paternelle*, p. 329.

brake the more . . . when, finally, it is known that no longer can a man betray the hopes of a too confiding woman."[34] The Napoleonic codes marked a great departure from this revolutionary distrust of the family; the codes explicitly considered the family a natural contract fulfilling necessary functions that required state protection.[35]

Under the National Convention, in contrast, most deputies believed that the state had to intervene to protect the rights of children against the potentially tyrannical actions of fathers, families, or churches. In many cases, such as education, the state actually took for itself the role of paternal authority. On 22 frimaire an II (12 December 1793), the Convention voted to establish state-run primary schools, and a week later it made attendance obligatory in principle. Danton proclaimed in the debate on whether primary schools should be obligatory, "Children belong to society before they belong to their family." Robespierre was even more forceful: "The country has the right to raise its children; it should not entrust this to the pride of families or to the prejudices of particular individuals, which always nourish aristocracy and domestic federalism."[36] Family prerogatives, in his view, were associated with particular interests rather than the general will, and particular interests in turn were associated with aristocracy and federalism, two major sources (though quite different in character) of opposition to the Jacobin revolution.

The republic had displayed its antipatriarchal direction: the political father had been killed, and ordinary fathers had been subjected to the constraints of the law or replaced by the authority of the state. As the radical revolution proceeded, the drama of the father disappeared from center stage, to be replaced by tensions about the nature of fraternal bonds and the place of women in the new republic. Was the family romance of fraternity to be a romance in which the brothers united gloriously to fight their common enemies or a tragedy of conflict and division? Were women the trophies of victory, the dangerous harpies of division, the helpmeets in struggle, the idealized representatives of virtue, or simply to be ignored? If the father was now absent, should one or more of the sons be imagined as taking his place, or would they remain brothers?

One powerful answer to such questions can be seen in an engraving from August 1793 that depicts three soldiers saluting a fallen brother. This print echoes David's *Oath of the Horatii* in the new atmosphere

---

34   Speech by Cambacérès, quoted in Brinton, *French Revolutionary Legislation*, p. 34.
35   Pierre Lascoumes, "L'Emergence de la famille comme intérêt protégé par le droit pénal, 1791–1810," in Théry and Biet, eds., *La Famille, la loi*, pp. 340–8.
36   Garaud and Szramkiewicz, *La Révolution française et la famille*, p. 142.

created by the republic at war. It evokes romance, in the literary sense, as the brothers-in-arms eagerly take up the challenge to go off and fight the forces of evil. Frye calls romance the "nearest of all literary forms to the wish-fulfillment dream." It is the projection of the ideals of an age, and it always revolves around adventure. Romances have three main stages, according to Frye: the perilous journey, the crucial struggle, and the exaltation of the hero.[37] The sequence of stages is implicit in the narrative of the print; the three young men have been through a battle and are ready to go onward to fight again and thus establish their heroism. Their united, brotherly action is the incarnation of the ideals of the republic, the realization of the dream of fraternity.

The transformation from David's earlier oath is striking. In the print we see an oath between men who are perhaps brothers of the same family but who are in any case revolutionary brothers. The army of the republic has created its own family composed entirely of brothers. The three brothers swear their fidelity to the republic in front of a man who himself is more fraternal than paternal, despite his reference to "mes chers enfants [my dear children]," and who in any case is dying and supine, in contrast to the father in David's *Oath*. The father is now absent or about to disappear, and the brothers are uniting to take his place. Whether the father is good or not is irrelevant because the brothers are now the focus of the story. The feminine world is now entirely outside the scene of action.

In the new family romance of fraternity, the revolutionaries seemed to hope that they would remain perpetually youthful, as the heroes of romances always were; they wanted to be permanently brothers and not founding fathers. Even the good sans-culotte family man imagined himself as a heroic young soldier.[38] In the iconography of the radical period of the French Revolution, consequently, there were virtually no emblems of fatherhood.[39] The male representation of the people in the form of Hercules was shown as a virile brother; we know that he is a

37 Northrop Frye, *Anatomy of Criticism: Four Essays* (Princeton, 1957), pp. 186–8; the quotation is from p. 186.
38 As Antoine de Baecque explains, "Le sans-culotte s'idéalise . . . en jeune soldat héroïque, alors que l'on sait, depuis les études sociologiques effectuées sur les sans-culottes parisiens et marseillais, qu'il est en fait un père de famille boutiquier." "Le sang des héros: Figures du corps dans l'imaginaire politique de la Révolution française," *Revue d'histoire moderne et contemporaine* 34 (1987): 573–4.
39 The exception seems to be the famous Père Duchesne, the figure who adorned the masthead of Hébert's newspaper of that name. Hébert's Père Duchesne has a wife and children, but he refers to the latter very rarely. See, for example, "La soirée des rois, du Père Duchesne, ou son souper de famille avec Jean-Bar," *Le Père Duchesne*, no. 4, where the Père refers to "mes bougres enfans" (he never refers to them by name).

brother because he is shown with his sisters, liberty and equality, who cannot be imagined as wives, much less mothers, if only because there are always two of them.[40]

The French brothers of 1793–94 thus seemed to be refusing to follow the Freudian script as laid out in *Totem and Taboo*; they insisted on "the original democratic equality" of each member of the tribe and refused to venerate those individuals who had distinguished themselves above the rest. In Freud's terms, they were stuck in that phase where no one was able to or was allowed to attain "the father's supreme power."[41] In contrast to the Americans, the French did not mythologize a living leader (at least not until Napoleon organized his own cult). Mirabeau, Lafayette, Marat, Danton, and Robespierre all passed from the scene without establishing an enduring cult of their own persons. Moreover, they did not successfully represent themselves either collectively or individually as fathers of the country.

The nearest French equivalent to Washington was not one individual but rather the cult of dead heroes. The first of these was Michel Lepeletier, the regicide deputy who was assassinated by a royalist on the eve of the king's execution. On the order of the Convention, the artist-deputy David organized a public exhibition of Lepeletier's body on 24 January 1793. On the pedestal of the destroyed statue of Louis XIV in the Place Vendôme, David built a raised base with lateral steps. The upper body was exposed to show the wound, and during the ceremony the president of the Convention crowned the body with the laurels of immortality.[42] The body was then carried to the Pantheon, where revolutionary heroes were entombed.

The ceremony for Lepeletier served as a kind of answer to the doubts remaining about the killing of the king. It showed that the deputies who voted for the king's death were not cannibals but rather men ready to die for their country. Lepeletier's wound was the sign of his political martyrdom and hence of his sacredness; for this reason, it had to be visible to everyone. Moreover, Lepeletier's body was still whole, unlike the king's; like a saint's body, it possessed the magical power of seeming still alive. The newspaper *Révolutions de Paris* explicitly compared the rapidly decomposing body of Louis with the "apotheosis" of Lepeletier and argued that the Convention had been able to "profit from this sad episode in order to sustain public morale at a suitable level." When Bertrand Barère delivered his eulogy for Lepeletier at the ceremony, he concluded

40   I discuss the significance of the Hercules seal in *Politics, Culture, and Class in the French Revolution* (Berkeley, 1984), pp. 87–119.
41   Freud, *Totem and Taboo*, pp. 148–9.
42   For a description and analysis of the ceremony, see Herbert, *David, Voltaire*, pp. 95–6.

by proposing that all those present swear an oath "on the body of Lepeletier to extinguish all personal animosity and to reunite to save the country."[43] In this way, the body of the martyr was supposed to help cement union between the remaining brothers.

Observers noted that this was a new kind of spectacle because dead bodies had never before been exposed this way in public. When David presented a painting of Lepeletier on his deathbed, *Lepeletier sur son lit de mort* (a painting that was subsequently destroyed), he explained the importance of the composition of Lepeletier's body: "See how his features are serene; that's because when one dies for one's country, one has nothing with which to reproach onself."[44] Lepeletier's body itself justified the deputies' confidence in their action; his serenity proved that they had no reason to feel guilty (itself an admission that many people thought guilt was in order).

When Jean-Paul Marat, journalist and deputy, was assassinated on 13 July 1793, his death became the subject of the most extensive cult organized around an individual political figure. His funeral prompted a major popular outpouring of grief, and in the following months and years, his death was the subject of scores of festivals, engravings, and theatrical representations.[45] After his assassination Marat's blood seemed to have taken on the sacrality that the king lost on 21 January. During the funeral procession on 16 July 1793 the members of the women's club called the Société des Républicaines Révolutionnaires threw flowers on the rapidly decomposing body and gathered the blood that still seemed to flow from his wounds. One of the orators cried, "Let the blood of Marat become the seed of intrepid republicans," and the women replied by swearing to "people the earth with as many Marats as they could."[46]

This vague notion that Marat's blood might engender brave republicans was the only connection of Marat with political fatherhood in the festival (a notion entirely lacking in the case of Lepeletier). For the most part he was the martyr-brother, as in David's famous painting of him in death or David's staging of the funeral procession, where Marat's body was carried on a Roman-style bier. The orators saluted him as the friend

43   *Révolutions de Paris*, no. 185, 19–26 January 1793.
44   Quoted in William Olander, *"Pour transmettre à la postérité*: French painting and the Revolution, 1774–1795" (Ph.D. diss., New York University, 1983), p. 248. See also pp. 244–5 for reactions to the funeral.
45   Jean-Claude Bonnet, ed., *La Mort de Marat* (Paris, 1986) and Marie-Hélène Huet, *Rehearsing the Revolution: The Staging of Marat's Death, 1793–1797*, trans. Robert Hurley (Berkeley, 1982).
46   Quoted in Jacques Guilhaumou, *La Mort de Marat* (Paris, 1989), p. 63. This scene is described as a ritual massacre in Bonnet, ed., *La Mort de Marat*, p. 71.

of the people (his newspaper was named *L'Ami du Peuple*), the apostle and martyr of liberty. Marat was immortal, courageous – in short, the tragic brother and example, much like the fallen brother in the engraving discussed earlier in this chapter. Or as his fellow journalist Hébert reminded his audience a few days later, Marat liked to think of himself as the Cassandra of the Revolution, certainly far removed from the image of a founding father.[47]

References to Marat as the "father of his people" only appeared after the assassination and may have been part of an effort to rehabilitate father figures that slowly took shape in late 1793 and 1794. If the father was going to reappear, however, it was only as the good father, a friend to his children, rather than as a stern, forbidding figure. In the festivals organized by the Parisian sections in the fall of 1793 to celebrate the memory of Marat, one hymn referred to "our father" ("Nous avons perdu notre père!"), but in the next line it reverted to the much more common "friend of the people" ("L'ami du peuple ne vit plus!").[48] A hymn published in the year II made the same link between father and friend of the people: "Of the people he was the father, the friend most ardent."[49]

Plays written about Marat after his death show the same pattern. Camaille Saint-Aubin's *L'Ami du Peuple* ended with the line: "An entire people acclaim him and call him their father." Gassier Saint-Amand's *L'Ami du Peuple, ou la mort de Marat* ended even more pointedly: "We all lose a father, a friend." Yet as Marie-Hélène Huet has argued about these lines, only Marat's death confirms his paternity, and his paternity is a fatherhood without lineage and without heirs.[50] The very memorializations that emphasized Marat's greatness seemed to imply that his contribution could not be imitated.[51]

---

47   Guilhaumou, *La Mort de Marat*, p. 85. For a sense of the wide variety of parallels drawn between Marat and Greco-Roman, modern republican, and even Biblical heroes (Moses, Jesus), see Jean-Claude Bonnet, "Les Formes de célébration," in Bonnet, ed., *La Mort de Marat*, pp. 101–27, especially pp. 110–11.

48   Guilhaumou, *La Mort de Marat*, p. 107, civic festival organized by the Section de la Cité, 21 October 1793.

49   "Stances en l'honneur de Marat," par d'Hannouville fils, *Le Chansonnier de la Montagne* (Paris, an II), quoted by Lise Andries, "Marat dans les occasionnels et les almanachs (1792–1797)," in Bonnet, ed., *La Mort de Marat*, p. 96.

50   Quoted in Huet, *Rehearsing the Revolution*, pp. 75, 79. Huet concludes (p. 83): "In the framework of the Revolution . . . there was a rupture and a discontinuity: no inheritance could be counted on, no transmission was possible: the father had children but no heirs."

51   Thus the engravings of Marat that aimed to be favorable to his legacy never presented him as father, but only as martyr, as public figure, sometimes as Christ figure. Lise Andries, "Les Estampes de Marat sous la Révolution: Une Emblématique," in Bonnet, ed., *La Mort de Marat*, pp. 187–201.

The cult of dead heroes extended to young boys who had died fighting for the republic, in itself a significant indicator that the revolutionaries were not interested in finding father figures to emulate. The young heroes were the model for the children of the republic, and they also represented the internalized self-image of the revolutionaries as young, romantic heroes. The best known of the child-heroes was Joseph Bara, a thirteen-year-old boy whose willingness to die in opposing the Vendée rebels was immortalized in an unfinished painting by David.[52] The heroism of Bara was brought to the attention of the Convention in December 1793 and taken up and considerably embellished by Robespierre soon after. He described the "extraordinary child" as someone who tried to satisfy both "filial love" and "love of country," but who in the end died for the latter.[53] As Robespierre himself had explained in November 1792, "the family of French legislators is the country [la patrie]; it is the entire human race, except for the tyrants and their accomplices."[54]

Bara, as many engravings on the theme explained, had worked hard to support his widowed mother with his soldier's pay. He had no father. David planned a festival for 10 thermidor (28 July 1794) to honor Bara and another young hero, Agricola Viala, an orphan from the south, who distinguished himself in fighting against the southern rebels. David's plan for the festival was published even though the festival itself was not held because of the fall of Robespierre, its chief patron, on 27 July 1794. The festival project reproduced the same absence of the fathers found in the young heroes' stories; David's plan called for two columns, one a deputation of children, the other a deputation of mothers.[55] Although the festival was not held, Bara and Viala were the subject of scores of songs and hymns and of many operas and

---

52   A discussion of the place of the painting of Bara within David's work would take me too far afield, but it should be noted that the figure of the young boy is very androgynous, even female. We can see here a major move away from David's pre-revolutionary paintings with their emphasis on virility, toward his post-1795 works and their revalorization of femininity. For a brief discussion, see Warren Roberts, "David's *Bara* and the Burdens of the French Revolution," *Proceedings of the Consortium on Revolutionary Europe, 1750–1850* (Tallahassee, Fla., 1990), pp. 76–81.
53   On the painting and Robespierre's support for the cult, see Olander, "*Pour transmettre*," pp. 293–302. It is tempting to make much of the androgyny of David's figure of Bara; is this an inadvertent rendering of the very blurring of sexual boundaries so feared by the revolutionaries themselves?
54   Marc Bouloiseau, Jean Dautry, Georges Lefebvre, and Albert Soboul, eds., *Oeuvres de Maximilien Robespierre*, vol. 9, *Discours, septembre 1792–27 juillet 1793* (Paris, 1961), p. 94.
55   *Rapport sur la fête héroique pour les honneurs du Panthéon à décerner aux jeunes Barra et Viala, par David; Séance du 23 messidor, an 2 de la République* (Paris, 1794).

plays.[56] Similar in thematic reference were the engravings of the young Darrudder, a drummer boy of fourteen who, seeing his father die at his side, grabbed his pistol and shot at the enemy. In this story too, the father is dead, and it is precisely the absence of the father that makes the courage of the son so moving.

In their own self-image, then, the French revolutionaries remained brothers. They were romantic heroes willing to fight for virtue and the triumph of the republic against the forces of evil and corruption. They were prepared to become martyrs for their cause, either on the battlefield or in the line of official duties. They expected the gratitude of the nation, but their chief reward was their sense of solidarity with their brothers.

Sisters had an equivocal place in the new family romance of fraternity. Their place as inheritors from the father had been assured by revolutionary legislation, and new questions had been raised about their rights as citizens. But republican men also expressed great uneasiness about women acting in public ways. These doubts began to crystallize when Marat was assassinated by a woman. Charlotte Corday took for herself the role of the three sons in David's *Oath of the Horatii* and the role of the father in his *Brutus*. She wielded the dagger in defense of her vision of the republic. Corday portrayed herself as the good daughter willing to sacrifice her life to rid the republic of a tyrant. "Pardon me," she wrote to her father, "for having disposed of my existence without your permission. I avenged many innocent victims, I prevented many new disasters. The people, disabused one day, will rejoice at being delivered from a tyrant."[57]

In response to newspaper reports that were deemed too favorable to Corday, the government distributed an article that attacked her sexuality and her impertinence as a female acting politically:

> This woman, said to be very pretty, was not at all pretty; she was a virago, brawny rather than fresh, without grace, untidy, as are almost all female philosophers and eggheads. . . . Charlotte Corday was 25 years old; in our customs that is practically an old maid, especially with a masculinized bearing and boyish look. . . . Thus, it follows that this woman had thrown herself absolutely outside of her sex.[58]

This rejection of Corday's self-attributed political role soon extended to all women who wished to act politically, including the same Société

---

56   James A. Leith, "Youth Heroes of the French Revolution," *Proceedings of the Consortium on Revolutionary Europe, 1750–1850* (Athens, Ga., 1987), pp. 127–37.
57   Guilhaumou, *La Mort de Marat*, p. 150.
58   Ibid., pp. 74–5.

des Républicaines Révolutionnaires which had been so prominent in the sacralization of Marat. Women who acted in the public sphere of politics would be described as transgressing sexual boundaries and contributing to the blurring of sexual differentiation. Their actions made them look like men; they were seen as taking on a sex not their own.

Women were not absent, however, from the iconographic family romance of the radical republic. Most representations of the republic were feminine, and they almost always showed young women, often virginal, but sometimes with very young children. Young women appear almost promiscuously in official representations, for they could be and were used to represent every imaginable political attribute such as Liberty, Reason, Wisdom, Victory, and even Force. Whenever a political message required an allegorical presentation, the allegory almost always centered on female figures.

The predominance of female figures in revolutionary iconography raises many questions. Were they present for entirely symbolic reasons or did their importance suggest something significant about women and the public sphere in revolutionary France? The reasons for the prominence of female figures are many.[59] The iconographic tradition had it that abstract qualities were best represented by female figures even when, as in the case of Fraternity or Force, for example, the representation by a female figure seemed to suggest a contradiction. This feminization of abstract qualities was reinforced by the fact that most such qualities were feminine nouns in French (and Latin and Greek) and also no doubt by the Catholic veneration of the Virgin Mary.

There were political reasons too for the apotheosis of the feminine allegory.[60] The founding of the republic required not only the destruction of every institution associated with monarchy but also a system of signs that was as distant as possible from monarchy. Since only men could rule directly in France – Salic law prevented women from succeeding to the throne – there was an obvious virtue in representing the republic by a female allegory; she could not be confused with the father/king. Moreover, French democracy operated in a manner which made any symbolic investment in individual political leaders quite problematic. If the brothers were determined to maintain what Freud called "the original democratic equality" of each member of the tribe and they refused to venerate any particular individual, then the singling out of

59   For a brief and useful discussion, see Maurice Agulhon, *Marianne au combat: L'Imagerie et la symbolique républicaines de 1789 à 1880* (Paris, 1979; English version, Cambridge, 1981).
60   See my discussion in *Politics, Culture, and Class*, pp. 87–119.

individual male political figures as representations of the people, the nation, or the general qualities of citizenship would be unacceptable. No individual politicians appeared on French coins or paper money. Female allegories could not be associated with particular political leaders, if only because all officials were male by definition.

The presence of the female figure in iconography was not, consequently, a sign of female influence in politics. As Marina Warner has argued for the nineteenth century, the representation of liberty as female worked on a paradoxical premise: women, who did not have the vote and would be ridiculed if they wore the cap of liberty in real life, were chosen to express the ideal of freedom because of their very distance from political liberty. Liberty was figured as female because women were not imagined as political actors. Yet the embodiment of political ideals by female figures also opened the door to a different vision. As Warner remarks, "a symbolized female presence both gives and takes value and meaning in relation to actual women, and contains the potential for affirmation not only of women themselves but of the general good they might represent."[61]

However overdetermined the choice of the female allegory might have been during the Revolution, the choice nevertheless had consequences. Women were shown as actors, and even if these women in plaster and metal were not imagined as particular women, they were still women and hence potentially threatening.[62] The constant criticism of the use of live women to represent virtues in festivals and the struggles over the female figure during the nineteenth century show that the female allegory had powerful resonances that went beyond the merely symbolic.

Although there is never a father present in the official vignettes of the republic, young men, especially Hercules, did sometimes figure in tandem with their sisters. In the representations of Hercules with Liberty and Equality, the female figures often appear as trophies held in the hand of the conquering hero/brother. Thus, in iconographic terms, the incest taboo is not being very well enforced in the absence of the father. This is an iconographic family without parentage and without a lineage. The relation of the brothers and sisters to each other in this family is ambiguous and ambivalent.

Deputies, artists, or writers were hardly ever explicitly concerned with incest, but many saw a connection between the experience of the

61   Marina Warner, *Monuments and Maidens: The Allegory of the Female Form* (New York, 1985), pp. xx, 277.
62   In my analysis of the Hercules figure, I show that the deputies chose a masculine representation when they wanted to eliminate the ambiguities created by the female allegory. *Politics, Culture, and Class*, pp. 87–119.

Revolution as a political and social upheaval and fundamental anxieties about family relationships. In a fragmentary manuscript written in 1792, Saint-Just argued that incest was a virtue when it was undertaken innocently: "It is virtue on the part of him who gives himself over to it in innocence and is no longer incest. . . . Observe the customs, read the laws of different peoples. The most corrupt also had the most horror of incest; innocent peoples never had a concept of it."[63] The same Saint-Just who argued so forcefully for the immediate execution of the king as a rebel here claims that the people most horrified by incest are also those who are the most politically corrupt. Incest, it might be said, was nothing but innocence about the force of the father's law, and those who were thus innocent were less likely to be contaminated by the experience of the father's despotism.

Incest seems to have disappeared from the novels produced during the radical revolution, and the novel itself went into decline. From a high point of 112 new novels published in 1789, the number steadily diminished from 66 in 1790 to 40 in 1792, 20 in 1793, and to the low point of 15 in 1794.[64] We do not know from direct testimony why novelists ceased producing new works, and there are many possible reasons for the decline, including a serious paper shortage.[65] Yet the production of new plays and the publication of new songs did not decrease in the same way. At least 1,500 new plays were staged between 1789 and 1799, and more than 750 were presented in the years 1792–94. Similarly, the number of new political songs rose steadily from 116 in 1789 to 701 in 1794.[66]

Apparently, the novel had come to seem suspect as a genre because it was private not public, and perhaps also because it was associated with women, both as authors and readers. By the last quarter of the eighteenth century, it was a commonplace of criticism that women were especially drawn to the novel. Laclos wrote in 1784 that he considered women especially apt for writing novels. Rousseau warned of the effect on girls of reading his own novel, and he associated novels in general

63   "De la nature, de l'état civil, de la cité ou les règles de l'indépendance, du gouvernement," in Louis-Antoine Saint-Just, *Oeuvres complètes*, ed. Michèle Duval (Paris, 1984), pp. 946–7.
64   These figures are compiled from the information given in Angus Martin, Vivienne G. Mylne, and Richard Frautschi, *Bibliographie du genre romanesque français, 1751–1800* (London, 1977).
65   On the paper shortage and related matters, see Carla Hesse, *Publishing and Cultural Politics in Revolutionary Paris, 1789–1810* (Berkeley, 1991).
66   Beatrice F. Hyslop, "The Theater during a Crisis: The Parisian Theater during the Reign of the Terror," *Journal of Modern History* 17 (1945): 332–55; Robert Brécy, "La Chanson révolutionnaire de 1789 à 1799," *Annales historiques de la Révolution française* 53 (1981): 279–303.

with corruption. In his *Tableau de Paris* of the 1780s, Mercier concluded that novels by women were "the happiest and most agreeable luxury" of great societies.[67] If in the period 1792–94 excessive privacy, luxury, and feminine power had come to be viewed as problems – they were all explicitly attacked by the Jacobins as conducive to corruption – then it is no wonder that the novel itself might become problematic.

Those who did publish novels between 1792 and 1794 often favored the pastoral myth, apparently because it was well suited to the republic's emphasis on the didactic presentation of virtue.[68] In the pastoral tale, the heroes are pure, courageous, and generous. "Sacred duty," "simplicity" of life and love, and clear-cut distinctions between those who are good and those who are evil are the constant themes. A. T. de Rochefort's novel *Adraste et Nancy V.Y.* (1794), for example, tells the story of a French officer during the American War of Independence who is convinced of the advantages of a republic by the virtues of the Americans, especially their hospitality and generosity. The pastoral also could be adapted to contemporary settings. Dulaurent's tale *Joseph, or the Little Chimney Sweep* (1794?), presents a young boy from the Vendée region whose father is killed during the uprising against the republic. Despite being forced to leave his tranquil and happy home (the pastoral setting) by these events and having to take a job as a chimney sweep, he maintains his consistently generous character throughout. In the same vein, Ducray-Duminil wrote short stories during this period that showed that love of the countryside, love for one's fellow humans, and love for the republic were all inextricably linked. One of his best-known stories from this period, "The Oak of Liberty," centers on an old man telling tales to children whose fathers have been killed in the revolutionary wars.

As these very brief descriptions make clear, the fiction of 1792–94 is preoccupied with the deaths of fathers, and the writers favorable to the republic seem eager to demonstrate that fatherless children can be bastions of republican virtue. The children in these tales do not have particularly interesting personalities; they are simply good through and

---

67   Georges May, *Le Dilemme du roman au dix-huitième siècle* (Paris, 1963), especially chapter 8, "Féminisme et roman," pp. 204–46; the quotation is from p. 219.
68   In my discussion of the pastoral tale I am following the analysis of Malcolm C. Cook, "Politics in the Fiction of the French Revolution, 1789–1794," *Studies on Voltaire and the Eighteenth Century*, vol. 201 (Oxford, 1982), pp. 290–311. Henri Coulet argues that the pedagogical novel in the style of Fénelon was especially suited to moderate republicanism, whereas the heroic story situated in Rome, Greece, or the Orient was suited to patriotic Jacobinism. This may be true, but his own analysis so mixes chronology that it is hard to evaluate. "Existe-t-il un roman révolutionnaire?" in *La Légende de la Révolution*, actes du colloque international de Clermont-Ferrand, juin 1986 (Clermont-Ferrand, 1988), pp. 173–83.

through. The fiction writers of 1792–94 thus appear unc
with the ambiguities of the family romance of fraternity; th
reassure their readers that a fatherless world poses no pro
same insistence that everything will be alright can be founu ᵤ. ᵤ
tale which directly takes up the issue of father killing. One of the pieces
in P. F. Barbault-Royer's *Republican Novellas* tells the story of Démophon,
who kills the tyrant Alcionaus on the urging of an oracle, only to discover that the tyrant was his father. The gods urge Démophon to reject
any feeling of guilt: "When it involves the happiness of everyone, when
by a divine stroke you have broken the most fierce tyrant, must you send
forth lamentations? It doesn't matter that he was your father; the
country and your brothers must come before everything else."[69] There
is little suggestion in any of these novels and stories that the death of
the father will lead to conflict between the brothers or to some form of
retribution.

Similarly, the paintings of the radical period 1792–94 rarely hinted
at conflict between the brothers. David's paintings of Lepeletier and
Marat both showed saintly martyrs in poses of self-confident serenity.
They were martyrs to the egotism, corruption, and evil designs of the
counterrevolutionaries, not to the struggles between brothers within
the revolutionary family. The violence of the Revolution was transcended in the composition of the paintings, which emphasized the
humanity, sensibility, and generosity of the victims as well as their
exemplary character for other republicans.

Painting did not diminish as an activity during the radical revolution,
but most of the established names withdrew from public view. The Salon
of 1793 attracted some 800 images by 350 painters and engravers, but
most of the well-known names in art stayed away (including David, who
exhibited his paintings in the hall of the Convention itself), and few
critics wrote about the exhibition, no doubt for some of the same reasons
that the novelists stayed out of print. Portraits remained an important
category in the 1793 Salon, accounting for one-fourth of the images
submitted. Since nearly two-thirds of the individuals in the portraits
were unidentified in the catalogue of the Salon, the portraits might be
seen as capturing the anonymity of the revolutionary crowd. On the
other hand, portraiture by definition singles out an individual from
the crowd. This tension about the role of the individual was central
to revolutionary ideology; the Revolution required great individual
heroism, but everyone was imagined as capable of it. By 1793 at least
five collections of engravings of important figures of the Revolution had
been published, but these conveyed the same message: the Revolution

69   Quoted in Cook, "Politics in the Fiction," p. 300.

had been made by many individuals acting together, and it was their sheer number, not their individuality, that guaranteed success. No one great figure stood out.[70]

Killing the king/father clearly aroused great anxiety among the supporters of the Revolution. The most radical republicans denied that there were any grounds for anxiety, but their forms of denial – whether in speeches, newspaper articles, novels, engravings or paintings – usually betray the existence of nagging questions. They seemed to be answering unseen critics. The more moderate republicans hoped that the king and his death could be forgotten, or at least remembered only in a distant, orderly fashion. Neither group proved right. If the king was the scapegoat for the community's fear of its own violence in a time of great change, killing him did not work to displace or transcend that threat of violence. Thousands more victims of every social class, both men and women, proceeded to the guillotine after him.

70   In this account of the Salon of 1793 I am following the analysis of Olander, "*Pour transmettre,*" pp. 254–84.

9

Church, State, and the Ideological Origins of the French Revolution: The Debate over the General Assembly of the Gallican Clergy in 1765

Dale Van Kley

Originally appeared as Dale Van Kley, "Church, State, and the Ideological Origins of the French Revolution: The Debate over the General Assembly of the Gallican Clergy in 1765," *The Journal of Modern History* 51 (1979), pp. 629–66 (Chicago: University of Chicago Press).

Editor's Introduction

Throughout the long reign of Louis XV (1715–74) a number of crucial political conflicts centered around the Catholic denomination known as Jansenism. Named for its originator, Flemish theologian Cornelius Jansenus (1585–1638), Jansenism promoted an austere morality and the doctrine of predestination, features that induced some to compare it to Calvinism and other variants of Protestantism. Despite the fact that the French Wars of Religion had concluded at the end of the sixteenth century, any departure from Catholic orthodoxy, and in particular any apparent affinity for Protestant doctrine, remained dangerous long into the eighteenth century. Louis XIV had oppressed Jansenists along with Protestants, and persecution continued under Louis XV. The principal theological adversaries of Jansenism were the members of the Society of Jesus (i.e. *Jesuits*) and in particular the *Molinists* or adherents to the theology of Luis de Molina

(1535–1600), a Spanish Jesuit who had opposed predestination and insisted on the doctrine of free will. Pope Clement XI (1649–1721) favored the Molinist position and in 1713 condemned Jansenism in a bull known as *Unigenitus*. At various points during Louis XV's reign, and especially during the 1750s, Molinist bishops supported a policy of refusing sacraments, including the crucial *extreme unction* administered to the dying as a precondition for their salvation, from men and women suspected of opposing Unigenitus. Although it is impossible to know how sympathetic the *parlements* or judicial courts were to Jansenism as a theology, many of their members denounced the cruel practice of withholding the sacraments from gravely ill believers and repeatedly declared it illegal. Whatever their religious beliefs, by intervening in the sacraments controversy the magistrates raised the question of the appropriate powers that the church, courts and crown should have in France. In the parlance of the time, they raised the question of France's *constitution*.

The political implications of religious controversies were also informed by a tension between *Gallicanism* and *ultramontanism*. Gallicanism advocated the independence of the French Catholic Church from papal control, and as such can be regarded as a precursor to or early form of nationalism; ultramontanists, by contrast, looked to Rome (literally "beyond the mountains" separating France from Italy) for guidance in matters of Church policy. Although nothing in Jansenist doctrine necessitated the espousal of Gallicanism, by the eighteenth century Jansenists and their supporters tended toward this position. By contrast, the episcopacy (i.e. the bishops) tended toward ultramontanism. This had not always been the case, and indeed the body of bishops that so frequently provoked the *parlementaire* supporters of Jansenism was called the assembly of the Gallican Clergy. That group had reiterated its independence from Rome as late as 1682, when it issued its Gallican Declaration. By the 1760s, however, the bishops had largely repudiated their autonomy and embraced ultramontanism.

Finally, Catholics were divided over the question of how the French Church itself was to be governed. The bishops, perhaps unsurprisingly, advocated a hierarchical, *episcopal* system in which bishops ruled (in accordance with guidelines from Rome), ordinary priests had little power, and their flocks had still less influence over Church governance. This ideal was opposed by *lay conciliarists* who called for a more democratic structure according to which "the faithful" in general would govern the church, as had been the practice, they claimed, in ancient times.

It is in the context of these three sets of tensions – Jansenism versus Molinism, Gallicanism versus ultramontanism, and episcopalism versus lay conciliarism – that Dale Van Kley places a controversy that erupted when the assembly of the Gallican Clergy published its *Actes* in 1765. The *Actes*

[Handwritten marginal notes at top: "Free will suggests that God is not all-powerful; predestination doesn't" and "Calvin claims that God is: 'not a loaf...'"; left margin: "Pandora's Box"]

included an "Exposition of the Rights of the Spiritual Power," which re-affirmed the bishops' exclusive prerogative over such matters as the administration (or refusal) of sacraments and denounced the *parlements* for having intervened in the controversy over Jansenism. This "Exposition" also implicitly criticized the king for having made adherence to Unigeni-tus optional (by not recognizing it as a "rule of faith") and for his *Law of Silence*, which forbade polemics about the papal bull. By criticizing the tem-poral power not only of the *parlements* but of the king himself, Van Kley maintains, borrowing the words of a prior historian, the bishops had made a declaration of "almost revolutionary audacity."

Van Kley briefly describes the ensuing "three-cornered slugfest" between the *parlements*, which denounced the Acts, the royal council, which annulled the denunciation (under financial pressure from the well-heeled episcopacy), and the bishops. Yet he focuses for the main part of the article on an examination of the many pamphlets that accompanied the publication of the *Actes*, most of which, he observes, defended the *par-lements*. Van Kley identifies two ideologies that crystalized in the pamphlet war. Those who opposed the bishops tended to combine elements of Jansenism, Gallicanism, and lay conciliarism. This last tendency, the author claims, suggested an affinity with the ideology of the *parlements*, since both justified their positions by locating "rights" in a supposedly ancient "con-stitution" and criticized their opponents as "despotic." Some anti-episcopal pamphlets invoked the idea of the *social contract* (most familiar from Rousseau) as well as the Enlightenment idea of a right to happiness, and the most radical among them envisaged the nationalization of Church property, precisely the measure that revolutionaries would take in 1790. Those authors who supported the *Actes*, by contrast, combined elements of Molinism, ultramontanism and episcopal power as described above. At the same time, and despite their obvious competition with the "temporal power" of the state, they presented themselves as firm supporters of monarchy. Thus, Van Kley argues, the *liberal* and *conservative* ideologies that most historians see as inventions of the nineteenth century were already firmly in place in the 1760s.

Furthermore, Van Kley observes that the conservatives were as adept in manipulating the vocabulary of the Enlightenment as the liberals. They were perfectly capable of invoking the concepts of reason, nature and social contracts to justify a hierarchical society headed by "throne and altar." If this appears paradoxical, it is only because post-revolutionary lib-erals appropriated the Enlightenment and treated it as the origin of their ideology, while post-revolutionary conservatives repudiated it as a purely revolutionary movement, even as they used its own concepts to attack it. Van Kley's observation that both groups spoke the language of the Enlight-enment, moreover, is relevant to the perennial question of the "ideological origins of the French Revolution," as indeed his article's title suggests. Although published in 1979, prior to Keith Michael Baker's important article, significantly titled, "On the Problem of the Ideological Origins of the French Revolution,"[1] Van Kley's piece represents an early assault (in which Baker similarly engages) on the long-held assumption that one could find the origins of the Revolution in the writings of the *philosophes*. Although lacking the concept of *discourse*,[2] which Baker would adapt from Michel Foucault (1926–84) to explain the relationship between ideas and politics in pre-revolutionary France, Van Kley's article makes a similar point. By arguing that the Enlightenment was a "vocabulary" or "language" available to anyone capable of using it to make political claims, he suggests that it did not *cause* the revolution, and that it was indeed no more inherently revolutionary than counter-revolutionary. Yet he departs from Baker in his argument that the controversies examined in this article "were central, not peripheral, to the unraveling of the Old Regime and the coming of the French Revolution." In this respect he has placed the history of religion, previously overlooked in the historiography of the French Revolution, squarely on the agenda of those seeking to understand its origins.

1 See chapter 2.
2 In his magnum opus, *The Religious Origins of the French Revolution* (New Haven and London: Yale University Press, 1996), Van Kley incorporates the concept of discourse into his analysis. *The Religious Origins*, although more recent than the article reprinted here, is a work of great erudition which, precisely because of its mastery of complex detail, appeared to me impossible to excerpt.

Church, State, and the Ideological Origins of the French Revolution: The Debate over the General Assembly of the Gallican Clergy in 1765

Dale Van Kley

I Introduction

The lot of the provincial parish priest has no doubt always been a hard one, but it seemed even harder than usual to Hubert Chalumeau, curé of Saint Pierre in Vézelay, in the spring of 1766. It was bad enough that numbers of "pernicious books" had penetrated this remote Burgundian town, most notably some by Jean-Jacques Rousseau, and that the curé's parishioners had been "devouring" them. At least for this evil a powerful antidote was at hand – or so the curé thought. For as it providentially happened, the general assembly of the Gallican Clergy had just anathematized some of these books, specifically Rousseau's *Emile*, *Social Contract*, and *Letters Written from the Mountain*, and had moreover published their condemnation as part of its *Actes*, which some bishops had sent to their parish priests.[1] So when the vigilant Chalumeau received his copy toward the beginning of 1766, he could think of no better means of countering the "extreme peril" threatening his parishioners' souls than to read to them the section condemning the "books against Religion" as an introduction to his sermon. But who should have thought that for this gesture of edification the local *procureur fiscal*, who had not even attended the sermon, would denounce the good curé to the attorney general of the parlement of Paris as a rebellious subject and a disturber of the public peace? Yet that is in fact what happened. "Ah, monsigneur," he sighed, in a letter to the attorney general on April 29, "how unhappy is the lot of the curé these days." It is hard to disagree.[2]

---

1 *Actes de l'assemblée générale du clergé de France sur la religion, extraits du procès-verbal de ladite assemblée, tenue à Paris, par permission du Roi, au couvent des Grands-Augustins, en mil sept cent soixante-cinq* (Paris, 1765), "Condamnation de plusieurs livres contre la religion," pp. 3–9, esp. p. 9 (hereafter cited as *Actes*).
2 Bibliothèque Nationale (hereafter BN), Collection Joly de Fleury, fol. 1480, MS 345, Billon, procureur fiscal, to attorney general, Vézelay, February 13, 1766, and MSS 348–9, Chalumeau to attorney general, Vézelay, April 29, 1766.

What had this curé done wrong? How could his modest stand against provincial apostasy have merited the martyrdom of a scrape with the law, which for its part had "lacerated and burned" Rousseau's *Emile* as recently as 1762? On one level, the answer is quite simple. Only the first and smaller portion of the *Actes*, published by the general assembly of 1765 dealt with the "criminal productions" of the French Enlightenment; the second and far larger portion defined the rights of the Church in relation to the State.[3] Now this second part of *Actes* had provoked the ire of the parlement of Paris, which therefore condemned the entire document and tried to prevent its dissemination. So when Vézelay's *procureur fiscal* obtained word that the curé of Saint Pierre had publicly read these *Actes*, he wrongly concluded that the curé had read the whole document, rather than only the part against the irreligious books. It was all a pathetic mistake – avoidable, no doubt, had the *procureur fiscal* only gone to mass.

But on another level the incident is rather more complicated than that, and invites a closer look at the whole range of issues dividing the clergy from the parlement which had culminated in the publication of the *Actes*. Important no doubt in their own right, the issues separating the two major *corps* of the realm seem all the more so in the light of the pamphlet literature the controversy provoked, for a careful examination of this literature reveals a "liberal" France in confrontation with a "conservative" France long before the nineteenth century or even the Revolution to which these divisions are generally credited. The controversy moreover reveals a ubiquitous Enlightenment cutting across these divisions, seemingly without specific political direction of its own. So let us leave this poor curé to his provincial misery, and proceed directly to the episcopal *Actes* which occasioned it, and the controversies of the capital which caused it.

It was most unusual for a general assembly of the Gallican Clergy to promulgate a doctrinal statement such as these *Actes* contained. For the general assembly was not strictly speaking a Church council, but rather a delegation of the clergy in its temporal capacity as first order of the realm. Its origin was fairly recent, as Old Regime institutions go: the monarchy virtually created it at the Colloquy of Poissy in 1561 when it guaranteed the clergy's corporate autonomy and fiscal immunities in return for a large financial contribution. Since then the first estate's assembly had ordinarily met every five years in order to renegotiate this contract, verify its financial accounts, and present remonstrances to the

---

3 *Actes*, "Exposition sur les droits de la puissance spirituelle," pp. 11–46, and "Déclaration sur la constitution *Unigenitus*," pp. 47–51.

king.[4] All the same, the assembly had occasionally made doctrinal judgments, most notably in 1682 when, cajoled by Louis XIV and guided by Bishop Bossuet, it defined the four famous "liberties" of the Gallican Church uniting adherence to the Council of Constance's assertion of the ecumenical council's supremacy in matters of faith to a declaration of the monarchy's complete independence of any ecclesiastical authority in temporal affairs.[5] But on this and other occasions the assembly had acted at the behest or at least with the blessings of the monarchy. In contrast, what the assembly first did timidly in 1760 and 1762, then with great fanfare in 1765, was quite without precedent: it published a doctrinal statement against the "temporal power" in spite of the unexpressed but sufficiently known displeasure of its crowned head. It was indeed, as one historian has called it, an act of "almost revolutionary audacity."[6]

The circumstances accounting for the clergy's belligerence in 1765 are not obscure. In the course of the previous decade, the macabre campaign by a group of episcopal zealots to deny the Eucharist and extreme unction to penitents suspected of Jansenism had broken against the inflexible resistance of the parlements which, led by that of Paris, defended the right of all Catholics to public participation in the sacraments. At first the king had seemed to side with the episcopacy against his Parisian magistrates, who sustained the unmistakable marks of royal displeasure in 1753 and again in 1757. But in September of that year the parlement returned triumphant and, under cover of the king's Law of Silence, thereafter ordered priests to administer the sacraments to appellants of *Unigenitus* and harried them out of the land if they refused. In sum, not only had the parlement "Thrust its hand into the censer" and seized ultimate jurisdictional authority over the Church's most "august" sacraments, but it had seriously undermined the episcopacy's control over its parish priests. Then came the parlement's suppression of the Jesuit Order, entailing two additional profane tramplings upon the holy ground of ecclesiastical jurisdiction. First, the parlement annulled the Jesuits' vows as abusive and pronounced the whole order to be "perverse." Then, not content with having arrogated to itself a purely spiritual authority by condemning a collection of extracts from Jesuits' theological treatises – the infamous *Assertions dangereuses* – the parlement added the effrontery of sending this collection to all the

---

4 Louis Greenbaum, "The General Assembly of the Clergy of France and Its Situation at the End of the Ancien Régime," *Catholic Historical Review* 53 (July 1967): 156–9.

5 On Gallicanism, Bossuet, and the assembly of 1682, see Victor Martin, *Le Gallicanisme politique et le clergé de France* (Paris, 1929); and Aimé-Georges Martimort, *Le Gallicanisme de Bossuet* (Paris, 1953).

6 Bourlon, *Les Assemblées du clergé et le jansénisme* (Paris, 1909), p. 274.

realm's bishops, not for their judgment, but for their instruction and edification.[7] Decidedly, by 1765 the bishops had had enough. For them the time had again come, as it had for Saint Flavian in the fifth century, "to raise our voices and proclaim our doctrine."[8]

So proclaim they did. The resultant "Exposition of the Rights of the Spiritual Power" began innocuously enough with a proclamation of Gallican banalities. Two powers had been established to govern man: "the sacred authority of priests and that of kings"; both came from God, from whom emanated all "well-ordered power on the earth." The goal of the second of these powers was man's well-being in the present life; the object of the first was to prepare him for eternity. In establishing these two powers, God had intended not their strife but their cooperation, so that they might lend mutual aid and support. But neither power was to be subordinate to the other, for each was "sovereign, independent and absolute" in its own domain. For that reason "the Clergy of France" had always taught that the Church's power was confined to "spiritual things," and that kings were "not subordinate to any ecclesiastical power . . . in temporal things," because they held their power from God himself. But if kings commanded in temporal affairs, "the universal Church" had always taught that they were "obliged to obey priests in the order of Religion," to whom "alone the government of the Church belongs."[9]

But it was not so much the glittering teeth of its principles as the tailend whiplash of their applications that constituted the *Actes'* chief force. ". . . Silence," the *Actes* for example proclaimed, "can never be imposed upon those whom God had instituted as His mouthpiece." This was a not very covert condemnation of Louis XV's Law of Silence of September 2, 1754, which had forbidden mention of the bull *Unigenitus* and polemical terms such as Jansenist and Molinist. Again, ". . . The Civil Power . . . cannot . . . be permitted to contradict the Doctrine received by the Church, to suspend the execution of her judgments, or to elude their effects. . . ." Instead read: the parlement of Paris flagrantly exceeded its authority on April 18, 1752, when it declared that no one could be refused the sacraments by virtue of opposition to *Unigenitus.* Moreover, "the Laws of the Church can receive no qualifications except from the authority which pronounced them." In other words, even Louis XV exceeded his authority in his Declaration of December 10, 1756, by

---

7   On these developments, see Dale Van Kley, *The Jansenists and the Expulsion of the Jesuits from France* (New Haven, Conn., 1975), pp. 108–36; and D. Van Kley, "The Refusal of Sacraments Controversy in France and the Political Crisis of 1756–7" (paper presented at the meeting of the American Society for Eighteenth-Century Studies, Chicago, April 1978).

8   *Actes*, accompanying circular letter dated August 27, 1765, p. 91.

9   Ibid., pp. 15–27.

saying that *Unigenitus* was not a "rule of faith," thereby implying that the bull's opponents were not really heretics. Further, "The Keys of the Kingdom of Heaven would have been remitted to [the Church] in vain, were she able to authorize a corrupt ethic . . . , and the judgment she pronounces on moral truths, is just as independent of Princes and their Ministers, as that which she makes concerning the objects of belief." That is to say that the parlement's condemnation of lax casuistical propositions taken from Jesuit authors was both unnecessary and jurisdictionally illicit. And finally, ". . . The refusal of the most august of our sacraments can never be the object of the competence of the civil authority." This passage speaks clearly enough for itself.[10]

The general assembly's *Actes* were no sooner printed than the parlement of Paris declared them "null" and condemned an accompanying circular letter as "fanatical and seditious" in judgments on September 4 and 5. These judgments in turn initiated a spectacle of jurisdictional and corporate anarchy – a three-cornered slugfest between the parlement, the episcopacy, and the royal council – to which the realm had grown strangely accustomed since 1750. Not wholly devoid, for its part, of means of "temporal" persuasion – the clergy had been dragging its feet on the 12 million *don gratuit* requested by the government – the general assembly promptly solicited and on September 15 obtained a royal order in council annulling the parlementary judgments. The royal action predictably enraged the parlement of Paris, which set to work on remonstrances, but also left the clergy imperfectly avenged by reserving for the king the cognizance of the contested matters. The provincial parlements now entered the fray: in the parlement of Aix-en-Provence, the solicitor general Le Blanc de Castillon delivered a *réquisitoire* so virulent against the *Actes* that the general assembly felt obliged to ask the king to disavow it. A conciliar order obligingly did so on May 24, 1766, but not strongly enough to suit the clergy: the same day, another conciliar order articulated the royal position on the proper boundaries between Sacerdoce and Empire, which predictably satisfied neither side. A parlementary judgment on July 8, which outlawed episcopal attempts to solicit adhesions to the *Actes*, provoked yet another conciliar order of annullment on November 25, which nonetheless displeased the clergy by adding its own prohibition of soliciting signatures.[11] The controversy

10 Ibid., pp. 31–9.
11 Nouvelles ecclésiastiques (henceforth NNEE), March 27, 1766, pp. 53–65 (December 9, 16, and 24, 1767), pp. 197–207; *Procès-verbal de l'assemblée générale du clergé tenue à Paris, au couvent des Grands-Augustins, en l'année 1765, et continuée en l'année 1766* (Paris, 1773); on *don gratuit*, pp. 55, 122; on assembly's immediate reaction to the parlement's *arrêts* of September 4–5, pp. 309–11, 320; on king's response, pp. 836–7; and clergy's complaint that royal condemnation of Le Blanc

slowly melted away during the spring and early summer of 1767, then disappeared altogether beneath the avalanche of the La Chalotais-d'Aiguillon affair in the following years.

II   Jansenism, Gallicanism, and Parlementary Constitutionalism

Before disappearing altogether, however, the controversy over the general assembly of 1765 set off a minor avalanche of its own in the form of anonymous polemical pamphlets and a few full-scale treatises, the great majority of which took the side of the parlements. Among these were some *Observations on the Acts of the Assembly of the Clergy of 1765* by the canon lawyer and Jansenist polemicist Adrien Le Paige, who could generally be counted on to contribute one or two pamphlets per *affaire*. But the *Actes* were also the object of *Reflections, Diverse Remarks, Anathemas, Legitimate Complaints*, a *Preservative Against*, and even a *Request on the Part of a Great Number of the Faithful*, to say nothing of numbers of *Letter[s]*, including one by a *Military Philosophe*.[12]

The point of view, or "mentality," common to most of these pamphlets might be described as a peculiar mix of Gallicanism, Jansenism, and parlementary constitutionalism – or perhaps distortions of all three.[13] The mentality's Gallicanism, first of all, was not in principle antiepiscopal and professed great reverence for the authority of Bishop Bossuet. But its taste for antiquity carried it beyond the episcopal conciliarism of 1682 to the more radical lay conciliarism of the fourteenth and fifteenth centuries, which invested the bibical "keys" with the entire "assembly of the faithful," not the episcopacy alone.[14] The consequent

de Castillon's *Réquisitoire* of October 30 was not strong enough, pp. 788–9. For parlement's *arrêts*, see Jules Flammermont, ed., *Remontrances du parlement de Paris au XVIIIᵉ siècle* (1888–98; reprint edn, Geneva, 1978), 2:596.

12   Of these titles, only *Plaintes légitimes, ou Réclamation contre les Actes de l'assemblée du clergé de France* (n.p., n.d.), is not cited on the following pages.

13   For another attempt to describe this mentality with the emphasis, however, on Jansenism, see Van Kley, *The Jansenists*, pp. 6–36.

14   Most immediately, this brand of Gallicanism harks back to such seventeenth- and early eighteenth-century figures as Edmond Richer, Vivien de la Borde, and Nicolas Le Gros. On these, see Edmond Préclin, *Les Jansénistes du XVIIIᵉ siècle et la constitution civile du clergé: Le développement du richerisme, sa propagation dans le bas clergé, 1713–1791* (Paris, 1929), pp. 1–12, 41–51, 60–5. But both Carroll Joynes and Keith Baker have called my attention to its direct and major dependence upon such late medieval conciliarists as Pierre d'Ailly, Jean Gerson, Jacques Almain, and John Mair. On these figures, see Martimort, pp. 17–70; Victor Martin, *Les Origines du gallicanisme*, 2 vols. (Paris, 1939), 2:31–54, 131–47; Quentin Skinner, *The Foundations of Modern Political Thought*, vol. 2, *The Reformation* (Cambridge, 1978), pp. 34–50; and Brian Tierney, *Foundations of the Conciliar Theory: The Contribution of the Medieval Canonists from Gratian to the Great Schism* (Cambridge, 1955).

pouring of the new wine of eighteenth-century religious and ecclesiastical controversy into the old wine skins of late medieval conciliarism
produced a Gallicanism prejudicial not only to the papacy but to the Gallican bishops themselves, making them "simple dispensers of the holy
mysteries" accountable to the equally "holy canons" and – ultimately –
to their lay congregations.[15] All gestures of independence of judgment
on their part were so many displays of "despotism" and the "spirit of
domination."

To curb the bishops' "despotism" and confine them to the "holy
canons," this mentality looked immediately to the crown, although its
democratic conciliarism and frequent appeals to the "nation" raise the
suspicion that it was here, if only half consciously, that it tended
to locate sovereignty. In any case the appeal to the king was authorized
by the royal and parlementary strains in its Gallicanism, enshrined
in the first article of the Gallican Declaration of 1682 guaranteeing
the temporal power's independence of any ecclesiastical – specifically
papal – supervision. But it hammered this axiom into a formidable
engine of war against the Gallican bishops themselves and what little
remained of their independent jurisdiction – called their "system of
independence" – and against even the king to the degree he tried to
maintain this jurisdiction.

The oppositional outlook's use of royal Gallicanism against the king
is warning enough that its strident royalism in the matter of Church–
State relations is somewhat deceptive and not without constitutional
limitations. To be sure, this constitutionalism was not self-consciously
antimonarchical and owed something to theorists as royalist as Jean
Bodin (although considerably more to the constitutionalism of the
Fronde and even the scholastic political analyses of the late medieval
Sorbonnists).[16] But it so venerated the immutability of "fundamental"
law and the parlements' immemorial role in the matter that it tended to
view every irregularity in monarchical behavior as another example of
"despotism," and it so impersonally conceived of the monarchical state
– not always sharply distinguished from the "nation" – as to leave little
room for flesh and blood monarchs who were "nothing but its adminis-

15   *Lettre de M. l'évêque de xxx à monseigneur l'archévêque de Rheims, sur les Actes de
l'assemblée de 1765, envoyés à tous les évêques du Royaume* (n.p., n.d.), p. 6.
16   On parlementary constitutionalism during the eighteenth century, see Roger
Bickart, *Les Parlements et la notion de souveraineté nationale au XVIIIe siècle* (Paris,
1932); Jean Egret, *Louis XV et l'opposition parlementaire, 1715–1774* (Paris, 1970);
and Elie Carcassonne, *Montesquieu et le problème de la constitution française au XVIIIe
siècle* (Paris, 1926). On the constitutionalism of the Fronde, see Paul Rice Doolin,
The Fronde (Cambridge, Mass., 1935); and on the political thought of the late
medieval Sorbonnists, especially Jacques Almain and John Maier, see Skinner, pp.
113–23. Again, I owe to Carroll Joynes and to Keith Baker my awareness of the
mentality's dependence on these sources.

trators."[17] As in the case of its Gallicanism, then, the mentality was fearfully preoccupied with "despotism" and "domination," although in this stage of its development the opposite of these spectres was not so much the Whiggish "liberty" described by Bernard Bailyn in England and the American colonies as it was the majesty of impartial "justice" and "law."[18]

The element of Jansenism is the most elusive and difficult to isolate because it seldom took the theologically explicit form of adherence to the Augustinian doctrines of predestination and efficacious grace. Yet like Le Paige, most of the pamphleteers in this instance were probably Jansenists in even this rigorous sense, and in any case numbers of originally Jansenist themes had become so thoroughly a part of the mentality that they functioned within it quite independently of the theological convictions of those who shared it. The Jansenist component most clearly surfaced in the convictions that the bull *Unigenitus* had endangered Catholic dogmas, that Jansenism itself was an imaginary heresy, that the eighteenth-century Catholic Church was corrupt doctrinally, morally and structurally, and finally, in an omnipresent tone of righteous indignation. Specifically, the mentality so accentuated Jansenism's long-standing theological quarrel with the Jesuit Order that, in explosive combination with Gallicanism's antipapalism, it became a xenophobic hatred of the "court of Rome," everything Italian or "over the mountains," plus a conspiratorial-mindedness capable of believing that the Jesuit Order lurked behind everything which had run amok in Christendom since the mid-sixteenth century.[19]

It was moreover the various papal condemnations of Jansenism, culminating in the bull *Unigenitus*, which had fused the originally distinct elements of Jansenism, the several strains of Gallicanism, and parlementary constitutionalism in the first place. Promulgated in 1713, this bull offended both Augustinian and Gallican susceptibilities, and the monarchy's persistent attempts to enforce it succeeded only in swelling the ranks of the opponents and in adding the crown as a target of their arrows.[20] As early as the 1730s the resultant coherent (if not altogether internally consistent) mentality of opposition was at once

17   [Gabriel-Nicolas Maultrot and Claude Mey], *Apologie de tous les jugements rendus par les tribunaux séculiers en France contre le schisme . . .* , 2 vols. (France, 1752), 2:357.
18   Bernard Bailyn, *The Ideological Origins of the American Revolution* (Cambridge, Mass., 1971), pp. 55–93.
19   Van Kley, *The Jansenists*, pp. 6–36, 233–7. See also René Taveneaux, *Jansénisme et politique* (Paris, 1965).
20   Jacques-François Thomas, *La Querelle de l'Unigenitus* (Paris, 1949).

denouncing the Jesuits' "Molinism" in the name of all good Catholics, the "court of Rome's" alien influence in the name of "all good Frenchmen," the Gallican bishops' "spirit of domination" in the name of the king's loyal subjects, and the monarchy's "despotism" in the name of the "fundamental laws of the realm." Conceived, in a word, by Jansenism, born of the bull *Unigenitus*, this mentality suffered greatly but waxed in obscurity under the archbishop of Paris and his infernal *billets de confession*, only to rise full-blown and triumphant over the Jesuits in the 1760s. It was more than ready for the general assembly's *Actes* in 1765.

This pamphlet literature fell upon the *Actes* with a violence which made the parlement's official reaction seem polite by comparison. Le Paige, for example, more melodramatic as pamphleteer than as parlementary *éminence grise*, proclaimed that the *Actes* "tend towards nothing less than to make a universal revolution in the Church of France and to engulf everything in the State," to constitute a regular "war declared by the Sacerdoce against the Empire."[21] The "enflamed style" of the circular letter which accompanied the *Actes*, the publication of these documents in various dioceses, the quest for adhesions and signatures – were not these together the "signal of reunion" of an "episcopal League," similar to the one in the sixteenth century?[22] If not all were as certain as Le Paige that they witnessed the renaissance of the Catholic League, most detected the hand of the sinister and omnipresent Jesuit Order, the same yesterday, today, and tomorrow despite its definitive dissolution in France a year earlier. "This imperious and vindictive society," warned one polemicist in the name of a *Great Number of the Faithful*, "in the days of our father the heart of such a terrible confederation [the League], is today perhaps more than ever animated by the same spirit . . . ; and the Public is persuaded that it is she who by her members spread out in every direction is the secret motor of all the operations of Your Assembly."[23]

If any part of the general assembly's *Actes* could have won the approval of these polemicists, it would surely have been the condemnation of unbelief. And indeed, acknowledged the anonymous fulminator of *The Anathemas*, "one cannot sufficiently praise the attention of our prelates to stop its rapid torrent. But our Bishops will in vain raise their voices against irreligion," he hastened to add, "as long

21 [Le Paige], *Observations*, pp. 1, 68.
22 Ibid., p. 126.
23 *Requête d'un grand nombre de fidèles adressée à Monseigneur l'archévêque de Reims, président de l'assemblée générale du clergé, qui se tient actuellement à Paris, pour être par lui communiquée à tous les prélats de ladite assemblée, au sujet des Actes qu'elle a fait imprimer* (n.p., 1765), pp. 94–5.

as they do not add the luminous principles and holy maxims of the Faith."[24] Too little, too late: such, in sum, was the general verdict. "The Assembly of 1765," intoned the Jansenist weekly *Nouvelles ecclésiastiques*, "points out in its *Actes* a part of the evil; but it applies to it only a powerless remedy: so long as [ecclesiastical] censures, especially censures as vague as these, preempt the place of instruction, religion will be badly defended."[25]

If such was their reaction to the *Actes*' first section, what were they to think of the next section concerning the "rights of the Spiritual power"? Here, predictably, they discovered yawning cavities beneath the pearly white of the principles themselves. To what mischievous end, for example, did the author of the *Actes* place the comma in Rom. 13:1 after *Deo* rather than *sunt*, where the Vulgate put it (*Non est enim potestas nisi a Deo; quae autem sunt *a Deo* ordinatae sunt*). Whereas the Vulgate's punctuation conveyed the message that every power on earth was ordained by God, the *Actes* clearly cajoled the verse into saying that only "well-ordered" powers had God's blessing. Who, in the latter case, was to decide whether a given polity was "well-ordered" or not? The bishops? The Pope? And if not "well-ordered," was obedience suspended?[26] The fact that Boniface VIII had punctuated the verse in this eccentric fashion in *Unam Sanctam* (1302), or that the archbishop of Paris, Christophe de Beaumont, had done likewise in a *mandement* published in the wake of Damiens's attempt to assassinate Louis XV in 1757, could scarcely be expected to allay suspicions.[27] These were instead reinforced by the *Actes*' failure to imitate the Assembly of 1682 in explicitly condemning Cardinal Bellarmin's theory of indirect ecclesiastical authority, which allowed for papal intervention in temporal affairs in cases where sin was clearly involved.[28]

To be sure, the *Actes* in principle concurred with the "divine right" theory of the Gallican Declaration of 1682 in teaching that kings were not accountable to any ecclesiastical authority in temporal matters, and that they received their power from God directly. But this high-principled dust thrown into the eyes of the inattentive citizen was not sufficiently dense to prevent the perspicacious editor of the *Nouvelles ecclésiastiques* from noting that "even the independence of the Crown is

---

24   *Les Anathèmes, ou Lettre à monseigneur l'évêque d'xxx sur la publication qu'il a faite dans son diocèse des nouveaux Actes du clergé* (n.p., 1766), pp. 6–7.
25   NNEE, January 2, 1767, p. 2.
26   *Actes*, p. 15.
27   *Lettre d'un solitaire sur le mandement de M l'archévêque de Paris, du 1 mars 1757* (n.p., 1757), pp. 9–10.
28   Jean-François-André Le Blanc de Castillon, *Réquisitoire du 30 octobre 1765* in Bibliothèque de Port Royal Collection (BPR), Le Paige 562, MS 562, pp. 22–3.

only presented in the *Actes* as the sentiment of the *Clergy of France*; whereas all the pretensions of the Spiritual Power . . . are presented as the teaching of the *Universal Church.*"[29] Other pamphleteers were quick to concur. The Declaration of the Assembly of 1682, explained the canon lawyer G.-N. Maultrot in *The Rights of the Temporal Power Defended*, had proclaimed the independence of the temporal authority "as a truth conformed to the word of God, the tradition of the Fathers, and to the examples of the Saints. In 1765 this doctrine is no more than the teaching of the Clergy of France. The reader is therefore entitled to conclude that it is a national opinion concerning which doubts are legitimate. . . ."[30] And if the *Actes'* pronouncements on the subject of the first Gallican article lacked constancy, the consistency of its commitment to the others was that of the purest sponge rubber. Its description of the bull *Unigenitus* as an "irreformable judgment," its publication of Pope Benedict's encyclical letter of 1756 without protestation against this document's presumption of papal infallibility – all this and more, complained Le Blanc de Castillon of the parlement of Aix, breathed an "ultramontanist spirit" in blatant disharmony with the conciliarist tradition of the Gallican Church.[31] Taken together, concluded the *Nouvelles ecclésiastiques*, these traits entitled one "to regard the *Actes* of the Assembly of 1765 as a revocation of the Declaration of 1682."[32]

Yet the polemicizing so far gives only an insufficient notion of the extent of the chasm dividing the rival conceptions of the Church and its relation to the State. On the episcopal side, a rigidly authoritarian and hierarchical structure dominated by the episcopacy in cooperation with the pope stood proudly on an equal footing with the State. On the Gallicano-Jansenist side, a more malleable and egalitarian structure allowing parish priests and laymen a role of active participation maneuvered exclusively within the confines of the State.

29 NNEE, March 27, 1766, p. 54.
30 [Gabriel-Nicolas Maultrot], *Les Droits de la puissance temporelle, déféndue contre la seconde partie des Actes de l'assemblée du clergé de 1765 concernant la religion* (Amsterdam, 1777), pp. 7–8. This belated contribution to the controversy was provoked by the reprinting of the *Actes*, along with the *Procès-verbaux* of the general assemblies, by Guillaume Desprez during the 1770s. For stylistic and organizational reasons, this pamphlet is treated as if it had appeared along with the others around 1765. If, as Barbier assures us, the author is the Jansenist canon lawyer Maultrot, it represents no advance over what he with the Abbé Mey and Le Paige were saying in the 1750s and 1760s. So if the pamphlet was not actually written in 1765, it clearly should have been. A few paragraphs from this work are reproduced in Taveneaux, *Jansénisme et politique*, pp. 190–5.
31 Le Blanc de Castillon, *Réquisitoire*, pp. 29–31, 97–8.
32 NNEE, March 27, 1766, pp. 54–5. The parlement of Paris, in its remonstrances of August 30–1, 1766, made the same comparison between 1682 and 1765. See Flammermont, *Remontrances*, 2:599–600.

Among these elements it was undoubtedly the latter, the degree to which Gallicano-Jansenist polemicists were willing to subordinate even the most "spiritual" of the Church's functions to the supervision of the State, that emerges most strikingly in the controversy. The authorities they most frequently cited in doing so were treatises on canon law written around the turn of the last century, especially those by Van Espen and Pierre de Marca, and the example of the early Church, especially under the emperors Constantine and Theodosius, as presented in the ecclesiastical histories of Noel Alexandre and Claude Fleury. Perhaps the chief principle they invoked and claimed to have found in these sources was that the Church was within the "Empire," and not the "Empire" within the Church, which in turn they took to mean that the State or "prince" alone possessed coercive power on earth, that the Church's ministry was in contrast exclusively spiritual, and that such authority as it did possess could be regulated by the "prince" in the interests of the temporal welfare of his subjects.[33] Even pagan or heretical princes were entitled to do this by virtue of their God-conferred capacity as "political magistrate," but since the regular establishment of Christianity after the conversion of the Roman emperors and the Germanic kings, the "Christian Prince" was further authorized by his role as "outside bishop" and "protector of the canons," enabling him to enforce and uphold the Church's own laws and constitutions – even against churchmen themselves, they stressed, should this become necessary. The very active role of a Constantine, Theodosius, or Charlemagne in decisions of ecclesiastical discipline and even doctrine were the historical examples they had in mind; they seemed imperfectly aware that the cultural context was no longer the same.[34]

Yet these principles could not have produced the radical consequences they did except in alliance with the corrosive and closely related distinctions between externality and spiritual internality, fact and principle. The latter represents one of the more authentically Jansenist contributions to the Gallican, Jansenist, and parlementary mix, and goes back to "the great" Antoine Arnauld's division between the questions of whether the five famous propositions supposedly extracted from Jansenius's *Augustinus* were *in fact* to be found in this treatise, and whether these proportions should *in principle* be regarded as heretical. Arnauld argued that the papacy was indeed infallible in matters of principle

33   Le Paige, *Observations*, pp. 38 and 102. See also Le Blanc de Castillon, *Réquisitoire*, p. 87.
34   The best examples of these principles at work are [Maultrot and Mey], *Apologie*; and Adrien Le Paige, *Lettres adressés à MM. les commissaires nommés par le roi pour délibérer sur l'affaire présente du parlement au sujet du refus des sacrements ou Lettres pacifiques au suject des contestations présentes* (n.p., 1752).

(*droit*) and hence entitled to declare the propositions heretical, but that it was quite fallible in matters of contingent fact (*fait*) and therefore incompetent to say that Jansenius's treatise contained these propositions.[35] Arnauld himself was only partially Gallican, as his concessions to papal infallibility demonstrate, but after the merging of Gallicanism and Jansenism in the wake of the bull *Unigenitus* his distinction was extended to ecumenical councils, indeed the Church universal, which was similarly held to be infallible in matters of doctrine but not of fact. Now all the territory annexed by the realm of *fait* and externality at the expense of the realm of *droit* and internality was territory opened up to the intervention of the "prince" and "reason," which could as competently judge matters of fact as any prelate, pope, or ecumenical council. As it turned out, moreover, there were few if any matters so vaporously spiritual that they could not be condensed into matters of temporal fact and thereby rendered accessible to profane inspection.

Not only were councils quite fallible in matters of fact, according to these pamphleteers, but whether they were ecumenical or not was itself a matter of fact which the "prince" was competent to judge. "Once the universal Church has pronounced, the laity has no choice except that of submission," conceded the self-annointed defender of *The Rights of the Temporal Power*. "But the Prince, the Magistrates, even the simple Faithful," he added, "have the right to examine the exterior character of the judgment which is attributed to the Church in order to see if she has really spoken, if it is not just a small number of Bishops who have usurped her name." They moreover "have the right to examine if the judgment has been reached freely and unanimously," that is, canonically, "and whether it has been formulated clearly, in such a manner as to abate the controversy."[36] And should any of these criteria remain unfulfilled, the prince, as "protector of the canons" was obliged to reject the judgment; or even if it met them all, as did the Council of Trent, the prince as "Political magistrate" had the right to see if under the name of doctrine nothing had "slipped by which is contrary to the rights of the Prince, to the interests of his Crown, to the tranquility of his Realm" and to accept or reject it "according to the utility or the danger of which it is susceptible in his States."[37]

---

35   Alexander Sedgwick, *Jansenism in Seventeenth-Century France: Voices from the Wilderness* (Charlottesville, Va., 1977), pp. 107–38. See also Louis Cognet, *Le Jansénisme*, no. 960 of "Que sais-je?" series (Paris, 1964), pp. 62–75.
36   [Maultrot], *Les Droits de la puissance temporelle*, pp. 26–7.
37   [Maultrot and Mey], *Apologie*, 1:348; and *Lettre d'un philosophe militaire à monsieur l'archévêque de Rheims, en qualité de président de l'assemblée générale du clergé de France en 1765; sur les affaires du temps, et sur les Actes du clergé* (n.p., n.d.), p. 8.

If such were the rights of princes with regard to decisions by ecumenical councils, how much more amply entitled was Louis XV in imposing silence on the subject of the bull *Unigenitus* – that mere product of Jesuitical intrigue – and in declaring that it was not a "rule of faith." By imposing silence, this prince was not, as the *Actes* implied, infringing upon the bishops' sacred right to teach, but merely forbidding them to make reference to the "exterior character" in which certain teachings were embodied. In rendering the bull this dubious "honor . . . , one can in truth no longer speak about it," elucidated Le Paige, speaking about it, "yet one can continue to teach the great and beautiful verities it has reputedly decided." In declaring the *Unigenitus* was not a "rule of faith," on the other hand, the king as both political magistrate and protector of the canons had only decided whether it taught "without ambiguity what should be believed and what should be rejected," and whether it was "more apt to augment the disputes than to terminate them.[38] "Such an examination," assured the *Request by a Great Number of the Faithful*, "has no article of doctrine as its object, but rather pure and palpable exterior facts of which the eyes are natural judges, and of which princes and magistrates can rightfully take cognizance."[39]

The same held for the *Actes'* other particular claims to independent ecclesiastical jurisdiction. The sole and infallible right to make moral judgments? "Who doubts that in certain doctrinal matters the prince cannot go much further" than what is purely factual and exterior, argued the defender of *The Rights of the Temporal Power*, with an eye toward justifying the parlement's recent condemnation of the Jesuitical *Assertions*. "There are certain points of doctrine" – namely, moral ones – "which have an intimate connection with the State. Is all cognizance of them to be denied to the Prince, because they fall into the category of a spiritual matter?"[40] The sole right to judge religious vows? One must distinguish – Le Paige again – between "*le droit et le fait.*" If it is a case of a simple vow validly contracted with God, "it is for the Ecclesiastical Power alone . . . to decide concerning its substance, to commute it, even to dispense someone from it. . . ." But whether the vow was validly contracted at all was a matter of fact, which the prince could judge "by the light of reason" alone.[41] The exclusive jurisdiction, finally, over the Eucharist and extreme unction, the Church's most "august" sacraments? One must again distinguish, with Le Paige, between the "interior dispositions required to approach the sacraments worthily" –

---

38   [Le Paige], *Observations*, p. 40.
39   *Requête d'un grand nombre de fidèles*, p. 64.
40   [Maultrot], *Les Droits de la puissance temporelle*, p. 27.
41   [Le Paige], *Observations*, pp. 71, 79–80.

altogether spiritual, this, and the business of the confessor – and the "conditions required to refuse them publicly," another matter altogether.[42] In the latter case canon law was the guide, and the prince – read: the parlement – as protector of the canons, could "bend a Bishop to the Laws of the Church when he has violated these overtly." As political magistrate, moreover, to believe the relentless defender of *The Temporal Power*, he had the right "to maintain a citizen in the possession of the exterior advantages assured to all Christians, because the legal possession [*possessoire*] of even spiritual things is a purely profane matter."[43]

Despite these and other audacities, all these pamphleteers stopped short before what they condemned as the heresy of "Anglican supremacy"; all, too, would have anathematized the "civil religion" of Rousseau's *Social Contract*.[44] Self-consciously Catholic, they sincerely believed that by granting the Church jurisdiction over matters "purely spiritual" they were safeguarding what was essential to ecclesiastical authority; the "capital error of the *Actes*," complained Le Blanc de Castillon, was "to have excluded the authority and even the Prince's right of inspection over everything which is not entirely profane, instead of restricting the innate power of the Church to what is purely spiritual," thereby opening the door, in his opinion, to the dreaded ultramontanist theory of indirect power.[45] Yet by restricting the Church to what was ethereally and internally spiritual and in fastening upon the temporal dimension of all that remained, these polemicists ran close to the opposite extreme of temporalizing the spiritual all the better to control it. The bishop of Le Puy, Lefranc de Pompignan, was not altogether sacrilegious in calling their "purely interior and invisible belief" a matter of "no consequence"; not wholly unjust in describing their theory of indirect princely power as different from ultramontanism only in the goal it proposed, but not in the means it employed. Neither the "Anglican supremacy" nor Rousseau's civil religion, he thought, had really pushed the subordination of religion to the State "any further."[46] Such, without doubt, was later his sentiment concerning the Civil Constitution of the Clergy, despite his tergiversations in the matter as Louis XVI's minister in 1790.[47]

42   Ibid., p. 91.
43   [Maultrot], *Les Droits de la puissance temporelle*, p. 82.
44   Jean-Jacques Rousseau, *Oeuvres complètes*, ed. Bernard Gagnebin and Marcel Raymond, vol. 3, *Du contrat social* (Paris, 1964), pp. 460–9.
45   Le Blanc de Castillon, *Réquisitoire*, pp. 57–8.
46   Lefranc de Pompignan, *Défense des Actes du clergé de France, publiée en l'assemblée de 1765, par M. l'évêque du Puy* (Louvain, 1769), pp. 285, 290, 304, 390.
47   On Lefranc de Pompignan's policy with regard to the Civil Constitution, see Pierre de la Gorce, *Histoire religieuse de la Révolution française*, 6 vols. (1912–13; reprint edn, New York, 1969), 1:285–9; and W. Henley Jervis, *The Gallican Church and the Revolution* (London, 1882), pp. 72–8.

III   Reason, Contract, and the Pursuit of Happiness

Lefranc de Pompignan however seemed less upset by the mass of pamphlets discussed thus far than by a few treatise-like productions which appeared later than the others, and which to his mind displayed an affinity to the principles of the "so-called *esprits forts* of our days," in particular Rousseau.[48] Nor were the worthy bishop's fears in this matter uniquely the figment of a paranoid episcopal imagination. The productions in question indeed differ from the others in their more frequent appeals to "reason," in their employment of the concept of political and social contract, in their easier acceptance of human nature and the pursuit of terrestrial happiness – intellectual traits one associates automatically with the Enlightenment in France. This "enlightened" conceptual apparatus perhaps enabled these pamphleteers to go somewhat further than the others in subordinating religious (or at least ecclesiastical) to purely political and social considerations.

Lefranc de Pompignan directed the bulk of his fire against a two-volume treatise entitled *On the Authority of the Clergy and the Power of the Political Magistrate in the Exercise of the Functions of the Ecclesiastical Ministry*, written by the lawyer François Richer and published in 1766.[49] Like the Rousseau of the *Social Contract*, Richer began with the question of why, given his natural liberty, man had everywhere accepted the restraints of society. Richer found the answer not so much in man's technological prowess as in the long period of helplessness preceding his maturity, rendering stable and authoritarian families indispensable. Large and extended families had therefore been the first sorts of societies. But after these had broken up due to the death of patriarchal chiefs, the "passions and the inherent vices of humanity" had created a state of perpetual war, whence the need to appoint a "conventional chief" in place of the "natural chief," thereby creating society. In the resulting social contract, the chief or "sovereign" agreed to promulgate "the most suitable rules" for the general welfare, in return for which the "nation" promised "the most prompt and blind obedience." The Hobbesian rigor of the contract's terms was nonetheless softened by their apparent compatibility with the sovereign's divine right – he

---

48   Ibid., p. 207.
49   [François Richer], *De l'autorité du clergé, et du pouvoir du magistrat politique sur l'exercise des fonctions du ministère ecclésiastique. Par M xxx, avocat au parlement*, 2 vols. (Amsterdam, 1766). On the authorship, see Préclin, *Les Jansénistes du XVIIIᵉ siècle*, p. 416. On the circulation of this book under Jansenist auspices in Maria Theresa's Austria, see ibid., p. 432.

accounted to God alone – and with his quality as a "representative" and even "mandatory" of the "nation."[50]

This somewhat precarious balance of constitutional authorities was revealed to the author by a combination of "reason," "nature," and the "essence of things," although it was also confirmed by biblical authority. These sources of inspiration again collaborated to produce another principle, that the "conservation and the agreements of terrestrial life" had been the "unique motive" behind the formation of civil societies. . . ." Religion had had no hand in it. For "the cult inspired by enlightened nature and guided by reason" (the only one which the Supreme Being had demanded before revealing "a more particular one") was not dependent upon society for its celebration. "Each man," in Emile-like fashion, had fulfilled all he owed to his Creator "within the most profound solitude and without any sort of communication with his fellows." Classical history here came to his aid by revealing that the "first legislators" had been almost solely occupied with temporal concerns; to the small extent that the "religious cult" had distracted them, it was "only as a subordinate dimension of politics. . . ." They were "almost always observed to accommodate the exterior ceremonies to the civil order they established."[51]

The intended effect of all this was obviously to give priority to the interests of civil society over those of religion, at least so far as temporal arrangements were concerned. Nor had the advent of Christianity much altered this primitive state of affairs. For Christianity had established an altogether different sort of society – the Church – consisting of a "corps of travelers on earth" en route to their "other country" or "the bosom of God himself." In contrast to the State, which employed physical force to rule corporeal bodies, the Church employed the gentler arms of grace and reason to persuade "our souls, or pure spirits" to accept its authority. The Church could proceed in no other fashion because our souls were "essentially free"; it was a "formal heresy" to suppose that even God coerced them.[52] Such spiritual authority as the Church rightfully possessed was moreover the property of the whole Church, or the assembly of all the faithful; the ecclesiastical hierarchy only administered the power of the keys. Though it was true that priests received their ministry directly from Christ, it was "no less true," Richer insisted, that they exercised it "only in the name of the Church" and could undertake nothing "without its presumed consent." The ministers were "only representatives" and

50   Ibid., 1:1–27.
51   Ibid.
52   Ibid., pp. 27–32, 39–40.

could only do "what the represented would do if he were acting upon his own."[53]

Despite the un-Jansenist emphasis upon the freedom of will, much of this seems vaguely familiar. It is as if Richer had imperceptibly strayed from the stark, austere heights of simple contracts and states of nature into a thickening forest of scriptural and early Church precedents below. Before descending any further, however, the ascent of another contract intervened, this one between the Church and the prince become Christian. For when the band of travelers which was the Church had first asked the prince for the "liberty of passage" through his lands, the prince's duty to maintain "good order" had obliged him to undertake a detailed examination of "all the views and intentions of these foreigners," including their doctrine, morals, liturgy, and government. None of this meant, to believe the author, that the prince had actually judged dogma; he had only ascertained that the "good order of the State" was in no way compromised. Now if as a result of this examination the travelers had obtained a safe conduct, they for their part had agreed to abide strictly by the Scriptures and the tradition of the early Church, while the Sovereign for his part had sworn "to maintain them in the free exercise of the dogmas, moral code and discipline" which formed "the basis of the contract" and its essential "clauses."[54]

With the conclusion of this second contract, however, the truth finally emerges. Like the Church he defines, our author has all along been a stranger in a foreign land, that of philosophical states of nature and natural religions. Yet far from impeding his homeward course, the last contract rather plummets him headlong toward the promised land of Gallicano-Jansenist conclusions. For this contract, not as two-sided as it might appear, has already put the "Sovereign" as "political magistrate" in control of everything affecting "good order," therefore everything external about the Church. The prince's promise to protect the Church's doctrine and discipline – read: his rights as "outside bishop" and "protector of the canons" – further entitles him to protect these rules against the ministers themselves. Hence, for example, the prince's obligation to oppose any novel doctrine – the bull *Unigenitus?* – that an ecclesiastical cabal might attempt to foist upon the Church. Hence, too, his obligation to examine all the exterior circumstances of the Church council to ascertain its ecumenicity, as well as his right to impose silence on religious disputes, invalidate unjust excommunications, prevent public refusals of sacraments – all this and more, without ever in-

53   Ibid., pp. 75–7, 107.
54   Ibid., pp. 125–9.

fringing upon the spiritual. But whether holy or not, most of this is familiar ground.[55]

Not so entirely, however. For the treatise's enlightened social contracts and states of nature do not simply serve as neutral containers of Jansenist and Gallican contents. They display, rather, a cocoon-like effect, in some cases making more explicit what was implicit before; in others, metamorphosing the contents altogether. More explicit are the author's transformation of the Catholic priest into moral henchman for the State – "the organ of those charged with announcing the divine word ought always to be at the orders of the government" – as well as his starker statement of Gallicano-Jansenism's criteria for infallibility on the part of Church councils – "only when human passions are silent" and "the necessary liberty to receive the Holy Spirit" obtains.[56] Some examples of metamorphosis are his advocacy of the marriage of priests – the "good order" of the State included the propagation of the human species – and his willingness to legalize divorce, which he justified by distinguishing between the civil contract, or "matter," and the inessential sacrament or its "benediction."[57] Under the same heading falls his attack upon ecclesiastical property as a contradiction in terms. The "improperly called property of the Church," he maintained, belonged not to the Church but to some clerics, and to these in turn not as clerics, but only as a privileged order of citizens. Having desacralized the property, he then subjected it to the "fundamental law" that all property was taxable. The "general will" of the "Sovereign" therefore demanded that the "particular interest" of these citizens cede, and that their property be, if not confiscated for the benefit of the State, at least taxed like "secular" property.[58]

It was this particular distillation of Richer's unique blend of Gallicano-Jansenism and "enlightened" concepts that several anonymously published pamphlets seized upon in their turn. The most spectacular of these, entitled *The Right of the Sovereign over the Property of the Clergy and Monks, and the Usage to Which He Can Put This Property for the Happiness of the Citizens*, appeared in 1770.[59] Unlike Richer, this pamphleteer began his pilgrimage in the forest of Gallicano-Jansenist appeals to the authority of the New Testament, especially the gospels and Saint Paul, and to the

---

55   Ibid., pp. 393–6, 414–21; 2:8–9, 38–43, 95–9.
56   Ibid., 1:211–14, 238, 247–8, 418. Note the similarity of these criteria to those which Rousseau lays down for an assembly's articulation of the general will.
57   Ibid., 2:146–59, 190–3.
58   Ibid., 1:149–94, esp. 151–3, 163–5, 174–5, 189–92.
59   [Cervol], *Du droit du souverain sur les biens fonds du clergé et des moines, et de l'usage qu'il peut faire de ces biens pour le bonheur des citoyens* (Naples, 1770).

example of "the first centuries of the Church." Thoroughly within this tradition, too, are his subordination of the clergy to the Church defined as the assembly of all the faithful and his insistence that the Church was purely spiritual and "not of this world" – all this, of course, to the familiar purpose of establishing the State's control over everything external, temporal, and factual.[60] Christ's precept to "sell everything you have, give it to the poor, and come follow me" was a formal condemnation in advance, he thought, of "every king of [temporal] pretension on the part of members of the Sacerdoce," most especially including the possession of property. Anyway, he argued, since the Church could not by definition possess property, all donations of property to priests "under the borrowed name of God or the Church" were legally invalid because they involved "an error of persons."[61]

Yet one might well enquire why he restricted the application of Christ's precept to the clergy alone. If the Church is the assembly of all the faithful, and if the faithful are the followers of Christ, then should not laymen and clergy alike sell all they have and give to the poor – or at least to the Church which succors the poor? Sensing this difficulty all the more acutely because ecclesiastical property constituted the grail-like object of his unholy quest, he retreated the better to advance. Having all but obscured the distinction between clergy and laity with the one hand, he then stealthily reintroduced it with the other, for we learn with surprise that "sell all you have" is not a precept after all, but rather a "counsel" applicable to the Church's "Holy Ministers" alone.[62] Yet his left hand knew very well what his right hand was up to – Christ's injunction to the contrary was undoubtedly just another counsel – for he was also aware that his task was now to justify the acquisition of property in particular and the pursuit of physical well-being in general.

His strategic retreat completed, he now jumps – indeed fairly catapults himself – onto the high ground of Enlightenment rhetoric. Like Rousseau's, his remaining "letters" are written from the mountain; the air grows abruptly chilly with appeals to "reason" and its "imprescriptible rights." Jolted, first of all, with the most un-Jansenist comment that it is not really necessary for a Christian to relate all his actions to God, that some actions are "indifferent in themselves," we are next astonished to hear that "*le bonheur physique*" is a gift of heaven, "that happiness and unhappiness are the results of our conduct," and that "the springs, producers of one as well as the other of these two states, are purely physical." Nor is that all. The proposition that society's

60 [Cervol], *Du droit du souverain*, pp. 11–14, 55–6.
61 Ibid., pp. 38–9, 87.
62 Ibid., pp. 13–14.

"inspection extends even to the precepts of Religion, not to contradict them, but in order to turn then to the profit of the State" may sound familiar enough, but not so the lengths to which it is taken. For not only is the Church's "exterior cult" purely "ceremonial and commemorative," but the State could eliminate it altogether and "restrict the Christian's cult to an interior act and the recitation of Dominical prayer, without forcing him to violate his religious obligations."[63] Now if the State may do all that, can the Church legitimately resist the "Supreme Legislator" should he cast covetous eyes upon ecclesiastical property, especially when "armed with the equitable and transcendent motive of the public good . . . ?"[64]

The answer is clearly no. The author then proceeded to imagine precisely the situation in which the monarchy and the National Assembly successively found themselves in 1789. The State owed 3 billion livres, and the payment of the interest on this debt, which consumed nearly half of the annual revenues, did not leave enough to meet the State's ordinary expenses. Taxes could not be augmented because of the "*cherté* of nearly all sorts of goods. . . ." What was then to be done? After considering and dismissing sundry alternatives, such as bankruptcy, economy measures, and additional loans, he opted for the "surgical, decisive," and "simple" solution also adopted in 1789, namely, the confiscation of all ecclesiastical property and its sale to private citizens, together with the transformation of ecclesiastics into paid "pensionaries of the State."[65] Nowhere, not even in the literature immediately preceding the Revolution, was the revolutionary solution to the State's financial problems more clearly anticipated than here.

IV Toward Throne and Altar

Quantitatively, at least, the episcopal cause mustered no more than a Noah's ark-like response to the deluge of writings submerging its *Actes*: the anonymous *Respective Rights of the State and the Church Reminded of Their Principles* (1766), the bishop of Grenoble's uninteresting *Dissertation* (1767), and the bishop of Le Puy's monumental *Defense of the Acts of the Clergy of France concerning Religion* (1769).[66] Taken together, however, these responses are not without some interesting features, one

---

63   Ibid., pp. 89–97.
64   Ibid., p. 120.
65   Ibid., p. 138 and in general, pp. 121–46.
66   *Les Droits respectifs de l'état et l'église rappellés à leurs principes* (Avignon, 1766), and [Jean de Caulet, bishop of Grenoble], *Dissertation à l'occasion des Actes de l'assemblée générale du clergé de France de 1765 sur la religion* (n.p., 1767).

of which is a marked preference for explicitly engaging the more "enlightened" of their opponents. In doing so, moreover, they proved themselves as adept at manipulating "enlightened" vocabulary and concepts in defense of their own cause as some of their enemies had been in attacking it.

Take, for example, the anonymous reminder of *The Respective Rights*, apparently an aristocratic defender of the first order rather than a member of it himself. His system, like that of the episcopacy's more "enlightened" opponents, made "civil" or "social" laws both chronologically and anthropologically prior to "religious" and "ecclesiastical" laws because of the more imperious character of physical needs. Further, these civil laws originated in "first conventions" based on natural law, more readily perceived, he thought, by "the vivacity of sentiments" than by some "method of reasoning." The resultant State, at first enlightened by means of natural religion alone, had accepted Christianity and the Church only subsequently, and on condition – a second contract, this – that its "ecclesiastical laws" did not run counter to its own. The State therefore reserved the right to inspect, approve, or reject ecclesiastical legislation, since it exercised an influence over "exterior morals" which in turn formed part of the State's "*haute police.*" The Church, although not expressly the ecumenical council, the author defined as the assembly of all the faithful, and he insisted that the clergy's functions had been "originally entirely spiritual."[67]

So far the author seemed headed down the path carved out by François Richer in *On the Authority of the Clergy and the Power of the Civil Magistrate*, which was published the same year. But at precisely this juncture his path diverged sharply. This was perhaps due in part to his accent on "sentiment" as opposed to reason, but mainly to his Montesquieuian, empirical, yet unimpeachably "enlightened" emphasis on the "strange circumstantial vicissitudes" and "conjunctural whimsicalities" encountered by different peoples. The main effect of these, in his view, had been to refract the application of natural law into the bewildering variety of particular laws we observe. Though natural law had inspired the formation of all constitutions, each "legislator" had had to adjust it according to the nation's physical and climactic circumstances, "factitious inclinations," and even errors, but infallibly with a view toward the "best possible condition." Even the most apparently bizarre laws were therefore "nonetheless respectable" because the "idea of the best possible" had dictated their formation; to understand them a detailed empirical examination of the circumstances which produced them was necessary. And the science of politics was therefore not

---

67   *Les Droits respectifs*, pp. 19, 28–30, 36–7, 57–9, 71–2.

reducible to a "system of geometrical order," but was rather a "calculus of proximities and simple approximations."[68]

The author's more empirical cast of mind thus led him to a proto-Burkean veneration for the delicately complex and infinitely variegated texture of all positive law, seen as the embodiment of the wisdom of the past. Consistent with himself, he did not exclude the clergy's privileged constitutional position from his all-embracing ken. The existence of a separate and even coercive ecclesiastical jurisdiction, the clergy's "titles of honor" and "exterior prerogatives," the Church's extensive property holdings – all these represented "universal reason's" infallible application of "natural law" to achieve the "best possible," which included the respect due to the ministers of a religion serving as spiritual foundation to the State. For "if in order to assure the repose of society, it was necessary to fortify the observation of human laws by means of a principle of religion and a motive of conscience," was it not "equally advantageous," he rhetorically asked, "to imprint on the people's soul a particular sentiment of respect for the censors of their conscience and the ministers of their religion . . . ?"[69]

Whereas the anonymous author of *The Respective Rights* thus anticipated counter-Revolutionary conservatism's veneration for traditional law and historic wisdom, Lefranc de Pompignan, in his monumental *Defense,* pointed no less clearly toward its theocratic and ultramonarchical tendencies. Yet he too, by pitting himself specifically against Richer's *On the Authority of the Clergy,* chose to do battle on unmistakably "enlightened" terrain. Though complaining throughout his treatise about "the false and modern philosophy" of "our day" and its addiction to states of nature and reciprocal contracts, he nonetheless accepted these concepts for practical purposes, and contrived to maneuver within their constraints.[70]

This maneuvering is not unimpressive, in a purely forensic way. Tactically postulating society's emergence from a state of nature, the future bishop of Vienne first argued the "enlightened" utility of religion by contesting the principle that mundane considerations alone could have effected such a transition. It was to "outrage providence," he protested, "to suppose that civil societies were formed without her, or that her principal purpose in presiding over their formation was not to unite men so that they could render the sovereign arbiter of their destinies the

68   Ibid., pp. 19–24.
69   Ibid., pp. 64–6, 71–3, 102–4. I fully accept the corollary that Edmund Burke himself is to be regarded as a legitimate child of Enlightenment thought. On this, see Frederick Drayer, "The Genesis of Burke's *Reflections,*" *Journal of Modern History* 50 (September 1978): 462–79.
70   Lefranc de Pompignan, *Défense des Actes du clergé de France,* p. 346.

common duties required of them." Although he conceded that terrestrial considerations might have been the occasion for the formation of civil societies, the deeper cause, he clearly implied, was religious. From Adam through Noah, the "first men" had indeed been recipients of a "particular revelation" which, however distorted with the passage of time in all but God's chosen race, made the father of every family at once a sacrificer and priest, rights inherited by the eldest son. Just as each family, then, had been basically a "religious association," so also the body politic, after men's "unchained passions" had led them to unite in civil society. Religion therefore entered into the very "constitution of every body politic, and it would have been impossible to associate men under a civil government if Religion, anterior to these human establishments, had not been the foundation and the tie." The redoubtable bishop thought it "easy to prove that, far from accommodating the exterior ceremonies of the religious cult to the civil order they established," the first legislators had more often "accommodated their political laws to the religious ideas established before them."[71]

Having sufficiently loosened Richer's social contract to incorporate religion at its core, the bishop of Le Puy proceeded to bind by his anathemas a principle he viewed as basic to the opposition's case, namely, that "by natural law and imprescriptible right" every society possessed the "power of government" and only delegated the usage to its chiefs. In ecclesiastical form, this principle gave the possession of the "keys" to the assembly of all the faithful, leaving the clergy with only their use; in political form, it located sovereignty within the nation which delegated its exercise by means of a contract. Now it goes without saying that the bishop vigorously combated the ecclesiastical manifestation of this principle, that he insisted that the episcopal hierarchy alone possessed the power of the keys and together with the pope formed a "very singular type" of "monarchy essentially tempered by an aristocracy." But in choosing Richer's book as his chief foil, de Pompignan cleverly linked lay conciliarism to national sovereignty and then concentrated his fire on the latter. It was a bit unfair, of course, for the bishop to insinuate thereby that the political form of this principle was explicitly attributable to *all* opponents of the *Actes*, or even that it was unambiguously held by Richer himself. But he was shrewd enough to see that it represented the profound current of their thought, and to aim his depth charges at the least avowable of their half-conscious assumptions.[72]

Accepting, again, the notion of a passage from a state of nature to one of civil government accompanied by a contract, de Pompignan contested the principle that it was sovereignty itself – the power of life and

71   Ibid., pp. 132–4.
72   Ibid., pp. 206–7, 233.

death over other humans – which the community had ever delegated to any government by virtue of natural law. Proceeding from the Rousseauean principle of men's "natural equality" in the "primitive state," the bishop cogently argued that nature gave to no man or group of men the right to human life. Sheer numbers or express conventions did not legitimize a power which no man rightfully possessed over either his own life or anyone else's, even if exercised in the act of self defense. Rendered powerless by this very equality to mitigate the fall's disorderly effects, men had received from the hand of their creator the gift of sovereignty necessary to create governments. "It is He who has come to their aid. His absolute power has enabled their impotence." With a stridency and accent which look forward to the early Lamennais or De Maistre, the bishop of Le Puy concluded that the "Supreme Arbiter of their life" was "also the unique and necessary principle of all sovereign authority."[73]

That religion was fundamental to the formation of civil societies, that God alone was the source of political sovereignty – neither of these principles led necessarily in a monarchical direction. The bishop acknowledged as much, and allowed that "all the nations of the earth [had] originally possessed the liberty to choose the form of government which suited them best." To the nations which had opted for monarchy he further allowed the choice of their first monarch, as well as between elective and hereditary monarchy. But could a nation so constituted subsequently rescind its original choice? Or could it ever dethrone a particular monarch by virtue of the nonfulfillment of some reciprocal contract? De Pompignan could hardly deny that some monarchical nations possessed such contracts, but he emphatically denied that these derived from natural law. He further failed to see how they could derive from the original liberty by which God had allowed men to choose their governments if this same liberty, "a gift of God's providence," could become the "germ of inexhaustible discords and intestine factions, of revolutions and catastrophes." Obviously, the bishop wanted to say no; the whole discussion put him out of sorts. What he clearly wished to affirm, on the contrary, was that the founders of hereditary monarchies could have very well tied the hands of their descendants and that, for the governance of their kingdoms, monarchs answered "to God alone."[74]

---

73 Ibid., pp. 207–10. The corollary is again intended and accepted that Lamennais and De Maistre are just as legitimately the Enlightenment's progeny as, say, Benjamin Constant or Madame de Staël. For the connections between Maistre's thought and the Enlightenment, see Jack Lively's excellent introduction to his translation and edition of *The Works of Joseph de Maistre* (New York and London, 1965), pp. 1–45.
74 Ibid., pp. 213–19.

In thus defending "divine right" monarchy against the threat of national sovereignty, the bishop was opposing the parlementary constitutionalism of the great majority of his opponents as much as the "*école de nos prétendus esprits forts*," Le Paige as much as Rousseau. That this was the case he made clear by an off-handed and less than reverent reference to the "fundamental laws" of the Realm, a key phrase in the parlementary constitutional rhetoric of the time.[75] Not, of course, that in 1765 either the parlement of Paris or the Gallicano-Jansenist press was publicly espousing a theory of national sovereignty or reciprocal political contract. But de Pompignan was not ignorant of the fact that the parlement, in its remonstrances, was then styling itself as "born with the monarchy" and the temple of its fundamental laws; or defining its duty as the defense of the "national constitution" against the "absolute power" of misguided monarchs, for which it was accountable to the "nation."[76] In view of this rhetoric, it was a calculated provocation on the bishop's part to define the French monarch as "absolute" and to add that his magistrates were "his first subjects, and nothing more" who "received his orders and gave none except in his name."[77]

Evidence suggests that the bishop of Le Puy spoke for a growing body of episcopal thinking on this score which, in predictable reaction to the constitutionalism of their Gallican and Jansenist foes, was redefining its conception of the monarchy in ever more absolutistic, anticonstitutional, or "despotic" terms.[78] But if so, had Lefranc de Pompignan and the episcopal thinking he represented progressed no further than Bossuet and the assembly of 1682? Were they still, albeit with naturalistic argumentation, defending the marriage of ecclesiastical conciliarism and royal absolutism which this celebrated assembly had solemnized? Hardly. Recall the *Actes*' dubious punctuation and translation of Romans 13:1; its spirited defense of the spiritual power as "sovereign, independent and absolute"; its insistence that kings themselves should obey priests; its ominous admonition, finally, that priests were to obey "God rather than men."[79] For if the episcopacy was extending the

---

75   Ibid., p. 217.
76   For some random examples, see Flammermont, *Remontrances*, 2:523–4, 534, 543, 546, 549.
77   Lefranc de Pompignan, *Défense*, pp. 232–3.
78   The evidence is not as satisfactory as it might be, partly because bishops had too few occasions to pronounce themselves on this subject. Nonetheless the evidence in Van Kley, *The Jansenists*, pp. 150–8, is applicable if the French Jesuits' thinking about the monarchy and its "constitution" can be taken as representative of at least zealously "constitutionary" (e.g., pro-*Unigenitus*) and ultramontanist bishops.
79   *Actes*, p. 43. Normal Ravitch first called attention to Lefranc de Pompignan's "hedging" in this matter in *Sword and Mitre: Government and Episcopate in France and England in the Age of Aristocracy* (The Hague, 1966), p. 23.

monarchy's power over the laity with the one hand, it was tending severely to curtail it in relation to the Church with the other. Unlike the assembly of 1682, after all, which had defended the temporal power against the Church, the assembly of 1765 rather defended the Church against the temporal power.

Now the demands of this new task, added to those of defending episcopal prerogatives against Jansenist laicism, put unaccustomed strains on the Gallican clergy, segments of which developed the symptoms of an identity crisis. Among these symptoms was a guarded disavowal of the whole Gallican Declaration of 1682 – thus confirming episcopal enemies' darkest suspicions. In response, for example, to the accusation that the general assembly had avoided the expressions consecrated by the celebrated assembly of 1682, the bishop of Le Puy confessed to the opinion that "whatever the respect" which subsequent assemblies of the clergy had paid to the one held in 1682, they had "never considered its authority as equal to that of the Universal Church or an Ecumenical Council." They had learned from this assembly itself "not to regard its Declaration as a symbol of faith."[80] A compromising admission, this, nonetheless outdone by Henri-Jacques de Montesquiou, bishop of Sarlat, who a few years earlier had informed his diocesan clergy in a *Pastoral Instruction* that God's word was "not the foundation of our [Gallican] liberties; for the word being unchangeable and uniform, all the Churches which do not possess such liberties would then be governed against the word of God."[81] At about the same time, the bishop of Langres, Montmorin-Saint-Herem, gave it out as his opinion that the Declaration of 1682 was more than just an opinion. But in the same breath he told his diocesan clergy that the "particular certitude" attributable to the article concerning the independence of the temporal power was "much superior to that of the other articles," leaving his clergy to wonder what precisely he thought of these.[82]

Not enough, in any event, to suit the Gallicano-Jansenist press, which snarled its condemnation in the pages of the *Nouvelles ecclésiastiques*, going so far as to accuse Montmorin of "treason."[83] For within the nationalized Catholicism of the *parti janséniste*, the four Gallican articles of 1682 had become, in the words of the bishop of Soissons, "holy

---

80   Lefranc de Pompignan, *Défense*, p. 472.
81   Henri-Jacques de Montesquiou, *Instruction pastorale de monseigneur l'évêque de Sarlat au clergé séculier et régulier et à tous les fidèles de son diocèse. 28 nov 1764* (n.p., n.d.), pp. 11, 16.
82   Montmorin de Saint-Herem, *Lettre pastorale de Mgr. l'évêque de Langres au clergé de son diocèse. 1 aout 1763* (n.p., n.d.), p. 9.
83   NNEE, January 23, 1764, p. 14. For the review of the bishop of Sarlat's pastoral instruction, see ibid., September 11, 1765, pp. 149–51.

truths which belong to revelation, which form part of the sacred *dépôt* which Jesus Christ confided to his Disciples, which has come down to us by the tradition of all the centuries. . . ."[84] If the universal Church in an ecumenical council had not enshrined these truths in a "formula of faith," it was only because for too many Catholics, especially Spanish and Italian ones, the eighteenth century remained a time of "obscurity" and "combat" – in short, they gnashed their teeth in outer darkness.[85]

As a concurrent controversy swirling around Fitz-James of Soissons's 1763 pastoral instruction made clear, not many of his episcopal peers shared this renegade Jansenist bishop's high view of the Gallican articles of 1682. At least the four bishops on the commission appointed by Louis XV to examine his instruction seemed more inclined to agree with Montmorin and Montesquiou that the Declaration represented a venerable but debatable "opinion" or "sentiment" which, however compatible with revelation, did not really belong to the realm of faith or dogma.[86] And it is not easy to see how they could have felt much differently in 1765. For to say that the Declaration enunciated articles of faith had become tantamount to endorsing nearly everything which Gallicano-Jansenism had construed it to mean: that is, the nearly total subordination of Church to State under the hammer of the Declaration's first article; the democratization and laicization of the Church itself under the cover of the remaining three. In the face of the former, the bishops felt bound to resist what Lefranc de Pompignan called the "shameful slavery" of the "ecclesiastical ministry to the secular Power."[87] Concerning the latter, the bishop of Le Puy again probably spoke for most of his peers when he said that given the choice between being "vicars of the Pope," on the one side, and "mandatories of the people" accountable to "laymen" and even "women," on the other, he

---

84   François de Fitz-James, *Oeuvres posthumes de monseigneur le duc de Fitz-James évesque de Soissons . . .* , vol. 1, *Ordonnance et instruction pastorale de monseigneur l'évêque de Soissons, au sujet des assertions extraites par le parlement des livres, thèses, cahiers composés, publiés et dictés par les jésuites* (Avignon, 1769), pp. 289–90.

85   Ibid., vol. 2, *Projet de réponse de m. l'évêque de Saint Pons*, pp. 374–5.

86   Ibid., *Mémoire au sujet de l'instruction pastorale*, pp. 197–200, 212–13, 224–5. The royal *commissaires* were Roche-Aimon, Montazet, Dillon and Jarente, archbishops of Narbonne, Lyon, and Toulouse, and bishop of Orléans, respectively. Ibid., vol. 1, *Vie*, pp. lxix–lxx. The general assembly's inclination to convene a provincial council to examine the bishop of Angers's 1763 pastoral instruction, which had similarly expressed a high view of the Declaration of 1682, perhaps also indicates something of the majority of bishops' thinking on this subject. See *Procès-verbal*, September 27, 1765, pp. 440–1; and Jacques de Grasse, *Ordonnance et instruction pastorale de monseigneur l'évêque d'Angers, portant condamnation de la doctrine contenue dans les Extraits des assertions* (n.p., n.d.), pp. 14, 16–17.

87   Lefranc de Pompignan, *Défense*, p. 348.

would choose the former. For all practical purposes, at least, the "ultra-montanist theologians" maintained the Church as a "mixture of aris-tocracy with monarchy" instead of reducing it to the "tumults" and "discords" of "popular Tribunals."[88] The bishop of Le Puy could protest all he wished his loyalty to the classically Gallican "*juste milieu* between these two extremities," but in spirit, at least – and decades before the French Revolution hurled them into the arms of the papacy – he and his peers were ultramontane.

Ultramontanism and absolutism or the Civil Constitution of the Clergy – that was how matters stood by 1765. Whatever the original intentions of the celebrated assembly of 1682, they were irrelevant now; whatever bridge classical Gallicanism yet maintained across the widening chasm was rapidly collapsing. Symptomatically, the royal council's judgment of May 24, 1765, which attempted to articulate and reinforce this bridge, was beset by both sides, as increas-ingly these sides had beset most everything the king had done affect-ing their relations since 1750.[89] The Gallican Declaration of 1682, that great legislative tapestry from the age of Louis XIV weaving con-ciliar Church and divine right monarchy together, was now in shreds.

New patterns and combinations were therefore in order, and they were not long in coming. For the emerging clerical party in France, it remained ahistorically to unite its new ultramontanism to its solici-tude for the monarchy against the perceived threat to both. Lefranc de Pompignan implicitly did this by identifying the same subversive principle of national sovereignty undermining both Church and State, maintaining that if it were really true, as critics of the *Actes* tended to say, that the bishops "in their chairs" were only "mandatories" and "representatives" of the people, then "the most absolute monarchs should be and are as much on their thrones."[90] But others were more explicit. *The Impartial Reflexions of a Papist and Royalist French-man*, the title of a pro-Jesuit pamphlet published in 1764 as part of the controversy over the suppression of that order, by itself speaks volumes, as does a *Letter from a Cosmopolite*, published the same year, which announced the formation and growth of a conspiracy against throne and altar.[91] Yet another clerical pamphleteer chal-

---

88   Ibid., pp. 203, 205.
89   For the text of the royal council's *arrêt* of May 24, 1765, as well as a good indi-cation of both parties' response to it, see NNEE, December 9 and 16, 1767, pp. 197–204.
90   Lefranc de Pompignan, *Défense*, p. 223.
91   *Réflexions impartiales d'un françois papiste et roialiste sur le réquisitoire de maitre Omer Joly de Fleury et l'arrêt du parlement de Paris du 1 juin 1764 qui suprime les brefs de n.s.p. le pape Clement XIII au roi de Pologne, duc de Lorraine et de Bar et à m.*

lenged Gallicano-Jansenism's hitherto quasi monopoly of what one Jesuit had already dubbed "the jargon of patriotism," and in his "double title" of "Catholic" and "Frenchman," raised a "cry of indignation" in reaction to Le Blanc de Castillon's *Réquisitoire*, especially its disrespectful attitude toward the papacy.[92] Well before it described a political reality of the counter-Revolution or became a watchword of the Bourbon and Catholic Restoration, Bourbon "throne" and papal "altar" began huddling together – if not in fact, at least in the minds of the emerging clerical party in France.

V   Conclusion

The controversy over the general assembly of the Gallican clergy in 1765 was really the last in a series of mixed religious, ecclesiastical, and political disputes which had dominated the eighteenth-century French domestic scene until then. The coming of the bull *Unigenitus* in 1713, the "miracles" of Saint-Médard in the early 1730s, the refusal of sacraments to Jansenists in the 1750s, the expulsion of the Jesuits in the 1760s – these were the major landmarks on a polemical road which gradually bifurcated toward both Revolution and counter-Revolution. By 1765 these directions were well established and clear enough. Not only had the Jansenist, Gallican, and parlementary syndrome conceived of the Civil Constitution of the Clergy and contemplated the confiscation of ecclesiastical property, but is it wholly fanciful to recognize the lineaments of future "liberalism" in its constitutionalism, protonationalism, and the thoroughgoing laicism of its ecclesiastical conceptions? And does it, again, stretch the imagination unduly to discern the basic contours of counter-Revolution – indeed, of early nineteenth-century "conservatism" generally – within the episcopal defenders' veneration for the past, theocratic social conceptions, and synthesis of anticonstitutional royalism and ultramontanism? Most conspicuously missing, at this stage, is aristocracy as such as a bone of contention.[93] But the

l'archévêque de Paris (à Alais, chés Narcisse Buisson imprimeur à l'enseigne du probabalisme, ce 12 juin 1764). For the *Lettre d'un cosmopolite*, see NNEE (August 28, 1765), p. 142.

92   *Cri d'un françois catholique après la lecture du Réquisitoire de m. Le Blanc de Castillon sur les Actes du clergé* (Soleure, 1766), p. 12. The Jesuit is Joseph-Antoine-J. Cerutti, *Apologie de l'institut des jésuites*, 2 vols. (n.p., 1763), 1:10.

93   The lines of division over aristocracy and privilege as such, when these became important towards the end of the century, tended to cut across and therefore confuse the issues outlined in this paper. It is this which in no small measure accounts for the gradual rapprochement between episcopacy and parlement after 1774. For examples of how at mid-century *both* parties to the controversy described in this

anti-aristocratic egalitarianism which played so important a role in the revolutionary mentality of the 1790s was a latecomer to the eighteenth-century scene; it was nowhere to be found in concentrated form during its middle decades.

If there is anything to this, then the marquis d'Argenson was not far wrong – in fact, much righter than he knew – when he observed of these midcentury ecclesiastical and religious controversies that they no longer so much pitted Jansenists against Molinists as "nationals" (*nationaux*) against "sacerdotals" (*sacerdotaux*).[94] It also follows that, at least prior to the Maupeou "revolution" of the 1770s, these mixed religious, ecclesiastical, and political controversies were central, not peripheral, to the unraveling of the Old Regime and the coming of the French Revolution. For they appear to have engendered the ideological and political divisions which later burst forth with greater clarity during the Revolution itself, which was hence as much a product of these divisions as it was a progenitor of them in its turn.

If the 1765 meeting of the general assembly touched off the last major *Unigenitus*-related controversy in France, it also occasioned the Gallican clergy's first explicit condemnation of Enlightenment works. This contrast raises the difficult question of the relationship between the Enlightenment and the emerging ideological and political divisions in France, which seem to have arisen quite independently of the celebrated "movement of lights." The question becomes the more difficult in proportion as one associates "Enlightenment" with "unbelief" because, as the study of this particular affair has indicated, these mixed religious, ecclesiastical, and political controversies tended to divide Catholic from Catholic much more than Catholic from unbeliever. Lefranc de Pompignan undoubtedly had doubts about the Catholicity of some of his opponents whom he called "enemies of the clergy," but he still distinguished between these and "unbelievers," and professed to respect the sincerity of the former who, he acknowledged, "call themselves Christians."[95] Not a single participant in this controversy fully qualifies as a member of Peter Gay's "little flock" of the truly enlightened, whose distinguished

---

paper could be "aristocratic," see n. 60 and the discussion of *Les Droits respectifs* in Section IV, above. For an example in a neighboring Catholic country of how controversy between "ultramontanists" and "Jansenists" lay at the origins of modern conservatism and liberalism, see Richard Herr, *The Eighteenth-Century Revolution in Spain* (Princeton, N.J., 1958). To a greater extent than in France, the Enlightenment was not very divisive; it was shared by both parties to the Jansenist–ultramontanist controversy.

94   René-Louis d'Argenson, *Journal et mémoires*, ed. E.-J.-B. Rathery, 9 vols. (Paris, 1859–67), 8:313.

95   Lefranc de Pompignan, *Défense*, pp. 132, 399.

bleating constitutes in fact no more than the most distant echo in any of these disputes.[96] In the debate over the general assembly of 1765 there is moreover across-the-board agreement among all participants that Catholicism should function as the moral and spiritual foundation of the State.[97] This much seems to suggest that even the very immediate origins of the ideological divisions of the Revolution and nineteenth-century France lie primarily in the century-long disputes between Catholic and Catholic, at best secondarily in the more loudly sung conflict between Catholic and unbeliever.

The privileged place which historians have traditionally accorded the Enlightenment *understood as unbelief* among the ideological origins of the French Revolution is surely in part the result of viewing the eighteenth century through the distorting lens of the Revolution itself, which in its frenzied pursuit of the refractory priest-*cum*-aristocrat had recourse to the most virulent form of anticlericalism available. But partly, too, it is a result of naively taking at face value a forensic device frequently employed by Old Regime defenders of the ecclesiastical establishment, that of concentrating all their polemical energies in corralling the most conspicuously "enlightened" of their opponents the better to brand them all with the stigma of unbelief. That is what Lefranc de Pompignan was really up to, of course, in choosing Richer's *On the Authority of the Clergy* as his chief foil; in a way, it was also the strategy of the general assembly's *Actes* in juxtaposing its condemnation of "impious works" to its defense of the rights of the "spiritual power." The Jesuits had earlier shown the way by lavishing all their attention, in the debate accompanying their expulsion, on the relatively "enlightened" *Compte rendu* of the attorney general of the parlement of Brittany while feigning ignorance of the hundred or more pamphlets of purely Gallicano-

96   Perpaps "enlightened" is not the right adjective to describe the "little flock," because Peter Gay distinguishes between "philosophes" and "other enlightened men of their age" who were presumably not part of the "little flock." The *philosophes*, unlike this broader category of the more or less enlightened, "used their classical learning to free themselves from their Christian heritage, and then, having done with the ancients, turned their face toward a modern world view. The Enlightenment was a volatile mixture of classicism, impiety, and science; the philosophes, in a phrase, were modern pagans" (Peter Gay, *The Enlightenment: An Interpretation*, vol. 1, *The Rise of Modern Paganism* [New York, 1967] p. 8, and, in general, "The Little Flock of Philosophes," pp. 3–20).
97   The abbé Bernard Plongeron has convincingly insisted upon the persistence of the idea of "Christendom" among the constitutional clergy during the Revolution in *Théologie et politique au siècle des lumières, 1770–1820* (Geneva, 1973), pp. 149–82, but more specifically in "Permanence d'une idéologie de 'civilisation chrétienne' dans le clergé constitutionnel" in *Studies in Eighteenth-Century Culture*, ed. Roseann Runt (Madison, Wis., 1978), 7:263–87. It is moreover to Plongeron that I owe the phrase "Gallicano-Jansenism."

Jansenist inspiration which were delivering them the most damaging blows.[98] But what was perhaps justifiable or at least clever as a forensic device in the eighteenth century seems precarious as a foundation of historical interpretation in the twentieth.

If, however, the Enlightenment is understood more broadly as a set of appeals, whether to reason, nature, or sensate experience, which replaced older ones such as to revelation and traditional precedents, then the problem of its relationship to the emerging ideological and political divisions of France is possibly susceptible of solution. And what this small study suggests is that "enlightened" concepts and vocabulary were sufficiently elastic to accommodate themselves to either side of the controversy, not just one, with perhaps a slight tendency for the Enlightenment's empirical side to run in a conservative direction, its natural rights inheritance in a revolutionary one. (This much, incidentally, might serve as a word of caution to those who wish to define the Enlightenment in exclusively empirical terms on the one hand, and persist in seeing it as the sole ancestor of modern liberalism on the other.) Can it be said, then, that the mixed religious, ecclesiastical, and political controversies generated the fundamental political and ideological directions of eighteenth-century France; whereas the Enlightenment, a broad cultural movement affecting the thought patterns of all literate groups, provided the conceptual apparatus and vocabulary in which either direction progressively expressed itself?

This is not to say that the choice of concepts and vocabulary was completely neutral or inconsequential. During the controversy in question, the recourse to contracts and states of nature obviously carried the Gallicano-Jansenist argument further than appeals to the early Church and distinctions between *fait* and *droit* by themselves could have done; something analogous could perhaps be observed on the other side. Nor is this to say that the Enlightenment did not develop affiliations of a more particular kind with either side. On the one side, both Bernhard Groethuysen and Robert Palmer have successfully called attention to the close similarity between "enlightened" conceptions of human nature and reason and those of certain segments of the French "devout" party, especially the Jesuits.[99] On the other side, this small study has attempted to underscore the very close proximity of Gallicano-Jansenism's subjection of Church to State to the ideas of the *philosophes* on this matter, particularly the "civil religion" of Rousseau's *Social Contract*.

98   Van Kley, *The Jansenists*, pp. 137–62.
99   Bernhard Groethuysen, *Die Entstehung der Bürgerlichen Welt-und Lebensanschauung in Frankreich* (Halle/Salle, 1927); and Robert R. Palmer, *Catholics and Unbelievers in Eighteenth-Century France* (Princeton, N.J., 1939), esp. pp. 23–52.

This takes us back, at long last, to the old pilgrimage town of Vézelay, and to Hubert Chalumeau, curé of the parish of Saint Pierre. The good curé could not have been more than dimly aware, as he resolved upon his diminutive stand against Rousseau and local apostasy, of the immense and somewhat irrelevant cross fire into which he was about to stumble. He wished only to sermonize against Rousseau, innocent of the fact that in using the assembly's *Actes* to do so, he was publicizing a document which the parlement of Paris had condemned for quite different reasons. On this superficial level, then, his affair was an accident, a mere and irrelevant anecdote, although illuminating rather poignantly the difficulties one could encounter in combating unbelief in eighteenth-century France. Yet Gallican and Jansenist thinking about Church and State, so close in some ways to the *Social Contract*, were also pretty much those of the parlement of Paris. In fact, the parlement's remonstrances of August 31, 1766, rather nicely sum up decades of Gallicano-Jansenist theorizing on relations between Church and State; it is as succinct a statement of these conceptions as exists anywhere. What is more, the authors of these remonstrances were malign enough to cite Chalumeau's case as an example of the "publication" of the *Actes* – in a footnote, to be fair – even though they almost certainly knew better by that time.[100] In view of these supplementary considerations, it is perhaps permissible to wonder whether, on some profounder level, the parlement's prosecution of the curé of Saint Pierre was so accidental, after all. What is in any event certain is that the lot of the curé was indeed an unhappy one in those days.

100   Flammermont, *Remontrances*, 2:638.

10

The Revolutionary Festival: A Transfer of Sacrality

Mona Ozouf

Originally appeared as Mona Ozouf, "The Revolutionary Festival: A Transfer of Sacrality," Chapter 10 of *Festivals and the French Revolution*, trans. Alan Sheridan (1988) pp. 267–82 (Cambridge, MA: Harvard University Press).

Editor's Introduction

Like Dale Van Kley,[1] Mona Ozouf is interested in the relationship between the French Revolution and religion. Unlike Van Kley, however, who focuses on the question of origins, Ozouf is primarily interested in the Revolution itself. Specifically, she takes as her subject the role of festivals in the Revolution. Historians have long been aware of the festivals that took place on specific occasions during the Revolution: from the Festival of the Federation (July 1790), at which patriots from every province converged on the Champs de Mars in Paris to commemorate the taking of the Bastille the year before, to the Festival of the Supreme Being (June 1794), where Robespierre declaimed on republican virtue, railed against atheists and defended the system of government by Terror. Most historians have mentioned these and a few other colorful festivals in passing, and those who examined them more seriously tended to see them as little more than mirrors of the revolutionary period in which they occurred or markers of the specific political factions that sponsored them.

Mona Ozouf's *Festivals and the French Revolution* distinguishes itself from its predecessors in two fundamental respects. First, it is based on an exhaustive search of archives in which official government reports on the festivals have been preserved. It is thus capable of shedding light not only on the well-known festivals in Paris, but on the thousands of smaller festivals that took place throughout France between 1789 and 1799. These

---

1   See chapter 9.

included, for example, not only the Festival of the Federation, but the many small and spontaneous *fédérations* at which National Guardsmen and other citizens joined their compatriots in neighboring villages to promise mutual defense and declare their loyalty to the Fatherland. Moreover, Ozouf examines in great detail the elaborate system of annual festivals established by the Law of 3 Brumaire IV (October 25, 1795) to correspond to the new revolutionary calendar: festivals dedicated to Youth, Old Age, Spouses, Thanksgiving, Agriculture, the anniversary of the republic's founding and that of Robespierre's fall. (Later a festival commemorating the execution of Louis XVI was added.)

Second, Ozouf sees in this multiplicity of ceremonies a single type, a model which she simply designates *la fête révolutionnaire* or "the Revolutionary festival."[2] Whatever the party that sponsored the festival in question, whatever the year and month in which it occurred, Ozouf sees each specific instance of the Revolutionary festival as having the same general features and the same reasons for existence. The most important of these are reiterated in the concluding chapter of her book, "The Revolutionary Festival: A Transfer of Sacrality," the greater part of which is excerpted below.

The selection begins with the claim that the revolutionaries, after banning public displays of Catholic worship, quickly felt a *horror vacui* or "abhorrence of the vacuum" that this assault left in religious life. Fearing popular immorality or resurgent "fanaticism," they sought to fill in the dangerous vacuum with a "new religion" and toward this end marshaled the ritual power of the Revolutionary festival. Their guiding principle in the creation of new religious practices, Ozouf argues, was a pairing of *imitation* and *purge*. From Catholicism itself they borrowed such familiar devices as catechisms, altars, tabernacles, sermons, and even envisaged the use of a "republican mass" officiated by priests. Yet they purged Catholic practice of those elements they regarded as superstitious, fanatical, unnatural, or tainted with "tyranny." The result was an airy, abstract religiosity that culminated in the cult of *theophilanthropy*, the deistic movement based simply on "love of God and man."

As to the imitative tendency of the Revolutionary festival, Ozouf notes that Catholicism was not the only source to be pillaged in search of raw material. Antiquity and the rituals of the Freemasons provided others. Ozouf raises the question of why the revolutionaries, who were otherwise quite innovative, took the apparently unimaginative route of reviving classical symbolism when creating republican forms of worship. She rejects

---

2   The title of the original version of Ozouf's book is *La fête révolutionnaire*. The emphasis on the singular type is lost in the English translation: *Festivals and the French Revolution*.

the argument that this was the "natural" thing for classically-educated people to do. Nor does she accept the argument that antiquity was chosen because it provided exemplary persons and deeds. After all, there were examples of heroism available in the intervening centuries, yet for Ozouf there was something special about antiquity as the revolutionaries understood it. Specifically, it stood for a time prior to the decadence that civilization would later bring in its wake. It appeared as a Golden Age in which equality and liberty coexisted and there was no contradiction between morality and natural inclinations. Most of all, Ozouf suggests, antiquity represented a time of *instituting*, of founding a society governed by wise laws and overseen by a sage lawgiver. It was therefore only appropriate that revolutionaries who saw themselves as embarking on a new path should have invoked a prior "founding moment." Regarding the presence of Masonic symbols, Ozouf links these to the "reasonable religion of the lodges" that emphasized the creative, hence sacred, power of human beings and their ability, through scientific study, to learn the secrets of creation. Moreover, Ozouf explains the frequent recourse to the largely astronomical imagery of freemasonry as indicative of a desire to link the human revolution to the heavenly revolutions, i.e. the orderly movement of the celestial bodies.

After interpreting the tendency of the Revolutionary festival to imitate Catholicism, antiquity and freemasonry, Ozouf returns to her discussion of the purging process that turned the borrowed practices into a distinctively revolutionary cult. She insists that this process was not "an attempt to extirpate the sacred," but rather an effort at "an elementary anthropology." By comparing different religious practices and eliminating aspects they found objectionable, Ozouf suggests, the revolutionaries hoped to learn what, essentially, human beings were and, by implication, what religion was most appropriate for them. Nevertheless, to inquire into the essential characteristics of humanity, was to call attention to the undeniable fact of difference. As Ozouf puts it, "This laying down of human identity, which testifies to the universal, leaves man alone." How did the revolutionaries attempt to resolve this paradox? For Ozouf, they repeatedly used the Revolutionary festival to emphasize the links between human beings, links that they portrayed as biological, domestic and civic. Thus, she suggests, the Revolutionary festival solved a problem of its own making by reconciling the individual with the community, emphasizing the homogeneous unity of humanity, and, finally, sacralizing that very humanity.

In the last section of the excerpt Ozouf observes that the Revolutionary festival was paradoxically conservative. Rather than encouraging "social turbulence," it sought to subdue the urge to revolt with reassuring impressions of "perfect intelligibility, order, and stability." Yet Ozouf insists on keeping the adjective "revolutionary" because it describes, in her view, the sense that contemporaries had of a new age unlike any other – even unlike antiquity, which was portrayed more allegorically than as a real historical period. For the first time, it was thought, humanity was on the point of reconciling all the contradictions of its condition – between reason and feeling, between the desire for eternity and a temporal existence, between the drive for civilization and the impulse to savagery. This utopian ideology, the author suggests, was conservative in its affirmation of happiness in the present, but revolutionary in its seeming inauguration of an unprecedented age.

Finally, Ozouf suggests that, despite its failures and shortcomings, the Revolutionary festival succeeded in achieving its greatest goal: namely, the *transfer of sacrality*. This concept, as we have seen in the essay by Lynn Hunt,[3] originated with the French sociologist Emile Durkheim (1858–1917) as a means of explaining the religious features (especially symbols) with which secular societies are paradoxically saturated. Yet if Hunt uses this Durkheimian concept to point to the failure of the revolutionaries to achieve their goal of creating a new society, Ozouf ends on a more optimistic note. She claims that when Napoleon came to power, "The transfer of sacrality onto political and social values was now accomplished." In other words, the ideals of the revolution were now considered sacred and the festivals through which they were raised to religious status could end.

3   See chapter 8.

The Revolutionary Festival: A Transfer of Sacrality

Mona Ozouf

Horror vacui

The men of the Revolution themselves had few illusions as to the meager nourishment offered popular religiosity by the Revolutionary festivals: "The poor conditions here on earth," the commissioner for the Ardennes wrote, "often transport the souls of the inhabitants of the countryside toward other hopes."[1] This is because the authorities chose not to follow the gentle methods recommended in 1789 by Rabaut Saint-Etienne in the memoranda of the Academy of Nîmes. Instead of "gradually reducing the processions, confraternities, ceremonies in square and street" – that is to say, being content to follow the simplifying tendency of the century as a whole – they chose to empty everyday life of religious acts, brutalizing, breaking up, and prosecuting them. Such a vacuum was abhorred on two accounts: either people were convinced that without rituals, any life declines into idleness or incoherence (this was the point of view of Dupont de Nemours), or it was predicted that the vacuum thus left by the expulsion of the marvelous might be filled by something even more fearful. Corruption and immortality or, worse still, a new, revived form of Catholicism might rise from its ashes. When a cult, even an unreasonable one, is destroyed, La Révellière declared, it has always proved necessary to replace it with others; otherwise, it has, so to speak, "replaced itself in rising from its own ruins."[2] The whole thinking of the Directoire, from Tracy to Madame de Staël, is agreed on the *horror vacui* left by the persecution of Catholicism and on the imperious need to replace it.

With what was one to replace what had been destroyed, and what could be substituted for Catholicism? How was the new religion to be established? The true answer, the leitmotif of the Revolutionary assemblies, was given by the imitation encouraged by the syncretic euphoria of the Revolutionary dawn. To replace was first of all to imitate – or to copy, said the critics. The new religion, like the old, had to have its sacred center, the altar of the fatherland, a place that was both religious and

1 F¹ C III, Ardennes 5, Arch. nat.
2 L. M. de La Révellière-Lépeaux, *Réflexions sur les cultes, sur les cérémonies civiles et les fêtes nationales* (Paris: F. J. Jansen, Year V).

civic, on which one might, as Benoist-Lamothe suggests, expose the bread of fraternity. There, too, there would have to be the sacralizing presence of a book, the sole receptacle of all moral precepts. This book would be the Declaration of Rights, which would be all the more capable of replacing the missal on the altar in that it contained the sacred statement of origins, that of the unchallengeable principles (a "children's alphabet" according to Rabaut Saint-Etienne, a "national catechism" according to Barnave), often preciously kept in an "august tabernacle," an ark of the Constitution. There would be a need for prayers and singing; hence the flood of patriotic anthems, "civic" sermons, "divine and constitutional" prayers, such literary confections as the "Village Sheet" intended to supplant "the old, superstitious prayers." A liturgical calendar would be needed, and ceremonies: thus a civic baptism was imagined, in which one saw the godfather, wearing his cockade, unstop a bottle, pour a few drops on the forehead of the newborn child, moisten his lips as the Republican Decalogue was recited, or someone read the commandments of the perfect member of the people's club.[3] And there would be a civic Lent, during which people would fast for the sake of liberty. There would be priests, who would be chosen not from among the "celibates" but from among family men. Apart from a few conditions – white hair and an upright life – they would perform exactly the same functions as Catholic priests, presiding at weddings, witnessing births, comforting the sick.

In all these suggestions there is a desperate wish to compete with religion – even to the extent of such physical features as the columns of the law and the altars of the fatherland. This furious rush of imitation is particularly apparent in the religious impregnation of vocabulary, a study of which has hardly begun. The mountain is "holy," the assemblies are "temples" and families "churches," a father is a "pontiff" and a mother his "loving and beloved vicar," the history of the Revolution is the "gospel of the day" and Paris the "true Rome," the "Vatican of Reason." The projects for a Republican liturgy, of which there was a proliferation at this time, illustrate this to the point of pastiche: there were, for example, suggestions that the Easter communion should be given twice a year, under the species of a cake at harvest time and wine from a ciborium at the wine harvest;[4] that the rogation procession be kept under the innocent name of "tour of the territory"; that Christmas be celebrated as the Festival of Birth (if the mother of the household had had a male child in that year); that All Saints' Day commemorate the

---

3 E. Fassin, "Les baptêmes civiques," *Bulletin de la Société des amis du vieil Arles* 2 (1904–1905).
4 *Décret de l'Assemblée nationale, portant règlement d'un culte sans prêtres, ou moyen de se passer de prêtres sans nuire au culte* (Paris, 1790).

great men who had died in the family; that on Good Friday, the wishes of the community be brought to those persons who, during the year, had suffered the most physically or morally.

We may laugh at the poverty of imagination of men condemned to reproduce a banished religion. This would not be entirely fair, for, in their conviction of the necessity of rites, the men of the Revolution were not content to borrow from what lay to hand. Antiquity provided them with at least as many models. There was, for example, the funeral ceremony, which Daubermesnil borrowed from the young Anacharsis and proposed to the organizers of Republican ceremonies.[5] Before the corpse the public officer would deliver the funeral oration. Then honey would be poured around the coffin in homage to the dead man's sweetness of character, then milk in memory of his candor, wine to commemorate his strength, and, lastly, incense so that "his good actions may fill the tableau of his life" like smoke. In their looting of ancient practices, the festival organizers and the authors of projects also found the powerful drama of the oath, with the curses that would befall the perjurer and the invocations that were not only a rhetorical resource but an attempt to equal the Romans, who, these men had read hundreds of times, believed that they were under a serious obligation only when they had sworn by Jupiter. It would seem, then, that in their obsession with ceremonies, they drew their models from different sources in quite unprincipled imitation.

And in fact there were no principles, or rather there was only one. By drawing on a mass of practices, wherever they were to be found, Revolutionary creation obeyed only a single law, that of the purge, which dominated both Revolutionary thought and Revolutionary action. Abolishing coats of arms, burning papers, striking out names, removing crowns and miters: a whole enterprise of subtraction and purification was directed at Catholic worship, with what was regarded as its excessive ornamentation and superfluous regulations. All this was regarded as so much bric-a-brac that needed to be swept away, if one were to see the true cult emerging from Revolutionary times in all its fresh beauty. A curious anonymous text of 1790 entitled *Décret de l'Assemblée nationale portant règlement d'un culte sans prêtres, ou moyen de se passer de prêtres sans nuire au culte* shows clearly the direction of the operation, the elimination of what Dupont de Nemours called "superfluity" – that is to say, toward the metaphysical heights and away from the depths of superstition. That is why the descriptions of the ideal

---

5   F. A. Daubermesnil, *Extraits d'un manuscrit intitulé "Le culte des Adorateurs,"* contenant des fragments de leurs différents livres sur l'institution du culte, les observances religieuses, les préceptes et l'Adoration (Paris: Imprimerie du Cercle social, Year IV).

Revolutionary worship are doomed to the grammar of "only" and "without." "Without recourse to trickery," writes Lefebvre de Villebrune in *La décade*; "without lustral water, without mysteries, without images."[6] Above all, this purging is the basis of all the others, without the slightest mention of sin. For the Revolutionary cult to live, all that was needed, it seems, was a mass of renunciations. As soon as the existence of the Supreme Being was declared as the first, unsuspecting cause of a formal, organized cult, a negative logic was set in motion.

At the cost of these purges, one could keep more or less anything, including the mass, for which Sobry wrote a strange apologia.[7] He had always loved the mass, he said, and never missed one under the ancien régime. And yet, in Year II, he applauded its suppression as the boldest act of the Revolution. There was no contradiction between these two attitudes. The hated mass was the mass overladen with baroque additions, weighed down by hateful dogmas, disfigured by a doctrine of tyrannies, persecutions, torture, and blood. Very little would be needed for the mass of which he dreamed to reappear in its true guise: it would be spoken in French; the priest would be allowed to say only certain words, laid down in advance; and, above all, he would say nothing about "those insignificant persons, who, under the name of saints, offer us only bad examples to follow." It is clear that the passion to purge was in no sense iconoclastic, but was an attempt to ensure the return of a primitive model. Furthermore, in their first, hesitant steps, the theophilanthropists very nearly called themselves "primitive Christians."

Indeed, this whole movement of simplification finds its culmination in theophilanthropy.[8] The hatred of the image, so often balanced in the festivals by sensualistic conformism, was here allowed full scope: no costumes (the priest would be an ordinary family man, correctly and simply dressed; the preacher of morality would renounce his robes); no exhibitionism (the examination of conscience would be silent); and a great cleansing (the temple would be swept clean not only of the tabernacle but even of the busts of the martyrs of liberty, the benefactors of mankind). This was to give rise to a great many conflicts when theophilanthropists and Catholics had to share their churches. According to its sectaries, the theophilanthropic temple was that austere place where one saw "neither emblems nor allegories, neither statuettes of saints nor pictures of miracles, still less *ex votos*, or offerings for the people." That was how Amaury Duval saw it.[9] The frantic desire to purge was such

6　February 8, 1797.
7　J. F. Sobry, *Apologie de la messe* (Paris: Sobry, Year VI).
8　On this point, see A. Mathiez, *La théophilanthropie et le culte décadaire* (Paris: F. Alcan, 1903).
9　In *La décade*, 30 Floréal, Year V.

that it even affected the book itself, whose presence on the altar seemed to be tolerated only as a temporary measure. Once the elders who presided over the worship were assured that the basic tenets were well established in everybody's mind, they ought, according to Siauve in his *Echo des cercles patriotiques*,[10] to burn solemnly the handwritten copy of the catechism, for "no book is needed for moral belief."

Since the outbreak of the Revolution, there had been plenty of people who rejected an enterprise that involved both purgation and imitation. Salaville, for example, protested against the civil cult advocated by the section of the Réunion, with its presentation of sixteen-year-old youths, which "resembles in every feature what was practiced in the churches."[11] This criticism was echoed by the counterrevolutionaries, keen to denounce, beyond the voluntary impoverishment of the purgings, the involuntary poverty of imitation. But Edgar Quinet, too, was appalled at the sterility of the Revolutionary imagination, which, in his eyes, was a disaster. Auguste Comte thought much the same. The liturgy that, in their fear of the void, the men of the Revolution were trying desperately to establish was, therefore, even for those who suspected its religious coloring, a failed liturgy. Very few regarded it as a transfer of sacrality.

The Meaning of a Few Borrowings

We must return, then, to those borrowings for which the organizers of the Revolutionary festival were so criticized and, above all, to that obsessive yet mysterious recourse to antiquity. While the quarrel between the ancients and the moderns had seemed to have been settled long since in favor of the moderns and emancipation, and at the very same moment when the Revolution was bringing modernity to birth, how is one to explain the imitative return to ancient models? Indeed, this choice raises several questions: first, yet again, that of the reality of Revolutionary innovation, and second, that of the extent to which the people understood this erudite revival. On March 24, 1792, *Les révolutions de Paris* declared quite calmly that the people were being "told" that the woolen cap had been the emblem in Greece and Rome of emancipation from all servitude and that, "from that moment, each citizen wanted to have such a cap." But the intellectualist optimism of the statement cannot make us forget how opaque the Revolutionary symbolism was in the eyes of even not-so-simple citizens. Lastly, and above all, we must ask

10 In *L'echo des cercles patriotiques*, no. 14.
11 *Annales patriotiques*, 9 Frimaire, Year II.

why the men of the Revolutionary festivals chose antiquity as their source of reference.

Let us now examine this last question, to which many answers have been given. According to Mathiez and Georges Lefebvre,[12] the enlightened bourgeois – those who were everywhere responsible for organizing the Revolutionary ceremonial – were imbued with a classical culture that was their lingua franca. Quite naturally, therefore, they borrowed the objects, emblems, and devices from their memories of the classroom. Not surprisingly, then, recourse to antiquity was the result of a thorough aesthetic and literary education, and, as Lefebvre puts it, of "the impregnation of a décor." This thesis, which assumes the cultural docility of indocile men, has good arguments in its favor. We now know a great deal more about what those men read in their schools;[13] and what they read was exactly the same as was read by the handful of opponents of antiquity (Volney, Condorcet) and by the overwhelming majority of its admirers. We know how potent such an impregnation can be. Yet was it irresistible, as Louis Hautecoeur suggests? For him, men living in that setting had necessarily to believe that they were the successors of the ancients. Necessarily? In architecture, painting, and furnishing, antique decoration had been current since the middle of the century, and it is difficult to understand how a Revolutionary generation could see forms that had become a repertoire of fashion and all too widespread as representing a break. Indeed, a certain lassitude could be detected before the flood of Reguluses, Catos, and Belisariuses at the Salon.[14]

This was no less so in the literary sphere: the image of Camille Desmoulins and Madame Roland in tears at a reading of Plutarch is often regarded as a new one; but that is to forget that in 1740, Vauvenargues had confided in a letter to the Marquis de Mirabeau: "I wept for joy on reading those Lives; I did not spend a night without speaking to Alcibiades, Agesilas, and others."[15] One also forgets that the comparison with the Roman Republic seemed such a rhetorical device that it aroused Argenson's sarcasm as early as 1764. In short, the Revolution did not invent the Romans, and its taste for them cannot be explained by some educational peculiarity. Yet one more thing, of course, should not be forgotten. There is something very convincing in Parker's thesis

12 G. Lefebvre, "Compte rendu de l'ouvrage de H. T. Parker," *Annales historiques de la Révolution française* (1938).
13 H. T. Parker, *The Cult of Antiquity and the French Revolutionaries* (Chicago: University of Chicago Press, 1937).
14 Faced with which Cochin suggested that the great subjects should be sought in the history of France, which is proof that the model might have had competition.
15 Letter to Mirabeau, March 22, 1740, in Vauvenargues, *Oeuvres*, vol. 3 (Paris: A la cité des Livres, 1929).

that a veneration for the ancients was for all those people – for Brissot as well as for Madame Roland – an episode of juvenile intransigence, followed by accommodations with present reality. Once the coming of the Revolution had suddenly swept such accommodations away, it is understandable that they should have returned to the beloved antique models of their youth. Antiquity was also the youth of history.

Another very traditional but more profound interpretation suggests that antiquity provided these men above all with models of greatness. Filling one's dreams with great examples would help one to live and sometimes – as in the case of Romme's suicide – to die. We know that Plutarch was the most frequently read author and that it was through him alone that the men of the Revolution knew Greek antiquity. This is as if to say that they were concerned not so much with knowing it as equaling it, as if, in the transparent perspective of the Enlightenment, cleansed of all "superstitions," one felt the need to cling to a few great figures. Legendary antiquity helped the men of the Revolution, therefore, to rise to the level of the events through which they were living. Yet one thing remains perplexing: why the Romans and Greeks but no other models? This world, "empty since the Romans," had not always been so. Not so long before, historians had peopled it with other exemplary figures. To take only one of those whom the revolutionaries read most assiduously – the "illustrious Mably," as they themselves said – they could find in him the model of the Franks, sovereignly free in the forests of Germany, or that of the ancient deliberating assemblies, open to all the talents, that once met in the "May fields." Why, then, when the hour of the Revolution sounded, were all traditions, even the most prestigious ones, swept aside, leaving only those of antiquity? And why that self-assurance, of which we get some idea when we listen to Babeuf, in the Committee of General Safety, glorying in having taken the name of Gracchus in preference to that of any Christian hero: "What ill can result from the fact that I took as my godfather a great man rather than a small one?"

The study of the festival can certainly throw some light on the riddle of the overwhelming choice in favor of antiquity. As we know, the festival reconstructed antique decor (usually some ideal type reduced to the simplicity of the idyll), paraded the busts of the heroes of antiquity, and heard interminable speeches in which one can glimpse what the history of Greece and Rome meant to the speakers. According to them, ancient history – and in this it is quite unlike Mably's version of the history of France – is a history of origins. Mably's history, by contrast, is a history of transition, of a period that has fallen from grace, in which one constantly notes the signs in societies of that decadence that was the century's obsession. It might be objected that Greek history and, above all, since Montesquieu, Roman history ought necessarily to initiate its readers into the theme of decline. But here we come to the type of history being taught in schools. The ancient authors then being taught, as Parker sees very clearly, described their present against the background of a republic of their dreams, and used a double palette, a dark one for their present and a bright one for their past. This has the result, which is of crucial importance for us here, of dehistoricizing early ancient history, utopianizing it as a simple, frugal, equitable life. The antique was scarcely historical, and we can understand why the century that, as Koyré has shown, invested so little in the past invested so much in antiquity. Antiquity seemed to the men of the Revolution to be a quite new, innocent society, in which words were a perfect match for deeds; when they did have to confront the theme of the decline of ancient society, they defused it by moralizing it, attributing the decadence of history to a taste for wealth and the loss of virtue; and they tried to see that decline occurring as late as possible.

A very fine text by Billaud-Varenne tells us much about the ancient history so dear to the festival orators:

> In the times of the Ancients, in those times that may be called the true golden age, when every nation decided its own rights and duties, times when oppression and oblivion affected only a class of exotic slaves, then the people, gathered together in what was often a very tight circle and sharing more or less equally the advantages of a collective administration, seemed to be at the same level as far as genius, tastes, manners, and idiom were concerned. The two passions that predominated in the civil order, namely, love of glory and lust for gold, must alone have introduced a jarring note into that political government, though that contrary movement became evident only after many centuries.[16]

It is all there: nostalgic evocation (the golden age); the model to be imitated (equality mythically obtained at the cost of the exclusion, scarcely felt as such, of a few "exotic" slaves, as easily forgotten as those excluded from the Revolutionary festivals); the explanation of social decline by the psychology of passions and the extreme slowness of decadence to make itself felt, which makes it possible to conceive of the ancient world as stable. Billaud-Varenne shows us what the men of the Revolution wanted from antiquity: the image of an ideal Republic, purged of despotism, in which the most obscure citizens enjoyed personal liberty and were protected from arbitrary rule. It does not seem to have been very important whether the model was more Spartan or more Athenian, whether a Spartan Mountain was to be contrasted with an Athenian

16   Billaud-Varenne, *Les éléments du républicanisme*, pt. 1 (n.p., n.d.).

Gironde,[17] whether the dramaturgy of the oath was copied precisely from the antique ceremonial or whether it was young Anacharsis who provided its distorted image. There is not a great deal of scholarly application here. What matters is being able to conceive of a society in which the instituted is still not too far removed from the instituter. Indeed, it is in this sense that the festival is itself, for the men of the Revolution, their great borrowing from antiquity, for the festival is instituting. When Saint-Just tried to copy Sparta in his *Fragments sur les institutions républicaines*, he borrowed two things: the school and the festival, that is to say, the two teachers of the nation.

This also helps us to understand why those men tried to bypass their own history. The obsession with decadence drove them to eliminate the mediocrity of those intermediary stages that could not, in any case, be founding moments. Their minds were still in the grip of the omnipotent idea of beginning, and for them the initial was also the founding moment. Even Condorcet, who was more susceptible than anyone else to the cumulative effect of human knowledge, transmitted from generation to generation, considered that the American Revolution, which escaped the radicalism of the French Revolution, had not been a true revolution. The good fortune of the French Revolution was that it broke with all tradition. The ancient festival was seen, therefore, not as a tradition to be rediscovered and copied but as an eternal model of communal togetherness, simplicity, and joy. Even in Pluviôse, Year IV, a sinister time, and in a reactionary newspaper, *L'historien*, a certain Vérus continued to justify the festivals conceived by the law of Brumaire: "Here is something that conforms to the simplicity and majesty of antiquity; reading the law to which we owe such festivals, one might think that it had been drawn up by Zaleucus or Solon."

Festival, law, origin: what we have here is an association suggestive of a sacralization. The great figure invoked by the festival organizers was, as Pierre Vidal-Naquet saw very clearly,[18] that of the legislator, the possessor of the power to institute, capable of bringing about a mutation of the savage world into the civilized world. Solon or Lycurgus: it hardly mattered which for such men, seeking in antiquity a model that had the reputation then of being the highest achievement of mankind. "Legislation," says Billaud-Varenne, "is the most difficult art, so much so that from the beginning of time the greatest geniuses have almost

17 On this theme, see E. Rawson, *The Spartan Tradition in European Thought* (Oxford: Clarendon Press, 1969).
18 P. Vidal-Naquet, preface to the French translation of M. I. Finley, *Democracy, Ancient and Modern* (*Démocratie antique et démocratie moderne*) (Paris: Payot, 1976).

wasted their time looking for it." A whole generation, which seemed to sense that the career that was open to all the talents in a period of revolution was that of the lawyer, played not at "if I were king" but at "if I were legislator" – so sighed Manon Philipon (not yet Madame Roland) at the age of twenty-four. The need for sacrality was concentrated entirely on the figure of the lawmaker. Jesus was not only a man, he was a legislator, declared Léonard Bourdon in rather poor verse. The humanization of Jesus was compensated here by the sacralization of the man who began or began again, placed his energies at the service of social happiness, and seemed by the same token endowed with supernatural powers. One is no longer surprised by the arrogance of certain orators, such as Camus, declaring at the session of January 1, 1790, "Assuredly we have the power to change religion."

So we may risk this conclusion: recourse to antiquity in the Revolutionary festivals expressed not only the nostalgia of the aesthete or even the moral need to replace the great examples that had disappeared with the old order. It expressed also, and above all, in a world in which Christian values were declining, the need for the sacred. A society instituting itself must sacralize the very deed of institution. If one wishes to found a new order, one cannot be sparing of the means to do so; beginning a new life cannot be imagined without faith. This is the key to the paradoxical victory that the Revolution accorded the ancients over the moderns. To opt for the moderns was obviously to opt for the instructive accumulation of experience, for the beneficent continuity of the generations. To opt for the ancients was to say that in going back to origins, no purpose is served in pausing at the intermediary stages. Thus each generation conquers its autonomy and its capacity to break with the past. Antiquity itself is not at all a moment in human history like other moments. It has an absolute privilege, for it is conceived as absolute beginning. It is a figure of rupture, not of continuity; and the fervor that it arouses is not diminished but enhanced by this.

The myth of origin is also the instrument of a teleology: to make conceivable and credible the transition to the New Jerusalem presupposes a memory of the past Eden. Indeed it is by no means certain that the memory can coexist in men's minds with the belief in human perfectibility. Madame de Staël states this better than anyone else:

> It is as if we felt at one and the same time regret for the few fine gifts that we were gratuitously granted and hope for the few benefits that we may acquire by our own efforts: just as the doctrine of perfectibility and that of the golden age, combined and merged together, arouse in man both pain at losing and ambition to recover. The feelings are melancholy and the mind is audacious. One looks back and the other forward. Out of this

daydream and this enthusiasm is born man's true superiority, the mixture of contemplation and activity, of resignation and will, which allows him to hitch his life in the world to the heavens.[19]

To hitch one's life in the world to the heavens: that undertaking, which is also that of the Revolutionary festival, helps us to understand the meaning of a borrowing: it is not so much an imitation as a beneficent invocation.

Can the same be said of the other elements borrowed by the Revolutionary festival? The presence in the festivals of Masonic symbols has been seen as the very signature of the "Masonic plot," almost as if caught in the act – and, by the same token, one ignored, or concealed, by those historians favorable to the Revolution. The listing of Masonic emblems in the medals and banners (the level, of course, but also the compasses, the square, the columns of the sun and moon, the eye of Reason piercing the clouds of Error, the joined hands, the triangular altar), or Masonic rituals in the ceremonies (the steel vault over the newborn infants, the goblet from which one drinks, the procession in which one carries the symbolic tools), the Masonic vocabulary in the speeches ("temples of virtues," "hiding places dug for vice") was first made by hostile commentators.[20] As soon as things were looked at rather differently, in the sense not of a political plot but of a long cultural impregnation, the enormous influence of Freemasonry on the French Revolution, the noting of detail passed into other hands. Thanks to Roger Cotte, we now know more about the profound influence of Masonic musical ritual on the Revolutionary festival. And thanks to Jacques Brengues,[21] we are discovering, beyond even the borrowings from Masonic symbolism, the profound kinship between the Masonic ritual and the Revolutionary festival: in both Masonry and in the Revolution, every assembly is ipso facto a festival.

But it may be said of Freemasonry what was said of antiquity: the borrowing that is attributed to it testifies not only to a cultural inertia. No doubt, just as the revolutionaries had been initiated in school into the culture of antiquity, so, accustomed to meeting in the studios, those other classrooms of the provincial elite, they could easily pile Masonic references on classical reminiscences. The interpretation is, in both cases, a lazy one. What strikes one in the Masonic borrowings of the Revolutionary festival, far more than this or that emblem, is the reasonable religion of the lodges, the evident dialectic from the Temple-

19   Madame de Staël, *De l'Allemagne* (Paris: H. Nicolle, 1810).
20   See, for example, G. Gautherot, *La démocratie révolutionnaire* (Paris: 1912).
21   Jacques Brengues, "L'apport de la franc-maçonnerie à la fête révolutionnaire," *Humanisme* (July–August 1974).

Building to the Temple-Universe, the sacralization of a life deserted by the sacred around the artisan figure of man the creator. When Daubermesnil was looking for a place that would be suitable for certain ceremonies that he wanted to establish, he imagined an "asylum,"[22] that is, a sacred place, crowned with an observatory stuffed with instruments and books, where scholars would come and study the course of the stars. With the signs of the zodiac on the walls and, inside, frescoes depicting the seasons, the temple is, significantly, both the place of astronomy and the place of the civic cult, a living illustration of the link established by the famous, and then quite recent, book by Dupuis on the origin of cults.[23] Indeed, it is here that the sacrality of a revolution, which is both a scientific and an astral figure, is most surely expressed.

The Meaning of Purging

Let us now abandon, then, these borrowings, whose eclecticism will be endlessly studied, and examine the essential operation of purging practiced by the organizers of the Revolutionary festivals on their harvest of practices. This operation is generally regarded as an attempt to extirpate the sacred. This seems to me to be a somewhat hasty judgment. In the revolutionaries' treatment of their discoveries, one is struck by the obstinate search for an elementary anthropology. The historical and ethnological justifications offered by so many writings on the festival bring together Chuvash, Tartar, and even Cherkess festivals with Greek and Roman ceremonies, as if, out of such a comparison of the ceremonies of these child-peoples, the fundamental would emerge. These proliferating practices give us a glimpse of the origin of all cults and the hope, too, of inferring the original cult. What the men of the Revolution were seeking was certainly the essential identity of religion as an expression of human identity. In Year IV, Rallier wrote to Grégoire: "In meditating on these objects, I remembered hearing a wise man say, long ago, that one could make up an excellent religion out of what the others have in common. Would it not be advantageous to collect the maxims common to all the religions accepted in France or likely to be and to compose out of them a formula for invoking the Supreme Being?"[24] Once the tragic, mournful, dark apparatus of religion had been eliminated, everyone seemed to believe that one would find that basis of worship in which the

22   Daubermesnil, *Extraits.*
23   C. Dupuis, *Origine de tous les cultes ou Religion universelle* (Paris: H. Agasse, Year III).
24   *Lettres de Rallier, membre du Conseil des Anciens, au citoyen Grégoire, membre du Conseil des Cinq-Cents* (Paris: Desenne, Year IV).

religious foundation gave place to the sociomoral foundation, but on which a new sacrality would have to be constructed for a newly homogeneous mankind.

It was a passion for unity and unanimity that governed this act of purging, therefore. Because it failed in this, the much-vaunted Festival of the Federation won its first detractors,[25] "for whom its *'oramuses,'* its 'barbarous chants in [a] foreign idiom' seemed to condemn the non-Roman fraction of the nation to the condition of schism. A purified religion, however, freed of dogma, should be capable of sealing the unity of the human community in a sense of the sacrality of the human being. "The only true religion," wrote Cabanis, "is that which ennobles man, by giving him a sublime idea of the dignity of his being and of the great destinies to which he is called by the human orderer."[26] The festival organizers set out, therefore, to reconstruct unity. This aim was sometimes naively pursued in the detail of the rituals, as in La Révellière's essay,[27] which proposes, according to methods inspired by Frederick II, a system of signals capable of repeating sacred words to an entire amphitheater at once. And this aim was always affirmed in the overall arrangements of the ceremony; for although the festival might have had its excluded elements, they had previously been excluded from the ranks of mankind. The Revolutionary festival worked for the homogenization of mankind. This explains the meaning of its renunciations: it was not a demolition enterprise but the search for a sacralizing foundation, of the mother religion, just as others at the same time were seeking the mother language and the humanity in all men.

This laying down of human identity, which testifies to the universal, leaves man alone, of course; that is the price to be paid for this discovery. The task of the festival is then seen to be that of redeeming the platitude of that psychosociology of the homogeneous, of saving the isolated individual from himself, and of reconstructing a new sacrality on the elementary elements thus revealed. This would take place, as we have seen throughout these pages, in the triple choice of the biological, the social, and the civic. The biological because it provides the strongest image of the reciprocity of human relations in an ideal community: this explains the importance given by the Revolutionary festivals to the ceremonial of the ages, the place they gave to the rituals of exchange and giving, the eminent role they accorded to the father and mother; it was

25   On this theme, see L. A. De Moy, *Accord de la religion et des cultes chez une nation libre* (Paris: Au presbytère de Saint-Laurent, Year IV).
26   P. J. G. Cabanis, *Lettre posthume et inédité de Cabanis à M. F. sur les causes premières* (Paris: Gabon, 1824).
27   La Révellière, *Essai sur les moyens de faire participer l'universalité des spectateurs à tout ce qui se pratique dans les fêtes nationales* (Paris: H. J. Jansen, Year VI).

a biological that had already been socialized into the domestic, and would soon be sacralized into a religion. We then come to the social link in its almost pure state, as revealed, throughout the Revolutionary festival, by the unusable scenography of the oath. Once again, one senses that this is not purely and simply a plagiarism from antiquity. The sacrality of the oath, for the men of the Revolution, derived from the fact that it made visible the act of contracting, which was conceived as the fundamental feature of sociability. Combined with those invocations that linked it to a necessary transcendence and those curses intended to show the extent to which the contractual commitments presupposed individual abdication, the oath of the Revolutionary festival was the sacred theater of the social contract.

Lastly, we come to the civic, the fatherland. This was the long-lost sacral reality. In 1754, the Abbé Coyer complained that this "old word of fatherland" had been purged from the language under the ministry of Cardinal Richelieu.[28] "Children have never learned it," he said sadly, and he went on to define it very confidently in terms of power: a superior power, based on nature, a divinity that accepts offerings only to redistribute them. It was a forgotten power, then, that was rediscovered by the Revolution and was henceforth recognized, proclaimed, sworn by. It was all the more unchallengeable in that it was eternal, more able than any other to oppose its resistance to the decline inherent in history. The fatherland may have been physically absent from the Revolutionary festival, in which, as we have seen, the tutelary female figures were Liberty, Victory, Reason, or the Republic, but never France, never the fatherland. Never shown, the invisible fatherland was nonetheless the focal point of the whole festival: the altar was the altar of the fatherland; the defenders were the defenders of the fatherland; the battalion of children was the hope of the fatherland; the duty of every citizen, as every speech hammered home, was to be worthy of the fatherland; and the injunction on all the banners was to live and die for the fatherland. Between this invisibility and the heroics of the festival there was an obvious link; and it is not irrelevant to this subject to note that the festivals in which the victories of the fatherland were celebrated maintained to the end of the Revolutionary decade a very special enthusiasm. The fatherland, the commonwealth, was the true expression of collective unity.

It was not difficult to find servants for these new values, domestic, social, and civic, sacralized by the festival: family men, schoolteachers, legislators, a whole benevolent team of "ministers of nature." The

---

28 G. F. Coyer, *Dissertations pour être lues: la première sur le vieux mot de patrie, la seconde sur la nature du peuple* (The Hague: P. Gosse, Jr., 1755).

priests of the new cult were so solely by virtue of the fact that they possessed the power to engender: the family man, at once progenitor and teacher; the schoolteacher, a father of the collective family; the legislator, the father of the fatherland. This conjunction of terms shows the extent to which Revolutionary sacrality was a sacrality of birth. It also explains what precisely was the function of the festival for the men of the Revolution, whatever political tendency they belonged to: it was to demonstrate to man the transcendence of mankind and to establish mankind in his humanity.

So the Revolutionary festival referred to a world of perfect intelligibility, order, and stability. In this it was faithful to its utopian aim of redeeming society from the obsession with decline that had haunted the entire century. There were few thinkers who, like Condorcet, considered with lucid pessimism that the ancient legislators, who had aspired "to render the constitutions that they presented eternal, in the name of the gods, to the enthusiasm of the people," had, by that very fact, placed "a seed of profound destruction" in those perpetual constitutions. His was an isolated voice, so strong did the connection between origin, law, and the sacred then seem. The Revolutionary festival, which saw itself as establishing an eternal society, was an immense effort to conjure away decadence, that sickness of society, to regularize the time of the Revolution, and to conceal its false starts and sudden changes.

After this, one would hesitate to call the festivals of the French Revolution "revolutionary," since such a charge of emotion and subversion has been invested in the adjective of social turbulence. One may agree that these festivals were "revolutionized": their break with the ancient rituals and their contempt for the traditional, popular religious festival are sufficient evidence of this. Whether they were "revolutionizing" is another matter: their organizers did not expect them to be. Once the immense event had taken place (which they obstinately conceived in terms of order, not of disorder), they saw the festival as doing no more than strengthening the Revolution, expected of it no subversion, and attributed it to no more than a power of conservation. On 8 Thermidor, Year VII, Grenier expressed this purpose in a striking formula: "We had to be revolutionaries in order to found the Revolution; but, in order to preserve it, we must cease to be."[29]

Must we, then, at the end of this book on the "revolutionary festival," abandon the magic of the adjective and be content simply to speak of the festivals of the French Revolution? One would be tempted to adopt

---

29   J. Grenier, *Opinion sur la question de savoir si l'on doit supprimer de la formule du serment civique les mots de haine à l'anarchie* (Paris: Imp. nat., Year VII).

this solution, which would avoid any suggestion of contempt, were it not that the men of the Revolution, already struck by the abuse of the adjective, had themselves taken the trouble to say exactly what they meant by "revolutionary": "A revolutionary man is inflexible, but sensible; he is frugal; he is simple, but does not display the luxury of false modesty; he is the irreconcilable enemy of all lies, all affectation. A revolutionary man is honorable, he is sober, but not mawkish, out of frankness and because he is at peace with himself; he believes that grossness is a mark of deception and remorse, and that it disguises falseness under exuberance." The virtues listed by Saint-Just[30] in defining the private man may also, when magnified, define the public festival. That was certainly how the festival was seen and was intended to be. So why not dare to call it revolutionary?

Furthermore, if it was revolutionary in the eyes of the men of the Revolution, it was because it seemed better equipped than anything else to reconcile the rational and the sense perceptible, time and eternity, the savage and the civilized. The festival announced the advent of that unified man of whom Diderot declared that he had traveled through the history of the centuries and nations and failed to find. He had seen men "alternately subjected to three codes: the code of nature, the civil code, and the religious code and forced to transgress alternately each of those three codes, which were never in agreement; hence it is that there has never been in any land either man, citizen, or religion." What the festival tried to do was to demonstrate the compatibility of the codes, and its result seemed to be the emergence at last of the reconciled man.

Yet it will be said, it failed to create him. But Brumaire, which saw this astonishing system of festivals disappear, nevertheless did not see the disappearance of the new values that it had sacralized. Rights, liberty, and the fatherland, which the Revolutionary festival bound together at the dawn of the modern, secular, liberal world, were not to be separated so soon. The transfer of sacrality onto political and social values was now accomplished, thus defining a new legitimacy and a hitherto inviolate patrimony, in which the cult of mankind and the religion of the social bond, the bounty of industry, and the future of France would coexist. How can it be said that the Revolutionary festival failed in that? It was exactly what it wanted to be: the beginning of a new era.

---

30   Saint-Just, *Rapport sur la police générale, la justice, le commerce, la législation, et les crimes des factions* (Paris: Imp. nat., n.d.).

Index